Baptist Pilgrims on Mission

Baptist Pilgrims on. Mission

Starting Churches

from Shore

to Shore

Charles A. Jolly Sr.
Dorothy P. Jolly

PROVIDENCE HOUSE PUBLISHERS
Franklin, Tennessee

To all of our family
and all of our churches

———◆◆◆◆———

Printed in the United States of America

03   02   01   00   99   99   1   2   3   4   5

Library of Congress Catalog Card Number: 98-68651

ISBN: 1–57736–135–0

Cover design by Gary Bozeman

PROVIDENCE HOUSE PUBLISHERS
238 Seaboard Lane • Franklin, Tennessee 37067
800-321-5692

Contents

Preface and Acknowledgments

Someone has said, "Life is an enigma enshrouded in a mystery." The poet has said, "I go on not knowing. I would not know if I might. I only know I'd rather walk with Him in darkness than to walk alone in the light."

These two thoughts come to mind, as we think of our journey thus far in His blessed will. We can only say that His hand has been on our lives even from our beginning days, with godly forebears who always encouraged us and prayed for us. It's almost as if we have had myriad friends of Christ Jesus along our way, and always our goal has been to reach more people for His Kingdom on earth and His Glory forever. The marvelous places He has led us and the connections to make it possible overwhelm us with deepest thankfulness for His bounteous mercies. Many of these are now gone and we look forward to meeting them in Glory. Others are still around, and they still reach out to us in love. The journey is not completed, but we look forward to His further blessings and to continuing to be a blessing in His dear name.

Throughout these journeys I have told about precious people who have helped us and ministered to us in Jesus' name. It is impossible to justly tell about all because there have been so many. Those least ones in all of our churches have been great ones to share with us their lives and journeys in Christ, our Lord. Only a pastor can really know about these. Therefore, I thank God for these dear souls along the way who have taught us what the deep and abiding love of Christ truly means. I thank my God upon every remembrance of them and for those who have so graciously helped us, especially, to tell our story. For you see, our story has run parallel with your story and we are a vital part of all we have met along the way. To God be the Glory, great things He has done, and His blessed work is never finished on this earth. The thrill of it all echoes in our memory and beckons us on to see what He has in store for those who love Him. Our greatest privilege has been, and is, to try to represent these dear people of God. What blessings have been ours and are ours in the ongoing process.

Our former secretary, in Madison, New Jersey, Jewel Weaver, now living in retirement in Surfside Beach, South Carolina, has been an encourager and volunteer typist in the production of this book—a labor of love.

Our one-year privilege as Supply Pastor at Victory Baptist Church, Des Moines, Washington, has been a special and blessed experience with a very special congregation—December, 1997–December 6, 1998.

1

Grade School and High School

1927–1939 (Charles) • 1929–1941 (Dorothy)

Dorothy moved from Warsaw, Kentucky, at eighteen months of age to live in the Mississippi Delta town of Anguilla until 1928. Dorothy's father, Reverend R. B. Patterson Sr., was pastor of Anguilla and Catchings churches, both half-time (two Sundays/month). The pastor's home was in Anguilla.

Because Dorothy's mother had had previous birth difficulties, losing their first son on April 16, 1921, she went back to Louisville, Kentucky, where she had had her previous birth by Caesarian section, to give birth to Robert Jr. (Bob), in 1925.

The Pattersons were later called to the Davis Memorial Baptist Church in Jackson, Mississippi, where the Mississippi Baptist Orphanage Home people, especially the children, would march to the church in a group on Sunday morning but rode the bus on Sunday nights.

Their ties to the orphanage went back to 1920 when Dr. J. R. Carter, the Superintendent of the Home, married Brother and Mrs. Patterson there on June 30. Ernestine Lowther, Dorothy's mother, had gone to the orphanage at ten years of age. As Ernestine grew older, she helped with the younger children who included Brother R. B. Patterson's (Bob's) younger brother David and his sister Hannah, who had been taken there by their older brother Bob from New Orleans where their father, Morgan, and mother, Fannie, had died from some type of epidemic. Brother R. B. Patterson's older brother George and his sister Leola had also died. I recall Brother Patterson saying the hearse backed up to his home three times in two weeks.

Brother R. B. Patterson's father, Morgan Patterson, an excellent artist, was not a Christian until Mordecai Ham came to New Orleans, held a great revival in which the family, Episcopalian in background, was saved (Mordecai Ham was the same one preaching in North Carolina when Billy Graham was saved).

1

We have a marvelous painting done by Morgan Patterson in 1884 depicting horses at the famous Jackson Square horse-drinking trough. In this painting, you can see the veins in the horses' faces and the water streaming down as they drink and lift their heads.

There was an Aunt Bonnie, a Baptist, who took the younger children and Dorothy's father to Grace Baptist Church in New Orleans. A Brother Clarke was pastor of the Grace Baptist Church, North Rampart Street, close by McDonough Boys' School #12 where Dorothy's father and others attended. In New Orleans at that time, boys and girls were segregated in school. It was this Brother Clarke who knew about the Mississippi Baptist Orphanage Home and recommended that the frightened Bob Patterson take his younger brother and sister there. Ernestine Lowther, now older, helped look after these younger Patterson children and met her husband-to-be when he came to visit for a Christmas party.

We went back to these places in June of 1969—the old home place, the Grace Baptist Church, McDonough Boys' School #12, et cetera, when the Southern Baptist Convention was in session in New Orleans, Louisiana.

Brother Patterson died suddenly on August 10, 1969. Therefore, this time with him and his New Orleans brother and wife and family was very special. The beautiful New Orleans Southern Baptist Theological Seminary was close by the motel where we stayed with Dorothy's father and stepmother and close by where the younger brother, Palmer Patterson, and his family lived (2654 Verbena Street). We rode the street cars, toured the famous French Market (walking tour), drank the thick, chicory coffee, and walked Bourbon Street. We saw the New Orleans old French-style buildings with wrought-iron balconies, the home of P. G. T. Beauregard (the Civil War general who fired the first shots in Charleston, South Carolina, harbor) and the places where Brother R. B. Patterson grew up. It was a significant event to treasure and to remember.

Dorothy remembers many early experiences as a child in the Mississippi Delta including: the Anguilla and Catchings churches and leaving on the train to Memphis, Tennessee, to escape the great Mississippi flood in 1927. Mrs. Patterson and her two children were going to Memphis on the last train out, to be with Dorothy's aunt and uncle, her mother's sister and brother-in-law, the Leon Murphys. Brother Patterson stayed behind to endure the flood and to minister to his church flock.

She remembers more vividly living in Jackson, Mississippi, where she had to walk to school. Miss Margaret Ledbetter was her first-grade teacher and a member of their Davis Memorial Baptist Church.

The Pattersons moved to Calhoun City, Mississippi, in the summer of 1930 when the country was in the throes of the deepening depression. Dorothy's brother, Bob, was five years old, and Dorothy was seven. Calhoun City was a very special place and a challenge in the lives of the Patterson family. The seven years in Calhoun City were formative years in the lives of the children and parents. Teachers' salaries were low as well as everyone else's salary. However, it was the time when some of the best were in the teaching profession! Dorothy remembers all of these teachers and especially her music teacher, Miss Lutie Temple, from Seminary, Mississippi. The people of Calhoun City were very special people who loved their pastors and their families.

Calhoun City was the home of Dennis Murphy, longtime lieutenant governor who served several times as governor after a sitting governor died in office. He and Brother R. B. Patterson became very close friends through Dennis Murphy's brother, the editor of the local paper. As a result, Brother Patterson was invited to be the chaplain on the "Know Mississippi Better" train to Mexico, where Mississippians got to know the inside of Mexico's political life from the palace down to the people on the street. We have many priceless coins from this experience. Brother Patterson attended a bullfight and became very proficient in reenacting a bullfight to fascinated children during the four-week summer Vacation Bible Schools held in those days.

Those Bible schools majored strongly on character training, and Brother Patterson always told the character stories. Some of the subsequent Vacation Bible School greats for Southern Baptists were involved in that Vacation Bible School experience including Charlie Treadway who was also a youth revival preacher at First Baptist Church, Calhoun City. Various Southern Baptist denominational people were in and out of the Patterson home. Dorothy became a Christian at seven years of age about the time of the move to Calhoun City in February of 1931. She was in second grade and was baptized on Mother's Day of that year.

Dorothy's mother loved working in the yard with flowers along with her helper, a black man named Hosey. They also raised much of what their food in a garden. In the summer they ate fresh produce; and in fall and winter they subsisted on the canning from the summer. That was a fact of life then, and still is now, in most Mississippi homes. Then, it was glass jar canning and later it was marked sealed cans. Today, there are freezing techniques. In those early days in the summer, the homes were dependent on the ice trucks to bring ice for the iceboxes. The children loved getting the ice chips in the process of getting a twenty-five pound block or sometimes the fifty-pound block of ice.

There were three special girls with whom Dorothy became very close then, and still is now. Mary Frances Van Landingham (Mrs. Tom Wofford), lives in Alexandria, Virginia, on land once owned by George Washington, and is a special volunteer worker in the White House. Her husband died suddenly several years ago. Their son-in-law was a military aide to President Jimmy Carter. Bobbie Ruth Aycock, daughter of the Patterson family physician, lives in Macon, Mississippi, and is married to Bernard Senter, who is in the hardware business. Both are involved in their churches and other special Christian ministries. Mary Elizabeth McGahey, daughter of the other doctor in town, was a member of the Lewis Memorial Methodist Church. Mary Elizabeth and her husband, Ullin Lee Hudson, a retired Army Colonel, now live in Texas. It has been years since we have seen her—1944, to be exact.

The Methodist pastor and his wife were Reverend and Mrs. A. Y. Brown. She was a former third-grade teacher in the Okolona school and taught my brother Joe. Miss Lucille Fatheree, as she was known then, was always remembered by Joe with deep affection. The Browns subsequently served as pastor and wife of the Okolona Methodist Church where my grandfather, Lawrence Jolly, was a member and from which church his funeral was preached. I remember well in January of 1932 when a Brother Gregory was the pastor. It was also the church where my mother attended when she and my father were first married. I heard our next-door neighbor, Mrs. Ida (John) Stone Sr., tell about the occasion: "Your mother was the most beautiful, little thing I'd ever seen." After ten children she changed, and it really cost her her life at an early age, but such love she had for all those children.

In Calhoun City, the Methodist church was right across the street from the Baptist church. Dorothy remembers often staying with the Browns when the Pattersons had to be out of town. Dorothy declares she always wanted to join the Methodist church because they let out earlier than her dad's church. Her brother, Bobby, had other friends with whom he, too, was closely involved, especially George Lacy Van Landingham, brother to Dorothy's friend, Mary Frances. Dorothy recalls she and Bobby doing chores together including stacking and bringing in stove wood, which was a major source of heating in the wintertime in Mississippi homes—aside from cooking. They were fortunate to have a bathroom in their home whereas so many in those days did not. There were chamber pots at night and outdoor toilets for the day. The Jollys took a Saturday-night bath in a zinc tub behind the warm stove.

Bobby loved making things with his hands, especially from wooden apple boxes. He, too, was an excellent student. When a boy would walk Dorothy home from church, she and the boy had to sit on the front porch swing. Dorothy's parents required Bobby to sit on the front porch to keep watch. Early on, Dorothy really had the boys who were interested in this pastor's pretty daughter. She reluctantly tells, when pressured, about her boy friends. There was a Billy Baldwin in Calhoun City, now a retired mail carrier in Pittsboro, Mississippi. In Okolona, W. H. West Jr., our barber's son, now a retired druggist in Jackson, Mississippi, was another. He and I had some competition in our early courting days but things worked out for the best for all concerned. I recall W. H. from Boy Scout days in Okolona. He was always kind and considerate toward me. He seemed to have money for treats when I had none and he would share.

Dorothy recalls Saturdays when she and her mother enjoyed the Texaco Metropolitan Opera Hour of music on the radio. Dorothy became one of the best musicians over the years and had a superb singing voice. This was a very great blessing and asset in our fifty-seven years of ministry, even to this day.

There were always missionaries and special denominational people in and out of the Patterson home and this was a very great asset in our ministry because Dorothy always so easily related to these and greatly helped me in this regard. She reports that she always loved her growing-up years in a pastor's home, her school, and in a city where her parents were always leading citizens and influential people. I was rather shy and reticent. She was always able to relate more or less positively to every situation. Her training and background have enabled her, by God's grace, to be positive and uplifting and always encouraging. There have been times when, without this, I tremble to think what might have happened. She has easily related to women, men, and the youth, and is a most positive influence and asset in our entire ministry.

And, she has been, and is, a most marvelous mother to each of our children. Their problems—and there have been many in these changing times—have always found her wise and giving loving Christian counsel. She stays in touch with each of our daughters, and each grandchild is special. All involved relatives, all my brothers and sisters and their families dearly love her and remember her and her family influence in all our lives! You see, her parents were our pastor and family, too, and the Pattersons lovingly ministered to and helped every member of our families, scattered everywhere. This, aside from all of her cousins (she is the only girl), who have depended on Dorothy for intimate family connections and relationships on her mother's side as well as her father's. She is known as the family eight-hundred number. She was able to pull together Patterson family help and support for the only other Patterson surviving girl, Hannah Patterson-Jones, long-time teacher, who was always especially close to Dorothy. She just recently, at ninety-one, went to join others in Heaven! Dorothy helped her cousin, David Patterson, and his wife, Ola, to take Aunt Hannah into their home. Other aging, ailing family members were also involved. We, and others, gave financial support. Dorothy was always the loving and connecting link, and through her we have kept in contact with every family member—her side and mine. Without exception, all relate easily to Dorothy and love her dearly, averting many a family explosion. Even now, this day of December 5, 1996, she is sending our annual Christmas letter to all these friends and family who have always been as interested in us as we are in each of them.

In the southern states and the rest of the country, the racial after-effects of slavery lingered more than one hundred years after the Civil War. What whites did to the blacks was practiced by many and overlooked by most. Black women, especially the young, were often victims and fled in terror. Many were unsuccessful and there were often mulatto children. The care of these children was thrust on the black race. The blacks were confined to certain areas in most southern towns. They were servants to the whites, taking care of many of their needs, by arrangement, and at lower than justifiable wages. In the terrible depression times, the blacks were on the farms as sharecroppers. One-half of the value of the crops they raised was supposedly theirs. They would be furnished by the landowners and usually at the end of the year had little and were even in debt. So, the landowners would let the tenant farmer leave for some other farm and boss man and bring in another tenant-farmer family that had suffered the same elsewhere. The black families usually lived in low-class shanties. The food was often scanty and loaded with hog grease, heavy molasses, et cetera, to enable the continued hard, grinding work on the farms and in the towns. It was often said that the Southerner hated the black race but loved the individual black person, and the Northerner hated the individual black but loved the black race. There were strong family ties in many cases and blacks and whites shared their families and needs in strong bonds of genuine love. The schools were segregated and if a black got any substantial education, he or she was looked on as a smart-aleck. The mule was the beast-of-burden and was the means of tilling the soil before the day of the tractor. The mules, therefore, had to be carefully fed and cared for and rested on Sundays.

The blacks usually had Saturdays off (at least a half-day) and were in town. They thoroughly enjoyed Saturday nights especially. The whites conceded this and sold their goods at cheap prices and got most of what the blacks made in the week gone by. There were segregated water fountains, or none at all. There were no restrooms for blacks, except the mule barns where the white boys, hidden in the barns, often threw rocks. And the blacks really had no soul anyhow, as subhumans, or so it was thought. If the whites molested the black women or their young, it was mostly overlooked as a normal outlet for sexual energy. Many times this was abhorrent to the white women. I know of no case where a white person was ever hanged for molesting a black girl or woman. If on the other hand, a black threatened or trifled with a white girl, there was hell to pay.

Such was the case in Calhoun City and in most other southern towns, mostly small, in an agricultural economy. In Calhoun City, a young black man did follow a white woman home after work and scratched at her window. The result? Certain white men took this man out of jail, tied him up, and took him south of town to a bridge over water, put a rope around his neck, and made him jump off. In many cases in the south, it was a tree and subsequent burning of the body. The Ku Klux Klan was strong and often contained many of our forebears, a holdover from "Old Bed Forrest Days." Dorothy and all others in Calhoun City were deeply stirred and affected by this incident. She remembers going, out of curiosity, with others to the black church neighborhood and seeing the simple pine box where the mutilated, black body lay inside. Brother Patterson deeply opposed this action and said to his family, "You will see that bad things will happen to those who committed this crime." His prediction came true.

I speak from personal experience about such matters. We had tenant farmers on our farm with usually a very good, mostly loving, relationship. My mother and the black mother would share about new babies as they shelled peas together. The blacks lived in a tenant cabin which was not adequate for winter, though we tried to fix it. Not so tasty brackish water was drawn from a cistern nearby, and, as in most white and black homes, there was the proverbial outhouse. I recall going to this home to see a new baby. I saw a very beautiful child and was asked to stay for dinner. It consisted of corn pone and mustard greens, laced strongly with greasy fatback. Later my father severely reprimanded me for eating with them. I never did again but I have never forgotten.

I can only thank God for the Martin Luther King days and the lifting of the black people in the South. There was terrible bitterness, hatred, and killing of children during the Bull Conner days in Birmingham. The federal troops used force to get black people into the University of Mississippi and the University of Alabama, first under Eisenhower and then under John F. Kennedy. Murdered people were buried under a dam in Philadelphia, Mississippi. The guilty were later tried and convicted. There was also the murder of Medgar Evers in Mississippi. Today things have changed all over the South, slowly and with deep resentment. For example, our town of Okolona is now strongly black. The schools and the good football teams are mostly black. The blacks are now predominant in major sports. For the first time, their economy, sometimes exceeds the whites.

The Great Depression was another major factor in our early lives. The stock market crash of 1929 wrought a major upheaval in every area of life. The heydays of the 1920s, as if there were no tomorrow, brought Wall Street to its knees and utterly ruined the major financial wizards and the country with it. I remember the words of a famous depression song, "Eleven cent cotton and forty cent meat; how in the world can a poor man eat?" Fortunately, we still had a strong agricultural way of life, and most folks raised what they had to eat, plus there were wild berries and nuts to use as surplus proteins. Even then, there were the terrible dust bowls and red clouds of soil blown away because of poor agricultural ways in the Midwest. The same crops were grown year after year on the same soil.

All the stores and businesses were individually owned and operated. There were only the beginnings of the Clarence Saunders trend (Clarence Saunders founded and owned the Piggly-Wiggly chain of grocery stores). Fifteen million people were out of work, and many sold apples and pencils on the streets of New York City. People became deeply depressed. The counties meagerly took care of old folks in the county poor houses. Our Congress today is coming back to the same ways. Let the states do it! They can do it better. There was no major federal or even state government support. I recall my father, as a postman, had his salary cut from $175 per month to $150 per month for a short time. We had the farm, however, and that saved the day for us and for various tenants on our farm. Many Americans committed suicide or died early. Franklin Roosevelt's New Deal and federally supported Civilian Conservation Corps (CCC) Camps and other federal programs helped more people to make some money and gave some hope to the hopeless people. We vividly recall those days! However, it was not until terrible World War II that full employment took over, with the defense industry "saving democracy for the world," and things slowly and then dramatically improved.

In connection with these terrible depression years, the Tennessee Valley Authority (TVA), which made electric power available for the common people, was a Franklin Roosevelt project. Tupelo, Mississippi, eighteen miles north of Okolona, became the first TVA town. My father, my mother's father, Clabe Freeman, his younger son Bill, my older brother Joe, and I made a night trip to Tupelo to be on hand for this great event! The streets were literally crowded beyond anything we had ever seen. We spent the night in our car when we were not on the streets with the tremendous crowds. The next day, the great day, my resourceful father got us a place on the street near where President Roosevelt would speak. Today, that area is a dedicated playground in honor of that great event. We stood on the street waiting with the multitudes for the president to come. Finally, we could see his open touring car coming slowly up the street. The president was waving his hat, and had his mouth wide open, with that inimitable smile of assurance that all was well in our stricken country—just give him and God time. I remember Mrs. Roosevelt seated beside him dressed in a black dress and hat, a smile of assurance on her face as well.

Then came a very agonizing scene as we watched our seriously crippled president painfully walking up the steps, with aid, to take his position behind the prearranged rostrum. We heard that singing voice speaking words of commendation and reassurance about TVA and other such government-sponsored programs and their ability to revive our stricken country. It was no wonder to me that my grandparents, Clabe and Lizzie Freeman, had a huge picture of a smiling Franklin Roosevelt hanging above their bed in their simple farmhouse in the piney woods of Mississippi. I often wonder whatever became of that treasured picture.

I well remember what we called the "Hoover depression days" versus the "Roosevelt hopeful days" in the midst of stark hopelessness. Later we visited the Muscle Shoals, Alabama, area with my grandparents to marvel at that dam to be succeeded by many such dams, some much larger, throughout the country, bringing the luxury of electricity into our cities and farm homes. America was changed by such bold attacks on poverty and destitution. Today we need more spiritual light to come into the deep spiritual darkness of our times. God was there then and He is still in control in our world to bring hope instead of despair—based on the promises of His Word.

The First Baptist Church of Calhoun City began to feel that they could not afford a full-time pastor, illustrative of so many churches—only one quarter to one-half time in the rural areas, especially. Also, the teachers' salaries were tragically low. However, these times brought forth the best in the people because we were all in the same boat and sought to lift and encourage one another. A great deal of talk and pessimism caused the church to have a business meeting to decide whether to go to half-time. Prayerfully and thankfully, the church voted to stay full time. Dorothy recalls those times and the effect on her family and others.

I got my first public job in 1937 helping to build the first concrete road from Shannon, Mississippi, to Okolona, Mississippi, with the Carey-Reed Construction Company. When the concrete was poured, only a two-lane highway in those days, it had to have two inches of dirt on it and be kept wet for two weeks before the road would be useable. My job was to pull a heavy hose and to water the two inches of dirt. My pay was twenty-two and a half cents an hour and I was just sixteen years of age. I actually lied about my age and got my job on a Sunday. My father, a deacon, took me to the place of employment and encouraged me in the process. (I did not face the results of this lie until I was to retire with Social Security in 1986. I was listed as born in 1919 instead of 1921. I had to confess my lie and the woman said, "Don't worry. My mother did the same thing and we can fix it." And, they did!) My dear mother awakened at 3:00 A.M. to get my lunch ready and get me to the job on time by truck from Okolona to the work-place in Shannon and back in the evening. I remember pineapple sandwiches and my black lunch box placed under the new bridges to keep cool.

Actually my brother Joe and I had gotten jobs even earlier at the first industry in Okolona, the Okolona Cheese Plant. The farmers brought their milk in to be processed into cheese and took the resultant whey back to mix with feed for the hogs that furnished our meat. Our job at first was to make the cheese boxes to contain the blocks of cheese that had to mature under relatively cool refrigeration by ice blocks. After many smashed fingers, we graduated to shoveling the cheese cubicles into a tremendous shining vat while we stripped to the waist with sweat pouring. I rather thought that the sweat gave the cheese its salty flavor plus the portions of salt used. For a long time, I could not eat cheese. Flies were a major problem. Even shortly before going away to college, I made less than five dollars a week, twelve hours a day (or night when needed), at five cents an hour in the local Brett's Café. The boss did let us eat anything we wanted—including treats for our dates. We made up for the low pay!

My boss, Mr. Addie Brett, lent my father and me the one hundred dollars to get into Mississippi College (ten-dollars-a-month notes which I finally had to pay back when my father was unable to do so). Dorothy's best friend, Mary Frances Brett, was Mr. Brett's daughter from a previous marriage. My Uncle Peden, who worked at Brett's Café, got us the jobs (that we were glad to get), even though it took us off the farm. We had eleven cows up until that time which we milked by hand, morning and night. We put the milk in a ten-gallon cream can to haul to the cheese plant. We kept it cool in well water, often dipping the flies out. My father built a platform holding area on the back of our Chevy car. When Joe and

I left for our more sophisticated jobs, our younger brothers took over. Hallelujah, we made it and thank God for his gracious mercy and blessing. Out of five boys and five girls, three boys were called to preach and one girl married a preacher. All of us are in special ministries and our father finally surrendered to do what God had early on called him to do, full-time ministry, after retiring from being a postman for thirty-five years. He preached very effectively the last ten years of his life in Mississippi country churches with help and books from Dorothy's father.

In reading a veterans' magazine that came to my father, I noticed an announcement of an American Legion oratorical contest. I mentioned this to Mr. A. W. James, our school superintendent, and he greatly encouraged me to enter. He also helped me prepare my speech. Where there were weaknesses, he helped me strengthen that area. He would also listen to me, time after time, give the speech. He personally took me to the first place where I was to speak. Thereafter, I was one of fifteen to enter the state-level contest. Mr. James took me to Jackson for my presentation there. I am including a copy of my speech (see Appendix A). Previous to that experience, I had been a high-school debater with Romie Morgan, Doris Dallas, and Alva Tate Rowan. With the excellent help and encouragement of our debate coach, Miss Lilah Maxwell, a history teacher at Okolona High School, we did a creditable job. This experience was excellent preparation for the national oratorical contest and, later on, the Mississippi College Debate Team.

I came up in the Cub Scouts of America under the leadership of a fine Jewish man, Mr. Ed Elias. I was often in and out of his home and was always received with love. This led to participation in some outstanding early Cub Scout competitions. We had a jamboree on the parade grounds of our local, outstanding children/youth/adult playground. This playground, called Wilson Park, included: swings, a merry-go-round, tennis courts, a large fishing lake, a classic swimming pool for youth and adults, a wading pool for children, and a fairground area. It was conceived and developed in the mind of our one-eyed mayor, Mr. H. S. Wilson, a Mobile and Ohio Railroad top employee. This man and his wife were absolutely great in our minds. It broke his heart when he was subsequently defeated for mayor by Dr. J. C. Luper. Dr. Luper was a very popular dentist in Okolona who had a yen for dry, good humor, and was beloved by all. Mr. and Mrs. Wilson later left Okolona for their final home in Meridian, Mississippi.

In subsequent years, because of racial tension, Wilson Park was placed under control of a private board in order to exclude the black people. Even now it is run down and a sad remnant of its glory years. Beauty pageants, family reunions, picnics, and horse shows were held under the shade of the great oak trees. Also, there were Mississippi Boy Scout jamborees. I recall literally running, on a hot summer day, two and a half miles west of Okolona to the park to get into the cool swimming pool and to swing on the swings. I had to be careful of the swings because somehow the swinging would upset my equilibrium and tend to make me ill. There was Bill Hixon, who lived just beyond the gateway to the park area, who had several boys in his family. One, Gay, was our special friend. Joe and I would often spend Saturday night and the weekend with the Hixons having rolicking fun. We would go into the park where there was a small children's wading pool. We went at night, careful to be quiet lest Mr. Wilson catch us. I remember eating the noon meal on a Sunday at the Hixon home. This was a godly home. After Mr. Hixon said the blessing, he told us boys to enjoy the meal of chicken and dumplings because he did not know where the next meal would come from. Times were just that hard in those depression years.

I started school with my older brother Joe. We were inseparable. I thought Miss Hurley picked on Joe. He had "haystack" blond hair. Our father cut our hair, and that's the way he did it. It hung down in our eyes, Joe's especially. Miss Hurley took time out to make Joe a spectacle. He would cry and she would send him to the nearby bathroom to straighten up. She'd pin his hair up with a bobbie pin. We did not learn much on those occasions. I recall marching into class and spitting on another boy, L. R. Ross, who picked on me. Miss Hurley took me to the superintendent, Mr. Moore, who gave me a whipping with a belt. I never spit on anybody else! On passing from first to second grade, Miss Hurley sat on one of the little chairs, lined us all up, and kissed us goodbye. We were sad, yet glad to go.

The first time I met Deedee Anderson was in the first or second grade of school in the boys' restroom. Deedee said to me, "My daddy is Hob Anderson and my daddy can whip your daddy." I didn't defend my daddy and rather remembered Cob for Hob. But from then on my older brother Joe and Deedee were the closest of friends—really blood brothers, even to the year 1993 when Joe went to Glory. Indeed, during Joe's final days of illness with leukemia, Deedee would go by to see him, and they would share old times. Our family members were often in Deedee's (Dewey Hobson Anderson's) home. He was named for the famous U.S. Admiral Dewey. We were welcome in that home and always remember the cordial welcome we received from all members of the Anderson family. I recall a Saturday afternoon when Joe and I went with Deedee to pick up pecans from a large pecan tree acreage of the Andersons. I also remember the time when Deedee tangled with a skunk, or polecat, as we called it. Despite long lingering over a cedar-brush fire and smoke, the skunk scent had to wear itself out. On another occasion, Deedee and Elbert Corley, another special childhood friend, went swimming nude in the Okolona Wilson Lake with several others of our gang. Joe and I got out earlier than the rest, dressed, and on a lark, Joe hid Deedee and Elbert's clothes! We sat at the upper end of the lake and watched as they searched frantically. Finally they started to walk out naked. Mr. Wilson stopped them and helped them find their clothes, as they whined, "Joe Jolly hid our clothes."

I recall Mr. Hob Anderson, along with the many others who came in love to visit and share when our little brother, Merrill, was so ill. Mr. Anderson brought a chicken, and sat in our hallway to visit. This was the only adequate place in our home and was adjacent to Merrill's bedroom. On the walls of that hallway was a chalk-talk painting by our friend, Reverend James Fairchild, of the two ways of life. At our request, he gave it to Dorothy and me at a State Training Union rally. It vividly illustrated the two ways of life Jesus talked about: one, the way of life; the other, the way of death. I recall Mr. Anderson and I talked at length about its meaning. There were some sad events later, and I have often recalled that visit in our hallway and take hope in the grace and promises of God. Today, Deedee and his two lovely sisters, Jamie and Geneva, like their beautiful mother, still live in Okolona. A younger sister, June Rose, is deceased. We thank God for loving friendship with these and others during our growing-up years in Okolona.

I was in Boy Scout Troop #21 and tried to make first class. I never quite made it. Our Scout leader, Mr. A. W. James, became increasingly my mentor and was almost a father-figure in the oratorical experience. He was an American Legion member and got that whole organization of outstanding Okolona businessmen behind me. They bought my first, real uptown, dark green suit, suitable shirts, and other attire for the train trip and were my boosters all the way. Joe was in Troop #11, led by our football coach, Mr. Walker. There was strong competition between us. In my Scout development, with tests to pass, an older boy, redheaded Jimmy Palmer, took me under his wing and spent hours with me on those tests. There were so many people who truly took a great interest in me. How could I ever repay them?

In the high school band, Mr. Frank Heard was our excellent director. I played the clarinet. Joe played the tuba and also, on occasion, the drums. We made all the football games. The cheerleaders were great, especially one Dorothy Patterson who never knew that I had my eye on her until much later. She was into piano music under a marvelous teacher, Miss Ruth Ainsworth. In the band, we played and cheered for our football team until Joe and I got on the team. I recall playing a night game on our new football field, a special project of our Superintendent of Schools, Mr. James. First, we played in the mud; later, a grass field. I was in a game, very excited, and ran into the opposing line of scrimmage and got seriously kneed over the heart area. I was hurting so much I had to beg the coach to take me out. It took weeks for me to get over that injury, and it left some lingering problems. I remember playing one night game on a muddy Mississippi loblolly field in Louisville, Mississippi, where we had gone by bus. There were sheets of ice on the field. We played because we had to, to get it over with, trying to avoid plowing our faces into the icy mud. We lost and didn't much care. We just wanted it over with! All of these experiences were just prior to World War II, and several of our youth went away, never to return alive.

We took band trips on the beautiful GM&O trains to Jackson, Mississippi, our state capitol. We stayed in the fabulous Edwards Hotel, marched on broiling hot Capitol Street, and rested on the lawn under the giant oaks on the old Mississippi Capitol grounds, dating from pre-Civil War times. The old capitol building, from Jefferson Davis times, is still one of the most beautiful architectural gems of that pre-Civil War era. We always placed in the top bracket of band competition. There were subsequent band directors, Mr. Charles McBride and Mr. O. B. Taylor, all good but none could quite come up to our first, Mr. Frank Heard. I made the mistake of calling him Shorty. He heard about it and my punishment was the "Board of Education" in front of the band. I never made the same mistake twice!

My high school teachers, as well as all others, were the best in those times, receiving low wages like everyone else. But what great teachers they were who truly sacrificed, though they never gave the impression of thinking so! We had one of the three top schools in Mississippi, competing with Jackson and Grenada, Mississippi, high schools. I don't know how the Jolly brothers managed to be in all the attendant activities involved, because with ten children we were always cash poor. But, somehow, we made it!

I recall the first battery-operated radio to get our favorite program, *Amos and Andy*, white comedians pretending to be black. I recall *Lowell Thomas and the News, Lum and Abner,* the *Jot 'Em Down Store*, and *Nurse Miller*.

We always had a fairly good car, though we spent much time pushing it on muddy, gravel roads, miring up to the hub, coming into Okolona from the west and coming off that road to the worst, muddy road on earth which came up to our house on the hill. We stayed stuck in winter and rainy times as we pushed and shoved. We were always getting a bad dose of Mississippi mud in the face and on our clothes until the blessed, hot, summer dried out the mud. Finally, we put into practice a Civil War trick. We cut down small, live, oak trees and corduroy-paved the road. These trimmed trees were laid side by side on the muddy roads and the car sailed right on up the hill. I recall our first car, a Model T Ford, on that muddy road. My father brought her through a barbed-wire gate up to our house. My mother tried driving once, but some minor accident so frightened her that she would never try to drive thereafter. As long as Daddy was at the wheel, we felt safe, even on one occasion when we had graduated to a Chevrolet touring car with celluloid side protectors. We got caught in a storm and those side protectors saved our lives.

I remember another time on a hot summer day when we had a flat tire. That was always a problem in those days on gravel or dirt roads. We were in the process of fixing it when a fast-flying larger Buick car came rushing by and someone in that car threw ears of green corn into our car and faces, denting the car and left front light. My father thought he knew the culprits, the Hadleys, from famous Hell's Half-acre, northwest of Okolona. My father's father, Lawrence Jolly, a constable, had had some run-ins with the Hadleys. I could never figure out how they could know it was our car they hit. Thereafter, my father carried a little pearl-handled thirty-eight revolver in his car for some time. This older Mr. Hadley had reportedly been cut with a large, sharp, pocketknife razor across his belly. He had sense enough to flee to a nearby fish pond where he stood holding his entrails in until our local doctor, B. DeVan Hansell, could come and sew him up. We were proud to have a grandfather who could create such exciting episodes. What a time to grow up and what a time we had making the grade!

Let me tell you about a little girl, Miriam Stone, sister of our very dear friends, John Jr., Richard, and Idanelle Stone, our across-the-field neighbors (one hundred yards or so). Their dear parents, very special to us in those years, are now in Glory.

John Stone Jr. and Miriam were first in their family. We were constantly back and forth in each other's homes. Their parents were always especially dear to me. Miriam was the oldest. She and my brother Joe started school together. I can remember her coming home with Joe in our car when our father came home from work. He got started as a mail carrier, rural substitute, in a covered hack buggy with an old mule named Sue, in the very early days of automobiles. He drove the rural route when needed—rain, sleet or snow, summer weather, winter, and in between. I recall the sad day when old Sue, the faithful mule, died, and we all gathered around and wept.

Miriam loved to dress up and boss her little brother John around. He does not remember her. She loved to use her mother's rouge, lipstick, and other makeup. She was a delightful little girl and playmate.

On a particular Saturday, when she had wanted to come to our home, she went instead to the home of her mother's brother, Mr. Bill Gregory. He had a pistol, not unusual in those days, which he placed on the mantle over the fireplace, as I recall. Somehow Miriam got that pistol and accidentally mortally wounded herself. She died that Saturday night while the whole community prayed. How very sad and heartbroken we all were words cannot describe.

I recall my first funeral service as she was buried in our Okolona cemetery in the Stone lot—very prominent, early people in our area. I stood by that grave when they lowered the little casket. I recall the white hearse, with red doors inside. A first cousin, J. C. Stone Jr., stood by the grave, weeping copiously, as all of us were. We never got over that great tragedy. Her dear father, later struck by a car as he turned into his driveway off the main road, died shortly thereafter.

Miriam never lived to grow up but her precious memory has lingered, and I feel her story, short and sweet, should be told. God bless your lovely memory, Miriam. You are now with your mother and father and others of your dear ones in Heaven's Glory, and we shall join you one day by and by when the battle's over.

There were always people in and out of our home, spending the day or the night. We older boys especially enjoyed the coming of the attractive young ladies to visit our sisters. One of the most special later on was Dorothy Faith Patterson, and for fifty-four years she has been a steady in my home.

We lived in the best of times of the Great Depression and always made it, though we were heavily in debt like most everybody else. However, my father gave the impression that he was in charge and, somehow, by God's grace and the loving support of our pastors and families and others who really liked our family, we made it. They often kidded my father about the number of children in the family. His reply, "I wouldn't give a dime for another but I wouldn't take a million dollars apiece for the ones I have," made me feel special, that I was worth that to him.

Our family was so large that all of us could not go to church at the same time. One-half went on one Sunday, and one-half went the next. My dear mother usually stayed home to have lunch ready for us, as we were usually starved beyond words. One beautiful Sunday, I was in the "in group." I remember saying to my father just as we were turning off the main road onto our road up the hill, "Daddy, I believe Jesus is the Son of God and died for our sins. Am I saved?" (The pastor had stressed that truth.) My father did not reply until we got up to our home and got out of the car. Then he said, "Son, when you are saved, you will know it." And I surely did know it, and have never doubted since, as in my salvation experience described.

When I was about eleven years of age, I became concerned about my soul's salvation. I had heard about revivals and people being saved, especially the black people. They would talk about so and so "getting" saved and baptized. I began to have a heavy burden about my own need to be saved. In this concern, I walked one hot, summer day after dinner down through the hog lot—so called in those days—on our farm and across a barbed-wire fence. There was a home-made ladder step-over at this crossing. Immediately upon crossing, to the right, were a shady post oak tree and a rather hidden area. I sat down under this tree and poured out my heart and need to be saved to God. He was so close in that moment. I asked Him to come into my heart and life and save me. And, then, to help me to be what He wanted me to be. In that moment a wonderful, assured peace came into my inner being and I knew the full forgiveness of God in Christ, though not as mature as later. I did know assuredly that I was saved and accepted. It was as if God came down in that place in answer to my prayer. I had an emotional burst of tears and thankfulness for at least fifteen minutes. I knew then and there that God had charge of my life.

I recall getting up from that place and walking down a path beside the stump of a tree with the consciousness that these were my first steps in the will of God— in full confidence that I was His and He was mine. Where would it lead me? I walked over across a railroad track that divided our farm and where my brother Joe and our black tenant farmer, Booker T. Hughes, were (he recently died in St. Louis, Missouri, at eighty-two years of age). I joyfully told them of my experience in detail. I remember Booker Hughes, whom we all loved and respected, rather made light of my "findin' de Lawd over there under a little bush." I felt affronted but it didn't daunt my newfound faith and spirit, nor have I had any doubts since.

In a revival meeting in our Okolona Baptist Church, I went forward to confess my faith. My younger sister Marguerite also came forward. She later married Reverend Hubert Hammet and lived in the west as a minister's wife for thirty-five years. We were baptized at the same time, although she later had an experience of deeper faith and was baptized again.

I do recall that when I went forward my pastor, Reverend D. L. Hill, took my hand in greeting and welcome. We dearly loved this man who preceded my future father-in-law, Reverend R. B. Patterson. Brother Hill and his family left Okolona for a church in Arkansas. Later when we were in Pineville, Kentucky, he was pastor of First Baptist Church, Somerset, Kentucky. He later was pastor of First Baptist Church, Corinth, Mississippi, which today has a beautiful, commanding building in the north of Corinth. We were there in a World Missions Conference in 1988.

So, only God knew, that day when I walked down that path, how many directions He would lead in my prayer, "help me to be what You want me to be." And, the end is not here yet. I must say here that my life was not always as devoted to His will until after our (Dorothy's and my) call to full-time ministry, described elsewhere. I enclose a copy of my Ordination to the Gospel Ministry in 1940 by my Okolona Baptist Church (see Appendix H). That in itself was a most unusual occasion!

My father-in-law-to-be gave me a copy of Dr. E. Y. Mullins' book on the doctrines of the Christian faith. I read it completely and later more understandably in seminary. Dr. Mullins was the great and distinguished president of our Southern Baptist Theological Seminary when most of my council were students under his leadership.

I expected a really deep examination from the distinguished ordination council. I told them of my pastor's counsel and the help in the Mullins' book. The chairman of my ordination council, Reverend W. C. Stewart, pastor of First Baptist Church, Houston, Mississippi, after only a couple of questions were answered, said, "We can see that this man, (nineteen years of age, I was), is well prepared thanks to our friend, R. B. Patterson. I move that we recommend his ordination to the gospel ministry in this church, and that he continue under Brother Patterson's counsel and in the further pursuit of his education." The motion was seconded with several positive expressions of confidence and expectancy, and I was able to breathe freely.

On a subsequent Sunday morning, I was ordained by my home church, at the request of my first church, Franklin Baptist Church, Flora, Mississippi. Dorothy, my one and only sweetheart, had a good box camera. On the day of my ordination, later at our family home, she took the only surviving picture of my whole family which all of us treasure to this day. Several are gone now to Glory, and we can see what we all looked like on that beautiful, meaningful day. Several of our family then were later in full-time ministry: my brothers, Joe and Fred, sister Marguerite, and much later, our father, Joe L. Jolly Sr. All of our then family and subsequent children are thankfully Christians and serving our Lord in many places.

All of the distinguished members of my ordination council are now in Glory except Col. Warren Earl Ferguson, USAF, retired, long-time special friend in the Patterson family, and subsequently to all our family, especially my brother, Lt.-Col. Joe L. Jolly Jr., Chaplain, USAF, retired. And so, the connections in our lives have always been there, by God's wonderful Grace in Christ Jesus, our Lord, to whom be all glory now and forevermore! Indeed, all

The Joe L. Jolly Sr. family on the day of Charles's ordination, September 1, 1940. Left to right, standing: Joe Jolly Jr., LaVerne, Joe Jolly Sr., Estelle Jolly, Charles, Merrill, Marguerite, Fred. Left to right, seated: Joanne, Mary Frances, Yvonne (in front of Mother), and Donnie.

our Jolly family became Christians and followers of our Lord under the ministry of Reverend and Mrs. R. B. Patterson Sr., who could not go as missionaries to Argentina, but were true, effective missionaries where God placed them.

Now, a further word about the little town of Buena Vista, Mississippi, and other related matters in our early lives. Buena Vista was the place where my great-grandfather on my mother's side, Michael Freeman, came back to live and rear his family after the Civil War. He fought at the Hornet's Nest at Shiloh, Tennessee, where the horrible shock of the war first hit the nation. He had a cadre of six sons and only one daughter, Aunt Lilly Freeman Patterson. She was the darling of her father, mother, and brothers.

The Buena Vista Normal School was equivalent to today's Junior College. There were relatively poor schools in Mississippi at this time, and even Mississippi State University was known then as Mississippi Agricultural and Mechanical College—emphasizing the two major industries of that time.

My grandfather, Claiborne Freeman Sr., lived in Buena Vista with his wife, Elizabeth (Lizzie) and reared their family. Here my father, Joe Jolly Sr., and Lillian Estelle Freeman met, fell in love, and were married following World War I.

My father's mother, Mollie Fowlkes, was a schoolmate of my grandfather, Claiborne(Clabe), according to a letter Clabe Freeman wrote to my father giving his consent to the marriage. My Aunt Lilly, a schoolteacher, lived here with her only son and family. All are buried in the old Buena Vista cemetery kept up by my uncle Claiborne Freeman Jr., and a Mr. Pulliam whom he enlisted, served until Claiborne's death. With invested money collected from all of us, the perpetual care of the cemetery was assured in Buena Vista and Woodland, Mississippi, where part of my mother's family is buried. Later, my grandfather Clabe and family lived in the Woodland area. That little Buena Vista cemetery is the burial place of most of our early relatives on my father's mother's side. The little town is dead as a place of business, scattered residentially, but still a very sacred place in my early memory and in my youngest recollections. The cemetery has monuments of beautiful angelic statues and tombstones where on resurrection day the dead in Christ will arise and ascend according to God's Word.

My uncle Claiborne Freeman Jr. married his first wife, Betty Russell, daughter of a cotton gin operator in Woodland, Mississippi, and had one daughter, Betty Ann, and later, one son, Kenneth. After his divorce and a broken family situation, Kenneth never seemed to settle down, and so far as is known, he died early. The little girl lived with her loving mother and father in Okolona in a roomy railroad car brought to the Wilson Recreation Park by Mr. H. S. Wilson. Uncle Claiborne lived there rent-free in return for looking after the rather large Wilson Park area. Betty Ann developed a summer sickness, extreme colitis, and in spite of the best medical care, she died. She is buried in the Woodland cemetery, where my mother's youngest sister, Frances, who died early, and my mother's oldest brother, Charlie Freeman, who was murdered, are also buried. Hence, the importance of these two cemeteries in the Freeman and Jolly families.

My mother's oldest sister, Kathleen Freeman, married to Georgette Davis, had an only child, Louise. Kathleen and my mother, Estelle, were very close until the early end of my mother's earthly life at forty-nine years. Daughter Louise married Johnnie Mihelic whose mother and brother came from Czechoslovakia. They all lived together in the Davis home in Houston, Mississippi. Louise, in our younger years, was like a sister to our family and our early playmate, and was looked on as one who managed us in delightful and acceptable fashion. We were very close even until the end of her life in October of 1992. She and Johnnie named their son John Merrill, out of loving memory of my brother who died of Hodgkins disease when he was thirteen, in April of 1941. They also had two girls, Donna Mihelic McMillian, who lived in the Dallas, Texas, area, and

Sandie Mihelic Porter, who lives in the Tupelo, Mississippi, area. John Merrill is married and lives with his family in Tupelo and is in the oil-rig business in Texas. The youngest son, Tony Mihelic, is married and lives with his family in Arizona.

Following her husband's death from serious depression, Donna came to Houston, Mississippi, to live with younger daughter, Dawn. Dawn recently married Steve Pate and lives in a mobile home in Woodland, Mississippi. A lovely home was built, and the property was deeded to the Davises (later Mihelics) in return for some land which was deeded to the new Houston High School next door. We feel very close to Donna and have recently stayed as guests in her home. These are all very special people to us. Johnnie Mihelic died in 1969 of cancer. He and his family had a strong Catholic background and were faithfully involved in the on-going program of their church. We keep in touch and only recently she brought me a large assortment of early family pictures and treasures of my mother's family and our kin. We were visiting with my brother Fred and his family who now live in the late Joe Jolly homeplace in the Okolona area, where he is pastor of the Mt. Olive Baptist Church. Many of our Jolly kin were members there from the early days—as was recounted at a recent church reunion.

My Aunt Kathleen Davis (Kay) and her husband, Georgette, were Methodist, and both are buried in the Methodist church cemetery. I was very close to Aunt Kay who wrote me wherever I might happen to be living. She was a second mother to our large Jolly family. She died while we were living in the Pittsburgh, Pennsylvania, area. I visited for a whole week in an earlier Georgette Davis home in Houston, Mississippi, and became a homesick child from being away from my family home in Okolona for the first time. The Davises were very patient with me and I witnessed their loving affection for one another and their little daughter, Louise, on that week's visit. We sat on their front porch one night when my mother's sister, Thelma, a schoolteacher, and her new husband, Paschal Alexander, came rolling by. They had just gotten married and had a procession of cars and old trucks, all horns blowing, following them. Uncle Paschal was a bird-dog trainer, among other things. He even tried to train one for me but there was no success. Their one son, Ted, lives with his wife, Gail, in Olive Branch, Mississippi. I mention these family connections because they are important for us to know.

These growing up, developing years of our lives were for the most part a very happy and memorable time. The Great Depression had its effect but really did not daunt our faith in the future. World War II deeply affected us all. We never doubted that our country would prevail, and that we would live through it. We would find what the one God had in His great plan for us. We would fall in love, get married, have a family, and help make the future the best it could be.

It has worked that way despite so many who went away to war and never came back alive. The later tragic wars had their evil effect—the Korean War, the Vietnam War and the more recent Gulf War never destroyed our hope in the future of our country, the marvel of the whole world.

When I think of the present generation and the relatively mixed-up people who have tended to ignore God, the Bible, and "Whatsoever we sow we shall also reap," I seriously wonder about the future. With drugs, gambling, rising and shocking crime rates, AIDS, and other prevalent diseases, I question what constructive future our children and grandchildren have to anticipate. Modern technology and the computer age point toward a more impersonal future. Certainly without a vital faith, the future on this planet Earth is in dire jeopardy. We think in terms of colonizing the Moon and Mars, but with what impossible costs that would seem to be prohibitive. And above all, without a vital faith in God and Bible truth, we are on a dead-end street. For the Christian, we look forward to the most wonderful future in the Kingdom of God. For those without this blessed hope, the future is bleak. Everywhere the un-christian world is filled with increasing violence and destruction, with millions being the victims of decreasing food, fuel, and water supplies. Whole countries are devastated. Agriculture and environment are in serious jeopardy.

We are either in the last days of this earth or in the challenge of the greatest era yet in earth's history, all inherent in the will of God who is over all and "not willing that any should perish but that all should come to repentance."

2

College Years

1939–1943 (Charles) • 1941–1946 (Dorothy)

Even thinking about going to college in 1939 seemed an impossible matter because of the six-hundred-dollar yearly cost. I had worked in a railroad hotel/café for five dollars a week plus whatever I wished to eat. My father had ten children to feed and clothe on $175 a month as a mail carrier, and our farm was not yet paid for. We did raise enough food for our table and our tenant farmer and his family. The latter worked on a sharecropper basis, which included a house to live in. Their food was less than our own and they usually wound up at the end of the year owing us money they could not pay.

When Dorothy and I surrendered our lives to full-time Christian service in a thrilling summer youth revival led by a team from our Baptist colleges, we were encouraged to think and pray about attending one of those schools. Because of my high-school oratorical experience, and as one of five national finalists from an original starting field of twenty-four thousand, I had some special claim to various colleges.

I had originally thought of being a lawyer, and in my final year of high school had applied to the University of Alabama and was accepted. However, the surrender to God's call made a difference in such consideration. I visited the Koch, Mississippi, home of one of my high school mentors, Professor H. G. Worley. He took me to visit Hinds County Junior College and Mississippi Baptist College. Once on the campus of Mississippi Baptist College, I had the feeling, this is the place! Dorothy's father, my father in the ministry and my pastor, made a subsequent trip to Mississippi Baptist College with my father and me. He was very helpful and encouraged me to attend this school where he had graduated in 1919.

I needed financial aid. At my pastor's suggestion, we visited Professor George Hazilrigg Mackie, director of the Mississippi Baptist College 155th Infantry

Band. With my four years of experience playing clarinet in the high-school band, Mr. Mackie immediately signed me up. This military connection with the National Guard meant twelve dollars a month support for me. Mr. Mackie later gave me the additional job of cleaning the band room once a month, or more if necessary, for an additional fourteen dollars a month. I left campus full of hope.

To seriously get started at Mississippi Baptist College, I needed more money. My father and I approached my boss at Brett's Hotel/Café. He agreed to lend me one hundred dollars with the promise from us to pay him back at the rate of ten dollars a month. We signed notes for this security. My father was unable to keep the commitment, and I later took care of the loan.

A part of the ability to pay back the loan was the printing and sale of my book, *Youth Speaks*. This book included the speeches, photos, and biographies of the five finalists in the third American Legion Oratorical Contest in 1939—of whom I was one. The book also included a laudatory recognition of the American Legion. We were between World War I and World War II. The Legion made me a gift of books, *The Great War—World War I*. I don't know what happened to them.

The preparation of this book was rather extensive and required much correspondence and persuasion. My favorite college professor, Dr. Walter Fuller Taylor, professor of English and literature who was seriously crippled by polio, helped me with this preparation and encouraged me. He subsequently became my college debate coach and took other debaters and me on debate trips in his little green car. We had fun! My debate partner, Tom Douglas, later best man in my wedding, and I won the state championship in 1942 at the University of Mississippi in Oxford, Mississippi. Also on the team were Benny Smith and Carol Izard, who is now a professor at the University of Delaware. There is a trophy at Mississippi Baptist College today marking this event.

I also became a paper grader for Dr. Taylor, which made for some additional income for college expenses. On one occasion, I got rather carried away in grading a set of papers in which I felt the persons, whom I knew too well, were derelict in study and expressed it on their papers. I severely reprimanded several. Dr. Taylor pulled me aside in his gentle fashion and said, "Mr. Jolly, I agree with your findings but perhaps you had best erase those comments and hope they will do better in the future." I did as he suggested but they could still see the erasures. Even though, they stayed my friends.

Dr. Taylor took me to Mississippi State College in Starkville, Mississippi, for the State Oratorical contest in April of 1941. I won that contest, and Dorothy has the small trophy. She and our Okolona Baptist Church pastor and wife,

Brother and Mrs. C. A. Alexander, came for that occasion and took me back to our home in Okolona.

When I walked into our home that night, I immediately sensed that things were really bad for my thirteen-year-old brother, John Merrill Jolly (Merrill), who had been ill for four years with pernicious Hodgkins disease. The burden of prayer for him had been overwhelming. My father would take him to Memphis, Tennessee, for X-ray treatments and, for lack of money, slept in the car overnight in order to bring Merrill back home the next day. His disease had progressed to the point of having deep bedsores, and he agonized in pain as my mother and others ministered to him. Even turning him on his sheet brought terrible screams of pain! Merrill was able to look up from complete exhaustion and ask me why I was home. I explained where I'd been and had taken the chance to come to see him. It turned out those were his last words to us. He lingered on through the night. I stayed up with him while others who were exhausted tried to rest. I would literally hold him in my arms to help him breathe. Finally, toward daybreak, he murmured, "Lordy, Lordy," and breathed his last. His frail body was in such dire condition that the undertaker could not embalm him.

My father, who was always short of money, and I went into Okolona, two and half miles away, to find a casket and suitable clothes. We found a white shirt and tie and a medium-sized casket. We had to bury him the same day because of his body's condition. Back home, neighbors and friends were quietly working to get our home ready for the funeral in the afternoon. Marvin Stone, longtime bachelor friend who lived in our tenant house, and some black people, all of whom deeply loved my little brother, went to Buena Vista cemetery and dug the grave. Dorothy's father, who had moved to Memphis, came at our request to have the funeral service on our front porch. It was a hard experience to have to plant him in his grave on the same day of his death, but God gave us strength. I counted fourteen beautiful wreaths. His teachers and friends came to the funeral. That morning when he died, the oak tree outside his window was covered with beautiful purple wisteria and the mockingbirds sang. We all gathered in the room where his body was laid, thanked God for his short life and great influence on all his family and the entire community, and gave him back to God who had allowed us to have him for those thirteen years.

Late that evening when we got back to our home from the burial, my oldest brother, Joe, had a date with Kittie Fain, from Tupelo, Mississippi. He invited Dorothy and me to go along with him. As we left our home, I could hear the brokenhearted wails of our dear mother in giving up this beloved child. A copy of her memorial poem is included in this book (see Appendix B).

I have gotten ahead of myself about college days. My Uncle Peden, my father's only brother, helped me so much with clothes and the loan of his typewriter. He was very supportive and proud of my choice of life work and the college. He had helped Joe and me to get our jobs at Brett's Hotel/Café, a railroad stopover hotel/café between the cities of Mobile, Alabama, and Jackson, Mississippi. He subsequently married my boss's sister-in-law, Isadora Powe. Later they all moved to Mobile, Alabama, and the Waynesboro, Mississippi, area. My uncle became a brakeman and later an engineer on the railroad between Mobile and New Orleans, Louisiana, from recommendations of his friends he'd met at the hotel/café in Okolona a stop on the GM&O between Mobile, Alabama, and Jackson, Tennessee.

This uncle meant much to me in my growing-up years. He had no high school diploma but read and studied on his own and was a highly intelligent person. He liked Robert M. Hutchins, president of the University of Chicago. He took me to baseball games. On one occasion we went to St. Louis, Missouri, to see the famous St. Louis Cardinals, the noted "Gas House Gang," play a doubleheader. What a thrill that was! The excursion fare was $1.50 from Okolona to St. Louis. There I first saw black people using the same restroom as whites, and I resented these Yankee traditions. I got over it, thank God, and have come to rejoice in the black recovery of basic human rights—that is another story. I recall a trip to Memphis with my uncle when we stayed in the Claridge Hotel. I attended a Broadway play with him, my first such experience. He was not married then and spent much time in our home. He would bring bananas and we would make homemade freezer ice cream. Sometimes, there was fresh pineapple. At Christmas, he brought the fruit, firecrackers, and other goodies that made Christmas special for my father's ten children and his sister, Pearl Christine, who lived with us for a time (their mother died early from cancer when Pearl was about thirteen years old).

Now, back to my college days. My father and mother and John Merrill took me to Mississippi Baptist College in early September of 1939. When we arrived, a group of Baptist Student Union (BSU) young men welcomed us. These same young men had been in the youth revival in Okolona when Dorothy and I were touched by God and called into his service. They helped me get my trunk and other goods up to the third floor of Ratliff Hall. This was a special preachers' dormitory which cost thirty-five dollars a month for room and board. I lived there for the next four years.

We had come by Dorothy's home in Okolona before daylight. She remembers us blowing the horn. She and I had had several dates and I knew, God willing, and she willing, that she was to share the rest of my life. She was somewhat doubtful at this point, thinking that the college scene would maybe change me, as I would meet other girls and have new experiences. She had just finished her sophomore year in high school. She was a special leader in our high school and even now stays in touch with everyone.

I was sad when my family left me behind. For the first several weeks, I was so terribly homesick and missed Dorothy so dreadfully. Dorothy and I agreed to pray for one another each night at ten o'clock. And always, there was the constant prayerful concern for my brother Merrill.

I gradually became oriented into the full swing of college. There was the ministerial banquet on Friday night at First Baptist Church, Clinton, Mississippi. The freshman class banquet on Saturday on campus. Dorothy came to my freshman class banquet as my guest and stayed with her father's family friends, the A. L. Goodriches. Mr. Goodrich was then editor of the Mississippi *Baptist Record*. How proud I was of this strikingly beautiful young woman in the bloom of life. She has not changed much after fifty-seven years. All of my friends loved and adored her. They were jealous of my good fortune and teased me unmercifully. It was something for her family to allow her to come alone on the train. They said they felt I would take care of their pride and joy. Before it was over, we shared all of our college experiences and all subsequent experiences, and at this point of fifty-seven years of knowing each other, "The bloom is still on the rose." At my senior year Philomathean banquet, held at the top of the Heidelburg Hotel, Dorothy was my sponsor as I was president of that society. Her picture is in the college annual.

One episode I must share. On the night of July 20, 1939, I went by train to Koch, Mississippi, to visit with the Worley family. Dorothy came with my family to see me off. My mother and family were standing on the platform when the Rebel Luxury Liner came in. I kissed my mother and hugged others in the family. Then, spontaneously, I swept Dorothy up in my arms and kissed her hard! She stood there, stunned. The first kiss from me! She said she never got over it. My mother reprimanded me later for being so improper. But, instead, I improved as things progressed!

My college roommate was Clifton Earl Cooper, a twenty-five-year-old ministerial student and pastor of Franklin Baptist Church in Flora, Mississippi. When I came into the room, he was sitting on the top bunk bed working on his toenails. He was an orator/debater, and we had much in common and have remained close friends to this day. When he was called to a church in Jayess, Mississippi, I believe, he sent me with his letter of resignation to the Franklin Baptist Church and included the recommendation that they call me as their pastor. They did, on the spot, and so I had my first church. I have recently been in touch with him. He is now retired from Riverside Baptist Church in Jacksonville, Florida. He sent us one of the fruits of his special sculpting hobby, a striking bust of Abraham Lincoln. I called Dr. Cooper on the phone, on a Saturday afternoon, on a whim. He answered and I said, "Earl, you don't know who this is but I once dated your beautiful, redheaded wife." He simply said, "I congratulate you." I proceeded to remind him that during our time at Mississippi Baptist College, there was an occasion when he had to be away on a preaching mission at an important time for his fiancée at old Hillman College. With her permission, he asked me to fill in as her date. What an honor! Dr. Cooper, now in his eighties, creates the Lincoln busts, et al, as a hobby.

I immediately became active in college. I was heavily involved with the Mississippi Baptist College 155th Infantry Band, marching and practicing. We made tours and had concerts up and down the state with the military 155th Infantry convoy on these occasions. We stayed in the homes of people, by pre-arrangements, which brought me in touch with a whole new way of life, and I loved it. In 1941, on a warm Sunday afternoon, we went by train to Camp Shelby, Mississippi, for a week of special training. Our band was a part of the Service Company of the 155th Infantry. We were given sandwiches, and fanned and fumed on the hot trip down. The band's task was to play while the rest of the 155th infantrymen marched. Lo and behold, the next day it turned bitterly cold and snowed hard—over a foot back on the college campus. Instead of playing while they marched, the band had to go out and cut green firewood to heat the cold tents. Hence, we suffered through the week. Two things stand out in my memory: one is that we sang old gospel songs at night in the freezing tents, and the other is that the men had to knock out the tent flues which were stopped-up from burning green firewood all through the night. What a week that was! I also recall the time we spent at a new camp, Camp Polk, Louisiana, where it rained all week. This was also the place where Eisenhower came into prominence.

The time came when, because of Pearl Harbor and the expanding war, the 155th Infantry was mobilized into service. We had forty band members and only twenty-five could go. Mr. Mackie wanted me to go. I was pastor of the Franklin Baptist Church; therefore, I could be exempt. I consulted with my father and my great friend, Dr. B. D. Hansell, who was on the draft board in Okolona. They advised me to take advantage of my exemption and pastor that church. This meant that later I was there when loved ones were gone to war and families needed a pastor, especially when some did not come back. I have never regretted my decision. I only deeply regret that some of our band paid the full price.

I became active in our BSU, the First Baptist Church of Clinton, and our Ministerial Association that included preaching on the street and jail ministries in Jackson, our state capitol. I well remember preaching on Sunday afternoon in the Jackson city jail. The prisoners were all around us, up and down, and listening intently to the preaching. I put my loud voice to good use. I felt good about bringing God's message of hope into this sad environment.

Later I had the privilege of teaching a weekly Bible class for Mrs. R. A. Overton in the First Baptist Church of Jackson, Mississippi. They paid me five dollars a week. In those days that was a substantial amount of money and very helpful to me. I got this privilege through Mrs. Vashti Brunson of Meridian, Mississippi, wife of deacon Grady Brunson. I was their pastor and Vashti, before marriage, had been a member of Mrs. Overton's Bible class. I would ride the bus over, getting to Jackson from Clinton early, and go to the office of Dr. Overton, a chiropractor, and wait for him to finish his practice for the day and then accompany him to his home for dinner. I got to know this family quite well. Mrs. Overton was truly a fundamental, premillennial Bible believer and teacher. She gave me several cherished books from her little Bible bookstore in her home. On one occasion, Dr. Overton went a back way to the drugstore to get strong drugs for headaches. I kidded him about saying his chiropractic work took away the need for drugs, and he became embarrassed to get things for himself and his family. One of the younger Overton daughters, Carol, became the wife of a young man who later became governor of Mississippi, Bill Waller. She was instrumental in beautifying the governor's mansion. I wrote to her at the time and she graciously responded.

I also worked on the college campus for fifty cents an hour. My campus work boss was an older student, Jimmy Weatherford, brother-in-law of my third-grade teacher, Mildred Burris. We had a project to clear trees from an area being prepared for a golf course. We literally dug the trees out by the roots. Jimmy would assign us a task for removal, usually after lunch, and when we finished, it counted for so many hours, three I believe. The money and also work on other campus projects went toward my tuition.

Dr. D. M. Nelson, the college president, was a great golfer and quite an orator. I later had him for a layman's revival in Annapolis, Maryland, after he had retired as president. I took him to Gettysburg and he could not believe the gentle slope up to the high-water mark of the Civil War where only six hundred southern rebels got across from seventeen thousand who started up. Dr. Nelson insisted that they went up a mountain. I'm not sure I convinced him, even with the markers to attest to the fact.

One other special friend was Frank G. Voight, a specialist worker in the school clinic and dispensary where we received our shots and other medical care. His father was a riverboat captain at Tuscumbia, Alabama, in the Muscle Shoals/Wilson Dam area. Frank later invited me to Virginia where we spent eight and a half years of happy pastoring. He died suddenly of a heart attack while on vacation in Myrtle Beach, South Carolina, in 1982. Frank's oldest daughter, Mary Ann, is now the organist at our former pastorate, Ivy Memorial Baptist Church in the Hampton area of Virginia. We saw her on September 17, 1995, in a worship service.

One might wonder how I ever got to study and make my grades in college with all these activities. The truth is I studied day and night and was always able to be prepared. I dearly loved all my teachers: Dr. S. E. Cranfill, sociology; Dr. W. H. Sumrall, psychology; Dr. Murray Latimer, Greek; Dr. E. Bruce Thompson, history; Dr. Ernestine Thomae, German; Dr. W. O. Sadler, biology; Dr. M. O. Patterson, Bible; and later, Dr. Howard Spell who replaced beloved Dr. Patterson in Bible.

I heard this beloved Dr. Patterson conduct the marriage ceremony for one of his daughters at First Baptist Church of Clinton, Mississippi. His college assistant, Dr. Othell Hand, now retired in Columbus, Georgia, was one of my closest friends across the years and was in our wedding. I got permission to use his ceremony as our own. I have married countless people in many places using this ceremony which is simple but beautiful and adequate.

I was also privileged to serve on the Honor Council and as president of the Philomathean Literary Society, one of two on campus. I was listed in Who's Who on college campuses and graduated after four years with distinction, with the next-to-highest average.

There was one more job I came by toward the close of my senior year. I helped construct a prisoner-of-war camp south of our college town of Clinton, Mississippi. I went with several others, including special friend David Byrd, to apply for a job for which we were hired on the spot. I received the mail-clerk job and felt good since my father was a mail carrier for thirty-five years. My rate of pay was not quite one hundred dollars a month. This was most helpful since Dorothy and I were carefully saving toward our coming marriage. With permission, I stayed at the college an extra month after graduation. We rode back and forth in a pickup truck with a work crew, had a lot of fun, and made some new friends. I worked in an office area with a Lieutenant Vernon and about a dozen employees, mostly women. We all became fast, caring friends. All were conscious of our impending marriage plans. My last day was on a rainy Friday. It was really gloomy outside, but inside that office there was, unknown to me, a party of celebration in the making for us. They roasted, toasted, and thrilled me with gifts for our wedding. One gift in particular was a beautiful chenille bedspread that we used for a long time. Dorothy was thrilled!

With all of this and careful saving toward the future, I had some three hundred dollars, a tidy sum in those days. I needed a pair of white shoes and a white linen suit for my part in the wedding. I borrowed a suit from a French Acadian, Louisiana, pastor friend, Reverend E. Y. Solieau, at Mississippi Baptist College. I dyed a pair of black shoes white and, with other needed purchases, felt reasonably ready for my part in the supreme experience of my life. I left Mississippi Baptist College for the last time and headed for my church field, Union Baptist Church, south of Meridian, Mississippi. After preaching on Sunday, I left Meridian, with gifts from my church people, for my home in Okolona, 150 miles north.

Several weeks before, I had made arrangements for our honeymoon week in the lovely old Civil War town, Natchez, on the Mississippi River where sixty of the country's one hundred millionaires lived in Civil War times.

<hr />

Early in my college career, I was invited, along with my soon-to-be special friend, Frank Rose, from Meridian, Mississippi, to attend the American Legion State Convention in Natchez in 1939. I was invited because I won in the third Mississippi American Legion Oratorical contest, and Frank was invited because he was governor of our first Boy's State in Jackson, Mississippi. I also served on the State Supreme Court in that week.

I rode to Natchez with Robert Morrow, State Legion Executive, and another man, Ben Hilbun, the future president of Mississippi State University. I was in high company and well remember that ride. I stayed in the home of a fine American Legionnaire and his wife. I gave my oratorical speech, and Frank addressed the convention as youth governor. Frank was later pastor of First Christian Church of Danville, Kentucky, while I was in First Baptist Church of Pineville, Kentucky. He later became president of the famous Transylvania College in Lexington, Kentucky, and from there he went on to the presidency of the University of Alabama. He was one of the ten Outstanding Young Americans in that time.

The people of Natchez gave us a tour of all the beautiful antebellum homes, and I was more than impressed. Though Dorothy and I had had only a few dates, and she was not altogether committed as to what our future might hold, I knew my heart and have never veered. We wrote each other then. I told her of my thrilling experience, and that I wanted us to spend our honeymoon, four years away, in beautiful old Natchez!

Our host friends took Frank and me to Baton Rouge, Louisiana. On that trip I talked long and intimately to Frank about his call to the Christian ministry. He helped me greatly to know that God was calling me to full-time ministry. In the subsequent fifty-seven years I have never doubted God's call, though many times I have longed to be more adequate. He has always sustained me. I visited the Louisiana State Capitol and learned all about Huey Long, the assassinated senator who wanted to be president of the United States. His "Share the Wealth" theme is still a major issue.

Four years later, I wrote to Dr. W. A. Sullivan, pastor of First Baptist Church in Natchez, about spending our honeymoon there. I did not know then that he had previously pastored in Okolona. For a long time, I did not hear anything, and then I received his gracious answer. He said, "Charles, I have checked up on you and you have a good record at Mississippi Baptist College. If you and Dorothy will consider helping us in Vacation Bible School that week—in the mornings only—I will protect you from afternoon and night occasions. We will put you up in the Hotel Eola (very famous and restored now), pay all your expenses, and give you an honorarium at the end." Wow! What an offer! Very soon Dorothy was on board. We loved the people, and Dr. Sullivan was wonderful. We ate our noon meals at a favorite little restaurant where, strangely, we loved the tune on the nickelodeon, "The Beer Barrel Polka." We took walks at night down to the river. The weather was hot and steamy, and the plague of mosquitoes was awful.

We were assigned to Chaplain and Mrs. Murray Fuqua with whom we toured the area including Camp Earl Van Dorn and the beautiful old homes. The chaplain is now deceased but Mrs. Fuqua, in her eighties, does beautiful paintings. Recently, she sent us a still-life painting of a lovely flower arrangement that hangs conspicuously near our living-room fireplace mantel.

At the end of our VBS experience, Dr. Sullivan came to the Hotel Eola lobby to thank us, bid us goodbye, and handed us an honorarium for thirty-five dollars ($350 in today's money). What a help this was to us later!

I must close this section with my trip north to Okolona on the way to Memphis to claim my bride. My dear mother and my precious, five-year-old, little sister, Yvonne, our flower girl, and I made the trip by train from Tupelo, Mississippi. My father, unable to attend the wedding, took us to Tupelo. We missed him, as he was always an encourager to our courtship and was always thereafter. He loved Dorothy. I remember Yvonne was a study in motion and never stopped the pace! When we arrived in Memphis, Dorothy's father met us. He took my sister and mother to stay with her Aunt Stella Jones Adams with whom she had lived in her junior year in school. My mother, Estelle, was named for her. Soon all the rest of us were caught up in the myriad wedding plans.

Our wedding in the Longview Heights Baptist Church was all and more than could have been expected in those wartime conditions. On the groom's side, my three best friends in college were involved: Tom Douglas, Meridian, Mississippi; Clarence Watson, Yazoo City, Mississippi; Othell Hand, Ethel, Mississippi. These three, my brother, Joe, and I stayed in a large motel room in south Memphis. They all pretended to be looking after the groom while actually plotting my surprise and consternation as the groom. All through college we were close and had bushels of fun. Except Joe, of course, who was in the Seabees, in the South Pacific, New Hebrides Islands, where he took three showers a day to survive the terrible heat. Dorothy's party of friends included: June Patterson, Lundell, Arkansas, maid of honor; Virginia Frances Lady, Truman, Arkansas, pianist, later married to our long-time preacher friend, Frank Norfleet; Sybil Bullock, Tylertown, Mississippi, soloist; Mrs. R. B. Patterson Sr., matron of honor. Dorothy's brother Bob gave the bride away. Reverend R. B. Patterson Sr. and Dorothy's college pastor, Dr. J. S. (Sunshine) Riser, performed the ceremony.

Wedding of Charles Armon Jolly and Dorothy Faith Patterson on June 3, 1943, at Longview Heights Baptist Church, Memphis, Tennessee.

Longview Heights Baptist Church where Charles and Dorothy were married June 3, 1943.

On the day of the wedding, the wedding party minus the preachers went to Britlings Cafeteria for lunch. What a joyous occasion!

Tom Douglas suggested he should guard the key to our hotel room. I was really flattered and trustingly turned over our key to him. When we finally got to that Peabody Hotel room, accompanied by all of them, what a mess it was. I had ordered a dozen red roses, Dorothy's favorite, to which they had strung streamers which serpentined from the ceiling down to the roses. On a table nearby, there was a glass of water and some crackers, "preacher's rations for the next forty years." At times this was very nearly true. The commode and bathtub were literally filled with rice as well as the short-sheeted bed. We left the room to the maids and went out to the nearby automat for beef stew and orange juice. We were nearly starved. Then Dorothy reminded me that she was minus toothpaste, and my first purchase for her was a bottle of Teel, a popular wartime liquid toothpaste. The man who waited on us happened to be from Okolona and the father of Dorothy's special high-school friend, Miriam Jones, now a bank executive. Mr. Seymour Jones was happy for us. Then we returned to our room to find our bags had been liberally sprinkled with rice—some of which lingered in places for several years.

The next morning at 3:00 A.M., I received a telephone call from the hotel desk, "Mr. Jolly, a call to awaken you as per your request." I fumbled and mumbled, "Man, I didn't leave you any such call." "Yes, Sir, Mr. Jolly left such a request." Later I learned the truth, that it was Joe who had done the trick. Several years later when I married him and Sue, his first wife, I left a message at his Hotel Edwards, in Jackson, Mississippi, that they supply him, a preacher too, with beer, pretzels, and tomato juice during the night.

The next morning, Dorothy's mother called to make sure Dorothy was OK. I assured her she was. After breakfast, we caught the Trailways bus to Jackson,

Mississippi, where we spent our second night at the Heidelburg Hotel. We had originally scheduled an airplane trip to Jackson, which was unheard of in those times. Because of the wartime need for airspace, the flight was cancelled, thus the Trailways bus. We did meet Dorothy's Uncle Knox Lowther and her cousin, Marnita Lowther, on a Jackson street, breakfasted together, and then went on to Natchez, and the lovely Eola Hotel. We still deeply cherish that very special time. Our friends have remembered June 3, 1943, throughout the years.

———————◆◆×◆◆———————

About the wedding itself. It was such a breathlessly hot night with no air-conditioning. I arrived at the church early and mistakenly began to welcome the people. One dear lady, Miss Bessie Strong, gave me five dollars. My dear preacher brothers reminded me I should be behind the scene until the proper time in the wedding ceremony. Dr. Riser started in Genesis and went to Malachi; then Dorothy's father started in Matthew and went to Revelation, or so it seemed! We stood there in the steaming heat, perspiring profusely. I literally felt a stream of water running down my spine. We had a photographer but because of wartime film, there was only one good picture of the ceremony. Thank God for that picture which we cherish to this day.

Following the ceremony, Dorothy and I got in the car of the sheriff of Yazoo County, Mississippi. Our special friends, the John Watsons, had arranged to borrow the car from our mutual friend, Sheriff Billy Perry. I led a youth revival there in 1940 at the First Baptist Church of Yazoo City (later they called me to be their pastor but I felt that I could not leave our pastorate in Newport News, Virginia). Dorothy slid over close, and clinging to me she said, "Darling, we are married. We are married." I stepped on the siren, and Dorothy slid over to the door on her side and said, "Charles, stop! stop! The police are behind us!" We both got the needed relief of laughter. What blessed, special memories these are.

———————◆◆×◆◆———————

The churches God allowed me to pastor while in college were a great sustaining force in my life. I have already referred to how I was called as pastor of Franklin Baptist Church, in Smith's Schoolhouse area, near Flora, Mississippi, some twenty miles from the college. I traveled back and forth with other pastor/preacher friends, one of whom was Roe Wilson, pastor of Lula Baptist Church near Franklin. Sometimes the church people would take me back after the evening worship service. I often rode out on Saturday nights, with the Hill brothers, our members, and spent the night or weekend. They operated a store on a back street in Jackson and often sold spoiled, rejected food to poor blacks for the pennies they could afford. I struggled with my feelings about this situation (I was in the Wilson home on Pearl Harbor weekend, a rather gloomy day, weatherwise).

Dorothy's mother's family was from this area, and her mother grew up there. Mrs. Patterson's mother married Mr. Carlton Lowther, and three children survived this union. After his early death, she married a Mr. Benjamin Lilly by whom she had two other children, Glynn and Helen. We had many occasions of fellowship with these relatives, several of whom live in the El Dorado, Arkansas, area today. Recently Mildred Lowther Brown and her mother, Fannie Lowther, now deceased, took us on a tour of the Tenin area including the ancient cemeteries. We found the grave of Mattie Lowther Lilly and other family members. I met several of Dorothy's relatives in the area before we ever married and was made aware of much family history. They all knew the folks who were members of Franklin Baptist Church. It is important for present family members to know their roots.

One of the members of Franklin Baptist Church, Mr. Claude Price, rarely attended but professed to know all about the Bible. His brother, Coleman Price, was the first husband of Dorothy's aunt Helen Darnaby. Coleman Price was still in the area. I would visit Claude who lived up on the north hill close by the church. He loved to argue about the Bible. One of his favorite passages was, "Be ye, therefore, perfect as your father in Heaven is perfect" (Matthew 5:48). He insisted that unless people were as perfect as God, they wouldn't go to Heaven. Therefore, since that was impossible, none can be saved. I would try to get him to see that this required perfection is only in Christ. I learned later on in seminary that the Greek word *telion* means to fulfill a perfect purpose. My New Testament professor, Dr. William Hersey Davis, illustrated this with his worn pocketknife. He said the purpose of this knife is to cut an apple. It is perfect for that purpose. It has a nick in the blade, but that imperfection does not keep it from fulfilling the perfect purpose of cutting an apple. So do we fulfill a perfect purpose, though we ourselves are imperfect.

Joe, just starting to college after delaying it for military service, helped me in our first revival at Franklin. He led the singing and sang some solos, old-time hymns which Dorothy's mother had worked on with us in preparation for the revival. He later said our revival was the only time he ever sang solos. Joe subsequently had a long career as a pastor and military chaplain in the Air Force. He was a lieutenant colonel, retired, at the time of his death in 1993. He was little more than a year older than I.

On the first night of the revival in the little, dimly lit, one-room Franklin Church, I preached a strong message of evangelism. Claude Price was sitting toward the back in the shadows. In the close of the message, I made the statement my father often used, "Some people don't know anymore about the Bible than a jay bird knows about a doctor's book. Yet, they argue about the Bible as if they know all about it." I could see Claude turn dark, even in the shadows. At the end of the service, I walked out the only door of the church into a group of people gathered around outside. Claude said, "Preacher, why did you want to call me a jay bird for." I tried to calmly say to him, "Claude, I didn't call you a jay bird." I then quoted what my father had said. One of the other deacons spoke up, "Claude, why don't you quit acting like a fool." With that, Claude swung his fist at that deacon and, in a moment, a melee of bedlam broke loose! Everybody, men, women, and children, got into a scrap, fracas, swinging brawl. As someone else put it, "All hell broke loose." Our special friends, the John Watsons, from Yazoo City, Mississippi, were there. They cautioned Joe and me not to get involved in this obvious interchurch fiasco. One other deacon, Alfred Purvis, got his nose broken. I was literally horrified and paralyzed with fear. For this to happen the first night of revival, what can happen for good in these circumstances?

Joe and I went home with an older deacon, Jim Cox, and his wife. It was a suffocatingly hot moonlit night, and we tried to sleep on a featherbed mattress. We tended to sink down toward the center and had to struggle to get back up. Neither of us got any sleep because we were so deeply disturbed at what had happened.

Early the next morning, deacon Jim Purvis and his deacon son, Alfred, the one with the broken nose, came to see me as pastor. Jim Purvis had his cap on backwards. On the back seat of their car was a whole array of guns. I learned that morning why our church area was called Little Texas. They told me they were going to Flora to put Claude Price under a peace bond and wanted me to go with them. The Lord helped me to respond—he had to! I told them I thought they were right to do this but that I shouldn't be a part of it because it would ruin my influence with Claude and others who needed to know the Lord. They accepted this and went on their errand. They achieved their goal without any trouble since Claude was a well-known character in the area.

Claude, upset by now, came and asked me to ride around with him. I spent most of the day with him. Joe was with us. Claude was deeply concerned about the peace bond and seemed to be humbly repentant. I tried again to make my point about the Scripture. I realized that I had caused the reaction and prayed that God would rectify the situation for good.

Joe and I were to eat at three different homes each day—breakfast, noon, and night. We dared not refuse now and there was good, fried chicken at every home. The chickens were raised around barnyards and outdoor toilets. Need I say more? We were afraid of getting sick, but we ate the chicken and did not have any problems.

At each subsequent worship service, I preached on the love of God and the people came in droves to see what might happen next. Through the open windows, you could see people slipping around outside. People came to church with guns on, obvious under their coats, and by God's wonderful grace, we had a wonderful revival!

Somehow, God worked great good out of that situation. Mr. Jim Purvis and his son, Alfred, did not soon come back to church while I was there. The other Purvis brother, Talmadge, and his wife, Mattie, have remained our dear friends across the years. The day I left Franklin, Mr. Talmadge Purvis took me to Jackson. They are now in their nineties and live with their lovely daughters in the Jackson/Clinton area. The Franklin Church now has a full-time pastor on the field, a new building including education space, a beautiful lake in the area, and a lovely new community developing. I have more recently visited the area and the people were all glad to see me and gracious to a fault!

Let me mention one other dear lady in the Franklin Church. She was Miss Mattie Nichols who lived just up a hill from the church. Often I would go out to the church on a rainy day, with slushy Mississippi mud everywhere. No one would risk coming to church and I would spend the day with Miss Mattie. She would always send me back with a dozen eggs. She gave a quarter every Sunday, a big offering for her, and was always dependable. The offering each Sunday amounted to five or six dollars and this was what they paid me. I was glad to have this source of income that helped me tremendously.

Actually, I served as half-time pastor for three churches. I spent two Sundays per month at each church for a time. I was called to a church field south of Meridian to pastor the New Hope Baptist Church in Lauderdale County, Mississippi, and the Union Baptist Church in Clarke County, Mississippi, a field of two rural, yet "uptown people" and churches, four miles apart. I rode the Greyhound bus from Jackson to Meridian and was met by the family I was to stay with that particular weekend. What blessings were shared with some of God's best people.

I used a loaned car on the field, courtesy of the people I stayed with—the Grady Brunsons or the Luther Walkers. I would preach at New Hope first, then drive the four miles to Union where the worship service was in progress. I would arrive just in time for my message there. It was a very moving and blessed experience. I then alternated the Sunday evening services for the two churches. They always had Sunday School and Training Union and, in the summer, Vacation Bible School. I finally resigned the Franklin Church and gave full time to the two Meridian area churches. When I could not be there for services, brother Joe, friend Clarence Watson, or others filled in for me.

An old preacher, Brother "Fate" Williams, who was trembly, had false teeth, was a widower, and lived with his son, gave me my first preacher's manual and always good, sound advice to the young preacher. Men like him were such a blessed source of help in that early ministry.

I came to the Meridian-area church field on the recommendations of the former pastor, Reverend D. L. Stennis, and the family of fellow ministerial student, Brother R. M. Williams. Many of his family and relatives were in the area and in our Union Church. My first service was on Easter Sunday, 1941, just after we had buried my brother, Merrill. I remember hitchhiking to Meridian from Okolona for that first service and how sad-at-heart I was about the loss of my brother. But Easter was a time to rejoice in victory in Jesus.

On a cold November weekend, the New Hope Church people presented me with a new and much-needed overcoat, hat, and gloves. Man, was I dressed up! I stayed with the Lamar Brunson family that night and had a roaring fire in my bedroom. I could not sleep from excitement.

One of the New Hope young people, Myra Gulledge, later became the Baptist Student Union director at Louisiana State University for a number of years. Another person who helped in summer Vacation Bible School, (VBS), Evelyn Moore, later married Brother Kenny, longtime friend and fellow pastor in Virginia and superintendent of the Baptist Home for Aging in the peninsula area of Virginia. More recently, we met a group Furman and Evelyn were leading on a tour of Alaska when they came through our Seattle (Sea-Tac) airport. Furman's sister, a member of the tour, got sick and was in a hospital here, and at his request, I visited her. Friendships that last and bless over the years are precious indeed.

Reverend D. L. Stennis (Deb), nephew of our longtime, great senator John Stennis from Mississippi, came back to the two churches from New Orleans Baptist Theological Seminary. Deb was a first vice-president of the Southern Baptist Convention one year. He was nominated by our mutual friend David Byrd.

Deacon Grady Brunson in our Union Church was a farmer and later had a chicken (poultry) dressing business. He and his wife, Vashti, had no children and virtually adopted young Billy Williams, son of our deacon Richard

Williams. Today, Billy has inherited all of the Grady Brunson enterprise.

Grady had some kind of beef with me. I never really knew why, except he would try to run my life. He and Vashti actually seemed to oppose my marrying Dorothy. When Deb Stennis came back, Grady tried similar tactics on him and Deb let him know he was not dealing with a boy (meaning me), but a fully-capable man. Grady thought he had called a secret meeting at New Hope Church to get rid of Deb. Someone told Deb of the meeting, and he showed up to answer Grady's accusations. Grady and Vashti, thereafter, went into Meridian to the First Baptist Church. The night of our final service at Union, some special things had been prepared for us. Grady spoiled it, had it cancelled, and did not show up. Deacon Richard Williams told us about it, apologized, and gave us twenty dollars. I must say Grady and Vashti took me in and were most generous and helpful. They dearly loved each other and had pet names for each other. I recall hearing each morning in their home: "Wake up, Charlie, and count your money." This was an old stagecoach stop call to awaken. With six sleeping in the same bed, you needed to count your money to see if any thieves were in the bunch.

The church at Union became full-time on the occasion of a great biblical stewardship/tithing revival led by Brother Sollie Smith, pastor of nearby Stonewall First Baptist Church. On a rainy Sunday morning, he preached on biblical stewardship, scriptural tithing and the whole church was moved by the Holy Spirit to sign what he called the tithing covenant. For the first time, I was deeply convicted, have tithed and more ever since, and inculcated that message in every revival thereafter on the closing Sunday morning service. I have seen God move whole churches to the same experience that had touched us. Praise the Lord! The Union Church went full time, called me full time, and I resigned from New Hope. The New Hope Church was not especially moved by the stewardship message then, but it is full-time now in a lovely new building with a fine, full-time pastor.

When we came back from our honeymoon, Union had rented living quarters for us with Mrs. Charles Strange, a widow, and her daughter, Mamie Rea. We had a bedroom and adjacent kitchen. Her son, Dr. William Earnest Strange, and his wife lived nearby and he later became a good math professor at Mississippi Baptist College. Dr. D. M. Nelson asked for my assessment and recommendation of him. Bill Strange died suddenly of a heart attack at an Ole Miss/Mississippi State football game.

Dorothy decided she wanted to have the Union Church deacons and their wives for dinner. We started early in the morning with a wood stove. There was fried chicken, gravy, rice, vegetables, salad, and lemon icebox pie. Dorothy had not yet learned to cook everything together but just one thing at a time. The result was that everything was cold, even the mashed potatoes and watery tea. The only redeeming factor was the pie. You live and learn, and so ever after she has done superbly.

We left the Stranges on a chilly morning to go north to the Southern Baptist Theological Seminary, another part of our journey. Mamie Rea Strange took us, trunks and all, in her truck into Meridian, Mississippi, to catch the train to Okolona. We have kept in touch with her through the years.

Dorothy and I were invited back to Union for the seventieth anniversary in 1982. We were in Atlanta for our missionary orientation and appointment week. We stayed with Mrs. Luther (Sweet) Walker, in the same home. She died in 1986. At Union, we also stayed with the James Williams family. We renewed old acquaintances, preached at both churches, and rejoiced in all that God had wrought in every life. To God be the glory!

Reverend Deb Stennis invited me back for a revival in 1950 when we lived and served in Pineville, Kentucky. I stayed at his home with his lovely family and visited on both church fields. There was a drought in the area, and we felt the burden to pray for rain one bright, sunny day during the morning revival service. We knelt and prayed earnestly for rain. By the time that revival service was over, it had clouded up and was raining. It was a good rain. We visited Grady that afternoon. He said it was just a coincidence. I said, "Well, Grady, thank God for a good coincidence and that we were in accord." I was grateful for that experience. Deb had a sudden brain hemorrhage sometime afterwards and was rushed to Meridian. He was suddenly gone to be with the Lord he had served so faithfully. One day, by and by, when the battle is over, we shall see the King and all of His!

3

Seminary—Louisville, Kentucky

1943–1946

There was never any question of where we would attend seminary. If possible, it would be the Southern Baptist Theological Seminary in Louisville, Kentucky, where Dorothy's parents had attended and loved it. These parents had prepared for foreign mission service in Argentina but could not be appointed because the Foreign Mission Board lacked funds. Therefore, they determined to be missionaries in the places where God called them, and they did. Many lives were touched by their ministry including a number of men and women who surrendered their lives for the Lord's service.

Faced with a housing scarcity at Southern Seminary, especially for couples without children, we left our application intact but made application to Southwestern Baptist Theological Seminary in Fort Worth, Texas. Then we prayed daily for God's leading.

In that first summer of marriage, I had seven weeks of one-week revivals in which I preached and lead the singing, and Dorothy played the piano. One day a letter reached us from the seminary in Louisville saying that they had turned a number of rooms for singles into apartments for married couples without children, and we were accepted. We breathed a sigh of relief and rejoiced. The very next day we received a similar letter from Fort Worth. We took this as a direct answer to prayer and of God's leading, and we have never had reason to regret it.

Much happened during those seven weeks of revival. Each church gave us an offering, which was a great help when we went to seminary. During the loud preaching and singing, I injured my ears, and they are affected to this day. One other memory comes to mind. As we rested one day after lunch, we felt crawly creatures on us and found bed bugs. We did not rest anymore that day in that home! Indeed, the people in each of those places were wonderful and encouraging, and God gave us souls and revival in each place.

The day of preparation came for going to Louisville, Kentucky. Uncle Claiborne Freeman offered to sell us his 1936 Ford for $450, and we snapped it up! As we drove to Memphis, where Dorothy's parents lived, trouble developed with the car and considerable work had to be done on it. I told my uncle, and he agreed to take twenty-five dollars off the price and let us repay the loan at twenty-five dollars a month. God bless him! All our relatives went all the way for us. We paid the car off on time, and it served us well for more than five years. When we were in New Jersey, the rich Dodge estate sold one just like it for twelve thousand dollars. We wished that we might have kept it, but we had worn it out.

Dorothy and I had one other thing we had to do. We burned all our old love letters except the first one she wrote to me. I kept it and treasure it to this day. Some were almost too hot to burn!

We left for Louisville driving through Nashville, Tennessee, where later, in that vicinity, we spent more than three years in ministry and learned all about historic areas and places in connection with the Civil War. We still had car troubles along the way but since we could only drive thirty-five miles an hour because of tire and gas shortages due to wartime measures, we made it. We drove on single-lane highways, the only kind in those days. We passed near Portland, Tennessee, and noted an historic marker where the famous Jenny Lind, traveling by stagecoach, had stopped at a spring (water) area and sung for a great host of people. We lived and served in Portland after we finished seminary.

We finally made it to Louisville at three in the morning and found a room at the older John Tyler Hotel. We were dog tired and thankful for a place to lay our heads—even though there was no air-conditioning.

When I checked in the next morning at the seminary to pay initial fees, Dr. Hugh Peterson, registrar, held out his hand and said, "Welcome Charles and Dorothy Jolly." He made it a point to memorize every application (which required a photograph) and greeted each new seminarian by name. To say the least, we were most impressed and came to love him. We saw and waved to the president, Dr. Ellis Fuller, a tremendous man of God.

We found our room, purchased some needed furniture, and moved in our "plunder," in the words of Abraham Lincoln. We got the needed furniture, bedding, and a desk for study at a downtown Louisville secondhand furniture store. Friends who had helped us to find God's will for our lives back in Okolona, and later in college, were there, and with other volunteers helped us move in with only a broad, accidental scratch on the bed from one of the railings. My old study desk now sits in our son's room covered with his collection of outer-space vehicles.

Later that day, we visited a college friend of Dorothy's, Virginia Colvin, whose father was an executive in the Kentucky Baptist Convention. After a lovely meal and pleasant visit, we left for our new church field, Salvisa, Kentucky, in the lovely Blue Grass country near Lexington, Kentucky, a horse raising and racing paradise.

———————◆◆◆◆◆———————

That summer Dorothy and I had wondered how we would make it to seminary with our money shortage. We received a letter from Dr. A. A. Kitchings, professor of romance languages at Mississippi Baptist College, stating that he had pastored the Salvisa Church while he was in seminary, that they had always called students from Mississippi, and that he had recommended me and our friend, David Byrd, to them. If I was interested, I needed to write to the church. Letting no grass grow under my feet, I wrote immediately, and they asked me to come. Dorothy couldn't go. Salvisa, Kentucky, was named for two old-maid sisters by their father, an early settler.

I rode the bus to Salvisa and stayed in the home of Oscar Brown who owned and operated a general store in the small town. They soon sold out and moved to Lawrenceburg, Kentucky. In my first visit with him, he asked if I had a "machine," meaning an automobile. I assured him that I had one in view and he felt it was a plus, and a necessity—it was later obvious. He also talked about driving down the "pike" and over the "knobs" (hills). I learned some of the Kentucky lingo that day. I preached for the people on Sunday and Mr. Edmund Miller, an older, influential member and a great friend, talked about Mississippi being "famous for Jersey cows and Baptist preachers." They liked what they saw and heard, and called me on the spot. What a blessed relief and assurance that God was leading. David Byrd was called later to Calvary Baptist Church near Harrodsburg, Kentucky, and asked me to help him in revival.

Therefore, Dorothy and I were on our way to our church in time for the weekend on this day at Louisville and seminary. We stayed in the home of Mr. and Mrs. Edmund Miller. He had served as a legislator in the Kentucky Assembly when the famous Happy Chandler was governor. On that first Monday, Mr. Miller took us to Harrodsburg, famous in Daniel Boone's time, and old Fort Harrod. Some of the sights we saw included: the cabin of Abraham Lincoln's grandparents and the grave of Virginia Dare, the first white child buried in Kentucky.

The pastor who had immediately preceded us was Wayne Todd, the youth preacher who had led the youth revival in Okolona when Dorothy and I surrendered our lives to ministry. That first week in the area, he asked us to serve in a week of training for new Sunday School teachers at First Baptist Church, Danville, Kentucky, not far from Salvisa. In that same week, his first child, a girl, was born, and Wayne in telling us, in his usual jovial way, remarked, "I've added one to the cradle roll, go thou and do likewise." Another friend, Bill Watson, former president of the Mississippi State Baptist Student Union, went with us and helped that week. I recall going down in an open car, and Bill was still recovering from a bout of pneumonia.

Later, in 1968, the First Baptist Church of Danville, after careful consideration, wanted to call us as pastor and wife. Instead we went to Madison, New Jersey, which is a story in itself. One chief negative reason was that in Salvisa, we found that Dorothy was highly allergic to the tobacco-bloom pollen. It weighed heavily in our decision in 1968, but, most of all, it was because of answered prayer and God's clear leading to Madison, New Jersey, and the unusual blessings to follow.

That Salvisa Church provided us with an outlet to express what we were learning and to fulfill the call of God in our lives. We would move there during the summer between seminary sessions, and in Dorothy's case, college sessions. She finished her college work at the University of Louisville during our last two years in seminary. The first year, she received much from the Woman's Missionary Union Training School, where her mother had studied a generation earlier.

During those summer interludes, the Salvisa Church made it possible for us to have room and board in one of the homes. This was also the case on weekends. One of those homes was the home of Gabe and Ella Gill. Gabe, a tobacco farmer, was not a Christian, but he supported his wife in her dedication. Ella, a lovely homemaker, was a longtime adult teacher in the Sunday School and very active in her church. For over thirty years, she never gave up praying for her husband's salvation.

During a revival service with Dr. John Carter of First Baptist Church of Harrodsburg, Kentucky (later college president at Campbellsville College), I felt a strong urging of the Holy Spirit to leave the church early and go to the Gill home where I knew Gabe to be alone. I went and told him of my deep concern for his soul's salvation. He took my hand in acknowledgment that he had received Christ as his Savior. He did not, however, make a public profession of his faith before we left the church. Later, he fell down his cellar steps, and on the way to the hospital, he reaffirmed his faith in Christ and was subsequently baptized. They had a son and daughter in the Navy. This daughter was in love with a much younger naval officer. She asked my opinion if she should marry him. I suggested that she would age faster than the man would and he might look on her more as a mother in later years. She considered this, and they never married. In fact, she never married and died of cancer at an early age. My answer to her has troubled me. She might have married the younger man and found some years of special joy and pleasure.

I was at the Gill home on a Saturday night when I had what seemed to be a spell with my heart. When I went to the doctor, he assured me that all was OK. However, I went through a time of nervous depression and concern during the rest of the time in seminary. I had been under a heavy strain with seminary studies, work on campus and elsewhere, plus my church responsibilities. We had been in a special financial drive to raise twelve hundred dollars for a new hot-air furnace for the church building which was heated in wintertime by a coal/wood stove. I had challenged the deacons that I would give one hundred dollars if each of them would. There were enough deacons to raise the amount needed. One country tobacco farmer, Mr. Louis Trisler, later laughed and said he had to sell a cow and a calf to raise his one hundred dollars. He and his wife were raising a grandson, Bobby, who was from a broken-home situation. Mr. Trisler was instrumental in recommending my dear Mississippi pastor friend, David Grant, to the Bergen, Kentucky, church where he had previously been a member and deacon. David acknowledged, in his life story, that this had been one of his most blessed pastoral experiences. He went on to become one of Mississippi's most outstanding pastors and served at the Broadmoor Baptist Church in Jackson, Mississippi. The governor and the city of Jackson recognized him as such. He has died since we came to the Northwest. He came for a special assignment in Lakewood, one of our best churches.

David invited me for a revival meeting when he was pastor of First Baptist Church of Drew, Mississippi. My school superintendent and mentor, A. W. James, had gone from our hometown of Okolona to the same position in Drew. I stayed in his home during this revival. What a special week that was. This man, of whom I had often stood in mortal terror, was a most gracious host, bringing grapefruit and coffee to my door every morning. He was the one who had so helped and believed in me, heard me patiently, took me to the places I was to speak in Mississippi, at his own expense, and in general gave me every encouragement and had done the same for Dorothy. The people in Drew did not understand this side of him and could hardly believe it when I told my story. They were somewhat down on Mr. James and my story, given in one of the youth messages, astounded them, including Pastor Grant. Mr. James invited me to address his student body, and in the audience was the aging Miss Lilah

Maxwell, my former high school debate coach. Again, what a blessed week and all because of Brother Louis Trisler, deacon in our Salvisa Baptist Church.

Another home we stayed in during seminary summer intermission was that of Mrs. Edna Houchin, mother of deacon and treasurer, Lloyd Houchin. She was a dear, sweet person and shared graciously. Dorothy had gone to Mississippi to visit her parents and the nights were lonely. She came back by train, and things picked up.

I was against tobacco and preached on the harm it did to the body—including: cancer, heart problems, and eight minutes per cigarette off one's life. However, our men were tobacco farmers, and I would peel off my shirt and help them, free of charge, in tobacco season. The day we left Salvisa there was a heavy snowstorm. Since we were having a special guest speaker that night, we decided to go back to the seminary before nightfall. I went by the home of Mr. Lloyd Houchin for a check of fifty dollars that the deacons had voted to refund me on my one hundred dollars for the new church furnace. Mr. and Mrs. Houchin had a son who became a physician, Dr. Everett Gill Houchin. I had to reprimand him in church on one occasion when he was a teenager. All the girls hovered around him.

I was invited back to Salvisa for a revival when I was in New Jersey. The church had a new building, and I thoroughly enjoyed the experience. The pastor, Brother Koch, was interested in our Twin County Church and later came for a visit to New Jersey but decided to stay in Salvisa. I stayed in the home of the Esco Beasleys. He was more than ninety years of age. We had often stayed in their home while in seminary and appreciated their bathroom, though often out of order, especially when we came. They had two lovely daughters. Margaret married Phillip Eads who later became our minister of music in Roanoke, Virginia. When the second daughter, Jean, married a local boy, Delbert (Peanuts) Harlow, they came to our home in Roanoke on their honeymoon. The Beasleys lived in the local funeral home in Salvisa. He was the Boy Scout leader and I was his assistant. We shared many memorable experiences with the local boys.

Mr. Beasley was famous for his ghost stories. He swore to their authenticity, and I believed him. One involved a headless woman in a black velvet dress whom he witnessed as a young man on a return to his Kentucky home. He had to cross a dry gulch between his home and the barn where he left his horse. It was dark as midnight on the bank of the gulch. He felt a sudden tingling around his legs. Thinking it was their old tomcat, he called out the cat's name but got no answering meow. As he walked on down into the gulch, a sudden bright light shone all around him and the headless woman. Arriving at home, he could not eat his supper because he was so frightened. He told his mother he did not feel like eating. Can you blame him?

He told a number of such stories. He was still living during our revival and still insisting the absolute truth of that story as well as others I questioned him about. His wife, Delta, now over ninety-five years old, still lives in the now-converted funeral home.

Esco was a collector of antiques and gave us several. One which I later bought for eighty-five dollars was a large old-fashioned armoire put together by pegs. We brought it home on top of our station wagon, disassembled. I enjoyed assembling it on our return to New Jersey. Dorothy saw another like it in Chester, New Jersey, valued at three thousand dollars. Ours is now in the possession of Harry Jolly, brother Fred's son, who lives in Dallas, Texas.

Several other special friends in Salvisa are the C. D. Ransdells who recently visited us in Federal Way. He was in the military service, and his wife, Adele, and their then-little son, David, lived in Salvisa with her family, the Jack Garriotts. She was principal of our first Vacation Bible School which was in progress on famous D-Day, June 6, 1944. The Worley Yocum family—Mildred, Morris, Marvin, and nine-year-old Margaret Lee—were very special. They always shared their home. The mother, Hallie, had much sickness in her family, and we shared and ministered. She was one of the world's best cooks, and believe me, we have shared with hundreds of the best on our journey. Margaret Lee has a large family now with grandchildren. She is a superb antique collector and has had us in her home and shared antique glassware. As a nine-year-old, she invited her pastor to her playhouse one day for tea with her dolls. I have always cherished that experience. Before her mother and father died, we had fellowship with her whole family during the revival we held later in Salvisa.

So many are gone, the Will Keightlys and the Edmund Millers—whose beautiful home and gorgeous antiques were recently purchased by an outsider for a bed and breakfast. I hope to go back someday. I remember the beaten biscuits and milk gravy and all else Mrs. Edna Miller served on those antique dishes. We spent much time with her daughter, Frances, now married to a Louisville doctor, and Mrs. Edna's sisters, Ann and Lou Nelson—who was crippled. They lived with Sarah and Davis Gritton. Sarah was our wonderful organist whose husband, Davis, a photographer, took one of our first, cherished photos. Our girls have had it refinished as a gift. It still sparkles. In it Dorothy is sitting on my lap. The Wilbur Johnsons had a little redheaded son, Ronnie, grown up and recently deceased, who served as a deacon in the Salvisa Church where his father served in our time. The mother, Mignon Johnson, is still around and about, but more slowly. The Chapman family, south of town, was special to us, especially just before we left the church. The Will Keightlys took us to their family doctor in Lexington, Kentucky. We had no children at that time, which worried our people. The doctor told Dorothy to take wheat-germ oil and forget it. It worked at the very right time, and then we worried about how to quit when Dorothy was forty years old and had Rebecca (Becky).

One very special family, the Otto Satterlys (he was the funeral director), was always cordial, hospitable, and had special feelings for their pastor and his wife. They had twin sons. On one occasion, while at lunch in their home after morning services, Mr. Otto asked one of his sons what he studied in Sunday School.

"About Jesus."

"What about Jesus?"

"He wode on a hoss."

"Where did he ride to?"

"Up to Hawodsburg."

This was a nearby town to Salvisa. The child couldn't remember Jerusalem. Mr. Otto was the school principal and superintendent, and Sallie, his wife, was a home economics teacher. They took us once to Danville, Kentucky, where they bought me a new suit of clothes at the instructions of the deacons.

These were all precious people in our young lives while I was in seminary and Dorothy was at the University of Louisville. There were other members of our Salvisa flock who were precious, as was everyone in our pastoral ministry. We thank God for this church that He gave us while in seminary. We worked to make it a full-time church with the pastor living on the field, looking toward a developing community. With us, the Mississippi pastor-only angle lessened. The next pastor, Vincent Appleton, married Miss Olive Powell, who was a Mississippi Baptist College classmate. The church gradually developed to a full-time ministry and pastorate as it is today. It is a beautifully developing residential area, and the present pastor has been there for a number of years. We were there in 1989 and told about our Northwest missions work with the aid of a video.

I mentioned early in these recollections that I had a nagging health problem that made for an eating difficulty. I was affected in many other ways. This was the chief reason I did not go on further in seminary to get a doctoral degree, even though I was asked to stay. My grade average was in the high As in all subjects, although it was not uncommon to stay up all night to study for final exams. I remember reaching daylight several times before stopping my studies for the night.

I went to several doctors who tried everything to help me. In one instance, I stopped in Lawrenceburg, Kentucky, to see Dr. Overall. I told him I felt like I was going straight up. He smiled and responded, "Now I know you are a preacher but right now you'd have to be better than you are to go straight up." I had headaches and dizzy feelings that I have dealt with all my life. For example, I became extremely nervous in close places with a compelling feeling to run out. I'd be in funeral services, surrounded by flowers, and feel like I would smother. I have stood in the pulpit many times when I felt weakened by my health problems. I did not find the answer until I went to Portland, Tennessee, our first pastorate out of seminary.

As usual, I became involved in general community affairs. In the Rotary Club, I got to know a heart-of-gold man, member of the Christian Church, named White Hill. We were on a committee to deal with extreme-need cases, no matter the church or no church. I shall describe these cases in more detail in the chapter on our Portland, Tennessee, years. In talking about my health problems, Mr. Hill suggested I see a doctor in Nashville, Dr. Randolph Pate. He was so enthusiastic about his doctor that I took him up on it.

Dr. Pate put a tube down into my stomach, a normal fifteen-minute procedure for my type of complaint. He left it there for an hour or more. In conference, he told me that my health was perfect except for one serious finding. I had no hydrochloric acid, a basic part of the digestive system. He gave me a prescription to supplement this lack of acid. I began to improve from then on and only have difficulty when I stop taking the medicine. The problem has persisted, and I've had the same diagnosis wherever I have lived.

After Dr. Pate's diagnosis, I remembered back in my childhood, when at some ten years of age, I could not keep my food down. I would work in the fields of cotton, corn, or whatever, and about mid-morning would come to the house with stomach trouble. My mother would give me a glass of buttermilk, which would help. My father, out of concern, took me to the family doctor, Dr. B. D. Hansell, in Okolona. On the examining table, he felt my distended stomach and told my father that I had no hydrochloric acid. He prescribed ten drops of the acid in a glass of water to be ingested carefully through a glass tube so it would not discolor my teeth. From Portland, Tennessee, I wrote to him, thanking him for his early diagnosis confirmed by the doctor in Nashville.

I had been very close to Dr. Hansell in high school, even grade school. He was always a friend and booster, an encourager to me in oratorical work. He would send me telegrams and letters. He wrote me back and said, "Charles, you

serve our Lord in one way and I in another. We are both serving the same God."
He died sometime after that of a sudden heart attack from unselfish, untiring
service to black and white alike in our community. When my father asked him
one day what he owed him for all his service to him and his family, Dr. Hansell
responded with a "bushel of peanuts or a bushel of potatoes, Joe." He had a beautiful, mulatto nurse named Margie who went with him on his house calls, black
or white, and on muddy roads. She was the epitome of courtesy and all loved her.

On the day of my graduation from seminary, my parents and their pastor
and his wife, Brother and Mrs. George Gay, were in the assembly. I was so
nervous. I wondered if I could go up on the rostrum to receive my diploma. I
made it, by God's help, and it has been the same through the years whenever I
would be in trouble.

At graduation, my parents, their pastor, and his wife were driving in the
vicinity of Lincoln's birthplace in Hodgenville, Kentucky, and were stopped by
a policeman. When asked their last name, my father said, "Jolly," and Brother
Gay said, "Gay." The policeman thought they were kidding and didn't like the
idea. They had to show full proof of who they were. He did not write a ticket
when they told him why they were in Kentucky.

My teachers in seminary were absolutely the finest teachers of their type in
the world. Dr. William Hersey Davis, New Testament; Dr. Leo Green, Old
Testament; Dr. Sydnor Staley, church history, and later the first president of
Southeastern Baptist Theological Seminary; Dr. E. A. McDowell, beginners'
New Testament Greek; Dr. J. J. Owens, Hebrew; Dr. Gaines Dobbins, church
administration and education; Dr. Inman Johnson and Dr. Charles McGlon,
speech and preaching; Dr. H. T. Goerner, missions, and Dr. O. T. Binkley, sociology, who later served as president of Southeastern Seminary, were among the
best. Other older, retired men like Dr. John R. Sampey, Old Testament, and Dr.
W. O. Carver, missions, would fill in as substitutes or special guest lecturers. Dr.
Sampey, a native of Alabama, previously had been president of the seminary.
One day when I was on a work crew at his home, he was reading in his sunlit
garden. I asked how he was feeling. He replied that he "was a little numb in his
feet but glad it was not in his head." I would also mention our librarian, Dr. Leo
Crismon; our building and grounds administrator, Dr. Bob Allen, and assistant,
Mr. Bob Gordon, for whom I worked. Another was Dr. J. B. Weatherspoon,
sermon preparation and preaching-homiletics.

I recall an instance when the student body designated me to preach to the
group and the faculty on the subject of confessing our sins. It had been a

seminary revival emphasis all week. I prepared in fear and trembling and stood up and preached in chapel to that great body. I dwelled in detail on our sins as students who failed to prepare and postulated to cover up for poor preparation. The faculty and administration highly approved and applauded. When I got to faculty sins, I seemingly laid heavy stress on every professor, making his lectures, classes, tests, and exams as if they were our only class, and that this, coupled with pastoring churches, working on campus and otherwise to meet our bills, placed undue stress on the students. I mentioned the effect of near nervous breakdown, and that I had often studied all night until daybreak and then would struggle to the classroom for a two-hour exam, walking ever so carefully lest I spill some of the memorized information. Well, the faculty and the assembled group sat somewhat stunned at this bold confession of our composite sins. Then the whole group of students stood in thunderous applause. As I stood there afterwards, the faculty stared at me, especially Dr. Weatherspoon. It did make a difference in the religious education classes of the great Gaines S. Dobbins, a native Mississippian and especially beloved professor.

I also recall in this connection the case of Wayne Todd, our dear friend and preacher in the Okolona revival when Dorothy and I surrendered to God's will for our lives in ministry. He was in my graduation class but should have graduated earlier. He came to the seminary the last several weeks of the final year to write over one hundred required lessons for religious education assignments he had ignored. He had to stay up late to make up those assignments and did graduate. Later on in his highly successful ministry in his great church in Lexington, Kentucky, he placed great emphasis on the church library. All of the church library people from the Sunday School Board were involved. When Miss Florida Waite retired from the church library service, Dr. Wayne E. Todd became the new church library leader for all of Southern Baptists! He did a great job there, retired with full acclaim, came back to the Lexington Church, and later on, after a further fruitful ministry, died suddenly of a heart attack. His last warning to his children was, "Be very careful how you tell your mother." Myrtis Haney she was, and a very dear person from a preacher family herself. She and Wayne were a great couple and loved each other dearly.

After graduation, Dorothy and I went to the Louisville home of our dear friends, the T. E. Williamses. He was pastor of Third Avenue Baptist church, Louisville, Kentucky, an older, declining church that he was trying to resurrect —they did a good job. They lived in the pastor's two-story, old, but commodious, solid-brick home. We moved in upstairs with all our books and belongings for six weeks until Dorothy could finish at the University of Louisville. We could not pay anything, and they did not charge us. We tried to help out around the home and yard, and there was plenty to do. They had only one child, a severely retarded daughter, who could never speak. She died early, mercifully, but how they loved her and how they grieved. Mary died early also, and T. E. remarried. What an investment they made in us because I had been his family's pastor.

His mother and father were members of our Union Baptist Church in Meridian, Mississippi. Hers was the first funeral service I had ever shared in. She arose on Sunday morning, prepared breakfast as usual for her family, and as she helped her nine-year-old daughter, Joy, get ready for Sunday School, she began to feel a blackout sensation. She called to her husband, told him she thought she was dying, told him where to find the family lock box, and to take care of Joy and their twin younger son. I was in a revival in Morton, Mississippi, with the older son, R. M. Williams. I visited her in the Meridian Hospital where she was unconscious and lingered for several days. We came back for the funeral service and then right back to the Morton, Mississippi, Leesburg Baptist Church revival in progress. R. M. led the singing with unusual power that night. I preached, and God blessed. I remember vividly the funeral service and, particularly, T. E. leaning over for the last view of his mother with such an outburst of emotion. He was living away from home at the time, and it was such a shock to all.

T. E. held several revivals for me in different churches—Salvisa, Kentucky, and Portland, Tennessee—and he was always such a good biblical preacher. I learned much from his style of biblical preaching. These dear friends were our loving hosts and mentors during our last weeks in Louisville.

I talked with R. M. Williams and wife, Alice Jean, from our daughter's home in Dallas, Texas, recently. He has retired from the pastorate of East Sherman Baptist Church, Sherman, Texas. I more recently visited there and told about our mission work in the New York area. I held a revival for him in the East Sherman Church in 1948 when I was serving in Portland, Tennessee, when God blessed us graciously. R.M. has Parkinson's disease and could talk with me, but haltingly, via telephone. Alice Jean could not thank us enough for calling.

We drove back and forth to Portland, Tennessee—one hundred and fifty miles each way—each weekend, until Dorothy could graduate. We drove with our friends, Robert (Bob) and Mary Elizabeth Sanders. Her father, Dr. Charles W. Pope, was the executive secretary of the Tennessee Baptist Convention at that time. Dr. Pope was a great blessing to us in our Portland years. I recall coming back on a Sunday night from Portland with Bob Sanders driving, Dorothy and I were tired and half-asleep on the back seat, when suddenly the car swerved. A wheel had come off and we were stranded far from Louisville on the highway at black midnight. We persuaded the girls to stay in the car, windows up, while we went for help. We saw a light far up in a nearby field and walked in search of help. Our knock on the door brought a man to answer. Looking in, we saw the body of a man laid out for burial, not yet in his casket. That man was doing a service of love. In those days people stayed up all night with the dead until the burial on the next day. Of course, there was no help there. Back we went to the car and the girls. We all hiked up the road to a Trailways bus stop and took the bus to Louisville. The Williamses met us. Bob went back the next day and brought the car back to Louisville.

Finally, on June 26, 1946, Dorothy graduated from the University of Louisville, Kentucky, really a prestigious school. Her parents were there for this very special, happy occasion. They had wanted Dorothy to finish college before she was married, or her father would not marry us. They said if she did not finish college before marrying, she never would and I would need her to be able to help me—as a teacher or whatever. Dorothy finally threatened them with, "There's more than one fish in the sea. If you won't marry us, our friend, Earl Cooper, will."

Dorothy graduates from University of Louisville in 1946.

They relented and consented. Therefore, we were determined that Dorothy would finish college. She actually did so well that two of her teachers asked her on occasion to substitute teach their classes: Dean Oppenhimer, dean of the School of Liberal Arts, and Hilda Threlkeld, dean of women. I bought Dorothy a red coat and I always knew her across the seminary campus, at dusk, when she had ridden the city bus home to the seminary apartment. Sometimes she rode with Ruth Matthews, the wife of Dewitt Matthews, one of our fellow assistant teachers and student in New Testament. He kidded me about the red coat. Sometimes she would ride to school with her English professor, Dr. Elizabeth Burton, who lived in the St. Matthews area near the seminary campus.

So Dorothy finished in style and was able to teach, if necessary, which she never got around to doing. Dorothy has never had to work or to teach outside our churches. We have been a team, and all of our people have constantly recognized her as someone special and accomplished in every good grace. To this day, without her expertise, knowledge, memory, expert detailed mind, and record keeping (often in our churches she was called a walking encyclopaedia of valuable information), I would never have made it nor would our family have made it. What a gal! Dorothy, the eight-hundred number of our family.

Some additional things come to mind about our seminary days. There we met friends who have been steadfast and true across these years.

Frank Voight was special from Mississippi College days. He had a job working for the Young Men's Christian Association (YMCA) with local Louisville boys in the Parkland area. He enlisted me to help. I coached basketball while learning myself. Can you believe it? It also gave us extra money for bills. We always left with our bills paid up. Thank our Lord for helping us in this vital respect and to bless lives of boys in the process. I'll never know what happened to those boys.

A couple of special friends from Missouri were Vernon and Peggy Elmore. We were drawn together and enjoyed sharing leisure times. We went to the Louisville airport on a windy, April afternoon. Dorothy and I decided to take our first airplane ride—it cost $2.50, I believe. Peggy and Vernon elected to stay on the ground, and we soon realized why. We got up in that little airplane that shook and trembled like a feather in that strong April wind. We flew over the seminary area and over the vast Cave Hill Cemetery, where Dorothy's little brother, stillborn when her mother almost died, was buried. We wondered about us and if we were ready to go. We finally landed with no mishap—what a relief! It did get us used to the idea of flying, so essential in our work in later years. For a long time, before jet aircraft, I had this terrible fear of flying, especially in thunderstorms.

In the Cave Hill Cemetery area, there was a fine florist—Marret and Miller. For a time, since we were so recently married, I purchased a twenty-five-cent single rosebud for my bride each week. She loved it and red roses have been our favorites ever since. Now I wash the dishes every time instead of buying roses. Dorothy loves that, as well as some roses along the way.

We were always hungry in the evenings at seminary. We ate a lot of asparagus on toast in the dining hall, or so it seemed to me. We had a room on the second floor just above the sidewalk leading to the dining hall. We could see and hear all the comings and goings. In wintertime, we would buy milk and Ritz crackers and keep them in a space outside our window. Often, studying late at night, we survived the hunger problems with these snacks. With everything in one room, our quarters were close. We did occasionally get on each other's nerves, and eruptions would occur. But, we made up and made it through, by God's grace. We were too far from home to do otherwise.

More dear friends, Dorothy Dell and Nat Mayhall, now live in Corinth, Mississippi, where he has retired as director of missions for Alcorn County, Mississippi. We were recently invited back to share in a World Missions Conference in Corinth. We flew into Memphis, Tennessee, and borrowed my sister Mary Frances Stewart's Mercedes-Benz. Her husband, Joe Kelley, owns and operates a prosperous body shop business in the Memphis area. Folks in Alcorn County wondered about a missionary driving such a vehicle, and we explained and gave credit. We thoroughly enjoyed that week in the Corinth area where Dorothy's father had been the first area missionary when Sarah Pat, our oldest daughter, was a baby.

<hr />

On one occasion when we visited Dorothy's parents in Corinth, we had a car wreck. It was my fault for accidentally running a stop sign. An old man from the country didn't see me coming, and I ruined his radiator and knocked Sarah out of Dorothy's lap in the backseat. Fortunately, insurance from a Portland, Tennessee, agency, where we then lived, covered the damage. I have believed in good insurance from that day on. We visited Dorothy's parents there again in 1950. This time Mary Margaret was the expected baby. We were there in prospect of a call from First Baptist Church of Booneville, Mississippi, from Pineville, Kentucky. We did not feel, in prayerful analysis, that we should leave Pineville, Kentucky, and return to Mississippi. Dorothy's parents wanted us closer to them, but only in the Lord's will. I will write later about places we might have gone and the dilemma of prayerful decision when people were sure we should leave where we were and come to their church field. They usually got a better pastor and we stayed put for a time longer. We met and prayed with wonderful people several times in these experiences. God's Baptist people are among His best.

The final story to relate about our Salvisa days involves our dear friends, the Nat Mayhalls. We had Nat and Dorothy Dell traveling with us from Salvisa to Mississippi for Christmas. After a long Christmas program at Salvisa, which lasted into early evening, we were all ready to go. The year was 1945. We were to drive all night until we reached home in Mississippi. When we left Salvisa, it was clouding up and spitting snow. As we drove the road to the main north and south highway, then Highway 31 West, the roads began to freeze quickly, and in thirty minutes they were covered in ice. We kept driving, praying, sliding, slipping, and almost made it to the main highway. Coming to a long hill, we could see the long line of traffic stalled and sliding. We could not get around the sliding car in front of us. Nat got out and pushed. He had some problem with epileptic attacks and had to ask Dorothy Dell for his medicine. We stopped dead. Nat got back in, and we slowly slid back down into the valley and stopped just in front of a nice, substantial farm home. Nat and I went to the door and were met by a man who turned out to be a strong Kentucky Southern Baptist who was active in his church. They offered us one large guest room with two double beds, took us in, fed us delicious chocolate cake, and prayed with us and for others stuck on that road. We learned how to have one couple undress for bed while we turned our heads and closed our eyes. We slept soundly through the night, were fed a delicious, full, country breakfast, bid our gracious hosts goodbye, and followed the tracks of a behemoth truck up that hill to 31West, and were on our way home.

We are still on our way home and to Glory, to join with all God's people one day. Even people like those dear Kentucky Baptists who so graciously ministered to us.

4

Portland, Tennessee

1946–1949

The day we left Louisville, Kentucky, and Southern Baptist Theological Seminary was the same day Dorothy graduated from the University of Louisville. We had already taken all our meager furniture and belongings to Portland using a U-Haul trailer that was sufficient, though rather heavily laden.

During the night, on our way to Portland from Louisville, as we came close to the Tennessee border, over a hill in front of us we saw a crowd with a car sideways across the road. Traveling too fast to stop with faulty brakes, the only thing I could do was hit the ditch in front of the broad-sided vehicle in the road and go around. Thank God for immediately directing us from certain death! When I got out of the car, a drunken woman cursed me, and I phoned the State Police from a roadside restaurant. I got my brakes fixed!

Arriving at our home east of Portland, we unloaded our belongings and moved in. The upstairs of this old home, originally owned by Miss Bessie Tibbs, was perfect for our needs. There was a large bedroom on the right front, a spacious hallway suitable for a living room area, another bedroom on the east side of the home, and a borrowed oil stove, sink, and all that was needed in the kitchen. The kitchen faced north giving an excellent view over the fields and open countryside. Also, there was a large bathroom with a huge tub, thanks to Miss Bessie. We loved living there.

We needed more adequate furnishings for our part of the home. Dorothy said she subscribed to the adage that "three moves were equal to a fire"; therefore, we must have furniture equal to the probable moves ahead, and she was dead right.

One of our members, Mr. Vernon Kerley, owned and operated the largest store in town, and we were able to meet our needs, on credit, paying as you go. We purchased beautiful cherry furniture which served us well until we moved to Hawaii and could not take it with us. Most of it is in Sarah's home in

Fredericksburg, Virginia. It has lasted and served her well with her family of three boys and through several moves.

The owners of the old home were the Henry Wilsons whom we called Ruby and Henry. We have kept up with them through the years. They had a daughter, Zella Mae, budding into young womanhood and always watching our every move. She was approaching twenty, in love, and soon to marry her beloved. We were elected to see it done right. I was acquainted with the young man, George Donald Austin, through leading a revival in his home church, Pleasant Hill Baptist Church. I came to know the pastor, James Foster, in Mississippi Baptist College and later in seminary. He was playing the piano one day in a large assembly hall in Mullins Hall while I was washing the windows. He asked me to help him in a revival that became a changing point in my life. He was winding up his ministry at Pleasant Hill with a week of revival (again the Mississippi College days connection). He was engaged to Zelma Van Osdol whom Dorothy knew from her Blue Mountain College days. The last day of the revival, Pleasant Hill Church gave them a shower of much-needed gifts. My final official act was to help him load everything in his car and bid him Godspeed. They were to serve on the foreign mission field in the Philippines and elsewhere, even to this day. I saw them on a recent return to the alumni event at Mississippi Baptist College, celebrating fifty years in 1993.

I fell in love with the Pleasant Hill people and was in a number of homes during the revival week. Unknown to me, there were people from First Baptist Church, Portland, Tennessee, visiting relatives in the area and attending revival services. This was the first connection to my first pastorate out of seminary. George Donald Austin's family was a vital part of the Pleasant Hill Church family. His mother, a strong German woman, was a gracious hostess together with her husband. From a prior marriage of Mr. Austin, there was Leslie Austin, a deacon in the Portland Church, who was a half-brother to the young George Donald Austin. There has always been a special bond between us. Therefore, it was an event to share with Zella Mae in her coming marriage to George Donald Austin.

There was also a younger son, Charles, in the Wilson home. He was fun-loving and worked hard alongside his farmer father. They raised strawberries, the special fruit of that whole Portland area, as well as tobacco, corn, and all types of vegetables which were shared with us; and even to this day we hear from these dear people now in their nineties. They were Cumberland Presbyterians and very active in their church. Ruby played the piano and often had church people and assorted relatives in their home, sometimes singing gospel music, Stamps Baxter style, far into the night. Charles has grown up, married, and is now a rather large landowner and successful farmer. You can see we loved this family and thoroughly enjoyed our time in their country home.

We were free to have family, friends, and church members in the Wilson home and also free to come and go in their part of the home. Often we were invited for a meal or dessert. They were really like family but greatly respected our privacy. To this place we came from seminary approaching my twenty-fifth birthday, and now I have just turned seventy-five. Praise the Lord!

There is a sad sequel to the beautiful ongoing romance of George and Zella Mae. They were married thirty-four years, and God blessed them with a lovely family, grandchildren included. On their thirty-fourth anniversary, January 9, 1983, they went to Nashville and had a beautiful, happy time of celebration. On the following February first, a cold, icy day, George break-fasted with his family, kissed Zella Mae, his usual habit on leaving for farm chores, and went out on his tractor to cut some tree branches that were in a transit area. Somehow the tractor overturned and instantly killed him within thirty minutes of leaving the warmth of his family and home. To Zella Mae, it was simply unbelievable, and she has sorely grieved this tragic death of her husband over these intervening years. We have shared with her from time to time. She writes to us and visited with us when our grandson, Alex Rasmussen, was just a constantly crying baby.

The First Baptist Church of Portland and my more than three years as pastor were wonderful, memorable, and lasting to this day. We were in an area of strong Seventh Day Adventists' presence since their headquarters are in Nashville. They had the only hospital in the area, and I made many trips to that hospital to visit patients. I became well acquainted with the Seventh Day Adventist leaders, and they were wonderful to deal with. Our Dr. Dittes was an Adventist and helpful in every way.

The Portland Rotary Club filled a vital role of unity and encouragement in a town of two thousand people where local business people were hurting. Our Sunday School superintendent, T. E. Booker, had been in bankruptcy and was just overcoming the damage. Mr. Sterling Dorris, Training Union director, was struggling to survive in his general store. At that time, Portland was the center of a burgeoning strawberry industry with a new plant that processed these berries for a demanding market. The annual Strawberry Festival was held at the peak of the season. People came from all around to partake of real strawberry shortcake. One Saturday night, the large, central area, strawberry crate factory burned to the ground. The owner and operator, Mr. White Hill, was decimated but "refused to lose" and slowly came out of the disaster. The farmers of the area

Rotary Club, Portland, Tennessee. Charles, standing in back row, fifth from right.

looked to the strawberry crop as a major source of income, along with tobacco. The north-south highway, 31 West, then under construction, needed to be considered. The 31 East highway ran east of our little town. All of these matters involved the local Rotary Club to coordinate, dissipate, and relate to. I attended meetings weekly and enjoyed fellowship with the business people of the town. I once served a term as president. One occasion of unusual interest was a "womanless wedding." It was a resounding success, and people came from all over to gawk, especially at me as a flower girl. Other important businessmen showed that they loved to have fun, and we all became closer as a result.

I was also involved with the local Masonic Lodge and have maintained my membership over the years. Dorothy and I were also in Eastern Star. Years later I was stopped on a Kentucky highway for slight speeding in a hilly area. When the patrolman asked for my license and saw my Masonic card, I became one of his crowd and received only a warning.

Mr. Kerley, owner and operator of the General Furniture and Plumbing business, lived across from the church in a large two-story white house. The wedding of his daughter, Nancy, was the first I performed. This was a big occasion since the Kerleys were leading people in the town. Her fiancé, Bill Miller, from New Jersey, later became heavily involved in the Kerley business. Today the home is gone, another Kerley building is there dealing in bric-a-brac, cosmetics, and gifts for every occasion, run by the surviving Kerley daughters. It is somewhat sad to realize the changes.

The Louisville and Nashville Railroad (L&N) ran right through our town, and our dear friend, O. O. Massey, was the depot agent. The local press, with people of decided editorial opinions, was right across the track. They helped me print my weekly church bulletin. In later years, clothing factories came in and other burgeoning industry constructed new buildings all over. Indeed, Portland is now a major commercial center. The strawberry industry declined in the process. We were there for the one-hundredth anniversary of First Baptist Church in 1990 and have kept in touch over the years.

I must elaborate the point of our special fellowship with the O. O. Masseys. They would take us in when we were traveling, no matter the time of day or night. From my first visit to hold a funeral service when we were still in seminary until today, their home is my home. After Mr. Massey's death, Annie Ruth married Reid Moore, the church music director, who had lost his wife. Now he is in his late eighties and she in her early nineties. They were able to visit us in Federal Way since Mr. Massey, her first husband, enabled Annie Ruth to have a railroad pass for life.

Charles, standing mid-door, with Vacation Bible School group, Portland, Tennessee.

Hugh Shannon, an insurance agent, was owner of property that has since become a major real-estate business run by his son, Douglas, and somewhat less so by older son, Robert. I knew Mr. Shannon's family near Franklin, Kentucky, and held a revival in his home church. Hugh, deacon chairman and always ahead of the game in leadership, and his wife, Mary Ellen, our church organist, were special in our lives. We had some differences and he decided to step aside and stop attending church. On a Wednesday night, noting his absence, I felt concern and prayerfully went by to see him. We reconciled our differences, and he became my friend and one of the best supporters of our ministry the rest of our time there. Mrs. Shannon's mother and her sisters, Annie Ruth Massey (later Moore) and Clare Thomas, were supportive in our ministry. They knew and were known by everybody, and that helped me. There was one brother, Presley Lanier, and his wife, Elizabeth. Two young sons who were in my pastor-led Royal Ambassador chapter have become outstanding family and businessmen.

We were often in the homes of all of our people and were so blessed in our fellowship. Our task was to preach God's Word and to serve with these people. We might have stayed right there for the rest of our lives. We had souls saved, constantly received new families, enjoyed tremendous Vacation Bible Schools, married the young, buried the dead, and grew in God's grace. We were young, and our church youth were always around us. This has been true wherever we have been. Many of these had special needs and family problems. They have gone out to live and serve in many places. These youth are always the hope of the future, in our Lord.

Our first child, Sarah, was born on July 31, 1948, my twenty-seventh birthday, in the Vanderbilt Hospital in Nashville. Dr. A. E. Dittes had ministered to us, as did Dr. Joseph D. Anderson in Nashville. We devised a plan to drive the thirty-five miles from Portland to Nashville. Dorothy woke before daylight when her water broke. We called the Wiseman Ambulance. With deacon Hugh Shannon ahead in his car, I in my car, and Dorothy, her mother, and Mary Ellen Shannon in the ambulance, we made it safe and sound, although we must have been some sight that morning. Dorothy finally delivered at 2:30 P.M. while I was reading a Civil War novel, which is always relaxing to me. The first time I saw Sarah she had a bump on her head from the difficult delivery. Dr. Anderson did his best that day, together with other excellent personnel in the great Vanderbilt University Hospital. My father-in-law paid the bill. Can you believe it was eighty-five dollars in that long ago time? We named her Sarah after several special friends and Patterson, Dorothy's family name. You can know she was a spoiled little girl by family and church people.

Sarah's birth was special in every way in my life, and I wrote a song and a poem for the occasion. The song, *How Good Is God*, can be sung to the tune of *Danny Boy*. I began to improve in my own health that day, to serve our Lord for the next forty-eight years, and I am still at it. Praise his name for this daughter. Sarah is a minister's wife in Virginia with three fine sons. Sarah's oldest, Donnie, is a graduate of Georgetown Baptist College, in Kentucky. Her second son, Timothy, has just entered William and Mary College in Virginia to study marine biology. He has a personal goal to help clean up Chesapeake Bay of the pollution that has befouled the fishing resources of that great section of our country. Redheaded Charles William (Charlie Bill), the youngest, is a whole institution himself! All have been inspired by their preacher father, Don Reid Sr., in fishing prowess. He has, at present, a rewarding fishing-lure business.

My parents came to visit us to welcome our first baby. Dorothy's mother was still with us, having come earlier to be present for the birth. We all rejoiced at the long-awaited birth of this child since there had been a question as to whether Dorothy could ever have children. Since then, there has been no doubt with our present five children and ten grandchildren. We all went to visit Andrew Jackson's Hermitage in Nashville on that occasion.

———◆━◆✕◆━◆———

The only time in our ministry we were privileged to live in a brand new house and to see it constructed from the ground up was in Portland. In that wartime, we had to have special permits to build. A group of deacons and I journeyed to then-Congressman Albert Gore Sr.'s home in Carthage, Tennessee. We were received cordially and given every promise of help. I believe our present vice-president was just a toddler at that time. Construction was begun on a snowy day and we watched the progress of the construction over several months and hovered over every step.

We had some frightening experiences in that house. One took place shortly after our home was finished. I came close to being electrocuted when the basement was flooded, and many stored items floated in the water. Another took place while the house was under construction. The garage was built first for practical purposes. One day Dorothy was standing under the lightweight aluminum door when I pulled it down. The door hit her and knocked her down. She was expecting our first child and I was frightened beyond words since she had had problems with her pregnancy. But she got right up, all well except for a tiny bump. Thank God it was a lightweight aluminum door!

Right after we moved into the house, Dorothy fried some fish and forgot to turn off the burner. In a moment, billowing, black smoke completely blackened the white walls of our kitchen! Insurance covered the damage and soon all was restored.

We spent our first Christmas with baby Sarah Pat in that new home. Together we went in search of our first Christmas tree on a hill near Gallatin, Tennessee. We put that small cedar tree with some rocks in a Maxwell House coffee can and stood it up. We had our best Christmas up to that time!

One other churchwide project was a summer canning project. In the harvest season the women, and men if possible, peeled, hulled, and canned food for the orphanage, and some for us, under the direction of our Woman's Missionary Union president, Mrs. Maude Elliott. These people were dear to our hearts. Oh, there were problems and difficulties but we helped each other through them by God's grace.

To conclude our Portland years, we need to tell the story of our Fountain Head mission and resulting church. Several of our people lived in the area south of Portland and wanted to start a new work for the Lord. The Freeman and Mullins families met by previous arrangement in the old, no-longer-in-use, Fountain Head depot on a rainy Sunday afternoon. They had done a good job of enlistment. James Henson, a young man in the Portland Church, felt called of God to preach. He was prayerfully led to take over the leadership of this work that involved getting property and a building. They are still in ministry, though many of the older families are gone.

When we first came to work in Puget Sound, a woman needed help in Sunday School work. Polly Johnson, our associational Sunday School director, brought in a woman from our Sunday School Board in Nashville. After the worship service in our South Hill Church, we found out that this woman was the daughter of a former pastor of Fountain Head and as a child had been blessed and helped to find God's will in that church. Her husband also worked for our Sunday School Board in Nashville. They had once attended our Waikiki church while we were in Hawaii.

━━━◆◆◆◆━━━

Starting new work has been a vital part of our ministry in all the places we have served. It started early on, even as early as Salvisa, Kentucky, in Bass Town on the Salt River, an area of very poor people with whom our predecessor, Wayne Todd, had worked. These people lived in cardboard boxes and corrugated tin and worked outside.

In our lives, God is always preparing us for the next step. In Portland, I became involved with the United Dry Forces (UDF) of Tennessee through our friend, Jim Furman, executive director of UDF. I attended meetings in Nashville and shared in the fight against beverage alcohol. Among my fellow members of UDF was Fred Tarpley, pastor of First Baptist Church of Donelson, Tennessee. We became close friends. He was later called to the First Baptist Church of Barbourville, Kentucky, not many miles from Pineville, Kentucky. When our mutual friend and classmate in seminary, Dr. Wayne Dehoney, left Pineville, Fred Tarpley recommended me to the pulpit committee. That led to the next ministry God had for us in his great will.

There has always been that person who knew us and recommended us. Dr. Fred Tarpley, now in Mississippi, has been most effective in ministry to churches and by serving as the director of missions in Hinds County, Mississippi, which includes the capital city, Jackson. He and wife, Ann, have a doctor son on the foreign mission field in Africa. Dr. Tarpley is now in his eighties and is still pastoring, but Ann died January 2, 1997. He has begun thirty churches in his ministry.

How God leads has been a great mystery and blessing. How good is God, indeed, in the words of the song I wrote when Sarah came to bless us and to bless the world.

HOW GOOD IS GOD
Charles A. Jolly
(Tune: Londonderry Air)

How good is God! My tongue could never tell you!
How wonderful His Grace that keeps me strong!
If all my days I spent in serving His dear Will;
T'would be but small compared to His great love!

How good is God! In Christ He came to save us!
He gave His life that no man has to die!
He lives on High each day to help His children.
One day He'll come and take us home above!

How much I owe to Him for all His goodness!
Ten thousand years I could not live and pay!
I only know my life does now belong to Him;
And hid with God in Christ I daily live!

Chorus

How good is God! My soul does long to sing it!
How great His love! My heart does fail to feel!
How good is God! How much, how much, He loves me!
My heart is full. How good is God. How good is God!

I WATCHED A MOTHER PLAY WITH HER BABE
The Baby's Father,
Charles A. Jolly

I watched a mother play with her babe tonight;
And in her face shone heaven's light.
The babe was tiny and fair and sweet;
With soft, curly hair and little, dainty feet.
The mother's soul was centered on baby's care;
With duties to perform, not hard to bear.
The mother was young and beautiful and strong;
With zeal for the right and soul against wrong.
All the future was centered in baby dear;
With fond plans and hopes so sincere.
Then, methought as I watched the mother there;
So tenderly cuddling her baby fair.
A few short years and time will erase;
The bloom of youth from the mother's face.
The baby will be the stronger one
With the battle over helpless infancy won.
Mother will be needful of baby's care
And baby's love will return, and to spare.
How wonderful the plan of God!
To provide for both in a world so hard.
The mother will care
For the baby awhile;
And rear it from a little child.
Then baby will lovingly cherish mother dear
As the sunset of life fast draws near.

5

Pineville, Kentucky

1949–1953

It was a struggle for us to think of leaving Portland, Tennessee, in beautiful Middle Tennessee. We made a trip to Pineville and were impressed with the church and the people, but the emotional ties were still strong at Portland. Our close friends there rejoiced with us when we decided to stay. Still, there was a lingering void about Pineville. Our phone rang on a Saturday night and on the line was Foley Partin, chairman of the Pineville pulpit committee. I knew his slow, drawling voice. He asked if I knew where he was. How could I? He was in the church, down on his knees, praying with the rest of the committee, and the Lord "tells us that you are supposed to be our pastor." Dorothy was holding her breath and listening in. After prayer with Foley, I told Dorothy, "I think God wants us in Pineville."

So the tide turned, and we began the slow, painful process of leaving people we had come to love as our own family. There were the last invitations to homes of our people, farewells, gifts, and thankfulness to God for letting us be there and the general submission to God's leading. The moving van left and we were not far behind. It was two hundred miles between Portland and Pineville, and that was not too far for some back and forth visiting. Portland was always a stopover place between our steep mountain country and our Mississippi family and home. Those ties have lingered over the years.

Pineville was a totally new and different experience for us. We were in Bell County not far from "bloody" Harlan, Kentucky, known for its coal mine strikes and people struggling to have enough to live on (always a worldwide problem). The beautiful mountains had been denuded of timber for lumber, and the coal mines were running out of black fuel as the country was slowly turning away from the use of coal to other sources of energy.

69

First Baptist Church of Pineville, Kentucky. The pastor's home is to the immediate right.

The First Baptist Church of Pineville was set right in the midst of these tides of change and was a key ministering center. A deacon, Dr. J. M. Brooks, a dentist, who had actually been chairman of the pulpit committee but had been unable to be too involved, told me, "Pastor, the First Baptist Church of Pineville is the biggest business in this town and you are its leader. We will support you and help you." Not realizing the force of his word, I felt proud and humble when I left his office. Pineville then had some four thousand citizens, and our church had over a thousand members.

There was the Clear Creek Mountain Preacher's Bible School close by and the inspiring story of how the previous, beloved pastor of First Baptist Church, Dr. L. C. Kelly, was inspired of God to found the school. He had been over-burdened in ministering to people dying from the Spanish Flu which killed so many in the aftermath of World War I. In his weariness, he walked down the railroad and along the banks of the flowing Clear Creek, and God spoke to him, saying, "I want you to build a school and place of recreation and study and peace in this beautiful area." Thus was born the vision from which Dr. L. C. Kelly founded and built the first segment of what is now Clear Creek Bible College. The present young president, Dr. Bill Whitaker, formerly led his church to graciously help the preachers with gifts of turkeys at Christmas and at other seasons. He has led Clear Creek onward with a budget of over five million dollars. At the time we were in the area, it was one hundred thousand dollars. The faculty has also increased. There is new housing and an increase in people enrolled for educational advantages that are unsurpassed.

Dr. Kelly and his second wife were still in our area and held a place in the affections of the older, wealthier members of our church. In his way, Dr. Kelly still tried to pastor the church behind the scenes. So here I was, twenty-eight years of age, following Dr. Wayne Dehoney, a pastor who had also had a powerful impact on the church and community. Indeed, Wayne, later president of the Southern Baptist Convention and now professor of evangelism at Southern Baptist Theological Seminary and operator of an overseas tour ministry, still deep in the affections of our people, had done about everything that could be done in pastoring and evangelism with Clear Creek. You name it; he had done it. I felt like a person in burnt-over new ground trying to utilize what was there, to work around the stumps and carry on in ministry. And, God still blessed!

Wayne had gotten Clear Creek included in the Kentucky Baptist Convention budget on a percentage support basis. This is still true, even to this day. There was an attempt to change that in my time, but it did not succeed. In fact, when I was pastor in Annapolis, Maryland, I wrote a letter favoring Clear Creek and received a serious reprimand from Eldred Taylor, a Kentucky Baptist executive, who said, "You are out of state, seeking to influence Kentucky Baptists' policy."

The president of Clear Creek at that time was Dr. Merrill Aldridge, now retired, but still starting new churches in the Kentucky mountains' worked-out coal fields where the poor are rampant. Dorothy and I visited Merrill and Kay Aldridge at Clear Creek before he left to go head another mountain school, Magoffin Institute, in Jackson County, now non-existent. It was entered only by a creek bed on a mule. On leaving Clear Creek, where he was the retiring professor of missions, he told me, "Charlie, I'm leaving Clear Creek but not necessarily for good." We had been good friends since seminary days. When we first came to Pineville, I was amazed at his skill and leadership in organizing an array of mission Vacation Bible Schools throughout the mountains using the Clear Creek pastors and families— thirty plus my first year at Pineville. He had box packets for all those preachers, even down to pencils. And, it was a tremendous success with God's bounteous blessings. Children and youth were touched for good in those craggy mountains. Before Merrill left the Pineville area, Kay gave birth to twin boys and Merrill came knocking on our door at daylight to tell us the good news.

When Dr. Kelly resigned as president of Clear Creek, Doc Creech, one of our deacons and always our personal friend, who was wealthy in coal, timber, lumber, and car sales, was chairman of the Clear Creek search committee for a new president. He called me to talk about it. They had looked at Dr. Ray Roberts, one of their trustees and pastor of First Baptist Church of Danville, Kentucky. Dr. Roberts was soon (in 1952) to go across the Ohio River and lead in the northward trek of Southern Baptist work. I knew this was happening and remembered what Merrill Aldridge had said to me before he left Clear Creek. I told Doc Creech that Merrill would make an excellent president. It happened that way, and for approximately the next twenty years, Merrill headed and continued to build Clear Creek. Later he and Doc Creech had serious differences over some financial matters regarding the school, and Doc dropped his support of Clear Creek and our work in general in the area. His wife moved back to her home in Fayetteville, Tennessee, following Doc's death and their wealth continued to support Southern Baptist work from there. One instance of this involved Brother Jessie Hawkins who is now one of our area missionary directors in the Northwest. He rejoiced that I knew Cora Creech. He lead her funeral in Fayetteville, where he was her pastor. She had so blessed him.

The new preacher students and their families and faculty members of Clear Creek Bible School poured into our Pineville Baptist Church. They were wonderful, dedicated people, and many became our personal friends. A couple of them came into our home to clean and fix-up under Dorothy's direction. One was Kendall Hatton from Bergoo, West Virginia. Through some members of our church, he met Sarah, a nursing student from London, Kentucky. Kendall had very poor eyesight, and Sarah became his eyes. He had a brilliant mind, went to college, and made excellent grades. He was called as a pastor in West Virginia and asked us to come to Webster Springs, West Virginia, for his ordination service. The other helpful young man was Gary Sowers who helped Dorothy during the February flood of 1951.

At the end of January 1951, I was asked to hold a revival in Bergoo, West Virginia, through Kendall Hatton's recommendation. His parents were very active in the Bergoo church. I shall never forget the scene of snow-capped mountains all around—like a deep bowl. I stayed in the home of Doc and Ann Warne, who had an only daughter, Barbara, who was soon to finish high school. She was constantly playing the piano and had obvious talent. I talked with her and her family about encouraging her to go to Carson-Newman College in Jefferson City, Tennessee. This came to be, and she met her future husband there. They were a wonderful family—like so many there in that Bergoo church. We had a good revival, and God blessed. The Warnes came to visit us later in Pineville during the famous Spring Mountain Laurel Festival, a big event in the Pineville mountain area in the gorgeous springtime. They also visited us later in Roanoake.

While in Bergoo, I received a telephone call from Dorothy telling me that Pineville was being flooded and they had to get out of our home. There I was, far away and unable to be with my family in trouble. I had to rest in the Lord and His people, as has often been my only means of peace. My younger sister, Joanne, was living with us following my mother's untimely death on March 2, 1950. She was a junior in high school and much involved with all the young people and head over heels in love with Bill Woolum. Thus, she was with Dorothy who by now had given birth to our second daughter, Mary Margaret, on August 30, 1950.

My mother's death before her forty-ninth birthday was a shocking experience. Returning from a revival with Brother Joe in Wagarville, Alabama, in December of 1949, we visited with my mother. Joe and Sue, his first wife, were still together and were to have their daughter, Martha Sue, in September of 1952. We had thoroughly enjoyed our week with them. I went on my one and only deer hunt there, early one morning after a breakfast "fit for a king's lodge" where the hunters congregated. I was placed on a deer stand while the dogs were sounding their cries all around us. Suddenly, a beautiful doe stood thirty yards from me looking at me completely unafraid. She must have known that we couldn't shoot a doe legally, only a buck. I was so paralyzed at the sight that I couldn't have shot, in any case. We returned through New Orleans and stayed with Joe and Sue in their seminary apartment. Sugar Bowl mania was on in the city of New Orleans. My Uncle Peden had come from Mobile to Wagarville to visit with Joe and me. He had always been close to our family and especially to us boys.

We had taken our black janitor, Ed Diamond, from Pineville to his home in Anniston, Alabama, on our way to the revival with Joe. Ed, alone since the death of his wife, lived out back in a little house close to our house in Pineville. He was always so solicitous toward our Sarah. He loved to give her Juicy Fruit chewing gum.

On this visit with my mother, she was very loving toward our baby, Sarah Pat. Following that visit, my mother wrote her last letter to us, which I cherish greatly. In it, she tells us how to treat our baby. She had been so experienced in giving birth to ten children. My mother died suddenly on March 2, 1950, from a blood clot that the doctors thought to be pneumonia because of spots on the X-ray. She had left her home in Okolona to spend a week with her older, favorite sister, visiting all the places where she had lived as a young girl. She went to the hospital with a supposed gall bladder condition and subsequent surgery. We had made an earlier visit from Pineville and were assured that she was going to be all right. We received the message of her serious condition and left Pineville for the second time in the late evening, driving all night to reach home. We reached Glasgow, Kentucky, stopped for gas and placed a call to the Houston, Mississippi, hospital inquiring about my mother's condition. There was a brief pause, then the voice on the other end said, "We are sorry but the patient has expired and the family has gone home." I was shaken but had to drive on to Portland, in pouring rain, to spend the night with our dear friends, the Masseys, before driving on to Okolona for the funeral service. It was a sad and trying time as we buried my mother in the Buena Vista Cemetery. It was close by where she had married my father at the Methodist parsonage and where she and my father had attended Normal School as it was called then. She lies beside our brother Merrill, who was so special to her. We returned to Pineville with all the loving concern expressed by our people who had so prayed for her and for us.

A word in this interlude about Mary Margaret's birth on August 30, 1950. We had accepted the gracious offer of our church member, anesthesiologist Jean McInturf at Pineville Community Hospital, to be on call if Dorothy needed her. Sure enough, one morning before dawn we called Jean. Dorothy was in trouble, and we had to get to the hospital! Jean called Dr. Asher, and he just made it in time for Mary Margaret's birth at about 3:00 A.M. I shall never forget the look on Sarah Pat's face when I took her into the room where her mother held a new baby. She had a startled, what-can-this-mean look on her face as I held her close. Sarah was with us on a beautiful Sunday at Clear Creek when we had been invited by Deacon and Mrs. Marvin Byrdwell for lunch at the school cafeteria. This was July 31, 1949, my twenty-eighth birthday and Sarah's first. She walked for the first time that day and was our adored first child. Well, she adjusted to the addition in the family and she and Mary Margaret became, and still are, very close. They called themselves, "Mrs. Jonkers and Mrs. Possydoots" in their play-make-believe times. What a mess their playroom was until they were made to clean up or move out.

Now, back to the 1951 flood in Pineville. The rains were pouring down when Dorothy and the girls went to bed after praying for Daddy all the way yonder in Bergoo, West Virginia. Dorothy heard a knock before daylight. When she got to the door, no one was there and she called the police. Wallace Britton, our education director, out of concern about the flood, had come to alert Dorothy and the family. After he knocked, he walked over to the side of the house next to the church to see the floodwaters rising at an alarming two inches an hour. The police came to the church next door where men had already begun to get ready for a flood like one that came in former Pastor Dehoney's time when the water rose two inches on the second floor of the parsonage. Just a little more at that time, and it would have floated that massive brick building. Gary Sowers, along with Deacon Jewell Farris and Wallace Britton, came swimming up our street, out of concern for our family and to take care of our family. They put all our furnishings except the stove and refrigerator on the second floor. Later, after cleaning and drying and fixing, they were still operable. Deacon Faulkner Byrd's redheaded brother, a Kentucky utility employee, came in a motor boat to get our family out and on up the hill away from the floodwaters.

Our family was taken into the home of Deacon and Mrs. Frank Baugh Sr. Mrs. Ann Baugh, who already ill from internal health problems, had to have surgery later for spleen removal and died within the month. All of this was such a shock. Frank was always so close to us. I had officiated at the marriage of their daughter, Jean. They had another daughter, Mary Laurantha, named for grandmothers Laura and Bertha and mother Ann. They also had two sons, Bobby and Frank Jr. Frank Jr. later married a daughter of a prominent Baptist leader, Otis Amis, in Lexington, Kentucky, and both served on the Pakistan mission field. Frank Sr. was devastated as I stood with him as he lovingly bade Ann goodbye. He later courted and married a widow in our church, Grace Muse, Martha Brooks's mother.

When I finally returned from West Virginia, it was just in time to help clean up the muddy mess both in the home and the church. The home was little damaged and was soon restored. The church basement had to be completely restored, which involved all of us. Sometime after this, Deacon Doc Creech was in the church office and said he thought it best to move the church to a location out of this valley. On the hill on Creech property, an old home was available for $25,000. I agreed and began to think and pray about it. I talked with all our prominent families and got their signatures in agreement. Some disagreed, probably from former pastoral influence, and a move was on foot to defeat this proposal. The flood was gone and no longer a threat. It was too expensive. The present site was historic and the only and right location. All these were given as reasons for a defeat of the proposal. The vote finally came to the church. I still have the record—nine votes more to stay than to move. People who never came to church on Wednesday night came that night to vote down the proposal. The old Creech property is still vacant.

The beautiful and imposing church building caught fire and completely burned as a subsequent pastor, Charlie Jones, was returning from attending the Southern Baptist Convention. He nearly had a nervous breakdown from this shocking experience. The new building was placed on the very same spot and a floodwall built around the town so there could never be another flood. Then, after all-day assurances from the floodwall officials that the wall would hold back any flood, just after midnight on April 4, 1977, the worst flood ever crashed over that wall! Most people now live with the dread of another flood.

Early on, I became involved with the Bell County Red Cross, formerly headed by Dr. McClurkan, pastor of the Presbyterian church. Having served so long himself, he enlisted me. We had a fine woman secretary. Dr. McClurkan and I rode up and down the creeks and hollows to enlist support of the Red Cross. I learned then that the Red Cross is the only agency that commands the full resources of the government to come in and help restore an area in times of disaster. This was true many times in our own area of Pineville, Kentucky. Yet, many of the people would talk of other agencies that always gave donuts and coffee when troubles came. They quoted a Red Cross event in Louisville in the Brown Hotel when there had been drinking. Nevertheless, the Red Cross was the one called on for substantial help. For example, during the 1952 coal mine strike, many of the people suffered and became destitute. Some generous businessmen raised money to buy food for them. They asked me to oversee the project from our First Baptist Church office. The church agreed. We had people lined up on every block around our church. I interviewed every family, talked with them about the Lord and their church and gave each a generous sack of food. I did not turn down anyone, the town's people paid the bill and a good community spirit was engendered.

The missions program through Clear Creek and our church heavily involved me as the pastor. The church had, and still has, a mission program reaching out into the mountains all around. The Clear Creek preachers usually are the mission pastors—as many as eight to ten while I was pastor. I was able to persuade the committee to allow me to enlist one of our more capable men to supervise this program under my direction. One we enlisted was Thelmar Harper from the great Independent Baptist Church in the Cincinnati, Ohio, area. Thelmar later recommended me to them as pastor, then for a membership of four thousand. More recently, the church has had a tremendous bus ministry outreach. There was prolific correspondence between us, but I felt then and now that I was a Southern Baptist and my ministry, then and now, would be in that context. Thelmar served us well and the program expanded under mission chairman Mr. L. G. Swofford. I would occasionally preach in one of the churches and visit with each of the pastors. It was always difficult for the churches to show steady growth. They were more like a lighthouse in desolate communities.

I recall a revival in Colmar, one of the churches in a coalmine area. I was in the homes of the people in a dirty coal area but every one of them was clean. The ladies were excellent cooks and gracious hostesses. Each night the people were on wooden benches, kneeling and praying out loud toward the pulpit. I would sit and pray quietly with them and then preach to loud "Amens" and agreement. God graciously blessed us. That pastor and his family were very special.

There was a radio preacher in the Harlan, Kentucky, area named W. W. Nails. He preached and ranted and always tried to relate to me. One Monday morning he walked into our church and said, "Brother Jolly, God has told me that He wants me to hold a revival in your church." To which I replied, "I'm sorry, Brother Nails, but God has not told me that." He insisted but finally accepted what I said. Later on, we were at a regular associational executive board meeting that usually occurred on Saturday mornings. I often rode with Dr. John Carter, one of Clear Creek's best professors and a member of our church. Our moderator, Beckham Carmichael, baldheaded and short, was in his glory. He was only an eighth-grade graduate but shrewd. Brother Nails was there and they got into an argument over some matter. Brother Nails got up and walked to the front to confront Beckham Carmichael who flipped open a carving knife. Other men had to separate them. I think Brother Carmichael said, "There is enough ignorance in Bell County to ignorance the whole world." Brother Nails thought he was referring to him, and he probably was.

I became involved with young Marvin Byrdwell Jr., at the Cubbage Mission on Brown's Creek where, up the hollow, they preached, shouted, and handled rattlesnakes. Brother Wayne Dehoney left a tent that he apparently used in evangelistic work. Marvin and I set up that tent on the other side of the creek from the little schoolhouse where the Cubbage church usually met. I called Cubbage our first Southern Baptist bus ministry. Marvin bought this old bus and spent half of his time working on it and often had breakdowns. He never got discouraged, had a good smile, and he believed in what he was doing. Marvin always had grease under his fingernails from working on that bus. I attended one of the best Christmas programs of my life out there—twenty miles away. The children from poor homes were superb and responsive. The week of our revival it poured rain but the people came, despite the rain washing the sawdust away and virtually ruining the piano. But those were good nights in those two weeks.

One night a group of rowdies came to break up the revival. I told them, "Under our constitution, I'm empowered to make a citizen's arrest in case no police or sheriff is available. Therefore, tomorrow night if you come back for these destructive purposes, I will arrest you in the name of the law. If you resist, it will be the same as resisting the sheriff." They did not return, and I was off the hook! We had a splendid God-blessed revival with nineteen people, several of them adults, saved. We baptized on a Saturday morning in a nearby creek. The people stood watching on an overhanging bridge.

I baptized two sisters that day. I later married one sister to Virgil Casey, a Clear Creek preacher, and later an excellent pastor in the Charlottesville, Virginia, area where I held a revival for him. He later sought to enlist me as the director of missions for the Charlottesville, Virginia, area. Dorothy and I seriously considered it but could not make the needed financial adjustment.

Later, I married young Marvin Byrdwell to Lillian, a local East Pineville girl. He left her for another. In 1980, at the Baptist World Alliance in Toronto, Canada, I saw his parents for the last time and his second, former, grieving wife. She worked in the Kentucky State WMU office. We told her of Marvin's earlier work. Sad things happen everywhere, preachers not excepted, and the trend seems to get worse. I pray, "even so, come Lord Jesus. Yet He may delay for some to carry His Word to some who've never heard, to some who have never believed. Perhaps it is for you or me He doth tarry. Someday He may charge you or me with their doom. Perhaps for you, me, He doth delay."

The full quote is from friend Joe Allman. We were on the way to Chicago in 1946 to celebrate seminary graduation and to visit with Dorothy's aunt and uncle Leon Murphy, then a Cudahy Packing Company executive, which company is now extinct. "Another day and Jesus hath not come. Why doth He tarry? Why doth He delay? Perhaps that you may carry the word of His first coming to some who've never heard, to some who have never believed. When, O friend, on that awful Judgment Day He charges thee with their doom. Perhaps for thee He doth delay!"

One of the very special people and her family whom we came to know at Pineville was Mrs. Mildred Oaks; her two daughters, Janice and Carolyn; and one son, Willie. She was secretary to Dr. L. C. Kelly, president of Clear Creek, and is now writing the story of Clear Creek at the request of President Bill Whitaker. Mildred had come to us from nearby Middlesboro First Baptist Church (Dr. Marvin Adams, pastor). I later held a youth revival for him and came to love this dear man and his family. He was such an inspiration and example and blessing to me and to all in that mountain area. He died suddenly sometime later from pneumonia and heart attack, which saddened the whole area. His wife and daughter went to Georgetown Baptist College where his daughter, Marjorie, was a student, and his wife was a housemother.

Mildred Oaks had a youth program, with the help of her family, at the Middlesboro Baptist Church. Dorothy and I were overwhelmingly impressed with Mildred, her family, and this unusual youth program. She did a recitation of *Old Rubi Plays the Piano*, and what a marvel of ability and leadership excellence. It's no wonder that she so ably served as our educational/youth director in Roanoke, Virginia, and Newport News, Virginia. She also served in the Tennessee Baptist Sunday School Department with Dorothy's brother, Bob, who was associate state Sunday School director. She was from Corbin, Kentucky, originally and lost her first husband in a tragic incident. With help from his father and mother, she reared and educated her family, often under difficult financial strain. All these years we have been close. Janice is wife to Dr. Paul Mims, the outstanding pastor of Ocean View Baptist Church in Myrtle Beach, South Carolina. Willie has been an outstanding layman with his wife, Lucy, in our Calvary Baptist Church here in Washington; Carolyn was married to Raymond Winstead, now deceased, and lives in Morristown, Tennessee. What a fine woman and family for God. They have been our cherished friends and coworkers across the years. She is one of the best, in every way, that we have ever known. She has given generously to our Mountain Highway Building project even to this day. She has retired to Morristown, Tennessee, where she was on the committee to start a new mission. Today that church, Manley Baptist Church, starting with two members, is the largest in Morristown with twenty-five hundred members.

Another dear man I came to know in Pineville was Handley Gaddie, secretary of the Chamber of Commerce. He was a seriously crippled man, apt and capable, and editor of the local paper. We worked and shared together in Kentucky lore and history involving Daniel Boone country and the trailblazing through Cumberland Gap to the new state of "Cain Tuck" (Kentucky). He knew all the history and we talked a lot. He told about chained rock—a huge chain attached to a tremendous rock hovering over Pineville—as if it were ready to roll down. For a long time, tourists were told, "It's chained up there," as if any chain could really hold it back. So the Chamber of Commerce decided to put the huge chain up there so they could be truthful in what they were saying.

There were financial difficulties in Pineville and the need to produce some new initiatives. Handley and I talked of inviting the famed Christian businessman R. G. LeTourneau to come and speak to a community-wide rally in the high school gymnasium. It worked, and Mr. LeTourneau came with his whole group by plane at his own expense. It caught the imagination of the whole area. He spoke at a special breakfast at Clear Creek. Mr. LeTourneau, formerly from Peoria, Illinois, where he had his first factory, spoke in our seminary chapel on a Missionary Day occasion. This was my introduction to him. He told how in a serious auto accident, in which he was pinned under a car, he promised God if He would get him out and let him live, he would build a business, by God's help, and give God ninety percent while he lived on ten percent. God answered his prayer and he became the world's greatest builder of heavy earth-moving and machine-lifting equipment.

During World War II, Mr. LeTourneau was struggling with an invention problem with a deadline the next morning. He left it to hold a prayer meeting, as was his custom every Wednesday night. His associates told him, "You can't go tonight. We need this invention!" He went to prayer meeting and prayed, came back to his work, and in a little while he worked out the needed invention. The rest is history. Both he and Mrs. LeTourneau are gone to Glory. LeTourneau Technical College is still right in the vanguard of training experts in this technological age. Now, this is the whole future trend.

There was also a community-wide revival in Pineville with Evangelist Eddie Martin. Many lives were touched and souls saved. Though there was some reluctance from one of the pastors, we did have large community-wide involvement, and God blessed.

Our associational missionary became involved with a woman who was not his wife when I was on the State Board of Missions for our area. A postcard he sent to the woman, asking her to meet him in the park on such and such a day and hour, came into the hands of his blind pastor. I called one of the missionary's best friends about the information, and he was in the park when the planned tryst took place. The layman friend, pastor, and the associational missionary came to see me and asked me what the associational missionary should do. I told them he would have to resign his job and leave the area. He must not come back, lest this become general information. He left and went to some area in northern Ohio. I never heard from him again. He was very popular with many of the mountain people. I believe we, under God, averted a disaster.

One message I preached early on created quite a furor, many debates, and hurt some of my best people. In a message on requirements for those serving as teachers and leaders in Sunday School, I said, "No divorced people should serve." There were several prominent families involved, and I had to go behind the scenes and help the people, as they would let me. Some didn't want any help from me. It got the attention of the whole area on the issue of divorce. Some were left or deserted by their mates beyond their desire or control. Some had young people involved. I was deeply hurt that they were hurt, but the matter stood.

Today, there is so much divorce, even in the churches, even in pastors' families, that I believe the churches have failed to take a stand under God. Would it do any good? Would it help? I have married many divorced people since and have had them elected to and involved in places of leadership and service. Where should our stand be, to make people more conscious of the no-divorce principle in the Bible, save for the cause of fornication, or unfaithfulness to the marriage covenant? Most people would say that this is the only reason they would consider a divorce. But many are ready for divorce when the first fight occurs, which is often over money, or when they are tired of one and feel that all is dead, and are ready for another person with exciting romance being the issue.

The divorce matter has deeply affected our nation and the lives of countless children who, regardless of divorce, have to love and respect both parents to have wholeness in their own lives. Most of us have experienced this horror in some form or other. It can easily happen in the next relationship for essentially the same reasons, and the next, and the next. One solution often used to avoid family or financial problems is live-in partners, countering the very basis of implicit trust that is so essential to wholesome marriage—above all, care of who and what, consequences before marriage. Sadly, divorce is rampant even among well-known pastors. I do believe that it is possible for the Spirit of Jesus to minister to hurting people and to heal their wounds. This is the essence of God's love in Christ. Several cases of divorce in our immediate families, not the fault of some and the cause in others, have made me more experienced of deep, inherent problems. Still, I believe something can happen to cause people to realize what the Bible really teaches about divorce—the words of Jesus, in spite of the example of David often quoted, involving adultery and murder and many wives. What a change from early days in our country and the world. We need to pray, repent and "be not unequally yoked with unbelievers." When we are unequally yoked and divorced, it's the children who are hurt the most—they who are our future.

In any case, the bombshell, as my Pineville sermon was called, had serious repercussions and is what I am remembered for by the older people and perhaps some of their children. Somehow we must account to God for our beliefs and actions in this serious bond that should be as Abraham Lincoln inscribed on the ring of his only wife, Mary, "Love is Eternal." Mary Lincoln never married again and divorce was serious and scarce even in the early times of Andrew Jackson and Rachel. It was all but impossible. The enemies of Jackson accused

Rachel of adultery. They were actually married a second time. Rachel died of a broken heart just before Andrew was to go to Washington as our seventh president. As Jackson stood looking down on her burial site, he said, "In the presence of this dear Saint, I can and do forgive all my enemies, but those vile wretches who slandered her, must look to Heaven for mercy!"

Because of felt reaction to some of our strong biblical stands, we were inclined to consider some other church situations.

In March 1950, shortly after my mother's untimely death and Dorothy's being far along in expectancy of our second child, we had an opportunity to go to First Baptist Church of Booneville, Mississippi. Our friend Brother Wayne Todd had been pastor there, and I assume he might have recommended us. Also, Dorothy's mother and father were living in Corinth, Mississippi, some twenty miles north of Booneville, where he was serving as director of missions for Alcorn County. They always wanted us closer to them and might have recommended us. We stayed with them on this visit.

We were in contact with a Dr. M. L. Anderson, chairman of the pulpit committee, trustee of Blue Mountain College, and a community leader. He showed us the local hospital where he was a dominant influence and practitioner and assured us that Dorothy would be okay in their care. After prayerful consideration, we felt we should stay in Pineville. Dorothy felt it would be too close to family.

In 1950, I held a revival in the Southside Baptist Church in Birmingham, Alabama. Brother C. C. Buckalew was the pastor. My dear friend and college roommate from Yazoo City, Mississippi, Dr. Clarence Watson, was the education director. They were an enthusiastic congregation in a beautiful new building but in a changing community. We had a very happy experience, and God gave us a revival. I stayed in the Buckalew home and learned all about their highly gifted family.

Brother Buckalew, in a revival with us later in Pineville, gave us an example of an instant answer to prayer. While in seminary at Louisville, Kentucky, he would drive to his preaching appointments on Sunday morning pondering his sermon notes. His beautiful little auburn-haired daughter would accompany her father, sitting in the back, singing. As he drove along, the back door suddenly came open, and the child was sucked out onto the pavement. All he could do was to say, "O God, save her." He was able to stop the car several yards down the road. As he looked back, he saw her crumpled up in the road. He slowly backed up, sure that she was dead or sorely injured. When he got to her, she jumped up, shook her hair, and laughed. There were no injuries. This child grew up to marry an outstanding preacher, Robert Norman, who pastored several outstanding pulpits. The Buckalews also shared about one of their sons and his family who had moved home from school bringing all their belongings and clothes. They were tired on arrival and left most of their things in the car overnight. The next morning they discovered everything had been stolen. They were deeply distressed because they had very little money to purchase new things. They prayed and asked God for the thieves to return the stolen goods. The next morning everything had been returned on the front porch, and they all rejoiced in the Lord.

Sometime later, Brother Buckalew felt led to go to a relatively new church in Atlanta, Georgia. I was still in a "stir" in Pineville. In the spring of 1951, the pulpit committee of Southside Baptist Church in Birmingham, Alabama, asked us to consider their pastorate. Our friend Clarence Watson was the education director and strongly wanted us to come. He is a doctoral graduate of Southwestern Seminary and has retired recently from longtime professorship of religious education at Carson-Newman College where he and wife, Frances, live.

Dorothy and our two girls accompanied me to Birmingham where we stayed with the Buckalews since they had not yet moved to Atlanta. We were in the church for the Wednesday night fellowship dinner and prayer service. Their call was unanimous and we asked for time to consider. We got back to Pineville and proceeded to resign. Shockingly, the church refused to accept our resignation. We wrestled with what to do. Old Brother Tom Ware, chairman of our deacons, a wonderful father and grandfather figure, was always giving me intimate and fatherly advice about most everything. I talked with all our leadership. Our Sunday School superintendent, Sneed Friar, thought we ought to go because of internal squabbles. Another, Deacon Frank Baugh, felt just the opposite. We called in Deacon Foley Partin and others. We talked and prayed and reconciled and decided we had best stay in Pineville, and the whole church pledged full and better support!

I called Brother Buckalew, and he confessed that they had been disturbed about leaving Southside. Things were not as he had hoped in Atlanta. He shared this with the chairman of the deacons in Southside, telling him that his going and contentment about his decision had been on provision that the Jollys would accept the call and come to Southside. The result was that Southside called him back and he served happily for five more years while the church went through a transitional period. The church is now in a solidly black neighborhood, and the blacks have a lovely new building at a greatly reduced cost. We stayed on in Pineville for two more years, and when we left for Waverly Place in Roanoke, it was with affirmation and the good will of our Pineville people.

Some of the people at Southside were still upset. On our 1951 trip west to the Southern Baptist Convention in San Francisco, we met some of those disgruntled people in the area of the giant Sequoias. They shared their feelings, and we prayed and left it with the Lord to work it out and he did.

━━━━●━●━━●●●●━━●━━━━

Also shortly after my mother's death in 1950, I held a revival in the great Southside Baptist Church in Pine Bluff, Arkansas. Dr. Lloyd Sparkman was the pastor. It was through the recommendation of Brother Lehman Webb, pastor of the West Helena, Arkansas, Baptist Church, later a missionary to Singapore, that I was asked. I had helped Brother Webb in a revival earlier in West Helena, and God richly blessed. Praise the Lord! Later my youngest sister, Yvonne, and her husband, Harry Lloyd Rye, and two daughters, Anne and Melissa, lived in West Helena when she contracted viral pneumonia and died at twenty-three—one of the hardest experiences of our lives.

The revival with Dr. Sparkman in Pine Bluff was graciously blessed of God. I stayed in the home of a doctor and his wife, who had a lovely garden. I was comforted by the garden because my mother and I worked so closely together in her flowers. Later on, when we came from Hawaii to the Puget Sound area, the chairman of our associational missions committee was Dick Ross, now director of missions in New Mexico. He was a grandson of the couple I stayed with during the Pine Bluff revival. There is always a connective link in God's leading in our lives—praise Him!

Immanuel, another church in Pine Bluff, twice came to me about being its pastor. It was in the same time frame as the revival in Southside. I flew from Knoxville, Tennessee, eighty miles from Pineville, to Little Rock in an old conventional-type plane. Then we could not fly above ten thousand feet and had to dodge numerous thunderstorms. I was sick when I got off the plane. Later, at their persistence, Dorothy, the girls, and I drove from Pineville, visiting relatives on the way. We met the Immanuel people, preached for them, and were blessed by the experience. I was paid forty-six hundred dollars in Pineville and the chairman of the Immanuel committee offered us fifty-two hundred dollars a year, plus a home and all utilities. What an increase that was in those days. How far this American economy has come. At the close of the evening service, I received an anxious telephone call from our dear deacon friend, Bob Turpin, in Pineville. He wanted to know how things had gone and I was able to say to him that I felt we would be back home in Pineville. So it happened. The Immanuel people came back, but we still felt the same. That Immanuel Church has gone on to do well, praise the Lord! And, so has First Baptist, Pineville.

A committee from Carthage, Mississippi, came to visit us in Pineville. They visited on a cold Sunday morning and met with us for lunch in the only hotel, the Continental. Having wrestled with the Arkansas situation, we felt we could not consider their church. We recommended our friends the Troy Princes, who served happily in Carthage, and he later served as executive director of the Alaska Baptist Convention. We had known them since college and seminary days. We served together on a Southern Baptist Seminary financial campaign while we were in the Madison, New Jersey/ New York area and were in meetings at the seminary together. Later on, Troy visited us in Hawaii. He wanted me to come to Alaska for a revival, but he left Alaska, and I left Hawaii before it could happen. The Troy Princes are now retired, living in Arkansas, and we are retired, living in the Northwest, "and never the twain shall meet."

On reflection, I do not understand why these several churches came to us. I can only say that it strengthened our conviction to stay in Pineville at the time, and at Waverly Place in Virginia later. I do not regret our decisions as I look back. I'm surer than ever that we made the right decisions in the will of God for us personally and for subsequent future leading of our Lord of us and all involved. Praise His dear name!

I'll close this section on a more positive note with reference to the East Pineville Mission that is now a thriving Baptist church. We started in a former roadhouse restaurant building that was closed after three people were killed by guns on an early Sunday morning. We sat in booths with bullet holes all over the place for the first meeting with our Pineville people. We were back to visit on a recent anniversary occasion and saw the beautiful new building, and the church lot was filled with Sunday-evening worshippers.

Along the lines of guns, shootings, and desperado-type people, I was called on one occasion to come to a home where a desperado gunslinger son was wounded and thought to be dying. I was led up the steps by one of his gunslingers with others around wearing guns. I prayed for the man and told him about Jesus and salvation and asked God to lead him and his fellow gunmen in right ways. A close friend and our doctor from our Pineville hospital, Dr. Ed Wilson, recently deceased, told me that people from Louisville and other prominent places came to Pineville to learn better how to remove bullets. They were skilled from experience in that hospital. Today it is routine everywhere, as senseless murder is on a rampage with younger and younger people involved.

I was privileged to meet and have fellowship with a number of outstanding denominational leaders who came to Clear Creek for various events. One was Dr. James L. Sullivan and his young family on the way to his new church, First Baptist Church of Abilene, Texas. He was my pastor in Clinton, Mississippi, during my college days, so we had easy rapport. We climbed the mountain to Chain Rock with his younger children and then rested and shared together in a cave-like area on the way down the mountain.

The Clear Creek professors were both members of our church and our friends: Dr. Tom Brown Sr., New Testament, and wife; Dr. L. T. Hastings, Old Testament, and wife, who later held a revival for me. One night as he preached, a storm knocked out our lights. He finished by car lights outside, and souls were saved. He came to Madison, New Jersey, and stayed with us on his way to his granddaughter's wedding. Nancy married Ken Sehested, and together they started Seeds Ministries, a Southern Baptist Convention outreach to the world's poor. She was later called as pastor of a church in Memphis, and the Memphis-Shelby County Association withdrew fellowship from her church—another controversial area in Southern Baptist Convention policy. Mrs. L. T. Hastings always had us pray on our knees, especially for her only son, Brownlow. I never knew Brownlow until later when he was the Home Mission Board liaison person with Roman Catholics and more recently the head of our Golden Gate Seminary adjunct in Portland, Oregon. We talked about his dear parents and about our often praying for him. More Clear Creek professors were: Dr. and Mrs. Sloan, church administration; Dr. and Mrs. John Carter, associate in New Testament; and of course, Dr. and Mrs. L. C. Kelly, president and administrator. Mrs. Gladys Kelly helped teach ministers' wives. One man, Gordon Mode, business manager and public relations man, with whom we often prayed and visited together, was instantly and violently killed when a heavy truck that he was driving, loaded with church furniture, went out of control down a steep mountain. The Clear Creek School manufactured beautiful church furniture that created work for the ministers and provided a source of income.

One Saturday, building teams from various local churches built the shell of houses for incoming ministers and families. Our church built one and came back to finish the inside. Seventeen such homes were constructed in one day! It was a great experience. The heating system later proved to be inadequate and had to be brought up to date.

In 1951, we attended the Southern Baptist Convention in San Francisco. Dorothy and I planned the trip with help from a Mr. Hoskins, a local car dealer. He had made the trip and suggested we go the southern route and return the northern route. We had just bought a relatively new, little used, Chrysler New Yorker in superb running condition. Martha Hoskins, a young single woman and an excellent musician (her life work), asked to go with us. Also, the old, retired, First Baptist Church pastor, Reverend J. A. McCord, who had led in the present First Baptist Church building in Pineville, asked to go with us (he was also a retired postmaster appointed by Woodrow Wilson). He offered to pay all car expenses, going and coming. Of course, we readily agreed since only a limited amount of money was available from the church. Dorothy's mother stayed with our girls and away we went. All roads were then two lanes and there were long lines of traffic at times.

We saw all the important places on the southern route including: Southwestern Seminary, Carlsbad Caverns, the Grand Canyon, the Painted Desert, Las Vegas—an all-aglitter oasis in a desert, Boulder Dam, and Death Valley. We worshipped Sunday morning at the First Presbyterian Church of Hollywood, California, Dr. Louis Evans, pastor, and Sunday evening at the First Baptist Church of Bakersfield, California. We viewed the Sequoia National Forest and went on into San Francisco for the convention meetings at the famous Cow Palace. We visited one of Dorothy's second cousins on her father's side whose mother was from Chile and had married Dorothy's great uncle, Charles, a merchant mariner. We also went to Chinatown.

At the convention one day, Brother McCord told me he just couldn't endure riding back by car, so he had decided to take the train back. Not a word was said of where this left me on planned expenses. We had to make it on what we had left. Martha Hoskins could only pay her own way.

On the return trip, we drove the Pacific Coastal Highway, attended a Southern Baptist church in Salem, Oregon, when there was only a handful of such churches at that time in that area. The work in that area was only three years old, having been started in the Northwest in 1948. Today, there are nearly four hundred churches with ninety thousand members in the Northwest Baptist Convention (Washington/Oregon). We headed east through the beautiful Columbia gorge, crossed the Columbia River at The Dalles, Oregon. Then we headed across the great eastern-Washington wheat fields to Spokane. We continued east through Coeur d'Alene, Idaho, out through copper mines in east Montana and to Yellowstone Park where we spent only two hours. Dorothy thought we would run out of gas, but we found five gallons at a roadside home, and this eased Dorothy's concerns. We saw the beautiful Grand Tetons at a distance out of Yellowstone, went to Lander, Wyoming, famous for the rodeo, and spent the night. From Lander we went to Cheyenne, Wyoming, and finally to Omaha, Nebraska, where we rested and spent a day and night with Dorothy's aunt and uncle, the Leon Murphys.

We drove seven hundred and fifty miles the next day to get back to Pineville, Kentucky. We had five dollars left when we arrived. The sun was coming up over our beautiful lush mountains. We rejoiced to see our girls and their dear grandmother, who was ready for us to come home. We drove seven thousand and eighty miles in seventeen driving days, and it was three weeks before my legs stopped trembling. It was truly a magnificent experience, especially as we look back and see how God has blessed the Northwest Convention and churches over these years. At present we are building a six million dollar building for our state convention headquarters and Golden Gate Seminary adjunct quarters in Vancouver, Washington. The future is bright with the promises of God. There are new pastors coming, and we have leaders for our state convention and associational leadership. That experience has inspired us in all the mission work still ahead in our lives in various areas of our Southern Baptist Convention. We will keep telling this story. May we be as faithful in the future as those who came before us, by the enabling Grace of God in Christ Jesus, our Lord!

In 1952, Dr. Frank Voight, my friend from Mississippi college days, invited me to hold a revival in Roanoke, Virginia, in the new Grandin Court Baptist Church. It was a blessed experience, and God blessed with saving souls and reviving the church. Dorothy and our two girls were with me. We were treated royally. When revival services were over, we went for my first visit to historic Richmond, Virginia, and Washington, D. C., where my brother Don was a page to Mississippi Congressman Thomas G. Abernathy. Don took us to every historic place. We saw President Harry S. Truman, at a distance, riding in style down the street with sirens sounding.

About a year later, Frank Voight called me about recommending me to Waverly Place Baptist Church in Roanoke. We visited that church in 1952 which was just entering a new building on Easter Sunday. Our mutual friend and pastor Ed Sandridge, from seminary days, asked me then if I might like to pastor that church since he was leaving. It proved to be God's leading for us to leave Pineville and go to Roanoke, Virginia. Ed became an associate in the Training Union Department of the Baptist General Association of Virginia.

6

Roanoke, Virginia

1953 –1956

Leaving a church has always been a hard task for me. We have worked and served hard and faithfully wherever we have been—even to the point of burnout. The Pineville experience, so many-sided, with so many ramifications, was probably like this. We have always loved the people where we were like our own family. We had some of our most precious friends in Pineville. We have kept in touch across the years in every place God has let us serve. I have to believe God understands the most and the best when he leads one on to another field of service and brings His next man to carry on.

When I received the telephone call from Frank Voight about considering the Waverly Place Baptist Church in Roanoke, Virginia, I remember my first words, "I would be glad to come to your beautiful state and to consider the Waverly Place Baptist Church." We soon made the trip to Roanoke and were guests in the Voights' home.

That night I was in turmoil because I believed some Virginia Baptists' interpretation of baptism was not biblical. If a person had been baptized, even by immersion, in other than a Baptist church, it was not acceptable. Dr. Voight explained to me that even when this happened the person was carefully questioned as to the genuineness of his/her salvation experience. If such person had truly been saved before his/her baptism (baptism to symbolize, by immersion, the picture of Christ's death, burial and resurrection), only then was that person received into membership and not required to be baptized again. In careful consideration of this crucial point of salvation symbolized, I recalled how we usually received a person who came on promise of letter from another Southern Baptist church. We usually raised little question about their salvation symbolized. The Virginia position seemed to be more real and valid because of such concern.

It turns out much later, when I was involved as a leader in the constitution of our Pennsylvania/South Jersey new state convention, this issue was heavily debated. It carried over in the later organization of the New York Baptist Convention and the New England Baptist Convention (see Chapter 9).

I preached a sermon before the Waverly Place pulpit committee in the Grandin Court Baptist Church where I had held the revival for Dr. Voight and the Grandin Court Church in 1952. It was a strong doctrinal sermon emphasizing my basic Baptist beliefs, since I knew that most pulpit committees were usually most concerned about these vital matters. I made the statement that these truths will stand, "come hell or high water." The older chairman of the committee, Mr. A. L. Parrish, took exception to this. He felt it was out of place. His fellow deacon, Brother Warren Huddleston, who spoke with authority, a businessman whom all respected, helped Mr. Parrish to see how I had said it and all was okay. The pulpit committee approved me unanimously. I preached before the church and the call was unanimous. We have never had a happier fellowship than at that church. With many younger couples and their families and with our own two little daughters, we understood the privileges of parenting in serving that great church. The Parrishes and the Huddlestons were among our best friends in our years at Waverly.

We had a program in Pineville that on Wednesday nights before our prayer service, we had a meal together and shared in helping for our Sunday School leaders. We had around two hundred people every Wednesday night with dinner served by our lovely ladies to people just getting off from work. We doubled and tripled our prayer meeting attendance and had ministries for children and babies in connection with the program.

Dr. Voight later became Sunday School director for the Virginia Baptist General Association. He was so impressed with our program that he asked me to accompany him over the state and tell others about the program. I believe it was generally utilized to great advantage in most of our churches, and I got to know about the work in different areas of Virginia—western, northern, and the tidewater. Each was different. I thoroughly enjoyed this experience and was later joined by other state leaders promoting their programs in a similar manner. I was told after leaving Roanoke and Virginia that I was up for consideration as director of evangelism/missions for the general association if I had not left the state. Our fellowship with the Voights continued across the years until his death in 1982.

The southeast Roanoke area people were heavily involved with Avisco, a so-called "silk mill" which furnished employment for many of our people at Waverly. It has ceased to operate in the Roanoke area which was a very adverse blow and to some extent has affected the church and its remarkable growth. My father and step-mother visited us in 1953, and we had a directed tour of this mill. This was the only time my daddy had been that far from his Mississippi home except during WWI when he was stationed at Ft. Sam Houston, Texas. We also visited Appomattox, Virginia, where the Civil War ended in the home of Wilbur McLean who fled the Washington area to get away from the war. My father had always wanted to visit some of the famous places. As for my family, I would always take them to visit such places even when they protested. Daughter Mary Margaret has commented that Daddy was always taking us to some historic place or some Civil War battlefield. Today, older and mature, they cherish the memories and will more so in the future.

Our ministry at Waverly Place Baptist Church was very much a family type of ministry with younger families and many children and enough older people to keep the balance. I married many couples there as I had in most places where we served. To name these families would be almost like calling the church roll. The older ones were precious saints of God and ministered to us even as we minis-tered to them. We had many young people and promoted youth revivals and activities. The leader of this program and of our educational area of ministry was Mrs. Mildred Oaks. We had a revival team from Carson-Newman College. Among them were Guy Patterson Jr., Larkin Howard, and Glen Dow. They have since grown up and become servants of our Lord in different places. I mention two special couples: Dr. Frank Campbell, president of Averett College, Danville, Virginia, married to Janet Faye Hale, and Dr. Fred Bentley married to Doris Phillips and recently retired as president of Mars Hill College in North Carolina. Both are Baptist colleges. I heard Frank preach one of his first sermons at the Cooper's Cove Baptist Church near Roanoke. Janet was our teenage babysitter and one of several enlisted by the Young Women's Association (YWAs) to help us from time to time to free Dorothy for ministry with me. Mrs. Mildred Oaks' two daughters, Janice and Carolyn, were much involved in our youth work. We always had churchwide picnics and various outdoor activities involving adults and youth.

One very special family was the Stoney Painter family. Elizabeth, his wife, was a nurse, and they had a son, Richard. Stoney was a farmer who grew hay, feed, hogs, chickens—you name it. He also worked for the N&W Railroad as did many other members in the church. Our family loved going to his farm where all the farm events were in progress. Stoney took our children to his heart. Becky and our son, Buddy, dearly loved Stoney. He would include rides with them on his tractor, hunting the hen eggs, and feeding his cattle and hogs.

There was a wooded area behind his home where I could go to hunt squirrels. The last time I hunted squirrels, I shot and killed the only one I saw. Shot twice, in fact. I came down the hill swinging the squirrel. Mary Margaret came running to me and wanted to hold the squirrel. I told her no because he was bloody and dead. She wanted to know why I wanted to kill that poor little squirrel. It so touched my heart that I have never hunted squirrels since. Elizabeth and Stoney were special youth leaders. At one time, he felt God wanted him in full-time service and even tried it for a time. They took youth groups to camp. When it came time to take several of these youth to Carson-Newman College, Stoney used his truck to carry the baggage. The rest of us were in a car caravan—an all-day and into-the-night experience. All of these young people have served our Lord in their calling. Elizabeth Painter developed cancer, breast at first, colon cancer later. She seemed to improve. Then Richard, excellent football player on the Carson-Newman team and later football/athletic coach at William Byrd High School (Vinton area), developed leukemia.

I must mention Frank Campbell in connection with our 17th Street Mission. We enlisted the leadership and help of Gordon and Dolly Wright for basic leadership in Sunday School. He enlisted Frank for the preaching and spiritual leadership of the mission. That work has continued to grow and develop with a great group of local people. There is now a beautiful building and church. The Roanoke Valley Association took charge of the work and has turned it into a facility that has ministered to many of the needy people in the southeast Roanoke area.

We returned to mainland United States from Hawaii for the first time in May of 1978. We went to the Washington/Annapolis area to celebrate the seventy-fifth anniversary of the College Avenue Baptist Church, now Heritage Baptist Church. We stayed with Austin and Ethel Stokes, our former neighbors when the three girls were small. They, along with son Howard, later called to the ministry, spoiled Martha Ruth who was one year old when we moved there. Therefore, our trip was very special and like old home week. We left Annapolis and flew into Roanoke and were met by our dear friend, Lois Bryant, who told us about Richard Painter. He was out of the hospital and with his wife, Lynn, was working on a used Airstream R.V. I helped them on this job, and there was no word about his illness that he expected to overcome. He looked the picture of health, but he lived only two years after that, battling the disease, in and out of the hospital, the whole time. I received a phone call from Stoney while we were in Hawaii. Richard was in the hospital and they both felt that God had answered their prayers and Richard was healed. They shared exuberantly and we cried and prayed. Richard was buried on May 1, 1980. Stoney developed lung cancer, apparently from smoking incessantly. We were often in his home, and he would cough hard and almost constantly. His cancer progressed rapidly. Dorothy was back in March of 1981 for a visit with Martha Ruth when her first son, Ryan, was born in Dallas. Dorothy visited with our oldest daughter, Sarah, in Hillsville, Virginia, where her husband, Don, was pastor. Together they visited in Roanoke and saw the Painters. Stoney died April 15, 1981.

We spent many nights with our dear friends, Clyde and Lois Bryant, of the Waverly Church. They, along with their two sons, Clyde Jr., and Roger, and Clyde Sr.'s mother, have always been special to us. Their lovely home was by a singing, rippling stream of water. They would spread pallets on the floor and treat us like family—even moving their two boys out to accommodate us.

On this occasion while Dorothy and Sarah were there, the Bryants had a celebration time in their home and invited many of our Waverly Place Church family to visit with Dorothy and Sarah. Stoney and Elizabeth were there, and it was obvious Stoney was very ill. He lived only a month longer leaving Elizabeth, the young widow Lynn, and her son, Jeffrey. Elizabeth was so solicitous of our welfare. She would spend time with us and go with us to visit Sarah and Don in Hillsville, Virginia. We visited with her last in August of 1983. She seemed up in spirit. Her young daughter-in-law, Lynn, had worked with her to beautifully fix up the whole downstairs of her home in pink, frilly curtains with an easy access to the bathroom. It was a work of special love and understanding.

On this day, I spent time with Jeffrey while the women went into town. We took a long walk with Stoney's old walking stick to keep the dogs at bay. A thunderstorm came up and we barely made it back to the house in time. We had a good time to remember because Elizabeth died on August 25th. Lynn and Jeff, now grown up, he a big football star, came to be with us on a subsequent occasion at the Bryant's home. They had built a new home in north Roanoke. Again we were at the Bryant's home. Clyde Sr. had died, and a good group of Waverly people had come to share. It was the occasion of my retirement year, April 26, 1986. I was invited back to Waverly for a revival—their sixtieth anniversary and my sixty-fifth birthday that year in July.

People had come from all over from various churches where we had served: the Austin Stokes from Annapolis, Maryland; the Charlie Browns formerly from Annapolis, Maryland; the Jones Fortunes from Madison, New Jersey, then living in Kingsport, Tennessee; the Jewell Farrises from Pineville, Kentucky; Bill and Ann Martin from Annapolis, Maryland; Pat Massey from Norfolk, Virginia; Lois and Dick Burks from Newport News, Virginia; Helen and Tom Morris from Newport News, Virginia; Mamie Todd, Elizabeth Brooks, and Norma Sandridge, widow of seminary friend, Ed Sandridge, and precious pastor prior to me at Waverly. Ed was killed in a head-on collision with a drunk driver at forty-one years of age leaving a handicapped son, Jimmy, with his mother. Ed had just left a church service on Friday night to return to Richmond, Virginia, where he lived. John Tubbs and his new wife, Ann Byrd, were at the reception also. His first wife, Doris, was our dispensary nurse in seminary. Later, he was state Sunday School director in our New York Baptist Convention.

David and Sanan Brazzeal and daughter, Corrie, from our Northwest area where he had served as music missionary were also there on their way to Richmond, Virginia, for missionary orientation to Brazil. He had not believed me when I talked about the people from various, previous places and churches in our Puget Sound staff meetings. He had no trouble believing that day! Also present were Carl and Edith Bush who had served all over the country in the Lord's work, then retired in Florida. He was our Sunday School director when we came to Waverly, and Red (D. L.) and Madeline St. Clair, he, formerly a deacon at Waverly, now retired in the Tampa, Florida, area. Thank God, our Heavenly Father, that "our lives have fallen in pleasant places" with wonderful people!

I really started out to say, before getting carried away in blessed memory, that Lynn and Jeffrey came to the Bryant party to give us an antique set of pearl-trimmed opera glasses originally from Paris, France. We had so admired them from Stoney Painter's antique collection acquired from everywhere. Lynn knew about our admiration and brought these as gifts, along with a special piece of beautiful carnival glass for Dorothy.

I have told this story because it is so many-sided and illustrates the type of spiritually thrilling ministry in which God has privileged us to serve across these years. Also, to wrestle with the why of the whole Painter family being wiped out because of cancer despite our long, and often anguished, praying. Did Stoney's smoking contribute to this sad tragedy? There are no easy answers, except to say that whatever the causes are here, they no longer apply where Stoney, Elizabeth, and Richard are now in Glory. What a party we will have when we meet together around the throne of God, at the feet of Jesus, our Lord. There are many other such stories about dear friends and gentle hearts who are gone so soon, but we'll meet again "in the sweet by and by."

One special friend from seminary days was J. C. (Carroll) Chapman. While in seminary, he married Betty Simmons in Johnson City, Tennessee. It was during the hard, trying years of World War II, when the Japanese were wrecking havoc in every place in Asia, that we got to know them. When Betty had their first and only child, Jean Carroll, Dorothy stayed with her on a cold snowy Sunday. In later years, this special relationship was to help in a visit with Jean in the New York area where she lived, apparently no longer in the Lord's will. Recently she came back to the Lord, and Betty, widowed in 1982, is awed that this could happen after so long.

We were very close in those years, and it filled a very vital need in our lives of struggle. Carroll had an old, battered car. The one opposite the driver had to hold the door shut when riding. I held a revival with Carroll in those seminary days at Long Run Baptist Church in a building that is set over the graves of the first Abraham Lincolns, killed by the Indians. He was the grandfather of our Civil War president. When we were in Pineville, Kentucky, I had the privilege to recommend Carroll to the First Baptist Church of Barbourville, Kentucky. He was pastor there when one of our members at Pineville, Mrs. Charles Matthews, left home, drove to a lonely area, and took her life. Her husband was in a panic about her whereabouts. There had been no real warning signs except a lingering depression. They found her, shot by her own hands, with a gun Charlie kept in a dresser drawer for protection. He was a Pineville businessman.

Brother Carroll Chapman came to Waverly to hold our revival in March of 1954 when Sarah was five years old. She told her mother and others that she wanted to "trust Jesus in her heart." Several people came forward for this purpose in a morning service. One of those who came forward to greet Sarah and others who had professed their faith in Christ was Tom Calfee, our milkman, who described to me what is taken out of raw milk in processing, some difference from raw milk. Tom, on that same day in the evening service, made his profession of faith and said, "When I saw that little girl make her profession of faith so confidently, I said it was time for me to take my stand with Christ." He was baptized at the same time as Sarah, April 4, 1954, Dorothy's thirty-first birthday. He had such a lovely family. Ethel, his wife, is still around and doing well. Their beautiful daughter, Ilona, subsequently married and died of cancer early in life. So Sarah, now forty-eight and a pastor's wife, had a vital influence for the Lord at an early age. Her life has continued this special influence for Christ in her family and in churches where they have faithfully served.

Brother Chapman invited me for a revival in his church, Litz Manor Baptist in Kingsport, Tennessee, later on. He subsequently had stomach cancer. He always had trouble and talked of "cancerphobia." He died in 1982. We have sorely missed him and his bombastic ways. He would come into our home, wherever we were, and always wanted to work on the furnace, the car, or whatever, and take pictures of us. We treasure those occasions to this day. He came to Annapolis, Maryland, when we were there, from his church at the Patuxent Naval Base in Lexington Park, Maryland. We were contemplating a new building, and he took pictures of the Naval Academy and all of us for a special brochure. That is another story.

One of our special delights as a family in Roanoke was to go up on beautiful Mill Mountain where a large electrical star is situated along with a very nice children's zoo. We thoroughly enjoyed such occasions.

When Mary Margaret, our second daughter, was saved and baptized on December 4, 1955, she was sitting between Dorothy and Dorothy's mother to observe her first Lord's Table. She partook, with help and direction, then smacked her hands together, brushing away crumbs, and said, "That was a nice little snack." She became very special to a young woman, Dorothy Kelly, who was married to a man in prison with psychiatric difficulties. They had no children. She lived with and came to church with an older couple, the Doc Stevenses. She touched our hearts from our first acquaintance, and Mary Margaret latched on to her. They became almost inseparable. She took Mary Margaret to various places. She would also paint her fingernails. Theirs is a lasting friendship. On a trip to the Baptist Children's Home in Salem, Virginia, nine-year-old Mary Margaret accompanied Reverend L. L. Jessup and me. We were taking some needy children to the home, and we visited Dot Kelly Blevins.

By this time, Dot had met a young man, seriously crippled from multiple sclerosis, who had been in the military. He was a marvelous artist. He owned and operated a newsstand on a downtown Roanoke street. It was later situated in the beautiful Patrick Henry Hotel in Roanoke. When Dot's first husband died, she asked Clarence Blevins to accompany her to the funeral home and help with funeral arrangements. They had become friends through the Waverly Church. From this, their friendship blossomed into love. They came to see me when we were guests in the home of Hildrey Pollard, a Waverly Church deacon, and his wife, to ask me to have their wedding ceremony. We were living and serving in Annapolis, Maryland, at that time. The wedding party came to Annapolis; the wedding took place in our parsonage home on May 17, 1957. What a special day, and what a special, precious couple. Clarence died in 1990, and Dorothy still lives

Waverly Place Baptist Church Seventieth Anniversary April 28, 1996.

in their lovely home in Vinton where we were guests in April of 1996. All around us there was Clarence's beautiful art. Everyone at Waverly Place Baptist Church dearly loved this special couple. Clarence was a deacon and Sunday School teacher later. My Dorothy got him to take his first part in Training Union. Clarence stood up there like a stalwart and spoke beautifully.

We were recently invited back to Waverly Church to celebrate their seventieth anniversary. It was an especially happy time for us. So many of those we had known, loved, and worked with were still involved and carrying on. We were hosted, with other special guests, by our friends the Mauyer Woods, the Hildrey Pollards, the Lewis Shartzers, the Lester Kellys, the David Justises, Lucille Bowling, and Mrs. Madelone (Guy) Austin. Guy is recently deceased. I was on the program for ten minutes with other former pastors. There was a lovely meal later, and before that a group photograph taken outside that we cherish dearly. Later in the evening, we had fellowship with our dear special friends, the Floyd Overstreets. He was our Brotherhood leader. We have prayed for each other across the years. He owns and operates a successful hardware business along with his family. Many Waverly Church member employees are also involved. He has been active and involved in another Baptist church with a mutual pastor friend and family, Landon and Dale Mattox, a retired pastor couple. Floyd and Olivia have given liberally toward our new Mountain Highway Baptist Church prospective building. He is an ardent Atlanta Braves fan, and I called him when the Braves won the 1995 World Series.

———————————•♦•⟩<•●———————————

In 1955, on May 20, in the old Lewis Gale Hospital, our third daughter, Martha Ruth, was born. Dorothy had some difficulty, but when Martha decided to come, she came. This was another blue-ribbon day in our lives. We are grateful for the skills and talents of Dorothy's doctor, Dr. Rufus P. Ellett. I left Dorothy at the hospital and went to the nearby S&W Cafeteria where our Janice Oaks worked. Even the doctor expected a long night, but then it happened, and things have never been the same in our lives! More about Marti, as she is now called, later.

———————————•♦•⟩<•●———————————

We have talked of Mrs. Mildred Oaks who came to us from being secretary to Dr. L. C. Kelly at Clear Creek Baptist Preacher's School. This was her first specific job in the field of Christian education. Dorothy and I saw her in action in Kentucky and have never been disappointed in the ability and skills of this dear lady. Mildred Oaks's first husband's aging parents visited us at Waverly, and we loved them dearly. To this day, Dorothy uses Miss Debbie's banana cake recipe. She was a pioneer of first magnitude from old Kentucky.

Coming to us later in the capacity of music minister was Brother Phil Eads, a native of Alabama who later served in Kentucky. He had the good fortune to meet and marry Margaret Beasley from our Salvisa Church. They had no children but were a special couple who have blessed both our lives personally and the Waverly Place Baptist Church. Phil had a marvelous voice. How he rang the bells when he sang "Down From His Glory," as well as many others. They were a great asset in our work there and also later in the Grandin Court Baptist Church in Roanoke, Virginia.

We were happy in Waverly and felt that we could be content to stay there for the rest of our lives, as God willed. The man who led in the organization of Waverly Place Baptist Church was Clifton C. Thomas from the Belmont Baptist Church in Roanoke, Virginia. He was beloved by all of our people, as indeed was true of all their pastors. Dr. Thomas was later pastor of First Baptist Church of Staunton, Virginia, and First Baptist Church of Noonan, Georgia. From there he was called as executive secretary of the Maryland Baptist Union Association.

He came back to Waverly on an occasion for a funeral service of one who had been close to him and his ministry. Of course I was involved in the funeral service and got to know Dr. Thomas briefly. Sometime later, I received a letter from him telling me of the pulpit vacancy in the College Avenue Baptist Church in Annapolis, Maryland, and that he wanted to recommend me as the pastor. He remarked that the Waverly people would "kill" him if they knew about this and thereby began the next story in our journey in God's call. It has been a thrilling story in every case, and the opportunity before us was to be one of the most unusual yet.

7

Annapolis, Maryland

1956–1959

A pulpit committee from Annapolis, Maryland, came to our church on a Sunday morning when we had a special speaker, the Honorable Eugene Siler, a gifted Baptist lay speaker and our longtime Kentucky friend and Congressman. He was a longtime advocate in Congress to proclaim the United States of America as a Christian nation. Would that we had done so and lived up to it. That was his goal.

The pulpit committee had discussed the possibility that I just might not be preaching when they came. I do recall the commotion in the church balcony when committee member and chairman of deacons at Annapolis, Bob Maddocks, burst into laughter when I announced the special speaker. The committee later met with us in our nearby home after the service. Congressman Siler and Mrs. Mildred Oaks, our education director and a relative of Mr. Siler, were in the kitchen and told Dorothy who these people were. Later, Congressman Siler came to Annapolis for a Men's Day emphasis. Deacon Bob Maddocks had had surgery for the removal of a cancerous growth from the back of his neck; when it reoccurred, he said that he felt the problem again on that visit to Waverly.

Our Waverly friends, the A. L. Parrishes, kept our children while Dorothy and I went to Annapolis and stayed with Bob and Pat Maddocks and their only child, an adopted son, Dickie. The Parrishes were special friends to Dr. C. C. Thomas, the first pastor at Waverly, the interim pastor at College Avenue Baptist Church and Maryland Baptist executive director.

We were given the grand tour of Annapolis, and we were more than impressed with the lovely old church building, built from reject stones left from the building of Bancroft Hall, the main dormitory for Naval Academy midshipmen. There was a beautiful stained-glass window depicting Christ holding a little lamb in his arms, which was given to the church by the architect of Bancroft Hall. This picture was in memory of a little son of this special couple who had died very young. The Merediths, the donors, were members of College Avenue Baptist Church. This window is now in a hallowed place in the new Heritage Baptist Church, located and developed on sixteen acres of lovely land in south Annapolis—a developing residential area.

The College Avenue Baptist Church was so called because it was adjacent to the beautiful St. John's College, famous for its curriculum of mastering one hundred special books for a college degree, and where our early continental forebears met under a still-standing, ancient tree. Samuel Adams and all the malcontents proclaimed their determination for a new and separate nation from British rule. The state of Maryland and its capitol of Annapolis later needed the land where College Avenue Baptist Church stood and offered the church one million dollars for the property. The church, under the leadership of its pastor, Dr. David Haney, formerly with Lebanon Baptist Church in the Cincinnati, Ohio, area, recommended by Ray Roberts and me to College Avenue, accepted the offer and moved to the new location with the new name Heritage. The new name was chosen by vote from individual solicitation. So much for recent history.

The College Avenue Baptist Church had bought the old original study chairs, on which the first midshipmen sat, from the Naval Academy which was founded in 1845. At Dorothy's request, they gave us six of these original captain's chairs. All are wired up with bailing wire and numbered underneath, as was the custom then. One has #666 on the inside back of the chair. He must have been a devil! They were a conversation piece in our Madison home around an antique dining table purchased for $135 from a lady in the Wilmington, Delaware, area. She wanted to sell it to cover expenses for a foreign cruise trip. We had to part with this furniture when we went to Hawaii because of the threat of termite infestation and possible damage.

When we came in 1956, the College Avenue Baptist Church was in the process of building a new educational building on their original property. It was finished and dedicated in our time there. On our visit, Mac McCarter, a Naval Academy official and chairman of our building project, told us all about this project. He was an exceptional man and handled his job with great proficiency and finesse, only taking time off once a year for the Miss America beauty pageant in Atlantic City, New Jersey, on the famous boardwalk.

The church office was in the old home of the first pastor. From its front window, Brother W. C. Wood, the beloved pastor, looked out to see 150 Naval Academy midshipmen marching in perfect union, three different companies of

Midshipmen arriving at College Avenue (now Heritage Baptist) for Sunday morning activities.

fifty each, to attend worship services at the church. It was official in those long-ago days that on Sunday mornings the midshipmen had to worship at either the academy's beautiful, commodious chapel or out in the town of Annapolis at the church of their choice. It was the same in our time.

Pastor Wood was the type of man who walked the streets of Annapolis with his Bible, seeking the lost for Christ. He was always loving to his flock and with his family. There was little money to build a new building, so Pastor Wood, believing in God's promises that it would come to pass, in pencil, put the name and date of classes and groups, who gave nickels, dimes, and pennies for the new building, on bricks used as an appeal. Several of those bricks were placed in the memorial space in the new educational building named in his memory.

One morning, his mind left him just before worship. Stress and strain were the cause of this, so the people thought. They took him to a special hospice for treatment. He never regained his mental strength, nor came out, before he died. His wife and family were still in the area in our time and were members of the Glen Burnie Baptist Church. Dr. Cline Vice was their pastor. I visited a patient in that hospice one time with one of our deacons, Mr. H. T. Pike. On that visit, Mr. Pike shared with me that the deacons would visit Pastor Wood, and this once-gentle and loving pastor would literally "curse them out." They were stunned. How could this happen? I suggested that any pastor bears many burdens and problems which he can only take to the Lord. Perhaps in his often-turbulent mind are also buried the dormant, negative feelings about this and that, which he cannot express. It simply came out in the end. Dorothy said later, talking with me, "I always knew that there was something down there" referring to me! This suggestion seemed to comfort Mr. Pike.

What a great, special day of rejoicing when we dedicated and moved into that lovely new educational building. All the Wood family and people from all over came for the dedication. The people rejoiced because there was space for all areas. They were so thankful for the memory of a good, godly man, Brother W. C. Wood.

One other thing that impressed me about the College Avenue Baptist Church sanctuary was the beautiful brass-eagle lectern given to the church originally by President Teddy Roosevelt. College Avenue had connections from its earliest days. Miss Margaret McCusker gave me a copy of a famous photo of President Roosevelt that had been given to her father by Roosevelt himself.

Before Dr. Thomas came to Maryland as executive director, there was a rather dormant Maryland Baptist Union Association which was changed to the Maryland Baptist Convention in our time there. This was more in keeping with the then Southern Baptist trends. According to some whom we knew, who knew the story, Maryland Southern Baptist work before Dr. Thomas was largely localized in three areas—Annapolis, Baltimore, and Frederick. The earlier executive director was a good-ole-boy type, and the leadership called him the "Pope." Dr. Thomas came into this situation with a vision to encourage new work, and the work developed into more than two hundred churches and is still growing. Indeed, the three areas mentioned are still the hub of the work.

Annapolis is built around two circles of traffic—the first, the historic St. Anne Church which is Episcopal; the second encompassed the capitol building which is the oldest state capitol building in the United States. In Annapolis, among other historic homes, is the former home of Francis Scott Key, who was in Baltimore when the British were burning it. He saw the flag still waving above the smoke and wrote the "Star Spangled Banner," our national anthem.

The United States Congress fled to Annapolis amidst the riots of Revolutionary War veterans demanding their back pay when there was no money to pay them. For two years, they met and struggled for survival in Annapolis. It was to this Congress, meeting in Annapolis at the now-historic old capitol building, that George Washington came to surrender his commission and to give his allegiance to the civil government. He was met coming into Annapolis by a delegation that wanted to make him veritably a dictator. Washington courteously refused and paid his compliments, first, to the president of the Congress. The next day, this "hunkered down" Congress met in the state senate chamber, their hats on, deep scowls on their faces, to show their authority. Washington, in full military regalia, sat quietly aside until called on. He arose and with a strong majestic bearing, came before the assembled Congress, presented his resignation, and then bowed graciously. Thus was born in the United States the subservience of the military to the civilian form of government. Then the congressmen arose, took off their hats, and accepted George Washington's surrender of his commission. It was near Christmas, and that night Washington danced the minuet with the ladies of Annapolis under the capitol dome.

The old State Treasury building still stands on the Annapolis state capitol grounds where the state officials could keep an eye on financial matters. Later, in Washington, D.C., President Andrew Jackson had to decide where to put the United States Treasury building. Some wanted it away from the White House area. Stalwart old Andy, walking stick in hand, walked out from the White House to an area close by, put down his walking stick and said, "Here, right here, the treasury building will be." So today when you go to Washington, D.C., the magnificent capitol building faces up Pennsylvania Avenue toward the White House at the other end. Then one has to go around the United States Treasury building to get to the White House. Old Andy and every president since has been able to keep an eye on the financial reins of the country. I write about these matters because, as a lover of history, I was about to be a part of it as pastor of the College Avenue Baptist Church, and it included the whole Washington, D.C. scene. This was all very impressive and stimulating to me in my ministry of three years.

One other impressive factor: a statue of Roger B. Tany in his Supreme Court regalia sits on the south side of the Maryland state capitol building. He was the chief justice of the Supreme Court who decided the Dred Scott case which stated "that a black person had no basic human rights to sue in a court of law." Of course, as chief justice in Andy Jackson's time, he led the Supreme Court to this renowned decision. He was the presiding justice at the first inauguration of Abraham Lincoln. He gave him the oath of office, and Lincoln led the nation through the terrible Civil War to reverse that decision and begin the prolonged wrangle that has ensued since.

Baltimore is a very old, historic city famous for row houses which were still in good condition in our time there. Famous Seventh Baptist Church was the headquarters of the southwide Woman's Missionary Union (WMU) where Miss Annie Armstrong held forth. She wrote so many letters by hand (there were no typewriters then) that she permanently injured her right hand. She was a member of the Eutaw Place Baptist Church. When we went to Maryland, Dr. Clyde Atkins, the church's, and Maryland's, oldest pastor, was still pastor of that church and remembered that as a young man with his first baby, Miss Annie encouraged him and his wife. That church, in the famous square, is no longer "lily white" but in an area of mixed cultures. I held a funeral service there for Mrs. Ben Bausum's mother and saw the ruins of older buildings where now the new prevail. It is also true that during the grave struggles of the Southern Baptist Convention in the Civil War era, it had its official offices and agencies in the boardroom area of the Maryland/Southwide WMU headquarters in Seventh Baptist Church. The women of the south literally saved the day for Southern Baptists in those turbulent years. When I went into that Seventh Baptist Church building, it was with a sense of awe. Dr. and Mrs. Winston Pierce (Winnie) were pastor and wife. He was one of the most used ministers ever at Ridgecrest, and she was special in her own right. Winnie was double first cousin of Dr. George Truett, former, deceased pastor of First Baptist Church of Dallas, Texas, for forty-nine years and a stalwart in the Southern Baptist Convention of that time. It was the time of the greatest growth and development in the Southern Baptist Convention, and Dr. Truett was always a loving, gracious healer.

For example, Charles Carroll, from the same family as the great B. H. Carroll, who was very distinguished in Southern Baptist life as founder and first president of Southwestern Baptist Theological Seminary, was a signer of the Declaration of Independence. Anna Ella Carroll was a member of this family. She was the famous female military expert during the Civil War era who helped to plan the Inner Rivers campaign that led to the southern collapse and finally the end of the war. All of these signers forfeited their rights and were maligned, persecuted, and hounded by the British in Revolutionary wartime. Charles Carroll's home was the beginning point and center of the great Johns Hopkins Hospital in Baltimore, Maryland. When one goes into the foyer of this hospital, as I often did, the first object one sees is the magnificent giant statue of the healing Christ. One must kneel to look up into His compassionate eyes. Out front of the Charles Carroll home area is a sundial. I showed it to my brother Joe when he visited us in Annapolis before going to England to serve as a chaplain in the military. On the sundial are the words, "The only time within Thy hand, is that upon which the shadow stands."

The famous Baltimore harbor was the harbor from which all of our Southern Baptist foreign missionaries sailed. Luther Rice, Adoniram Judson, and others were touched by God's spirit as they sailed under the auspices of another mission board. It was in the study of scriptural baptism, after one is saved, and in testimony thereof, the Baptist position, they left their own denomination. They became

Baptists and our first missionaries. They were the ones who were previously in the famous Haystack Prayer Meeting in Williams College, Massachusetts, during a rainstorm. This had the first American burden for foreign missions, even as Southern Baptists have believed and proclaimed it ever since.

Luther Rice was sent back to travel up and down the eastern seaboard in a horse-drawn surrey to tell their story and to raise interest and money for foreign missions. He was called "the dreamer" because of his dream of taking the gospel to the world, and more often than not met with rebuke rather than affirmation. Baltimore harbor also was the place where Nurse Miller got off the boat without the living Lottie Moon, only the box of her ashes in her hands. She had died on Christmas Eve, 1912, in Kobe Harbor in Japan. This is the place of a recent, deadly earthquake and the center of our foreign mission outreach to Japan. These facts have always inspired me as I have read about and shared the missions burden of those brave early pioneers, out of which the Southern Baptist Convention was born and has been nurtured ever since. One-half of our female foreign missionaries are single women who do everything necessary to carry on the work—even speaking and preaching. The other half are married to male missionaries and work with their husbands. If we will only keep our minds on missions, which is really what we as Southern Baptists are all about, we wouldn't be so divided in these desperate times.

◆◆)◆(◆◆

We had a final visit with Dr. C. C. Thomas in Baltimore, and he asked us to send a photograph for the state Baptist paper. Among other duties, he was the editor of the paper. Dorothy and I headed back to Virginia and to Waverly Place still perturbed over what decision we needed to make. We dearly loved Waverly and had no reason to leave. Instead, we felt we had every reason, personally, to stay. We traveled back by Harper's Ferry, Virginia, where old John Brown had holed up to threaten the National Armory which was located there. We saw the places involved, the beautiful area of Harper's Ferry, and the marvelous Blue Ridge Mountains in every gorgeous vista. We could imagine the horde of Federal troops, led by Robert E. Lee, storming the arsenal where several died; the surrender and trial of intransigent old John Brown; the day of his hanging when he rode on his wooden casket, pulled by wagon and team. His last words were "terrible war and strife will come and God will curse this guilty land." His body fell from the gallows, and men remembered his body swaying in the gentle breeze. Later on, at Lake Placid, New York, we visited the old homestead and the tomb of his burial place and his family, who were rebellious like their father. We imagined that day at

Harper's Ferry and the military leaders who would later be involved in the terrible Civil War. J. E. B. (Jeb) Stewart carried out Lee's orders. John Wilkes Booth, the to-be assassin of Abraham Lincoln, was there. All were there and countless others. Old John Brown's experience and warnings set the stage for what was to come. Many date the start of the Civil War from that experience. They sang "John Brown's body lies moldering in the grave." Julia Ward Howe turned the tune later, in the midst of the terrible strife, to "Mine eyes have seen the glory of the coming of the Lord." Glory, glory, hallelujah, His truth still marches on.

We got back to Waverly and to the Parrish home, loved our children, as we smelled Mrs. Parrish's canning of grape/muscadine jelly, and the smell of one of her famous pound cakes filled with the rich texture of real creamery butter. They heard all our story of where we had been and our reactions and questions still about God's will. Mr. Parrish, a man who used only regular fertilizer on his usually productive garden, always shared with his pastor. This man, chairman of the pulpit committee that brought us to Waverly, said, surprisingly, "Why, pastor, you are like Jonah, fleeing from the Lord." That proved to be the word that sealed our decision to go to Annapolis. It was God's word to our hearts.

We left Waverly on a day that was threatening. We traveled mostly two-lane highways to the Washington/Annapolis area where we came to Highway 301 that brought us to Annapolis and the Baltimore area. Coming into Annapolis, there was a tornado warning on the car radio and we stopped briefly under one of the overhead bridges until an especially dark cloud dissipated. That night we were to have a church nominating committee meeting at the home of John and Elsie Pettibone. I drove in blinding sheets of rain with Mr. H. T. Pike and our host, the chairman of the deacons, Bob Maddocks, Bill Martin, treasurer, and Austin Stokes, Sunday School superintendent. We soon forgot the weather in our consideration of the greater business of our Lord.

We were back and forth to Bob and Pat Maddocks's home until our closer neighbors on South Cherry Grove Avenue, Austin and Ethel Stokes, took us in. They became not only our neighbors but also dear and special friends across the years, along with their son Howard. Our last visit with Ethel, Howard, and his wife, Robin, and family was in Oxford, North Carolina, in 1990. Austin and Ethel moved there where their only child, Howard, lived and served in the ministry. Austin was formerly manager of the Sherwin-Williams paint store in Annapolis but became a shoe salesman in Oxford. Austin had recently died and was buried in a cemetery close by. Ethel has now been placed by his side where she always was, faithfully, in this life, for many years. She was originally from Malden, Massachusetts, and was truly a great lady. She was an operating room nurse by profession.

Our home, 203 South Cherry Grove, was to be a warm, special place for the next three years. It had a large backyard that was the ideal play area for our three girls, Sarah, Mary, and especially Martha. We had the usual sliding board, sand box, tricycles, and later bicycles. Our girls were happy in that home. Our next-door neighbors, the Hughes, were Catholic, warm, and loving, as were others on the street, such as the Bakers. Germantown grade school where Sarah and Mary went to school was just up the street. Sarah started to school in southeast Roanoke at the Jamison Elementary School. Her first beloved teacher was Miss Corrine Williams who was ever an inspiration to Sarah. Sarah is now and has been a superb teacher in special education for many years. All our girls were touched by the handicapped condition of their only brother, Charles Jr., and were always sympathetic toward others with similar developmental needs.

Our welcome and official church reception in Annapolis was a very special event and took place on my thirty-fifth birthday and Sarah's ninth. The Governor of Maryland, the Honorable Theodore Roosevelt McKeldin, and his lovely wife were there. He was a Republican and the one who nominated Dwight D. Eisenhower to be president of the United States. When President Eisenhower died and the bells of Washington tolled, Governor McKeldin was first on the scene for the official funeral service. We saw him sitting there, a lonely sight on that sad day as we watched television back in Madison, New Jersey. The governor's mansion was just up the street from our church and was always open to the public on New Year's Day with a reception and greetings by the governor and his lady.

Also present for our official reception was our Democratic mayor, a member of our church, Arthur Ellington. He became most special in the lives of our girls because he always brought bubble gum and candy to church in his pockets. His dear wife, Emma, was the real power behind the scenes. We were often in their lovely home. He, a Democrat, was not especially fond of the governor, a Republican. In fact, the mayor thought the governor, a Bible-believing Methodist, was a hypocrite, "that Bible toting hypocrite." The governor sat on the church rostrum beside me that night at our welcoming reception. He leaned over to tell me that at one time he felt the call to religious ministry but God led him into politics. One of our members, an older man, Mr. Basil, was an assistant to Governor McKeldin. Hence, ours was a special relationship. I was always welcomed in his office. I remember his beautiful gold telephone that I used once to call Dorothy and the lovely gift of a painting of Christ in the midst of the children. Martha Ruth stayed in the nursery. It was a steamy hot night with no air-conditioning. We were standing beside Governor and Mrs. McKeldin in the receiving line when someone brought Martha in to see her parents. The governor greeted her and wanted to hold her. Martha stamped her feet and said, decisively, "No!" She wanted her daddy to hold her. The governor was disappointed and so were we, but the way of a child is a mystery. The next day the governor sent special spiritual books for me and for Sarah Pat, officially inscribed in welcome to Maryland, and for our birthdays. He had already presented me with a Bible the night before.

I remember the occasion of the memorable graduation at the Naval Academy when President Eisenhower was the speaker. We were invited and had special seats right near the entranceway of the president. When he came in, all stood and the band played "Hail to the Chief." We saw the famous grin up close and the twinkle in his eye as he broke rank and crossed to the next seat in front of us to hug and greet one of his nieces. We were there when the graduates threw their white caps into the air. Dorothy looked beautiful in her maternity dress. She was expecting our son who was born later in Newport News, Virginia.

One of the unusual things about College Avenue Baptist Church was the fact that we had three women deacons who were very involved in the church's life. Two of them were widows of deacons who had died in service, and they were asked to serve in their husbands' places. They were usually in the background, with duties such as serving coffee at our meetings. They voted with us on issues to come before the church. The third was Evelyn Sites—"Mom Sites" to the Navy midshipmen who came to our church and our Baptist Student Union group. Evelyn was also a widow. Her aging mother lived with her and her only child, Johnny. Every Christmas we were invited to her house for an official Christmas party for the midshipmen and our other church young people. She led the young people's department in Sunday School and was the Training Union director for the church. The midshipmen always invited and hosted her to the Navy football games. Evelyn has only recently gone to heaven. She visited us in Newport News with the Stokes and their son, Howard, and we kept in touch across the years. We had a group of about thirty to forty midshipmen involved in our church life and they dearly loved our girls and they them.

Some of the midshipmen came to visit us when we moved to Newport News, Virginia. One, Dick Hartman, a naval pilot and officer from Clark, New Jersey, was captured in the Vietnam War and died there. Another was Ted Wu of Chinese descent, from Los Angeles, who became a lawyer in the Boston area. We talked with him when Dorothy went to the great Lahey Clinic for treatment of asthma. Ted had a marvelous voice and would thrill us at Christmas when he sang "O Holy Night." These young men were a very special, greatly influential group in the life of our church.

When we came to seek God's leading for an associate in education and youth, we had only one person in mind, Mildred Oaks, who was our great helper in Waverly Place Baptist Church. I had spoken to her before leaving Waverly, but she would only say, "We shall seek the Lord's will." I was deeply disappointed and even depressed when she finally decided to go to Morristown, Tennessee, instead. She did come for a visit with us in August after our coming to Annapolis in July. Everyone loved her, wrote her, called her, especially Mayor Arthur Ellington. Looking back, we can see now why God led her to Morristown, Tennessee. It was close to Carson-Newman College where her girls were to go to college and to meet their future husbands.

Finally, God led us to the person He wanted with us in Annapolis. We decided we needed an educational director, youth leader, and organist. Martha Stone was that person from Greenville, South Carolina. Her family was, and still is, in real estate there. I had fellowship and lunch with them in 1977 in a revival with Bob Reese from the Newport News, Virginia, church. Martha was a natural for the job. She fit right into the Annapolis scene. She was an attractive, younger, but mature woman. She was an accomplished organist/musician, and the local youth and naval midshipmen loved her. There was resentment between the local young men and that "flashy naval group" that so easily charmed the local girls. Martha was only partially able to bridge that gap. She worked well with Evelyn Sites. The church, in calling Martha, received six hundred dollars a year from the Maryland State Convention in connection with the BSU work. Martha, through our church as a base, was instrumental in starting the first BSU ministry in one of our military academies. Now, today, we have such a ministry in each of our military academies through the support of the BSU and Sunday School Board, and we were the brave pioneers. We "stranded" Martha when we left Annapolis and she went first to Kensington, Maryland, First Baptist Church before going back to Greenville to be with her aging father, who has since died.

There was one family who came into our Annapolis church that provided needed employment for several of our young men. The Bob Wagner family with the Diamond Construction Company fulfilled a special purpose regarding needed additional land for expansion of facilities for the United States Naval Academy. There was no more land available except for space in the Severn River, the shortest river in the world. The job of the Diamond Construction Company and Bob Wagner was to make more than fifty acres of land out in that Severn River, and it was done in due time. Those who see the beautiful additional buildings today little realize the gigantic task involved. Any young man who wanted a job and was willing to work could have it for the best possible remuneration.

A young man who came to Annapolis from Alpine, Texas, was Paul Hilbrich. He needed a place to room and board. He taught music at Glen Burnie, just north of Annapolis. I had some previous words from Mrs. Ben Bausum (Mildred) that she might be interested in such a person. She had two daughters living at home, Miriam and Virginia. The Bausum family operated the local dairy, and Ben Bausum was our milkman all the time we lived in Annapolis. I suggested to Paul Hilbrich that he knock on the Bausum door and he did. He and Virginia fell in love, and I married them in August of 1960. Today they live in Eau Clair, Wisconsin, where he has been a music professor in the university and is now retiring. They have three daughters. What a joy to be in the middle of that special relationship. At the end of Christmas holidays, Paul, not yet married, took Virginia to Washington to catch a plane back to her Baptist college in Georgetown, Kentucky. (Later, Dorothy's first cousin, Dr. Morgan Patterson, became president of Georgetown College. We had had special contact with that school during our Kentucky years and saw many fine young people get their education there. We visited the Pattersons there in the president's beautiful old home and enjoyed anew the special flavor of Kentucky Blue Grass country.) On Paul's way back from Washington to Annapolis, he hit and killed a man. This man had mental difficulties. He had run across the road to get his mail. It was dusk and Paul did not see him in time to stop. I was with Paul during the very detailed trial when he was acquitted, much to our great relief.

Another young man, David Johnson, conscientious objector in the Korean War from Hector, Minnesota, was sent to Annapolis to work on the Bausum farm. He met and fell in love with the other Bausum daughter, Miriam. He was of strong religious faith, though not a Baptist. I counseled them and was privileged to marry them. Today, they live in Mound, Minnesota, where he is a retired farmer and in the construction business. They visited us in Hawaii and more recently here in the Northwest. They have several children, but sadly lost one. What a very special joy to be involved in such wonderful experiences in Annapolis. David ran for Congress in Minnesota recently and was almost elected. Ida, the oldest Bausum daughter, is married to Tommy Russell of Annapolis. He is now deceased. We have stayed in touch with all of these fine families.

One of the Bausum brothers, Robert, was a longtime Southern Baptist missionary in the orient. His son became a teacher at Carson-Newman College in Tennessee. The Ben Bausums had an older son, Franklin, whose son was drowned tragically in our Baptist high school (Oneida Institute), in

Oneida, Kentucky. This school helps a lot of troubled young people.

One episode in the coming of the Bausum brothers to Annapolis is a rather amazing story. The older brother, John, and wife, Mary, were dairy farmers and members of our church. They had come from one of the Dakotas with their father and mother and others in the family. On their way by railroad, the father got off the train at a stop to get some food. He was hit and killed before the family's eyes by a passing train. They came to Annapolis at the time they were building the original College Avenue Baptist Church in 1899, and knew all the history of that special time.

Another Bausum brother, Fred, was instrumental in starting our mission church, Weems Creek, that is a strong church in Annapolis. It has been pastored all of these years by Roland Smith who came to Johns Hopkins to study archeology under the great archeology professor, Dr. Albright. I heard Dr. Albright speak once. Fred Jr. was in our Annapolis church where he met and fell in love with his wife, Jean. I counseled and married them. They have several children and came to visit us in Hawaii.

One other story involves midshipman George Murphy and Rose Mary Sturgis, a beautiful young woman from one of our special Annapolis families, the Bill Sturgises. Rose Mary was the idol of our Mary Margaret. When Rose Mary and George fell in love, I counseled them and married them in a beautiful, full regalia, military service in our church. Mary Margaret was the flower girl and she was darling, even if I do say so. We visited the Murphys in Groton, Connecticut, in the summer of 1958. Parke and Sheila Brown from the Naval Academy were with them also. Sheila was from England and died later from cancer. Parke was from Knoxville, Tennessee, and had served as the first president of the Baptist Student Union at the academy.

Wayne and Beverly Hatchett were also special to us and were at our fiftieth wedding anniversary in Hampton, Virginia, on June 26, 1993. He is a retired naval captain. Also, Clyde Morris and family came to Newport News, Virginia, and the Ivy Memorial Baptist Church. Clyde and Fran became leaders and were very active.

Roland and Betty Smith of the Weems Creek Church went with Dorothy and me to the Southern Baptist Convention in Chicago in June of 1957. We were so excited about Southern Baptist work in that great windy city. Betty was from Chicago and had visited with her parents that week. She was telling us all about it in her Chicago twang when we were approached by Ray Roberts, a great big red-headed giant of a man whom we knew from seminary days. He told us of his recent trip to New York City where he preached for a group of people on a hotel mezzanine. A strategic family, the Wil Dukes (he a student at Columbia University), was especially prayerfully involved. He said, "Charles, since you at Annapolis are the closest Southern Baptist Convention church to New York City, I want to ask you to sponsor that New York work." Ray was then executive director of the Ohio Baptist Convention and too far away to be involved. I was shocked and responded that New York City was two hundred miles from Annapolis. I had never sponsored work that far away from the sponsoring source. In any case, I'd need to talk with Dr. C. C. Thomas, our Maryland executive director, and with our College Avenue people. I told him I would pray about it and see what they had to say. Thereby was the start of one of the most exciting, thrilling, and rewarding eras of our lives.

We drove back to Annapolis pondering and talking about Chicago and what Dr. Ray Roberts had asked of me. I was in an associational meeting the week after that convention, and Dr. Thomas was there. I shared with him what Ray Roberts had asked of me. Dr. Thomas was a loving, enthusiastic man and saw no problem with this. He encouraged me to proceed, and so I did. I shared with our Southern District of Maryland director of missions, Dr. Paul Bard, and he became my encourager and stalwart supporter in every way. Then I brought the matter to our College Avenue missions committee. H. T. Pike was the chairman. They felt that if Dr. Thomas, their former interim pastor, was positive, they were for it. The deacons all agreed. They were excited and brought it to the church and received one hundred percent enthusiastic approval. I was ready to go forward and was in touch with our Home Mission Board and with Dr. A. B. Cash who was assigned to this project. It proved important that I had allowed no grass to grow underfoot.

One morning shortly afterwards, I received a telephone call from Dr. Thomas in Baltimore. He had found that there was significant opposition to the New York project. There was a feeling that Southern Baptists did not need to go north. They already had their churches there. He thought he had better call me before I got out on a limb. I was stunned again. First approval, and now, seemingly, disapproval. I told him I was already out on a limb having received one hundred percent approval from our men and our church, largely based on his previous, positive word. I just could not let it drop without going back to our people, and I would do that. He thanked me, and I was depressed. I went over to an exclusive men's store, The Men's Shop, where our missions chairman, Mr. Pike, a very close personal friend to Dr. Thomas, was the tailor. In fact, Dr. Thomas, the man who had recommended me to College Avenue Baptist

Church, had been seriously injured in an automobile accident only recently, and the whole church encouraged and prayed him through.

I explained matters to Mr. Pike, and I rather expected him to say, "We'll just drop it." A gentle man, he listened very carefully, which was his style—strong, quiet, and thoughtful. I finally asked him what he thought we should do now. He pondered his reply and I waited. He said, "Why, pastor, we'll just go right ahead." And that layman's word assured the College Avenue sponsorship of the New York work. I went back singing in my heart because I had become enthusiastic. I found out later that a prominent layman in Baltimore, Francis A. Davis, a furniture and tobacco merchant with close ties to the New York area and father-in-law of my doctor, Dr. George Murgatroyd, in Baltimore, was the chief opponent of our sponsorship of the New York work.

This movement was later ascribed as "Southern Baptists invading the North" Civil War lore. Thereafter, Dr. Thomas rather distanced himself from the New York work and assigned the Maryland educational director, L. J. Newton, to relate to us and the New York work. L. J. and I discussed the strategy at length. I must say that Dr. Thomas was soon facing retirement. In retirement he became associate to Dr. Theodore Adams, great pastor of First Baptist Church of Richmond, Virginia, and worldwide Baptist leader. The Thomases bought a lovely home there, and he became the hospital visitor for Dr. Adams. I later learned from Dr. Cline Vice that there had previously been an original Home Mission Board sponsored banquet in Baltimore. It was to talk about big cities missions and the Home Mission Board had set aside one hundred thousand dollars for such work. There was some internal Home Mission Board financial problem that rather blew the meeting and soured the Maryland laypeople. Hence, the resentment toward this new effort. There is now over one million dollars from the Home Mission Board in our Puget Sound area alone.

There was also the matter of rising opposition to the New York work from various pastors and leaders in the Baltimore area. Through the help of Dr. Paul Bard, Southern District Associational director of missions, we began to confront the possibility of rejection of the New York work in the upcoming state association general meeting. Our churches and pastors and association leaders were supportive all the way. They studied our state association constitution and found a clause that stated: "If a new work is approved and agreed upon by one of our District Associations, it is automatically acceptable in our General Association." That eliminated a floor fight in the Maryland General Association meeting at the University Church in Baltimore. Dr. Vernon Richardson was their excellent pastor and our friend. That is the church where Dr. Wade Bryant, pastor of First Baptist Church of Roanoke, Virginia, had been the pastor. When I was struggling with the decision to leave Waverly Place and come to Annapolis, I went to share and pray with Dr. Bryant who was always the pastor's loving friend. We got down on our knees and prayed, as was Dr. Bryant's custom. He said to me, "Charles, you can stay in Waverly Place Baptist Church, do a great work and be happy. However, I think it would be in the backwater of denominational life. If you go to College Avenue and Annapolis, you will be in the mainstream of denominational life." Never was a truer word spoken.

Here I was in the mainstream of denominational life in a very significant and strategic sense. We were very far along in relating to Dr. A. B. Cash from our Home Mission Board. He and Mrs. Cash visited us, with Dr. Paul Bard, in our home in Annapolis. In the process of planning, he reported the Home Mission Board had two men in mind who might lead this work in New York: Dr. Paul S. James, pastor of Tabernacle Baptist Church in Atlanta, and Dr. Elmer Sizemore, later to be involved and now retired from Alaska work.

The strong preference was for Dr. James. His father had pastored for twenty-one years at the First Baptist Church of Auburn, New York, home of Abraham Lincoln's Secretary of State William Seward, who was the strong favorite of most Republicans over the relatively unknown Illinois country lawyer. At the Republican Convention he confidently expected to be the nominee and next president of the United States. He had arranged a huge party on the lawn of his beautiful home and a cannon ready to fire a salute. A great crowd was present. A lone horseman rode up furiously to announce that Abraham Lincoln had been nominated. The Sewards, shocked, closed their doors to the throng and the sullen crowd dissipated. Afterward, in Washington, wisely chosen by a conciliatory Lincoln as secretary of state, Mr. Seward had, in effect, offered to the inexperienced Mr. Lincoln to serve behind the scenes as president. Mr. Lincoln assured his secretary of state that he intended to be the president. Later, Mr. Seward was to thoroughly understand why.

Dr. Paul James, along with his wife, Ava, was later to serve as pastor of the Auburn, New York, church for seven years. He came along in the time of the great debate over liberals like Harry Emerson Fosdick, pastor of the Riverside Baptist Church, versus the strong conservatives/fundamentalists (we seem to have a recurring debate about such issues in Southern Baptist life—even until now). Paul S. James, from his strong New York background, was God's chosen vessel to lead our New York work and to see it spread across the city of New York, and the state where ten percent of the country's population lives in a one hundred and fifty mile radius of the Statue of Liberty.

Our first visit to New York City was in July of 1957. We went with a busload of College Avenue Baptist Church young people and adults to attend the famous sixteen-week Billy Graham Crusade in the old Madison Square Garden. We visited famous sights in the city including the top of the Empire State Building before going into the crusade meeting. All of us were greatly excited. When we got into the Garden crusade area, we were early and obtained good balcony seats. We had no more been seated when a call came over the loudspeaker that Charles Jolly was wanted at the rostrum down front. Dorothy immediately quipped, "Charles, Billy is sick and they want you to preach!" This certainly relieved the tension. I met Jim Robb, Wil Duke, and others involved in the New York work for Southern Baptists. Our missions committee members, H. T. Pike, Alvin Jackson, and others, met with the New York group for the first time in the cafeteria of Madison Square Garden and talked about where we were in the process. I remember the "grab, and first come, first served" demeanor as we walked through the food line, different from my laid-back, southern courtesy style. That was New York, and we were to get used to it later on. We went back home rejoicing, knowing that we were a vital part of something unusual in God's Great Plan.

The Billy Graham Crusade, extended several weeks from their original schedule by strong, local request, and its remarkable impact on the city of New York, was the context of the beginning of our work in the New York area. We rejoiced in those meetings because their effect made it easier for our then-feeble flame to burst into glory. I shared this with Dr. Graham at a subsequent New York Crusade, after we had been in New Jersey for sometime, at a prayer breakfast at the Waldorf Astoria where Dorothy had always wanted to spend a week. Dr. Graham, a Southern Baptist and member of First Baptist Church of Dallas, Texas, and his wife, Ruth, a Presbyterian and daughter of the L. Nelson Bells, missionaries in China and founders of *Christianity Today* magazine, have always been a special treasure of God to the nation and to the whole world. He was impressed and encouraged when I told him that at that time we had over 125 churches in the New York area. Dr. and Mrs. Paul James had been on the scene and had done a marvelous job, by God's grace, and had been in touch with Billy Graham.

Our Annapolis missions committee members were guests at an old-fashioned potluck at the O. K. McCarter home in Carteret, New Jersey, in the fall of 1957 after the initial contact in New York. O. K. McCarter was an executive with the Kresge Corporation. The group at their home was to later become our Madison, New Jersey, church and the base church for our work in northern New Jersey. I remember how we felt so at home at that potluck—the south was north. Dr. Cline Vice, president of our Maryland Baptist Union Association and a former pastor in Virginia, was with us on this New York/New Jersey event. He remarked when we got back to his Glen Burnie, Maryland, home, "So far as I'm concerned, it's like the Book of Acts," referring to the New York work. *Like the Book of Acts* is the title of Keith Cogburn's excellent recent book that is a great coverage of all the historic events in the New York work.

In the meantime, Dr. and Mrs. Paul James came through Annapolis in the fall of 1957 on their way to become our sterling leaders in the New York work. We met with them by prearrangement at an Annapolis restaurant. We had planned for them to be with us in our Annapolis home but they were anxious to get on and to get involved. They were later with us in Baltimore at the Maryland Baptist Convention meeting when the New York work was approved without a floor fight. I was anxious about that meeting and rather held my breath when Dr. A. B. Cash spoke to us. This good man had recently had a heart attack and felt the tension at the Maryland Convention where we had headed off any tragic confrontation. I sensed that Dr. Cash, representing our Home Mission Board, was tense. Dr. James hosted a dinner following the convention session. All was a "go!" We were on our way!

On January 10, 1958, on a cold, wintry day, a busload of our Annapolis people made their way back to New York City for the organizational meeting of the Manhattan Baptist Church. This meeting, with arrangements made by Dr. Paul James, was in the old Hotel New Yorker, more recently owned by the Moonies. All the dignitaries were there from the Home Mission Board and elsewhere. Dr. James had rather thought he would be in charge of this organizational meeting which was so historic, as he had done the groundwork in the city. However, Dr. Paul Bard, our Southern District Association director, insisted that I should preside, as pastor of the sponsoring church. Dr. James graciously acceded and had all the details for me. There I stood in that very special meeting, trembling in my boots, literally, because the outside streets were covered with snow and melting ice.

There were people present from other denominations. Some Southern Baptists in Baltimore had raised the question of "invading the north." These people assured us that we were more than welcome. There were enough people, and more, in that "sin city" who needed Christ, and we were welcome.

At one point in the process, some question about procedure was raised by Dr. Solomon Dowis, Home Mission Board leader in new areas for Southern Baptists. I seethed inside and wrestled with what to say to Dr. Dowis. God, by His grace, helped me conquer my angry feeling and say, "Dr. Dowis is correct and we thank him for his great help and support, as for all of our Home Mission Board." We moved on as ninety-nine precious people were officially organized in our first Southern Baptist church in New York City. We have pictures of this group that was the base church for all subsequent work in the New York City area. Dr. W. C. Fields was there from our Mississippi Baptist Convention, formerly the pastor of First Baptist Church of Yazoo City, Mississippi. He was the editor of the historic *Baptist Record*, the Mississippi Baptist newspaper. He took the pictures. I always appreciated his being there and the interest of my native state in these historic happenings.

That Manhattan Church met subsequently in the Times Square area in a rented Seventh Day Adventist building. We attended there in the summer of 1958 while on vacation. Dr. James had his office there. What a thrill to see an excellent group present and to be recognized. The beautiful painting of Christ with His arms embracing that great city was a thrilling and inspiring sight dominating the whole area behind the podium. The Madison Baptist Church was the base church for northern New Jersey. The Greenwich Baptist Church was the base church for Connecticut and north. The Farmingdale Baptist Church was the base church for the Long Island/New York City area. Since then, the New York State Convention was organized on September 26, 1969, in Syracuse, New York, in Central Baptist Church. It is now mostly a caring, black congregation. On their recent twenty-fifth anniversary, there were three hundred churches and thousands of lives that had been touched by God's grace. Later, the New England Baptist Convention was to come into being.

<hr />

We had the new educational building at College Avenue. The grounds were beautifully situated. Bob Maddocks took great delight in this new building named for his friend, Pastor W. C. Wood. Bob, beloved and respected by all, had full-blown cancer. Bob had gone into the National Institute of Health Hospital in Washington, D.C., and I visited him just before we left on a mini-Christmas vacation to Mississippi in 1957. He hardly knew me and seemed to have some negative reaction to my visit that concerned me in leaving. Sure enough, we got a telephone call from Pat that Bob had died on the twenty-seventh of December; and we decided to drive home immediately, leaving on a Sunday afternoon and driving straight through. Former pastor, Bill Scurlock, and I led the sad funeral service. All of us felt the keen loss, especially for Pat and Dickie. Shortly after that, Pat, who had a terrible dental problem, was in an automobile accident and her teeth were knocked out. She was trembling in concern when I visited her at the doctor's clinic. In trying to comfort her, I was led to say, "Why, Pat, it's the best thing that could have happened. From now on you will have a mouthful of beautiful, perfect teeth," and Pat began to smile.

It was pointed out to me that the thin walls of the original church building could not be repaired. You could see light through them in some places. With the formation of a building committee, we began to plan. An architect drew a plan for a beautiful sanctuary that would cost $150,000 when finished. Wow! We got my friend, J. C. Chapman, to come up on a Sunday, getting a pulpit supply for his own Lexington Park Church where I'd been privileged to recommend him. He took pictures of all our activities including our family in our parsonage home. All of this was prepared in a beautiful brochure.

Brother Chapman brought a young friend from Lexington Park Naval Air Station with him. They had never really toured the Naval Academy. After church, we took the tour. We had come to the beautiful chapel building, and I was showing and explaining the burial place of John Paul Jones, father of the American Navy. As was the custom in those days, they put the body in a barrel of alcohol that literally pickled it, and buried the body in a huge sarcophagus on the back of four huge tortoises in the basement under the chapel building. A marine honor guard was always on duty. As I was explaining this, the Marine was listening. The young naval man with us looked at this marine, in stark military stiffness in a dead-serious pose, and said, "Man, just think, if you are a good boy and do your faithful duty, they may fix you up like that someday." The marine almost collapsed with laughter—so did we!

Ever since my arrival in Annapolis, the people kept referring to a Commander Lowell Shallenberg and his family. "Wait until he comes back," they would say. They had now returned and were building a beautiful home to cost some $90,000. Oddly enough, he opposed building a new building for College Avenue. I had gotten Southern Baptist leaders, including Dr. James Sullivan, Sunday School Board secretary and my former college pastor and friend, and Dr. Porter Routh, executive secretary of the Southern Baptist Executive Committee, to visit. I had had dinners to celebrate their visits, with the governor present, talking of our plans and asking for their support and help to get some money from outside sources on the basis of our Southern Baptist relationship to the Naval Academy.

It turned out that Shallenberg was right since under the next pastor, Dr. Haney, the educational building and old College Avenue Baptist Church were torn down to make room for a new Maryland government building. My heart was sick to think of all that had to be destroyed that we had planned and built on that spot. However, to go back today and see what we got in return, we can rejoice in the future that God foresaw and used Commander Shallenberg to discourage us in building more on that spot which would also have been destroyed. This had not yet taken place when we left Annapolis. On the day we left, I rather strongly rebuked Brother Shallenberg for building his own beautiful home and opposing the church building. The Shallenbergs have visited us here in Federal Way since we came to the Northwest. He was the national governor of the Kiwanis Clubs of America. They shared with us about others in their family. Indeed, Commander Shallenberg made a special trip to visit us in Newport News, Virginia, in full navy regalia. He was a fine man, and his family and I could see why the Annapolis people relied on his judgment.

There were several notable occasions of revival and special services while we were in Maryland. Our friend, Frank Voight, came for a revival and on the first night there was a heavy, deep snow, and the service was cancelled. However, the Bob Wagner family came and chided me for calling off the service that was to be "a fun night for their family." Bill Parker from Virginia led the singing. Dorothy's brother, Bob Patterson, Sunday School associate director for the Tennessee Baptist Convention, came and God blessed in another gracious revival. I had called it "special Easter services," but Bob said at the end that he thought we could call it a real revival.

Two other notables we had for special services during our pastorate were Dr. and Mrs. J. W. Storer from First Baptist Church, Oklahoma City, former president of the Southern Baptist Convention; and later, the unique and unusual Southern Baptist youth teacher of all time, Dr. Chester Swor, from Mississippi Baptist College and formerly a judge in my high school oratorical contest in Mississippi. Chester Swor was seriously crippled but turned that disability into a great plus.

Some very special people from our Annapolis years were Malcom and Pat Massey. He came to church but was not yet saved. Dorothy and I paid a visit to their home. While Dorothy and Pat stayed in the car and prayed, I talked with Malcom inside about the Lord and God's plan of salvation—repeated over and over in our ministry of fifty-seven years. Malcom accepted Christ as Savior and was later baptized. We rejoiced then and have ever since because Malcom died young. Pat has kept in touch with us and has come to see us on various occasions when we were back in the area. She later moved to the Norfolk, Virginia, area with her two boys, Troy and Malcom Jr. Malcom Jr. later married and with his family was, for a long time, a cold and an indifferent man to the Lord's work. God continued to deal with him, however, and he felt God's call to foreign mission service. He and his wife went to language school in Costa Rica to prepare for service in Bolivia. In December of 1996, they went to their field of service.

The Clarence Smith family was very special. He owned a dry-cleaning business and a service station. We used both services while in Annapolis. I married his son Carl and wife, Edythe. The Smith family owned a beach home in Ocean City, Maryland, and also a large fishing boat. They made it possible for us to spend some joyful vacation times with our family and one time with Dorothy's brother, Bob, and his family in a pouring rain. We had fun. I did some fishing and caught some beauties, especially flounder. On one occasion, Sarah stayed on the beach. The weather was overcast, and we thought she was safe from undue sunburn. She got the worst sunburn ever because the harmful sun's rays came right through the overcast. What a painful time for her and all of us. On these occasions, because of Clarence Smith's desire to worship the Lord, we started a mission in the local fire station that grew into a Southern Baptist church.

One of our faithful secretaries was Alice Coletta, whose husband taught at the Naval Academy. They had one daughter, Dana. Sadly, Alice developed cancer and died early in life. What a marvelous Christian, loved by all and superb in her secretarial work. The one who took her place was a younger woman, Ann Pittman, with a young family. She served faithfully and well and grew in her ability. She was always a loving, helpful Christian spirit. There were others who helped in the office from time to time. No pastor can function well without such excellent help to keep up with all that flows through the church office. I was always blessed.

I must mention Brother Alvin Jackson. The Jacksons had no children of their own but adopted a little boy who had a handicapped condition. They were so patient and loving in care of this child and in all their church relations. Brother Jackson would come to our home, cut my grass, and bring delicious fruit and vegetables in season. He loved our little girls and they him. He was always doing something special for the pastor's family.

There were others. One dear lady, Kathryn Grimes, the daughter of one of our older deaconesses, Mrs. Fullerton, gave our girls music lessons. Our music director, redheaded Jackie, married to Bill Owens, a teacher at the Naval Academy, did a marvelous job in the church music program and was so instrumental in reaching young people. Bill later taught at a college in Danville, Kentucky. We saw Bill and Jackie when I was there in a revival in 1968. He later became president of a Presbyterian College in Pikeville,

Kentucky. This was near Jackie's home in Whitesburg, Kentucky.

There were the Charlie Browns, a large and precious family; the Floyd Barkers and two children; and the Dale Dunlaps and their two boys. Dale was a teacher in the Naval Academy, a deacon, and chairman of deacons at the time we left Annapolis. Also, Norman and Nancy Hatfield who had a handicapped daughter. They are still most faithful in the church at this writing. We had a wonderful fellowship with all of these and others during our years there, and a special renewed fellowship on a special visit in the lovely new home of Pat Maddocks in the fall of 1991. Sarah and Don Reid allowed us to use their car to drive from their home in Fredericksburg, Virginia.

I need to mention also the Graham Gutsches. He taught physics at the Naval Academy. He had an unusually scientific mind and kept up and kept me up! His wife, Libby, was from a wealthy family in Chicago. Her mother, Mrs. Leslie, was a special dynamic Christian and was involved in the famous Pacific Garden Mission in Chicago where world famous evangelist Mel Trotter was saved, along with Billy Sunday. The Gutsches later joined the Presbyterian Church, which was Libby's church background. They were faithful teachers in our Sunday School. Libby was an artist, among other hobbies, and worked with our older girls. Mary won the Ann Arundel County Blue Ribbon Contest with a picture of historic St. Ann's Cathedral, across the Severn River. It was called an impressionistic painting. Sarah did one, a still life, a rural scene. Libby reprimanded me for thinking a pastoral scene of a church and some surrounding cottages should show some form of life. Sarah did the suggested change but Libby thought it detrimental to her own perceived artistic expression. She was right.

We had several older couples in our church and a number of single older people. One couple, Mr. and Mrs. Porter, had a fiftieth wedding anniversary and asked me to have them repeat their vows in a morning service. She was so pretty that morning and he so regal.

Another older couple was the Bennings. Several of their faithful children were in our church family. Mr. Benning, our church janitor, was a self-educated man and great at his job. He did fine until we brought in a younger black man to help him, as he was growing older. Mr. Benning resented this intrusion and let it get the best of him. His wife had crippling arthritis in her hands but did not let it deter her from her work. We celebrated their lovely golden anniversary in their home. He was a famous crab fisherman and invited me to go with him on several very special occasions. We would leave the dock in his rowboat at 3:00 A.M. Annapolis is surrounded by water. He would have his line, tackle, and bait all arranged in the back end of his boat where he rowed from and fed the baited line into the water. He used floating oilcans—a homemade type of contraption. We would row around the Naval Academy, a very beautiful sight with the rising sun reflecting on the buildings. I often thought of my early days in Mississippi and my special friend to this day, John Stone Jr., who went to Annapolis and graduated before our time there. Dorothy and I were with him in our courtship time, and he was most helpful to both of us. He now has the adjoining farm to the Mississippi farm where we all grew up. John and Mary Lou have retired on his father's farm. Both of his parents are gone and much land has been added to his holdings. We go back often, have stayed in their home, even their old home that is now owned by his only sister, Idanelle. What friends they have been across the years. His parents were special to me in my earliest years.

Back to crab fishing. Mr. Benning and I would lay out the lines across the broad expanse of the Severn River and then go back down to dip up the crabs. We would usually wind up with a bushel of crabs. We would take these back to his home where Mrs. Benning would have the water scalding. Mr. and Mrs. Benning would put the crabs in the boiling water in a lard can. Even with her hurting hands, she was an expert at picking out the delicious meat. We were often the beneficiaries of this Maryland delicacy. Maryland crab feasts were the usual thing in crab season. Every Christmas, Mr. Benning delighted in bringing us a quart of large Chincoteague oysters. In the winter of 1958, Mr. Benning got pneumonia from shoveling heavy snow. He never recovered adequately and died the same week we left for Newport News, Virginia. On our last day in Annapolis, I led his funeral service and left for our new pastorate in Newport News, Virginia, and Ivy Memorial Baptist Church.

There was a special instance of serving Maryland crab cakes to some distinguished friends. Dr. Will Cook Boone was our seminary pastor at Crescent Hill Baptist Church in Louisville, Kentucky, and a former pastor of First Baptist Church of Roanoke, Virginia. His father, Dr. A. U. Boone, was formerly a pastor in Memphis, and Dorothy's parents knew and loved him. Dr. and Mrs. Will Cook Boone were in the Baltimore area for some denominational event, and we invited them to come to our home for lunch. He was then executive director of the Kentucky Baptist Convention. After all the formalities, we came to sit down to Dorothy's elegantly decorated table, and she announced delightedly that she was serving famous Maryland crab cakes. There was silence, and as she was going about serving the meal, Dr. Boone called out, "Mrs. Jolly, have you got any bologna you can serve me? I can't eat those dirty little varmints."

Mrs. Boone was appalled and embarrassed. From absolute silence to a burst of laughter, Dr. Boone got his bologna while the rest of us thoroughly enjoyed the crab cakes. Dorothy did have a good dessert.

We had a mission church at the Edgewater area south of Annapolis. We had good land and ultimately a nice building. It was in the area of the home of Miss Eva B. Saunders, longtime missionary in Nigeria, Africa. Mr. Ed Wright and family, formerly in our Pineville Church and Clear Creek Baptist School, came and served in our time. Some fellowship difficulties ensued, and they left Edgewater for Tennessee. He is now retired in the West Memphis, Arkansas, area.

I must tell you now how we came to leave Annapolis to go to Newport News, Virginia, and the Ivy Memorial Baptist Church. Just before we left Virginia to come to Annapolis, I was asked to hold a revival at the Central Baptist church, Alta Vista, Virginia, by Brother L. L. Jessup. I do not remember how Brother Jessup even knew about me, but I thoroughly enjoyed the week with him. Mrs. Jessup was a great lover of flowers. The Greenways, in whose home I stayed, and all the Alta Vista people were great. God blessed us with a great revival. We talked that week about the decision to go to Annapolis. Brother Jessup pled with me not to leave Virginia. Well, we went to Annapolis but Brother Jessup did not forget. Ivy Memorial Baptist Church had been his first pastorate. He told me about how he and his young family had grown tired of the harsh New York winters. One day, in a doctor's office, he picked up a magazine and saw an article about the relatively nice, warmer weather in the Hampton Roads area of Virginia. Brother Jessup was an oculist and came to Newport News to practice as an oculist. He joined the Ivy Memorial Baptist Church, worked as a layman, and became enamored in the lives of the people. He became an efficient Sunday School superintendent, and God blessed that phase of the work especially. In fact, God so blessed, and with encouragement from his pastor, and the people, he felt God calling him to full-time pastoral ministry. He left Mrs. Jessup back in Virginia and enrolled in the Southern Baptist Theological Seminary. It was a hard struggle, but God helped him, and his family, and the Ivy Memorial people stuck by him. He was later to serve twice as pastor of the church. Therefore, when the people were without a pastor in 1959, they sought his counsel. He gave them my name, and they relentlessly pursued me. They came to visit us in the fall and pled their cause. When they came to me in Annapolis the first time, and the second, I turned them down and thought it was over. My leaving Virginia and going to Annapolis was a trying experience to begin with, like leaving the South for the North, and I struggled for a year or so until I was caught up in the New York work.

One day the Ivy Memorial pulpit committee called me and said, "We've gone through a whole group of men recommended to us, but God has led us back to you." I felt, after praying some more, and with Dorothy's prayerful assent, that God must be in this. The decision was made, and the day came when I was to announce it to the College Avenue Baptist Church.

Dale Dunlap was chairman of our deacons. On a rainy Sunday afternoon, we were at the county jail for a layman's service. After the service, I called Dale aside and told him of the call of the committee from Newport News. Our family had gone to Hampton Roads for a look-see visit in February and stayed at the famous Chamberlain Hotel right on the beautiful Hampton Roads. All of us were impressed. I preached on "This, I Believe," and they called me. In this process I had turned them down twice but felt compelled after this final call. Dale Dunlap was stunned to the point of tears, and I was sad. I was always hard put to leave a church.

Then the process began of moving back deeper south which proved for them and for us to be the will of God. And God moved on to bless and lead College Avenue Baptist Church.

8

Newport News, Virginia

1959–1964

We left Annapolis on a bright and sunny day which was quite a contrast to the dark and stormy day on which we had arrived. We drove all day save for essential stops for Dorothy who was expecting our son, Charles Jr., five weeks later. We got into Newport News after dark after listening on the radio to a pugilistic championship prizefight in which Floyd Patterson was the winner (Sarah was later dubbed "Floyd" by her school friends).

We had reservations at the downtown Warwick Hotel that is no longer in business because of the civil-rights issue. The downtown Woolworth store and lunch counter was one of the first targeted for service to blacks. Already a heavy black population was very close to the downtown area. Today the inner-city area is decimated. Sarah's high school building is no longer functioning. Most of the stores and banks are closed and boarded up. Businesses that are open are of the sleeze type, and all together it looks like a ghost town.

Newport News was a Norfolk and Western Railroad terminal near a big Sears store and the Newport News Shipbuilding and Dry Dock Company with its apprentice training school. Now owned and operated by Tenneco, it is still in business in the same location. The formerly white churches, buildings of great construction and beauty, have been taken over by black congregations. For example, our beautiful new Ivy Memorial Baptist Church buildings, valued at a million dollars in our time there, situated on beautiful, historic Hampton Roads, were sold to the Ivy black Baptist congregation for some two hundred thousand dollars, typical of the changes. Most of the homes have been sold to black families. Our former home, the parsonage, in full view of Hampton Roads, is now occupied by black families. Historic Stewart Gardens with expensive, beautiful homes on Hampton Roads waterfront are all now completely

126

gone. This has all happened since we left. I tried to encourage our people to realize that in this change and in the selling of our buildings to blacks, we had made an eight-hundred-thousand-dollar investment in black missions. I went back later and was allowed by the present congregation to come in and look around. They had lovingly cared for the building and grounds. In fact, the same fine black janitorial staff that kept the building clean and spotless for the former white congregation was cleaning that Monday after Sunday services.

◆✦✕✦◆

It was to the formerly all-white, middle-class area that we came on a lovely June day in 1959. Our church leaders were all around that day helping us to move in and to hook up everything. Right off, Martha Ruth opened the basement door and fell down the steps. We finally got it all together and began our five and one-half years of ministry in our home, 24 Park Avenue, Newport News, Virginia. The church was a half-block away in easy walking distance. What a special ministry and blessed days we were to have in that spot.

The changing social and cultural conditions in the older Newport News/Hampton Roads area made for an unusual projection of new mission starts as the white population of Newport News moved northward.

Dr. Herman T. Stevens, then seventy-five years of age (my age now), had been the interim and very effective pastor at Ivy Memorial prior to our coming. He was unique and unusual, and all of our people and every Baptist on the Peninsula of Virginia knew and loved this man. He had a doctor son who died during our time there of the same strange illness, viral pneumonia, as my younger sister, Yvonne. His funeral was in progress when we got back to Newport News from my sister's funeral. The husband of one of our Annapolis members, a relatively young man who was a chef on a large luxury boat in Florida, died of the same disease that same week. His boss had a doctor flown in from New York to Florida to try to save his life but to no avail. Dr. Stevens had a daughter, Elizabeth Stevens Flowers, the wife of Joe Flowers. At Dr. Stevens' recommendation, Joe had come from the Winona, Mississippi, First Baptist Church to a new area close to our church—a World War II housing area of poor, divorced, and problem people. Joe started Copeland Park Mission, now the great West Hampton Baptist Church. Joe Flowers was a nephew of Mrs. Ida Carter, the wife of the head of the Mississippi Baptist Orphanage who married Dorothy's mother and father on June 30, 1920. Therefore, Joe Flowers was very special to us, as was his wife, Elizabeth. I stayed in their home more recently in a World Missions Conference where I was one of the speakers. Both are since deceased. Elizabeth died first, and Joe remarried. He was on a tour in England when he died suddenly. They were two great people for God.

Dr. Herman Stevens was married first to a sister of Dr. C. C. Warren, a former Southern Baptist Convention president, in our time, and the author of the resolution called the "30,000 Movement," Southern Baptists' first effort to plant thirty thousand new missions and churches. It was almost accomplished. Dr. Herman Stevens and Dr. Warren would fish together off Hampton Roads in Dr. Stevens's old houseboat. Dr. Stevens was strong on mission starting and inspired Dr. Warren in his bold dream and vision for the Southern Baptist Convention. Would to God that we had such men of vision today for our convention because the dream is still alive. Dr. Stevens became my inspiration in starting new work on the Virginia Tidewater Peninsula area where the vast Civil War Army of Union General George McClellan bogged down in the effort to take Richmond in 1862. Robert E. Lee, who took the place of the wounded Joseph E. Johnston, stopped McClellan dead and built one of the greatest fighting armies of all time. History was made then and has been made since as the Lord's army moves out across that famous Virginia Tidewater Peninsula.

The work of mission starting began early in our ministry. We started four missions over a relatively short period of time. One was in the Hornsbyville area of York County in an abandoned building that has stood the test of time over the years. From this abandoned building, Dorothy was given two old pulpit chairs, true antiques. They were refurbished to their original state and have graced our home over the years. They are now in Sarah's home. We had a picnic-cleanup day on a Saturday at Hornsbyville, and one of our deacons, Glenroy Belvin, developed a severe case of poison ivy after clearing some of the grounds.

Seaford was another of our missions developed out of the Hornsbyville Mission. We asked the pastor emeritus of Ivy Memorial, Brother L. L. Jessup, to take over this mission work. It was like a community dump area and required burning of the accumulated trash and garbage. There was a squatter family living on the property, and it was difficult to get them to move on. They did not choose to help in the church development and finally moved. Brother Jessup worked hard and steadily at the job. One day he came to my office at Ivy Memorial to discuss his projected plans with me. He had the sketch of the planned first building. The cost was greatly in excess of reality according to Home Mission Board regulations. You cannot borrow beyond ten times the

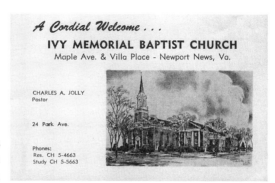

A Cordial Welcome . . .

IVY MEMORIAL BAPTIST CHURCH

Maple Ave. & Villa Place - Newport News, Va.

CHARLES A. JOLLY
Pastor

24 Park Ave.

Phones:
Res. CH 5-4663
Study CH 5-5663

Ivy Memorial Baptist church,
formerly in Newport News.
Now, in Hampton.

present income, then at four thousand dollars. Brother Jessup seemed stunned at this reality, but he did not let it daunt him. He went right ahead with his plans. Today, one of our most beautiful church plants, increased several times, sits on this property. They are planning a Christian Life Center now.

Shortly before we left Virginia for Pittsburgh, Pennsylvania, we were able to recommend Brother (Doctor now) Paul Mims from Brevard, North Carolina, as pastor. The first unit building was then in place, and next to it they were building the pastor's home, in sticky, black mud. I held a revival there later with Paul and Janice and stayed in this lovely home. Their two young children, Joe and Jenny, are both married and have children of their own. Joe is a fine surgeon in Atlanta and Jenny is in accounting. Paul Mims later served as pastor of First Baptist Church of Norfolk, Virginia, that had nearly died under a liberal pastor. While in the old downtown Norfolk area, a fire completely destroyed the building and Paul's library. They moved out to Virginia Beach where they built the present building. That church grew and thrived under Paul's ministry and later under Dr. Ken Hemphill who is now president of Southwestern Baptist Theological Seminary, the largest in the Southern Baptist Convention and, indeed, in the world. Paul and Janice are now pastoring the Ocean View Baptist Church in Myrtle Beach, South Carolina. They came from Druid Hills Baptist Church in Atlanta, Georgia, where the late great Southern Baptist leader, Dr. Louie Newton, was the lifetime pastor. Paul led his funeral.

The Seaford Church came to consider us as their pastor in the late 1960s when we were in Pittsburgh. They and we were so very close to a positive decision. It was our desire to be back in Virginia, so they had our permission to vote on a call on a certain Sunday morning. On that Sunday, in doubt about my decision, I called the pulpit committee chairman and asked them not to present my name. Seaford has moved right on and is still doing a great work for our Lord in the York County area of Virginia. There are always the lingering questions of the "what ifs." I have thought to write sometime on "What If?" we had gone to every place we might have gone.

Next there was the Grafton Mission. It was on new land and ultimately had a first unit building. It was rather more difficult to get started. That church has moved steadily onward across the years. We were recently back in that area in the lovely new townhouse of our special friend, Rachel Edwards. Her only son, Jimmy, and his wife, Sally, have a townhouse next door and look after his widowed mother. In taking my routine Sunday morning walk, this time in a slight rain, I walked past the Grafton Church that sits right in the midst of a tremendous developing area in every direction. Praise the Lord.

The Colony Mission met initially in an abandoned building next to the old courthouse. It was called Colony because the whole area was formerly owned by a colony of Mennonite farmers. I will never forget the hot sunny day when, with our associational director of missions, we went to inspect a five-acre plot of land on which we envisioned a new Baptist church. Dr. Herman Stevens was there with his old flop hat. We gathered in a circle to pray and to claim this land for the Lord. Dr. Stevens threw down his old flop hat and led our prayer. Lifting our heads, we looked down the road and saw a field of grain on another beautiful ten acres of property. We later bought the five-acre plot and then resold it to a developing housing area. It was rather the Lord's leading that we have that ten acres of property on which the new Tabernacle Baptist Church now sits. Fellow pastor Jack Tesh was, for a long time, pastor of that church in downtown Newport News. He is now deceased. The old Tabernacle Baptist Church was one of the churches that the black people bought for a minimum price and now use. Jack Tesh was very determined in his vision and very apt in designing. He led in building the new Tabernacle Baptist building on the ten acres and lived to retire there. He showed me all his unique areas of ministry for that new building.

After sponsoring the above-named missions from our Ivy Memorial Baptist Church, I was elected chairman of the missions committee by the Peninsula Association. In that capacity I was involved in the Fox Hill Road Mission development and new church building which was close to the water and subject to periodic flooding. Nevertheless, the church was built and has flourished until this day. York County, slow to develop for a long time, is now a booming development area. The Yorktown Battlefield is where the troops of George Washington defeated the British troops under Lord Cornwallis to end the

Revolutionary War and insure that the new nation, under God, would develop into the United States of America. Would that we might regain our nation, under God, unashamed and unafraid to proclaim our faith and cause, through Christ Jesus, our Lord, in the power and energy of His blessed Holy Spirit.

Other missions were developed in the Williamsburg area. One, Walnut Hills, now one of our best-growing and influential churches, was sponsored by old Orcutt Avenue Baptist Church. Brother Bill Milne was pastor and died suddenly of a heart attack while conducting a prayer service.

Hilton Baptist Church, with Brother Loyall Prior (now deceased) as pastor, sponsored the Stoney Point Mission. We purchased a beautiful piece of property and built a new building. It is now in a continually developing situation. Later, I was privileged to hold a revival there and to be in the home of the pastor, Norman Blythe, who is now deceased.

On and on I could go in this burgeoning mission and church growth and development on the Peninsula during and beyond my time as pastor of Ivy Memorial Baptist Church and which is still heavily involved in associational work. Today there is a new associational missions building and center, a new Baptist Home, a retirement area for aging Baptist faithfuls, new church buildings in many areas, and the work moves on. I have been privileged to be back in revival with Brother Henry Reynolds of New Market Baptist Church, in a World Missions Conference at Deer Park, and in the new Ivy Memorial Baptist Church in the new downtown area of Hampton.

One unusual event happened in the historic Union Baptist Church area where Charlie Jones was pastor. He related this story to us. There had been severe flooding and the church cemetery was just in view at the front of his church. As he was standing in the door of his church, he saw the graves burst open, one by one, and the vaults and caskets pop up out of the ground like corks under tremendous water pressure. A great reburying took place after the weather settled down.

East Hampton Baptist was a weak, struggling church, where Brother Virgil Casey, a former Clear Creek student in Pineville, Kentucky, served as pastor. He married one of the young women saved in a tent revival in Kentucky (described in chapter five of this book). They were a special group although on the downside in finances. Nevertheless, they built a lovely, simply designed building. I held a revival for them and God blessed us. The church still struggles, but they have reached people for our Lord that no other church could have reached. Virgil Casey and his family later moved to the Charlottesville, Virginia, area where I was privileged to hold a revival for him when we lived in Madison, New Jersey. Virgil became the chairman of a search committee for a first-time director of missions. Dorothy and I were invited to come and look at the situation. Again, there was the temptation to consider going back to one of the most beautiful areas of Virginia. The history of Thomas Jefferson, Monticello, the university, and location all appealed to us. They had a dinner meeting in our honor in order for questions to be asked and answered. They were ready to call us but were unable to offer a financial package sufficient to enable us to buy a home and to live—another of those might-have-beens. We passed through there on a recent summer-vacation trip. It was a suffocatingly hot day, and we were thankful for our cooler Northwest climate which is more suitable to our way of life.

When we were in Annapolis, we had a lovely black woman, Rachel Adams, now deceased, who worked in our church nursery. We would pick her up and take her to church. She knew Dorothy was expecting, and we talked about her need for help. Rachel was close to a naval captain and his wife and family who had moved to Little Creek in the Norfolk area. (This is the same area where Richard Rasmussen served for a time in the Navy. He is the father of our three grandchildren who live here in the Northwest.) Rachel had helped the naval captain's family get settled and lived with them in their home for a time. She offered to come from Annapolis and stay with us and help us with our baby due to come five weeks after we moved. I went and got her and took her back to the naval family after her live-in with us for a whole month. Her charges for this service of love were very minimal. What a blessing she was to all of us that month.

It was hard on Dorothy to make this move with all the essential adjustments at the time. She bore her burdens in the usual Dorothy fashion—welcomed new people, moved essentials, and so on. On a stormy and rainy Sunday night after church, we rushed to the old Riverside Hospital. All signals were go and soon. Dorothy's doctor, Benjamin Harrison Inloes, from Maryland, was a friend and classmate of Dr. Joseph Sheehan, Dorothy's Annapolis doctor. (We had a precious older member and friend in Annapolis, Mrs. Emily Winters, who baby-sat for Dr. Sheehan and his wife. Her only son was a Navy captain and we were included in several special occasions at the Naval Officers Club because of Miss Emily.)

On this Sunday night Dr. Inloes, our new doctor, had two women who were delivering at the same time—Dorothy and one other. I was standing downstairs at the nurses' station when the secretary on duty told the father of the other child that his son had died because the umbilical cord was entangled around his neck. It was a sad moment for this couple. We have often wondered if in such an emergency situation Dorothy may have been inadvertently neglected. Dr. Inloes was careful to assure us that such was not the case and he felt that every vital sign for our son was excellent. Our concern came later, when we found out that "Buddy" had a developmental disability handicap. In all our remaining time at Ivy Memorial, Buddy seemed in every way to be a normal boy, loved and adored by his three sisters and all the church family, and has been ever since. He has been and is most special in our lives since all the sisters are now gone from the nest.

Again, in seeking for additional help at Ivy Memorial, we turned to Mildred Oaks. She came to us from the Tennessee Sunday School Department where she worked with Dorothy's brother, Bob Patterson. She found a lovely place right across the street from our parsonage home with a single young woman, Sue Hutton, educational director in Parkland Baptist Church. They were good friends who shared about their mutual work. We were often in and out of each other's homes. Mildred especially loved the waters of Hampton Roads and often took long walks along the waterfront and said on more than one occasion, "that water talks to you." She was again very effective in her work with us, and our people responded accordingly.

Dorothy's brother was scheduled for a Sunday School conference in the Portsmouth area at the time a major hurricane was to cross our area. We all spent the night in Mildred and Sue's home because it was built of brick and concrete. The storm passed with minimal damage. It was a very sad day for us when Mildred felt led to accept a similar position at First Baptist Church of Hendersonville, North Carolina, in September of 1963. She would be closer to her daughters. She met her second husband, Henry Barringer, there.

When Henry's first wife died, he and Mildred became close friends and later married. They had a lovely home in Hendersonville that we enjoyed sharing on a subsequent visit. Mildred was elected to the County Commissioners' office in the Hendersonville area. She was a Republican and became the very effective chairperson of the group. All the rest were men and Democrats. I always said she should have run for Congress. She would have been great! What a great blessing Mildred and all her talented family has been in our Lord's work and to us personally since we first met in Pineville, Kentucky. She has just recently written the history of that period, including our ministry. It is a superb piece of Mildred Oaks's upbeat philosophy and writing. Mildred often visits in our area and we get to share many special occasions with her family. She has her beautiful home in Morristown, Tennessee, now and is very active in her church.

When Mildred left us at Ivy Memorial, it took us a long time to replace her. We finally found an excellent young man, Charles Jones, with his wife and baby.

Sadly for him, he had been with us only a short time when we were involved in a move to Pittsburgh, Pennsylvania. Charlie was a great help to Ivy Memorial during this changing period. He is now deceased.

We had been at Ivy Memorial only two years when the First Baptist Church of Yazoo City, Mississippi, became pastorless. I had held a youth revival in that church in 1940 when the pastor was Dr. Webb Brame. He was also the Chaplain of the Mississippi 155th Infantry that saw heavy service in World War II. I got to know and to love these Yazoo City people through my college roommate, Clarence Watson, and his family, the John Watsons. I knew and was close to Mrs. Watson's aging mother, Mrs. Sarah Bridges, and to other members of her family. I refer to them in chapter two. They literally made me a member of their family and became my family away from home. They were close to my family in Okolona and kept up with all of us. Dr. Clarence Watson has been a longtime teacher in religious education at Carson-Newman College and is now retired. Don Roark, chairman of the Yazoo City pulpit committee, was also an executive of the Mississippi Chemical Corporation. Owen Cooper was president and a member of the committee. He later served as president of the Southern Baptist Convention and even later, president of the Baptist World Alliance. Also, Jerry Clower, a famous humorist with the Grand Ole Opry, was on the committee.

The committee sent part of their group to visit us in Newport News. Later, they invited us to Yazoo City to meet with the entire committee. The Owen Coopers met with us and entertained us. The committee carefully talked with us about our view of civil rights for blacks, including intermarriage. We felt essentially as they did about mixing the races. They drove us around the area. We were disturbed at the general rundown condition of the downtown area. We were concerned about the black people selling their property up on the hill to white people and blacks coming down to the inter-city area with accompanying impoverishment and neglect. We were very impressed with the lovely new church building. They met with us again on a later visit to Dorothy's parents' home in Grenada, Mississippi. Dorothy's father was the director of missions in Grenada County. All of our families wanted us back in Mississippi. On the occasion of this visit, Dr. Brame was retired and we visited him at his barn with a prize bull. He affirmed that I was the one for their church.

We came back to Ivy Memorial with a very upset and divided mind. Our leaders at Ivy Memorial felt strongly that we had been there too short a time and we needed to stay. The people at Yazoo City voted to call us, even in our indecision. They actually had a brief article in the Mississippi *Baptist Record* that they had called us as pastor. This was without our permission. We were embarrassed for ourselves and for them. We were in a tremendous crisis decision stage. Our girls were in school, in a different culture from that in Mississippi so stirred by the civil-rights battle at the time. We earnestly prayed but could not find the peace we needed to leave Ivy Memorial and Virginia and go back to Mississippi. Finally, our decision was negative and I posted a letter to that effect. We made most of our Ivy Memorial people happy, but all of this deeply upset our Mississippi friends. We were never again considered for a pastorate in our native state. Our parents were sorely disappointed. That great Yazoo City church was very soon to call their next pastor, Dr. Jimmy Yates, who served long and effectively in Yazoo City and among Mississippi Baptists until he retired. He is still involved in Mississippi Baptist life. Looking back, I believe our decision was right for the sake of all concerned. God worked good for all. For our Ivy Memorial people, there was a renewed sense of mission for great changes ahead. Not only because of the racial factors but there was a positive facing-up to what was right and good for the whites and blacks, and all in between. God had yet a mission purpose ahead for us, and ultimately, Mississippi Baptists were a great source of financial help when we went to Hawaii.

Almost from the beginning of our ministry in Ivy Memorial, I had a number of funerals that I felt inadequate to cope with. In fact, it was always the tough part of my ministry, yet it was so important for the people most involved. Looking back, God has enabled me to be effective and comforting and helpful because His people were going home.

Our youngest daughter at the time, Martha Ruth, "Little Miss Busybody," was always reacting one way or another. One day our excellent musician, choir leader, and organist, Vera Rathkamp, called me aside. She told me, "Your little Martha Ruth has been saying something I think you would want to know about. She is saying, 'My Daddy is killing 'em off like flies.'" She was referring to about a dozen consecutive funerals. When I told Dorothy, she was shocked. We proceeded forthwith to help our little daughter to understand the needs of people in such times of the passing of dear loved ones. Apparently Vera heard it first, and when she told me, I had inadvertently said, "It sounds like something her mother must have said." That made for double trouble for me! Really, all the people took our girls into their hearts. They were then, and are now, very special, really sweethearts of our church. I'm sure that our people, a loving congregation, understood the nature of children and helped to set them straight.

Vera was great with children and youth. By profession she was a gifted music teacher in the Hampton, Virginia, public schools. Once each month on Sunday nights, we had a special youth night, and I brought a particular message for the needs and interests of the young people. This series began with my own experience, including my debate and oratorical experiences in high school in Okolona, Mississippi. In the process, I would tell about my travels by train, a new experience indeed for me, especially learning how to cope with sleeping in a Pullman car—also, how I came to compete in the final contest on a rainy afternoon in the high school auditorium in Springfield, Illinois, home of Abraham Lincoln. There were five of us there out of a starting field of twenty-four thousand youth.

I remember the auditorium was filled to overflowing because youth from all over Illinois had come in to share in these contests. The prize was a four-thousand-dollar college scholarship given by Eddie Cantor and at that time amounted to the cost of a four-year college course. I intended to become a lawyer and hopefully a politician. I would pray to God, in every hotel room in which I stayed, to win because I needed this financial help. I continued by relating that the greatest thrill of my young life was when I won out of a group of four in Ponca City, Oklahoma, the southwestern United States region, on a beautiful sunny morning. The Ponca City student body gave a rousing fifteen rahs for Mississippi. I remembered redheaded Betty Swidensky from Oklahoma who gave a superb speech on the Constitution of the United States and I thought she had won. I was declared the winner and was surely on my way to win the national contest. I felt in the Springfield contest that I did the best ever in my prepared speech. I fouled up in an extemporaneous speech on the Second Amendment to the Constitution. We had been told to prepare for an extemporaneous speech. We had only ten minutes to think through an assigned amendment before we spoke for three minutes about the meaning of that amendment. My school superintendent in Okolona had sent Mr. H. N. Worley to Springfield to be in that auditorium that afternoon. I can see him even now sitting way back under the balcony to my left. He was always special and encouraging to me. How disappointed and sad I was to lose to an excellent young man, Chester Padgett Jr., from Saluda, South Carolina.

In my first year in Mississippi Baptist College, I wrote the story in a little book entitled *Youth Speaks*. My English Professor, Dr. Walter Fuller Taylor, helped me in this project. The book contained the five speeches, the photos of those involved, together with a brief biography of each. Also, there was an introductory section on the American Legion, how it was formed and where and a tribute to those Americans who served in World War I, called the Great War. I had received a gift of books from the American Legion on this subject, as had the other speakers. My father was a Legionnaire, as was my school superintendent in Okolona, and all the men there had so helped me with new clothes, to make the national trip and have that experience. I went on to explain in my youth sermon at Ivy Memorial that God was leading all the while in my life. He did not intend for me to be a lawyer or a politician although I have had a keen interest in both. He intended that I be a minister and preacher of His blessed gospel. I went on to tell how that came about, how I found Dorothy, and that the story is not yet finished.

Vera Rathkamp said to Dorothy, "I knew I had heard Reverend Jolly's voice when I first heard him here. I was in that Springfield auditorium and heard him speak and was impressed. I was one of those interested university students invited to come in from over Illinois to hear those national contest speakers." What a small world and how reassuring of God that He knew all about it, and all about me, in this place, Ivy Memorial Baptist Church, and in this time, with one I had never known, Vera Rathkamp. How could we ever doubt His leading and His tender mercies?

I was very close to the Rathkamp family during our ministry at Ivy Memorial and have been since, to Vera and her daughter, Betty Rose, who is today involved in educational funding for children in Africa. She is quite excellent at it. Frank, Vera's husband, was some forty years of age, very overweight, and a retired military chaplain. He always attended our church and complimented my ministry and messages. He had a severe gall bladder attack and was in a military hospital. He had done well in the operation, which was a major and critical operation in those days. He had a severe incision all the way across the stomach area just below the navel. One day while eating, Frank choked on his food and coughed so hard he burst the incision and was rushed back to surgery. He had a strong heart reaction and died, most unexpectedly. His death devastated the young Jewish surgeon who blamed himself for this loss. The nurse asked me to please go aside in the next room and try to comfort the surgeon. Here I was a Christian minister trying to minister to a Jewish surgeon who seemed about to lose it. I sat down beside him. His head was in his hands, and he was obviously in great pain. I spoke to him. I told him who I was and that all of us felt he had done his best and that this was in God's hands. I had prayer with him and in the name of Christ whom many of us believe to be the Savior of the world.

I had heard this type of prayer back in Roanoke, Virginia, when a group of ministers of many faiths were invited to a Christian/Jewish dialogue and lovely meal prepared by the Jewish ladies. A black Baptist pastor had been invited to lead the prayer for our meal. At the dedication of a permanent memorial recon-struction of the "triumphal arch" there in Newport News through which returning World War I soldiers had marched, returning from the awful, bloody trenches of France, I was asked to lead in prayer. I prayed in the same manner as the black pastor had done. This arch was an historic place and commemora-tive of those men, lest we forget. My prayer was accepted as recognition of others' faith. The young doctor was responsive and grateful and thanked me. I led Frank's funeral in the First Methodist Church of Hampton, Virginia, which was another great opportunity to witness.

Frank had given me a book of his sermons in which one sermon was "Ride the Wild Horses," meaning there are many wild horses in our sinful, human nature. If we don't learn to ride them, they will ride us down to infamy and ruin. Sometime later when Dorothy and I and family were visiting our chaplain brother, Joe, in Florida, we attended Sunday morning worship in the Air Force Base Chapel. One of the Protestant base chaplains, not Joe but a guest, preached an excellent sermon and then I remembered Frank's sermon, "Ride the Wild Horses." I looked it up, and the chaplain had preached that sermon word for word without giving credit. Well, I wonder if it was Frank's sermon or whose? No matter, really, because it still spoke to our hearts.

The Ivy Memorial Church had a constant program of visitation to new people and the lost people. The hospital visitation itself was a heavy load. I recall going into the room of one of our male patients early in the morning. He and his wife were having breakfast and pleasantly chatting and were glad to see the pastor, even so early. In a few minutes, the patient began to hemorrhage through his mouth and nose. Despite every effort to save him, he was gone in a few minutes. Then I knew why I had gone early. I have often gone into such a situ-ation just when I was needed the most. I thank our Lord, the Great Physician, for his leading, healing, and care when time to leave this earth. I was called one night to be with a relative stranger to witness his signing of a will while he was hemorrhaging to death. Later I was called on in court to testify about my witnessing the deceased man's will. It held up in court.

There was a relatively wealthy man who was a builder of beautiful homes, including his own, right on Hampton Roads. I was often in his home. He was a fellow Mason. He was not too faithful in his church but active in the Masons, and his wife was right along with him, in high style. This man became deeply depressed. I would talk and pray with him as he contemplated suicide. Nothing I could say or do could deter him. He could not stand this besetting depression.

I really understood because I had had several serious bouts myself. One day this man went up on the high point of the James River Bridge, parked his truck, swallowed poison, and jumped off. It was a sad funeral and hard on me because I had been inadequate to help him more.

The Ivy Memorial Baptist Church had the full Southern Baptist program for men, women, girls, and boys. It was mostly a pleasant experience. The women were wonderful in their missionary zeal, giving, praying, and especially in programs for the Girl's Auxiliary and Young Women's Auxiliary. There were beautiful occasions that really touched the lives of our young people. There was an excellent Royal Ambassador program also. I reached my fortieth year there. There was a brief celebration by the church on Wednesday night and a gift of a lovely silver tray that Dorothy liked. We had the fiftieth anniversary of the church during our ministry. Our Brother Lloyd Jessup, former pastor twice and now emeritus, led us in a whole week of thanksgiving and celebration. We had all the former pastors back for a message during the week. It was truly a rewarding and renewal time for the church.

One young man, Ronnie Williams, who literally camped on our doorstep, had a terrible drinking problem. He was a good newspaperman in advertising until drinking destroyed his effectiveness. His wife couldn't take it and left him, despite all of Ronnie's pleading. When she remarried, her new husband was active in the church, and they had several fine children. He died early of a massive brain tumor. Ronnie kept in touch with us over the years and wanted me to come back to Newport News to head a joint Baptist/Lutheran Home project. He said he had the property, inherited from his Lutheran parents whom I knew and had shared with often about the burden of their son. I asked one of the members to check Ronnie's story, and there was no foundation to his claim. I had to tell him so and have never heard from him since.

A man lived across the street from our church who was not a member. He was intelligent, and we often visited. He lived next door to Wylie and Helen Jenkins and Wylie's aged mother, Nannie. Helen cut Dorothy's hair and was a good friend. She died early from cancer. They made us acquainted with their neighbor, George Golden. I believe his wife had died previous to our time in Ivy Memorial. George was a World War I veteran and loved to tell a story that made an indelible impression on his mind and life. There was a black man in military service in France. His routine on Saturday nights was to be in his tent praying, reading his Bible, and writing to his wife and family with their pictures around him. His fellow soldiers would kid him about going out with them on the city, *parlez vous*. They would say, "Your wife won't know about it and besides, there's not much to this religion stuff." He would reply, "Well, suppose there ain't nothing to it and you go your way and I stay here and pray and read my Bible. If there ain't nothing to it I'm still going to be better off than you are. But, suppose there is something to it, and you go your way and I go my way. You are going to be in one hell of a fix." It made an impression on George and he kept on telling that story.

Our older girls were all involved in the church programs and helping to look after their beloved little brother, Charles Jr. He was in every way an active growing little boy with short cropped blond hair. He delighted in playing and being underfoot. He also loved to play outside under our large sycamore trees and to pour the powdered dirt down on his head. Bathing him at the end of the day was a chore. Sarah and Mary both were in older grades at the Woodrow Wilson School. They loved their teachers and did well.

Martha Ruth had just started to school and had a vivid imagination. She declares to this day that she was frightened beyond words by a man and woman in a big black car who tried to get her to come with them. I had a telephone call from our effective secretary, Sadie Suddeth. She had been on the job since the previous pastor and was the wife of deacon Rodney. They had no children. His father, a preacher, was fired from his church because he befriended the Indians in his area. Rodney never forgot the final day, the loving response of his father, and his mother's copious weeping with her white lace handkerchief. Rodney and Saddie were fine people.

She said, "Pastor, Martha Ruth is over here at the church, hiding and trembling under my desk." I went at once and heard her story, trying to play it down, but to no avail. Considering what is happening today, I don't doubt her story. We tracked her to school after that and made sure she was with others.

Martha became deeply convicted of her need for Jesus before she was five years of age. Perhaps her fright had some bearing, but I have never doubted the validity of her experience. During this time, we visited my father in his church in Woodland, Mississippi. She stood beside me during the invitation time and held my hand. I could feel her trembling, and it troubled me. I left the family with Dorothy's mother and father in Amory, Mississippi, for a revival in nearby Leighton, Alabama, with our friends Dorothy and Ed Wright and family. Going over a mountainous area into Leighton, I got caught in a snowstorm. The snow was so deep that we had to cancel the first night's service. It warmed up, and we were okay the rest of the week. On the last day of the revival, my father-in-law brought the family over to the Wrights' to go back with me to Newport News. That afternoon Martha Ruth was with some church folk and talked with them about trusting Jesus as her Savior. That night at the invitation time, I stayed on the rostrum so it would not be easy for her. She was not to be deterred and marched right up beside me to give her heart to Jesus. No one else came. I raised a question about her being so young. The people she had been with said, "Brother Jolly, you need not worry. We have been talking with this child all afternoon, and she knows what she is doing." The church there approved, and when we got back to Ivy Memorial and told the story, the church voted unanimously and enthusiastically to approve her for baptism.

To know her life in teaching Christian music to over two thousand private preschool children in Dallas, Texas, the writing of spiritual music, and, more recently, her overcoming obesity, diabetes, and congestive heart problems that nearly cost her life, one does not doubt the validity of her experience. With the help of her Jewish doctor, she went from 330 pounds to a trim 135 pounds. We were in Dallas recently and went with her to one of her school's music programs. She stood on the stage for one solid hour and directed those children who enthusiastically responded and sang. There were seventy-five to one hundred children in the program. I marveled anew at the ability God gave her. She was involved in a doctor-directed, weight-control program involving over five hundred people and has been on national television on the Mike and Maty Show from Hollywood, California. Martha has left the doctor-directed program and is a marketing agent for an imaging firm—x-rays, magnetic resonance imagings, and cat scans, to name a few. Her husband, Kevin, carries Uncle Sam's mail. Their two boys, Ryan and Spencer, are okay and very special.

Another incident during the Leighton revival occurred when Brother Ed Wright took us up on a mountain above the town to show us the ruins of a Normal School, as they were called in those early days. There was also the town's ancient cemetery. He knew of my interest in history. I walked over the cemetery to where the most prominent citizen had been buried under a huge monument. The story was that it took a team of twenty oxen to haul that monument up the mountain more than one hundred years before. I looked under the monument, and there was nothing there to indicate a burial. Then I realized the Bible teaching about our end time on this earth. "It is ashes to ashes and dust to dust" no matter how much we may spend to keep it from happening. Hence, a box in Nurse Miller's hands contained the ashes of Miss Lottie Moon after a legally required cremation in Kobe, Japan. Those ashes are buried in a chained-off area in Crew, Virginia, where thousands go to view the sight. "It is still ashes to ashes and dust to dust."

Our plan, ultimately, is for cremation and the remains to be laid beside my wife's parents in Pontotoc, Mississippi, where Brother Patterson started and was pastor of the West Heights Baptist Church. The church people gave Dorothy's father twelve lots in the cemetery for the resting-place of any of his loved ones desiring to be interred there. His son Bob Jr. later served as pastor of the same West Heights Baptist Church. It is now one of the outstanding churches in Mississippi with a $800,000 budget. Bob was invited back on March 9, 1997, to preach for the fiftieth anniversary service. He was the second pastor, traveling by train from New Orleans Baptist Theological Seminary. The church grew from 66 to 324 members under his ministry. They expected seven hundred in Sunday School for the fiftieth anniversary.

We had good revivals at Ivy Memorial, and God blessed us with souls saved and "seasons of refreshing from the Lord." We had Dr. F. Crossley Morgan, son of the great Bible expositor, G. Campbell Morgan of England. We had Dr. Paul S. James, director of our work in New York and Dr. Frank Voight, Sunday School secretary for Virginia. Also, Brother J. C. Chapman from South Carolina, Dr. Andrew Hall from Fayetteville, Arkansas, and Dr. Ray Roberts, executive secretary of the Ohio Baptist Convention. All of these stayed in various members' homes. They always seemed to feel at home when we had them for meals. (Dorothy's marvelous cooking, when we were not eating out, showed tender love and care.) We had Dr. Wayne E. Todd who was the youth revival preacher in Okolona, Mississippi, when Dorothy and I gave our lives to God's call to Christian ministry in 1939, four years before we could be married, and it is still holding. We enjoy God's gracious blessings even to this day and hour. Wayne Todd is since deceased as have all the others, save Dr. Paul James and Dr. Andy Hall. One day, what a glad and glorious reunion there will be beyond the sunset. For the Christian, this life is not the end. It is just the beginning—oh glorious day!

While at Ivy Memorial, we took several bus tours. One was with a mixed group of youth and adults to the Gettysburg Battlefield that was the scene of the high-water mark of the Confederacy. We asked the Annapolis people to have us in their homes. Hostess Ottie Bassford had a lovely meal for us in the redecorated dining area. Our Ivy people thoroughly enjoyed fellowship with the Annapolis folk and vice versa. We took another mixed group to New York City. What an experience for those who had never been in the city and to experience some of what Southern Baptists were doing. Some tried the subways and lived to tell the story! Also, I took a select group of girls to Charlottesville, Virginia, for a picnic and a tour of Monticello and the University of Virginia. We also visited Bobbie White in the University Hospital. We took a group of youth to Washington, D.C., and toured the various national shrines. We gave explicit instructions to the youth to stay with us always, especially at the capitol building. One couple got off to themselves on the lower southwest corner of the capitol grounds. A group of black kids on bicycles came along and some words were passed. The blacks hurriedly recruited others, and they came back and stoned the couple. One boy had to be hospitalized. We stayed with the injured boy until he was released, while the others went back home on the tour bus. I got a taste of the difficulty that Washington police had in identifying anyone among so many in such an incident.

One of the older retired Ivy Memorial ministers from World War I days was a Brother Jamerson. He and his wife had one daughter, Evelyn, a military photographer. Brother Jamerson was pastor of the church during the Spanish flu experience of 1918 when so many died. One could go to work in the morning and be dead before night. People were so frightened at Ivy Memorial that they set up a large tent with cots provided and trained personnel cared for the people. I believe this was done by the military. Brother Jamerson visited each day, walked some distance, prayed for those who were ill, buried the dead, and comforted the grieving. In time, with aging, and with his wife deceased, he virtually lost his mental faculties. He came to church with his daughter. He was a very nice looking older man, with a half-smile on his face, and listened as if he understood. He would shake my hand at the door but was unable to speak. He later had to go to a nursing home in Matthews County, north of Newport News. We would take Evelyn to visit him. Evelyn, in gratitude, did a photo of Martha Ruth, a painting of all save her face that was one of Evelyn's photos. The face is so vivid that it seems to talk to you, a perfect portrayal of Martha Ruth at that time. It hangs in our bedroom and is most cherished to this day. As a child, she was always nosey, and it seems to show in this beloved photo. I led Brother Jamerson's funeral later on.

Evelyn had a serious, progressive, disabling malady, muscular dystrophy, that put her in Patrick Henry Hospital, a long-term facility for the disabled. She lingered for several hard years. However, when we would occasionally visit her, she was always upbeat and had that half-smile like her dad. Mrs. Jamerson died before we knew the family.

Several others of our precious members were finally in that Patrick Henry perpetual nursing care area and died there: wonderful, vivacious Emily Wade, our vital, strong WMU leader; and our church secretary, Sadie Suddeth, who just looked at me, unable to speak the last time I visited her on a return trip to the Peninsula. Todd Pointer, the developmentally disabled son of Mrs. Merle Pointer, and brother to our beloved Virginia Nichols, died recently. Virginia's husband, Bill Nichols, died several years ago. Virginia subsequently lost her son-in-law, vital and vivacious Jerry Hogge Jr,. from a sudden heart attack on the tennis court. This was devastating to his young wife and family, and Virginia who had so depended on him for help after Bill's death. Jerry was an outstanding banker who had suffered severe losses in bank difficulties that adversely affected him. Jerry was innocent and bounced back. He was former vice-mayor of Newport News and highly respected in the business community. Another patient was Curtis Edwards, my barber, special friend, deacon, husband of Rachel, and father of daughter Judy, and son Jimmy. He spent four years there with Alzheimer's disease. It broke Rachel's heart to see him slowly fade away. Their home was always open to us, and we spent many happy times together. More recently, Judy's husband, Rick Andrews, in Suffolk, Virginia, had a strange malady that nearly cost his life but through prayer and a never-give-up doctor, he has come through and will likely recover fully. This doctor knew of one other such case, and he conferred with the doctor in North Carolina. We have been especially close, and Dorothy flew from Pittsburgh to sing at their wedding on June 29, 1968. Thank God, Rick is making solid, steady progress! His parents are fine Christians and active in the Presbyterian Church. So much for those who were so close to us over these years and with whom we, by phone and occasional visits, even recently, have been privileged to share.

Another very unusual occasion in very cold weather occurred when I ran into a serious wreck as I was riding down the interstate toward Norfolk to get to a hospital. A truck in front of a carload of people had the hood suddenly pop straight up. The driver of the truck did the natural thing and stepped hard on his brakes. He had heavy traffic behind him and people plowed into him and others into them. I stopped and got out to see what I might do. A young man got out of his car in utter panic, not realizing how seriously he was injured, and was running around trying to help others who were injured. The traffic was so heavy that I could see that an ambulance or first aid crew would never make it. My station wagon was warm, and I loaded it full of the injured people and rushed back to the new Dixie hospital. One woman next to me had a broken hip and was in severe pain. I held her up while I drove. There was blood every-where, and it was freezing on their faces. I got to the hospital just as one shift was going off and another coming on. This meant all the doctors and nurses were there to take care of this emergency. I stayed with them into the night while surgeons worked—bone specialist, a spleen operation for the young man to save his life, and on and on. Fortunately, and by God's grace and healing power, all were saved. I visited them, some dozen or so, until they recovered. And, on a subsequent Sunday, they all showed up in church with their various families to thank me and to hear God's message. They brought a big batch of cookies on a silver, galleried tray as a gift to us.

It was in this hospital on a lovely, fall afternoon on September 26, 1963, that Becky was born. Dorothy did well. Dorothy had a hard time dealing with a pregnancy at this time at forty years of age with four children already. Deacon and Mrs. W. T. Baker, older and wiser, heard her patiently, and my encouraging words helped Dorothy to feel better. And so, Becky came to bless our lives in a very special way. I telephoned Dorothy's mother with the name Elizabeth Ernestine in mind, after Queen Elizabeth. Dorothy's mother said, "My grandmother was named Rebecca, and it would go good with Ernestine." That's how Becky got her name. This was another biblical name for our girls. They all had biblical names except Charles Jr., who was named for his dad.

When Becky was about eight weeks old, a great tragedy came to our country. The president of our nation was assassinated in Dallas on a political journey for his coming re-election. The vice-president, Lyndon Johnson, was in the long parade of cars. The governor of Texas, John Connally, and his wife were in the jump seat in front of the president and Mrs. Kennedy. It was determined later that the shots came from the Texas School Book Depository storage building. Dorothy and I had left our baby and other children at home with our maid, a black woman, Pauline Wilson, loved in our church by all our people. We had gone to do some Christmas shopping after lunch at a nearby restaurant. When we walked into the K-Mart, in the Christmas spirit, all was strangely quiet, and people were focused on the store's television sets. Walter Cronkite first said the president had been shot in Dallas and rushed to the Parkland Hospital. Then in painful, somber tones, he said, "The president is dead." All the following week, every eye was riveted on the television screens as the remarkable funeral arrangements by Jackie Kennedy proceeded. The entire world was hushed in sorrow. Vice-President Lyndon Johnson was sworn in by a local Texas judge friend as the new president, in the presence of Jackie who was in bloody clothing unchanged from the tragedy. The new president and his wife came off the plane in Washington, D.C., in the glare of searchlights, and said, "Today we have suffered a great tragedy. I will do my best with God's help and yours." This was to assure the stricken nation that he was in charge. And for over five years, he wrestled with the nation's problems despite harsh criticism and resistance to the Vietnam War.

At the time of this national tragedy, I had a youth revival in northern Maryland (Conowingo) with my dear friend, Brother Walter Burcham. I drove to Maryland on the day of the president's funeral not daring to think I could even get near the funeral procession. However, I decided to try. I was familiar with the Arlington area and found a place to park my car about a mile from the route of the funeral procession. I recall thinking that God did not intend for the Kennedy family to be so influential in our government and future. Kennedy money was made from gross sales of Scotch whiskey. The Scriptures state that persons of this background would not be in control. I was able to get close to the funeral procession just before it crossed into Arlington National Cemetery, the place of interment. I took pictures with my camera and noted across the way that the limousine of the new president was surrounded by a horde of Secret Service people. There were helicopters flying overhead, and I remember thinking, "All of this, and they couldn't get the president of the United States through Dallas." I rode on to northern Maryland and heard the twenty-one-gun salute, the final rites, and the lighting of the eternal flame over the car radio. When I got to Maryland, the pastor's wife met me. She was very upset because a little boy had been hit and killed by a car. Brother Burcham was involved with the stricken family. We had a good week—one night each in several churches. God graciously blessed us despite the events of recent days.

When Lee Harvey Oswald was shot by Jack Ruby on the following Sunday, that was even more shocking. I recall Danny Sanchez, who was our missions director then in New York, and later professor of evangelism in Southwestern Baptist Theological Seminary, telling of an unusual experience. He related taking a walk in a Dallas cemetery and hearing someone crying. Upon investigation, it turned out to be Lee Harvey Oswald's mother. She replied to Danny's inquiry, "They all are concerned about the president. I'm so sad because all have turned against my son. None weep for him!" I heard later that Lee Oswald had to cross a Baptist church area every day but somehow was never reached for Christ. He was a very mixed-up young man.

In my preaching responsibility in the Conowingo revival, I always took a daily walk. Even to this day, it is my habit to walk four miles a day Monday through Friday. It was as if God spoke to me to take Dorothy, our baby Rebecca, and the rest of our family to visit her mother in the hospital in their home area of Grenada, Mississippi. Becky was ten weeks old, and Dorothy resisted the idea of taking a baby and our family out across the country in winter-like weather. I insisted, and we went. Dorothy visited with her mother and took the new baby daughter several times. She had fallen and broken her hip the day the president was shot. She was never to get out of the hospital. She wasn't able to be too responsive, and we sadly left on December 15. She died on January 13. Dorothy's father told us later, "She gradually went into a coma but she seemed so happy and would smile sweetly so one of the nurses told me." We have always been grateful that we went and braved the wintry weather. One day, she will want to meet our Becky face to face.

On the day Dorothy and I left Newport News to board the train for the trip home for the funeral service, deacon and friend Hugh Adams brought us our mail. In that mail was our first request for information from the Pittsburgh Baptist Church.

Dorothy and I had to leave our children again in the loving care of deacon and Mrs. Hugh Adams while we made the long train trip back to Mississippi for the funeral services of Mother Ernestine who had suggested the name Rebecca Ernestine. On that trip, I wrote a poetic description of the places we passed through, much of it in the nighttime, places where Dorothy's parents had served our Lord so faithfully. The people who knew and loved Ernestine Lowther Patterson came from all over to pay their loving tributes—people whose lives she had influenced for our Lord. One special item of interest for Dorothy and me, that I had never known, came to our attention in the Grenada, Mississippi, train depot. The station agent was Robert Boone. When we told him who we were, he said, "Why, Charles, I stood up with your mother and father when they married in the Methodist parsonage [in their and my Normal School] in Buena Vista, Mississippi." My mother's best friend, Ellie T. King, had stood up with her. Her beautiful, old, white, two-story house is right across from my mother's grave. I have since stood there in sight of the Methodist parsonage and in the opposite direction, the old King home. I thought about those special days in my parents' lives. Ellie T. King has died in recent years at eighty-two years of age. This information came through my mother's brother, Claiborne Freeman Jr., who is now also deceased.

The Virginia churches gave us four weeks of vacation with pay. We thoroughly enjoyed that privilege. Elder deacon W. T. Baker and Mrs. Baker had a lovely little cottage in rural York County that they made available to us. Our girls loved to go there and so did we. The Bakers had things there for the girls and rather spoiled them. You could hear the bobwhites and other birds. A radio made it possible to keep up with the outside news. I recall being there during the presidential nominations and debates.

There was also the time Mr. Baker made it possible for our family to use the larger Baker summer cottage in Louisa County, Patrick Henry country, during a revival in the historic Goldmine church. Mr. Baker would come from Newport News during revival week, and we would visit together in the community where many of his relatives lived. Some were not Christians. His sister

Dorothy, a banker, and his brother Frank lived in the old home place. There was a huge swimming pool that our girls loved, as did I. Mr. Baker took particular pains to prepare the cottage for our comfort. Several of our Ivy Memorial people came, visited, and shared with us. The Tom Morrises and Dick Burkses brought and prepared delicious steaks. These two men were experienced cooks, and their wives thoroughly enjoyed such occasions. Dick Burks is recently deceased.

Sarah had a boyfriend, Jerry Pierpont, who had lovely parents. He came up to see her at the Baker cottage. He has never married. When we left Newport News, Sarah was brokenhearted to leave Jerry behind. Indeed, he came to visit us in Pittsburgh. When we were taking him back to the airport, we had a major auto accident in which the occupants of the car behind us just missed hitting squarely on the iron post of a street light. I was pulling into the right-hand lane when they scraped me and hit the lamp post but not solidly. They were able to scrape through. It was my fault, and my insurance paid without question because the other party was not killed or seriously injured. Jerry finally got back home but he was "shook up."

Back to the Goldmine revival experience. Mr. Baker and I visited in the home of an older lady who reached back to Civil War days. I believe she had been a member of a Presbyterian church but had never been saved until she heard the woman evangelist Kathryn Kuhlman from Pittsburgh. I later called the Kuhlman people in Pittsburgh to tell them her story, and they rejoiced. This lady opened her old trunk and gave me two original Civil War southern monetary bills with the original signatures evident. I have them in my coin collection. The Bakers were very special in our lives in Ivy Memorial. She has only recently died. He died much earlier. Both were well up in age. God bless their memory.

There was another family in Ivy Memorial who was very special in our lives, the Frank Littles. Frank was in the auto repair and tire business. He was not, and is not, a member of Ivy Memorial but is a faithful attendee with his family. He kept my car running and outfitted with adequate tires. I pray that Frank may yet make his full commitment to Christ. He has a lovely wife, Claudia, and a fine family (just today, March 11, 1997, I learned he is in the hospital). The Lee Smiths were not members of Ivy Memorial when I was pastor but joined later. He took care of my car in other ways. He made a car available for me to use in a revival in the Portsmouth area in the spring of 1982 with Dr. Lee Jones. Lee Smith died suddenly and his wife, Sarah, still survives. They had a lovely family. God has been good to give us such people in our lives in His ministry. I could name so many others.

I do wish to tell of one other very special family in Ivy Memorial, the Dr. Antonio Martinez family, who came out of communist Cuba to live their latter years among their Virginia relatives, in the joy of the Lord. Dr. Martinez came originally from Spain where in some civil upheaval, he and eleven other men fled to a cave. They were apprehended and were brought out of the cave to be shot. The captain of the military group asked them how many of them were in that cave. Dr. Martinez, the spokesman, said, "Captain, there were thirteen of us." The captain counted and there were only twelve. He said to Antonio, "I count only twelve." "But there were thirteen of us in that cave." "Well, where is number thirteen. Who is he?" "It was our Lord Jesus, captain. He was with us in that cave, and we were having fellowship with Him." The military captain was so upset that he dismissed the whole group, and they lived for another day. Antonio later married Teresa, the daughter of Don Carlos, renowned cattle and horse plantation owner in Cuba. During a financial disaster in pre-communist Cuba, the banks were closing. Don Carlos, who had become wealthy selling mules to the United States Army, rode on his white horse to the bank. He went in, laid his big pearl-handled revolver on the counter, and said, "I want my money. Just my money. I must have it for the operation of my business." He left with his money and a subsequent notable reputation.

Antonio Martinez was later a schoolteacher in Cuba and had as one of his pupils the beautiful, shy Teresa. He studied how to meet her and finally decided to do so in a scholarly context. He engaged her in conversation, and over time, they fell in love, and he asked for her hand in marriage. Her father, impressed with young Antonio, saw in him the best and gave his permission. They lived to have a large family of five offspring.

Antonio was ambitious and wanted to be a doctor. He enrolled in the Medical College in Havana and did well in all his subjects. Somehow, his main professor did not like him and purposed to fail him. The day came for a final examination to that end. He asked Antonio a question about a subject he had never discussed in class. The other students knew of the professor's diabolical dislike for Antonio—probably because of jealousy. To the professor's amazement, Antonio answered the question. The professor said, "How did you know about it? We never discussed it in class." Antonio politely replied, "You did mention a book about him once, and I bought and read that book." The professor had to pass him, reluctantly, to the bitter resentment of the other students. Antonio Martinez not only became an excellent physician but also one of the best-known preachers in Cuba to stir the hearts of youth. As a doctor, he was known as the physician who prayed for his patients. He had bought a new Chevy automobile and hesitated to take it out into the backcountry. The roads were poor and slushy in the rainy weather. He was called one day to visit a family in the back area that he had visited several times. He went resentfully. When he came into the room, he noticed bottles of his earlier prescribed medicines on the shelves. They were still unopened and he asked why. They said, "We bought the medicine but when you prayed for us, we got well without the medicine and didn't need it."

Fidel Castro came to power, and all non-communists were in trouble. Dr. Martinez had a beautiful home on Veradero Beach where you could see down seventy-five feet into the beautiful water off the white, sandy beach. This description came from Glenroy Belvin, a deacon in Ivy Memorial, who married Maria, one of Martinez's lovely daughters. The communists were taking over all such property for their own emissaries. Those who used the old Cuban money were executed. Dr. Martinez had seventy-five thousand dollars of this money in the walls of his home. He secretly burned it at night. They wanted to get out of this communist debacle and go to the mainland United States to be with their children who were already there. People never knew, even one hour ahead of time, when or if they could leave. One such day, they received word late in the evening that they could go. They could take two paper bags of clothes. He had to leave the keys in his car, leave everything in the house, and get to Havana which was fifty miles away, to get on the Red Cross ship. It turned out that the wife of the communist cadre had been in one of Dr. Martinez' Bible classes. He was able to persuade a friend to drive them to Havana. His younger daughter, Lydia, had a prosperous dress shop that she had to leave behind. They felt ill but were able to drink a glass of milk. When they got to Havana, they had to wait in line with some seven hundred others, standing several hours in the hot, Cuban sun. People were collapsing all around them and being cursed and spit at by their communist adversaries. Finally, they were able to get on the Red Cross ship. Dr. Martinez and his family later came to Newport News where he ministered as a doctor in the laboratory of the new Dixie Hospital. One Fourth of July weekend, he was working in the hospital lab. He had not been feeling well and noticed that his fingernails were white, not a normal pink. He diagnosed his own illness—acute leukemia. With treatment, there was some intermittent improvement but also a relentless onward progression of the disease with intense periods of suffering.

I wrote this story from careful research for publication by our Home Mission Board. The book editor felt it should be more embellished—a more personal love story. I did not pursue it. In my interest in writing the story, I visited him in his last days. I asked him how he really felt when they were leaving

Havana harbor the last time at the end of the day with the setting sun and blinking harbor lights. I was thinking he would tell me about his deep sadness. Instead, with a flash of his tired eyes, he said, "I tell you, Jolly, it was a taste of Glory." He died shortly after that, and we have stayed in touch with his dear family. In Newport News, he became known as "the Angel of Newport News" from Revelation. The enlarging Spanish population looked to him above all for spiritual guidance in their new country. His best job in declining days was this essential ministry of the Lord to the many lonely, lovely Spanish people in the area. This was mission work of the highest caliber. Teresa died suddenly in 1993 just after we had been back to Ivy Memorial for our fiftieth wedding anniversary. We were visiting with their daughter, Maria, and husband, Glenroy Belvin, when they received a call that Teresa had been taken to the hospital. We received a call the next day in Roanoke telling us of her passing and joining her beloved Antonio for the "fullness of Glory."

[A note from Dorothy]: I recall so well the night Dr. Martinez gave his personal testimony before our Sunday evening audience at Ivy Memorial. He was so very personable and spoke with unique animation. He recounted their coming to Miami and knew they had precious little money to spend before getting settled. They were hungry and planned to go to a cafeteria for their very first meal. He kindly cautioned Mrs. Martinez and Lydia to be unusually selective and to choose only one thing to eat. All caution blew to the winds when they went through the lines and Dr. Martinez told them to get anything their hearts desired. It all looked so tempting and so good. Another incident I'm aware of was during a prayer time at the church when the women were meeting during the Week of Prayer for Foreign Missions. This was some little time before the family was able to come to the states. Maria was in tears when she came in to the meeting to ask the women present to share with her the concern she had for her family in Cuba. They had so little to eat. We all had just recently enjoyed an abundant Thanksgiving, and Maria said her parents only had one small chicken. [Charles: God answered their prayers as per my writings].

One very dear and special lady at our Ivy Memorial Church who was on the original pulpit committee was Ruth Sims. We had dinner in her home on our first visit to Ivy Memorial. She was a gracious, charming lady whose life in the Ivy Church reached all the way back. Her first husband, Parris Aiken, had been killed in their home during a lightning and thunderstorm. They had some little chickens in those days that he had just brought in out of the storm. They had electricity and an old light hanging down from the ceiling. A bolt of lightning

The Jolly Family just before moving to Pittsburgh in October 1964. Left to right are: Sarah, Buddy, Charles (holding Becky), Dorothy, Marti, and Mary.

came in through the non-grounded light and killed him instantly. Later she married Mr. Sims who was in the ice and coal business with his horse and wagon. Ruth later built this into a good solid business, and we were privileged to be among her customers with our oil furnace needs. Her son, Parris Aiken Jr., lived almost as long as his mother, to lovingly look after and care for her. She had other children by her second husband, and most of them were faithful members of Ivy Memorial. She told us of early days in Ivy when close by there was a shallow pond area which iced over in the wintertime and the fun the young people had in ice skating. She showed us pictures of this era. Ruth was a beautiful young woman back then. She went with us on two trips overseas and was a great traveling companion who kept the balance. She was an older woman then.

I have referred to our original correspondence with the Pittsburgh Baptist Church when we left on the train for Dorothy's mother's funeral. I did not hear from them for a long time and we prayed about it. We had a keen interest in what was then called pioneer missions in Southern Baptist life in the great cities of the North. I wrote the people stating our interest. We had been to Mississippi and Dorothy's father had, in effect, given us his former Amory, Mississippi, home.

We let him collect the rent for two years, and we made the $175 monthly payments on the home for the two years. We had happily closed on this arrangement and were driving back to Virginia. We stopped over in Memphis to spend the night with my sister, Joanne, and her husband, Jimmy Lantrip. The next morning we received a telephone call from Mr. Ben Tatterson, associate chairman of the Pittsburgh pulpit committee. He had been with the original group who had visited us in Ivy Memorial on a Sunday in October of 1963. Others on the committee were John Holder and Carolyn Hendricks. Mr. Tatterson said they wanted me to come to Pittsburgh in view of a call to their church. We changed our plans, drove via Roanoke up the valley into Pennsylvania, and there was God's place for us for the next unusual four and one half years of blessed mission experience.

I recall a final meeting in the Peninsula area of Virginia in West Hampton Baptist Church. Our friend Joe Flowers was the pastor. God put in my heart that our place was not in large settled churches like that, itself a former mission church. Our place was to start new churches in the great cities, hopefully to become more, in size, like that church and reaching new people for our Lord—which is still our goal.

9

Pittsburgh, Pennsylvania

1964–1969

W e left Newport News, Virginia, on a rainy first day of October to drive to our new home in Pittsburgh, Pennsylvania. The girls were sad to leave old friends behind, but there was wonderment about the future. Rebecca, one week past her first birthday, was in her convenient carryall. As one last touch of old Virginia, we drove through Fredericksburg. We went out of our way to visit Guinea Station and the house where Stonewall Jackson died. Many believe that had he lived, we would have had a new nation dominated by "Southern Rights." That old Stonewall might even have been president. Jackson's last words when told that he was dying of pneumonia were, "As God wills," and God willed the future otherwise for our nation.

We drove up the valley of Virginia to the Winchester area to Shenandoah College to pay a last visit to one of our talented young women, Brenda Dansey, a first year student in music. She is the only daughter of Harry and Dorothy (Dot) Dansey, one of the first families we really got to know in Ivy Memorial Baptist Church. Their only son, David, had been hit in the head with a baseball bat and seriously injured. In visiting David with his father that first Sunday afternoon, I met several of our Ivy families with special needs. David recovered. He is now married and has a fine family. Brenda married David Brown from one of our other Ivy families and is the minister of music in one of our Richmond, Virginia, churches. We have been close to Harry and Dot across these years and to her single brother, Garland Latham, who lives with Dot.

We continued up the valley to the Pennsylvania Turnpike where we stopped for dinner. Becky was resting more comfortably than all of us as I took her in and placed her down at our feet. Following dinner, we drove to the home of the Jim Robbs who were so prominent in all our new areas of Southern Baptist work. He was from the little town of Neon, Kentucky. Jim, along with his wife, Pauline, and son, James Jr., and daughter, Patricia, was most influential in our New York, Pennsylvania, and Ohio work. Jim was an executive of the Koppers Company headquartered in Pittsburgh. It so happens that my last official visit in Pittsburgh before going to New Jersey/New York was with the Robbs. Pauline was in the Woman's Magee Hospital. They took us out to an Italian restaurant for a delicious spaghetti dinner before we left, and Jim took me to our first Ohio Baptist Convention in the very month we came to Pittsburgh.

I recall how small everything seemed to be compared to our Virginia Baptist meetings. I thought this state convention was more like one of our Virginia association meetings. Later I was to drive many miles back and forth from Pittsburgh to Columbus, for various state meetings. The Baptist Convention of Ohio headquarters are located in Columbus, and our dear friend, Ray Roberts, was the executive secretary. Until the Pennsylvania/South Jersey Convention was organized later, all of our western Pennsylvania work related to the Ohio convention.

I had been in the Kentucky Baptist Convention in Bowling Green when our Kentucky Baptist Convention voted to sponsor the Ohio work then located in the Dayton area (1952). Ray Roberts came from First Baptist Church of Danville, Kentucky, to lead the new work in Ohio. He was later one of three men considered for the position of executive director of our Home Mission Board when Arthur Rutledge was the one chosen.

I served on the Finance Committee of the state convention and later as the first vice-president in 1968. I was nominated for president but deferred by nominating the incumbent president who later served as pastor of our North Park Baptist Church in Pittsburgh. All of these relationships were a vital part of my own developing missions and new work concepts and areas of convention life as they related to our Home Mission Board and Southern Baptist Convention.

I took our youth to an Ohio and Pennsylvania Training Union State Convention meeting, and Sarah Pat placed second in an oratorical contest (I thought she should have been first). On our return trip to Pittsburgh, we were hurtling down the freeway when a large white Poland China hog lumbered across the road. I could not avoid hitting it—hard. I recalled my father saying that hogs did not budge easily. We killed the hog and stopped to tell the owners who were able to butcher it and to thank us for stopping. My front bumper stayed crooked until we found the money to repair it. The carload of girls was all excited because of this incident.

Well, back to our arrival in Pittsburgh at the Jim Robb home, not far from the Pittsburgh Baptist Church where we were to spend the next four and one half years of ministry in our Lord's great work. The Robb home was an old home beautifully situated in a row-housing complex with an upstairs and downstairs. We were to be upstairs. The garage and entrance way from the alley were to the back.

There was a steep hill (Pioneer Avenue) down to the main highway that led into the tunnel and the gorgeous sight of the city of Pittsburgh. Pittsburgh was historic from the time of the French and Indian Wars and the ascent of George Washington as a military leader, replacing English General Braddock who was killed in a battle close by. Braddock's body was buried in the much-traveled military wagon trail so the Indians would not know of his death. George Washington, Braddock's aide-de-camp, took over, and history was made before his military, civic, and home life ended. Up over the beautiful city of Pittsburgh is Mt. Washington, named for General Washington who called it one of the most beautiful sights he had ever seen. Fort Pitt, named for the English prime minister, was at the confluence of the Allegheny and Monongahela Rivers that formed the Ohio River.

Pittsburgh has developed from those early days to a great industrial city based on coal and steel. It was a virtual British-style ghost city due to pollution from the steel mills until more recent years. It is one of the great stories of cleaning up the environment. All around there were other cities related to the same industry, and many today are virtually ghost towns.

Andrew Carnegie, the great steel magnate of Scottish descent, was a typical example of the first builders of America. Back then, he was the wealthiest man in America. His greatest legacy perhaps was a free public library in every city in the United States with access for all who wished to read and learn.

The Pittsburgh Baptist Church is located on Pioneer Avenue at the edge of Dormont and in the Borough of Dormont. It was formerly a Lutheran Church building that Southern Baptists, new people on the block, were able to buy when the Lutherans moved to another area and built anew. The old building and property, still strategically located, is well built and has been changed and renovated to suit our Baptist needs. A new educational building was constructed. It has grown tremendously under Pastor Danny Crow, a graduate of Mid-America Baptist Theological Seminary in Memphis, Tennessee. Baptists are not new to the area of south Pittsburgh as we learned later from a street called Baptist Road which dates from the earliest Baptist presence and influence.

We had an excellent real-estate man and his family in our Pittsburgh Baptist Church, Amos Hughes, with his wife, Jo Ann, and their lovely children. Amos helped us to purchase a home at 1410 Bower Hill Road, Mt. Lebanon, for nineteen thousand dollars. We needed one thousand dollars for a down payment, an amount hard to come by in those days before rampant inflation. Because of Dorothy's father's generous help to us, we had the money. The Pittsburgh Baptist Church paid us $1,150 per month with $175 per month allowed for house payment. Because of this housing allowance, we owned a beautiful one-acre plot which ran downhill in back to a lovely creek area. We were fifteen miles from the Greater Pittsburgh Airport looking toward the mountains. Our neighbors had neat yards with shrubs and trees situated next to us. The overall effect was a beautiful park-like area ideally suited for a young family like ours, and believe me, we made the most of it. In wintertime when the snows were deep, there was the perfect miniature ski area, and we often had company to use it. St. Clair Hospital was close by. Sarah later worked there as a candy striper the summer after her senior year at Mt. Lebanon and between her freshman and sophomore years at Bluefield Baptist Junior College in Bluefield, Virginia. The Mt. Lebanon High School was listed as one of the ten best in the nation. Other schools around were in the same category. Our two older girls were to graduate from Mt. Lebanon High, and our other children were in excellent grade schools. How blessed we were.

It so happened that when we left Pittsburgh we rented out that house through the auspices of Amos Hughes and his real estate firm. The rental payments always paid the monthly payments and real estate fee. The house was renovated through the generosity of our excellent builder friend Wade Olsen, a member of our church who has visited us here in the Northwest. His lovely second wife, Dorothy, had died and Wade had married again. For $1,800, he renovated and repaired the home. On the day our Rebecca married, August 10, 1984, the home sold and netted us some sixty thousand dollars. We paid some accumulated debts and invested the remaining amount. This invested money has helped us to save the homes of two of our girls and has helped the others at various times of need, with loans against the principal. It has also helped us in the enlargement of the capacity of our present home. On a later celebration occasion in Pittsburgh Church, I remarked that even though the church actually paid us less than other churches, in the long run, they had helped us more by enabling us to own our home. The only real help for most people is the equity in a home made possible by government exemption.

The Pittsburgh Baptist Church was the strategic base church for all our Southern Baptist work in the developing Pennsylvania and South Jersey Baptist

Convention. The key leader of this developing work was Joe Waltz, a former pastor in the Fairborne Baptist Church in Ohio, where he worked closely with Dr. Ray Roberts. After Joe Waltz, Dr. Charles Stanley was the pastor and is now the longtime pastor of First Baptist Church of Atlanta, Georgia. I had never known Joe Waltz, but anybody so well thought of by my special friend, Ray Roberts, had to be somebody. Joe Waltz met me at the Greater Pittsburgh Airport when I first came to Pittsburgh. I picked him out of a multitude of people thronging through that airport that day. He had that restless aggressive personality and searching eyes. On the way into Pittsburgh, he filled me in and answered a thousand questions. The Waltz family was still in our Pittsburgh Church, and we became dear friends and coworkers. There was wife, Jane, older son, Marvin, older daughter, Carol, younger son, David, and younger daughter, Lynn. This younger daughter had been used to her father as the preacher/pastor. Every Sunday as he came out of the pulpit, while the people's heads were bowed, he and Lynn had a special greeting episode. Lynn was to miss that when we came with her father out and about in various mission endeavors. We were often invited to their home for lovely meals, cookouts with Joe as the cook. We got to know Jane's father from Floyd Knob, Kentucky, where later our future son-in-law Jim Ragains's father, Lowell Ragains, was the pastor.

When David was about twelve, he rode with Dorothy and me to some associational youth event. He told us that he felt God calling him into full-time ministry. Later, in New Jersey, we visited Princeton University with Joe and Jane when they were planning with David to attend that prestigious school. David went there and later graduated from Southern Baptist Theological Seminary in Louisville, Kentucky. He has since married, had his family, and today is the executive director of the Pennsylvania/South Jersey Baptist Convention where his father had been the first executive director. Joe Waltz had served only a short time when he died suddenly of a heart attack on a deer hunt in the Bedford, Pennsylvania, mountain area. Joe was on a deer stand with his gun in the crook of his arm. He fell in that position.

He and Jane came through Madison, New Jersey, on their way to their first trip to Israel and preached for us. They were on a bus tour in the dangerous Hebron area when their tour bus was attacked. Thirteen shots were fired. The last shot hit the bus but did not penetrate seat number thirteen where Joe and Jane were riding. One woman died who had been sitting in the front. The laws of Israel required, in such circumstances, that one should be buried in Israel, sealed in a simple wooden box. If they were an Israelite, the bottom of the casket was removed so the body could mingle more easily with sacred Jewish soil.

Therefore, this woman's body was placed in a wooden casket. Joe and Jane agreed that if and when one of them might go, they would like such a simple casket. When Joe died, Jane tried to fulfill this wish. She found it very difficult and much more expensive to carry out. We attended Joe's funeral and saw the casket. We even stayed for the sealing of the grave there in the Harrisburg/Hershey, Pennsylvania, area. Our new state convention offices were there and are located now in Hershey where you can smell the odor of Hershey chocolate. Dorothy and I went to the Waltz home following the funeral, and Dorothy had a severe asthma attack from the little dog, beloved of the Waltz family especially at that time. We had to leave hurriedly and apologetically.

I had come from Madison to an evangelistic week at Harrisburg when Joe was still alive and only recently appointed as full-time executive director. I noticed he looked very puffy. He, too, had trouble with asthma. Joe and I had worked so closely in planning the emerging Pennsylvania/South Jersey Baptist Convention, even to the name, in our motel room during state fellowship meetings. The Pennsylvania/South Jersey Convention related to two state sponsoring groups, Ohio and Maryland. I had related to both.

The Maryland convention, east coast, was much like the Virginia convention relative to baptism. If one had been baptized, by immersion, as a believer, he or she would be accepted in Maryland churches upon examination and approved. I had wrestled with this coming from Kentucky to Virginia. Kentucky related to and sponsored the Baptist Convention of Ohio. I came to feel that the Virginia/Maryland position was more honest even than the Landmark view from which I had come. If a person who came forward at the invitation time said, "I am Southern Baptist, et cetera," he or she would be accepted and approved without question. Very little effort would be expended to determine if such person had really been saved prior to baptism. In the Virginia/Maryland manner, every person was examined about his or her personal salvation. If saved before their baptism, always by immersion, of course, then their baptism was acceptable. As president of our emerging Pennsylvania/South Jersey Fellowship into a new state convention, I had asked that we have this issue discussed fully with both views presented and followed by debate as to what our new state convention constitution would say on the issue. We had a thorough presentation of both sides and a subsequent long debate. Wendell Belew, from our Home Mission Board and a longtime friend from Kentucky days, was present on the occasion. In the time of final decision, I stated that we could not, and should not, let our differences on this issue become a test of fellowship. Wendell stood and said, "This cannot be a test of fellowship in the new state convention." Each church, of course, would decide its own position. That was the last word on the issue in the new constitution. It was a great experience to work with Ohio and Maryland leadership in the formation of this new convention which today has some three hundred churches all across Pennsylvania and South Jersey.

I must say a word about the original Ohio sponsor of our Pittsburgh Baptist Church. In Pineville, Kentucky, at the Clear Creek Mountain Preacher's School, we knew Paul Nevils. He was a fine young man involved in our mission program in the mountains. Paul later moved to the Ohio area and became pastor of the Wierton, West Virginia, First Baptist Church. When the call came for work to begin in the Pittsburgh area in the early 1950s, Paul's church in Wierton, under his leadership, became the sponsoring church for our new Pittsburgh work. I would later meet with the Clear Creek Fellowship group at their request during the Ohio Baptist Convention. Later, my brother, Fred Jolly, served as pastor of that Wierton Baptist Church just before his retirement in September of 1992. "What goes around, comes around."

The Pittsburgh Baptist Church continued to be the sponsoring church for various missions during our four and a half years of ministry. A growing internal struggle came about over the sponsorship of missions in our Pittsburgh Baptist Church fellowship especially among those influenced by the Ben Tatterson family who had come from the First Baptist Church of Mt. Lebanon, an American Baptist church. The Tatterson family felt that the Mt. Lebanon church was not mission-minded enough. They came into the Pittsburgh Baptist Church (SBC) with some apparent consuming desire to outshine the larger Mt. Lebanon church.

In a fellowship meeting back in Newport News in the home of our good friends, the Joe Flowers, he received a telephone call from his pastor friend in the Mt. Lebanon Baptist Church in Pittsburgh. The pastor was a former Southern Baptist and a good personal friend of Joe's. The pastor's wife had died with a sad consequence. Their retarded son, who depended so much on his mother, took his own life out of his anguish and distress. The pastor, of course, was devastated. I could feel for our own handicapped son and how very much he depended on his mother, and does still, even to this day. We were all sad at Joe Flowers's sorrow and prayed for the family in Pennsylvania. When I got to Pittsburgh, I got acquainted with the Mt. Lebanon Baptist Church out of that sad happening. It has remained a great church.

Ben Tatterson was the men's Bible class teacher and had a great influence. Many of the men who came through his class were influenced to think in Ben's way. There came an estrangement and many temper tantrums, by Mrs. Tatterson especially. Mrs. Tatterson came from a pioneer family reaching back to the French and Indian days. She shared an historical family document with me. It was about her great-grandmother and a baby girl who had been captured by marauding Indians. The men had been killed. The Indians, not wishing the hindrance of this baby, took the baby from the arms of the mother and dashed the child's head against a rock killing her instantly. The great-grandmother had written, "The last sight of my darling baby was her little legs quivering from the death struggle." She subdued her grief and lived to escape, marry again, and here was Clerissa Tatterson to share the sad story with me. Later, the Tattersons grew bitter and left our church and their responsible jobs in it. They particularly resented the Jim Robbs, so positively involved in our total mission work. Ben and Clerissa are both gone now, and their two Tatterson sons have done well in Texas. I later met one of Ben's nephews and his family in our Annapolis church on an anniversary occasion. They were solid supporters in that church and freely talked and shared about Uncle Ben.

There was a young Christian in Ben's class, Fred Bissert, who was from a Lutheran background. His Catholic wife was a daughter of a doctor and a nurse herself. She had cancer and I was often in their home to visit, especially at Christmastime. I would visit and sing Christmas carols with the family and read the Christmas story. The mother was proud of her family and would lovingly and appreciatively join in. She died after we left, and Fred has married again. I believe all of his family is involved in the Pittsburgh Baptist Church. They have all done well with their father's support and positive leadership. Fred became, and still is, the men's Bible class teacher. Fred in every way has been an encourager in the work.

We had a great group of people to work with in the Pittsburgh Church. We worked out a way to install a beautiful baptistry, renovated an old garage building that became the children's Sunday School space, and did other renovations. Under Pastor Danny Crow there is a new educational building, and plans call for further expansion. Many of those we knew as younger families have been faithful, their children faithful, and have grown up to have families of their own. A number of them are still in the Pittsburgh Church.

We had excellent revivals/visitation under Dr. Ray Roberts; Reverend Carrol Chapman, Dr. Winston Crawley, associate executive secretary of our Foreign Mission Board; and Dr. Jack Wilder, pastor friend from the Newport News area and grower and builder of the great Liberty Baptist Church in Hampton, Virginia. This church had grown from a much smaller church in a still developing area under Pastor Jessie King who had died in the pulpit after we left. He became part of the inspiration for the growth and development under Pastor Wilder. We also had Dr. F. Crossley Morgan for Bible studies, and he did his usual wonderful job of teaching. We ran into a snag though, because he was not Southern Baptist. Two of our men, Steve Marmion, single, and "Chubby" Eubanks, our Sunday School director, made a case of offense against me. We had befriended Steve, sick of stomach ulcer, and took him into our home. These men were adamant in their criticism and caused some negative reaction in the church. We also had Bill Harbin from Maryville, Tennessee, and the pastor of our friend from Clear Creek days, Mrs. T. D. Brown. We had such lovely fellowship with her and Dr. T. D. Brown, professor of New Testament at Clear Creek Mountain Preacher's School. Their only son, Tom Jr., later became pastor of First Baptist Church of Harlan, Kentucky, some thirty miles from Pineville. These men (professors like Dr. Brown) were retired and gave their latter days to this vital teaching ministry.

One of our first missions involved the area of the Greater Pittsburgh Airport and West Heights. We started in the home of some fine people from Oklahoma who had come for twenty miles or so into our Pittsburgh Church. The work enlarged to the extent that we used the facility of the West Heights Grade School in Moon Township. I would drive out early on Sunday morning for worship services at 9:00 A.M. with Sunday School following, then drive back to our Pittsburgh Church in time for our worship service.

For a considerable time, I did the same on Sunday evenings in a mission that became our South Park Baptist Church. Worship service began at 6:00 P.M. with Training Union following. We went back to our worship service in Pittsburgh at 7:00 P.M. It was a hectic schedule for me, but I was young and "sold out" to mission starting. On the last Sunday before we left Pittsburgh for Madison, New Jersey, we had the dedication service for a new building in South Park on land given by an auto dealer friend to our associational director of missions, Joe Waltz. The special speaker for that occasion was Dr. Leonard Stigler whom we had known from Portland, Tennessee, days. Dr. Stigler had also been the pastor for the Joe Hunt family in Oklahoma. He later came to Madison for a revival and stayed in the Hunt home. Dr. Stigler was the state director of evangelism for the Baptist Convention of Ohio and thus related to all of our Pennsylvania/South Jersey work at the time of the dedication of the South Park building. This building now houses the associational headquarters for our Greater Pittsburgh Baptist Association.

An interesting side note: While my brother Fred was strategically involved in our Greater Pittsburgh Association mission/church starting program, he had invited Dr. Jim Henry and his family to visit in prospect of a call as pastor to the South Park Baptist Church. The church concluded he was not the man for them.

Since that time, Dr. Jim Henry has gone on to pastor the great Two Rivers Baptist Church in Nashville, Tennessee, and from there to pastor the great First Baptist Church of Orlando, Florida, and has just retired as the very able and effective president of our Southern Baptist Convention. He and his family have remained very close friends with Fred. Fred helped to start the Two Rivers Baptist Church, was its first pastor, and led in building the first unit building which still stands on the strategic Two Rivers land area facing the world famous Grand Ole Opry facility. The interim pastor of Two Rivers before Fred Jolly came, and who was actually instrumental in Fred's coming, was Dorothy's brother, Bob Patterson. He was with the Sunday School Board and later served as associate director and finally director of the Sunday School for the Tennessee Baptist Convention. Many of the Sunday School Board members were strategic in starting the Two Rivers Church. What a marvelous story of Southern Baptist mission church starting.

Now to the story of how Fred Jolly came to the Greater Pittsburgh area. Fred entered Mississippi College after his years in the Navy and then taught school and coached football in Port Gibson, Mississippi. It was there that he felt the call to the ministry. He graduated from the New Orleans Baptist Theological Seminary. He experienced some difficulties in the Two Rivers Church. He resigned and moved with his family back to New Orleans Seminary to get his master's degree in religious education. Upon finishing his degree work, he was invited to visit a new church start area in Ohio. I was in revival with my father in his rural church near Grenada, Mississippi, when Fred called my father to tell him about going to Ohio. I picked up the phone to listen in. When a break came in the conversation, I told Fred we had a ripe situation right in our Greater Pittsburgh Airport area. I sked, "How about stopping by to visit us on your way to Ohio and take a look-see at our situation?" Fred never got to Ohio. He anchored his life and ministry in the area mentioned, helped our mission there to build a new church building, and started some fourteen new churches before his ministry concluded at Weirton, West Virginia, Baptist Church. The same church had originally sponsored our Pittsburgh Baptist Church. It was one of our greatest sources of joy to work together as brothers in the Greater Pittsburgh Baptist Association. Among other things, I was moderator of the association for two years. In that time, we started a number of new churches with our Pittsburgh church as the sponsor and helped to lay the groundwork for our Pennsylvania/South Jersey Baptist Convention.

I recall the special joy of helping to enroll Fred and Maxine's children in the Moon Township school system. All five of them did well in school and later all finished college. Johnny got his doctorate in psychology and is professor of psychology in our mentor college, Mississippi Baptist College in Clinton, Mississippi. He is also on the curriculum advisory council. Harry, the oldest, worked in Pittsburgh for a steel company and is now vice-president of a steel company in Dallas, Texas. Jimmy teaches art in high school in Philadelphia, Pennsylvania. He is also one of our family and his mother's family historians. The two girls, both college graduates, Lillian Ann and Ladye, are married and live with their families in Texas. Maxine has worked all these years as a nurse to help the family finances. Fred and Maxine are now back home in Okolona, Mississippi, where they have worked relentlessly to beautify and keep up the family home place. One of our neighbors there has remarked that the place looks like a beautiful golf course. They have done this work with the help of all of our family, especially the Mary Frances and Joe Kelley Stewart family in Olive Branch, Mississippi. God has blessed the Stewarts with a great business in that area, and they have generously helped Fred and family to beautify the home place. The other members of our family have been equally involved in carrying out the initial agreement to restore the home place in a beautiful fashion. They are, namely: LaVerne and Bob Webber, Joanne and Darold Hebert, Marguerite Hammett, and Donald Jolly. Families of each of these have contributed hard work as time has allowed.

We are all so scattered. This farm has been a unifying force in our hearts as we, far away, ponder and treasure in our hearts and minds all the happenings of our lives. Ten children and their family members, some sixty or so, have nurtured and sustained the Joe and Estelle Freeman Jolly homestead since World War I days. All of us were born there or close by and all at home. Our parents bade us goodbye, then welcomed us home. It was the place of comfort when death took our youngest sister at twenty-three and our mother at forty-nine and little brother, John Merrill, at thirteen after four years of being ravaged by Hodgkins disease.

Older brother Joe left us in 1993. He was a lieutenant colonel in the Air Force. His wife, Toni, married Ed Stone after Joe's death, and they live in a retirement home in Austin, Texas. Joe is buried close by. Joe's oldest daughter by a previous marriage, Martha Sue, lives with her husband, John Chris Stephenson, and family in Ruston, Louisiana. Oldest son, Larry, is in the graphic arts business in Austin, Texas. Lilly and husband, Ralph, a pastor, and children are in Florida. Frank and Vickie, a nurse, and family are in Austin, as is Tim, a very special son.

Our sister, Marguerite, and family live in California where she and husband, Hubert Hammett, deceased June 17, 1993, served California Southern Baptist churches (and elsewhere before that in Southern Baptist churches for more than thirty-five years.) Hubert Hammett never earned more than four hundred dollars per month in those struggling churches. Marguerite also worked outside the home to help pay the bills and sustain their family. A still-unknown assailant cruelly and brutally murdered one daughter, Fontayne, in 1979. She left small children behind.

Our oldest sister, Laverne Webber, and husband, Bob, live in the Jackson, Mississippi, area where she still works and Bob plies his artistic skills. One son is a doctor, another is a lawyer, and another is with the telephone company in Atlanta. Daughter Susan is a capable art teacher and lives with her family in Lake Charles, Louisiana.

My sister Mary Frances and her husband, Joe Kelley Stewart, live in Olive Branch, Mississippi. Joe Kelley has a very prosperous auto body-shop business in Memphis, Tennessee. They have a family of four children and "grands." They belong to Longview Heights Church in Olive Branch now, the same church where we were married in 1943, when it was in Memphis.

Our youngest brother, Don, lives in Birmingham, Alabama, and his children are scattered. Their mother, Zi, has been a special source of strength to their family.

Sister Joanne and husband, Darold, live in Walls, Mississippi, with their large family of children and grandchildren and are a blessing indeed, especially in the Lord's work and His churches.

Youngest sister Yvonne's two girls, Melissa and Ann, live with their families in the Fayetteville, Arkansas, area and stay in touch with others in our large family. Yvonne died at age twenty-three, leaving them as little children.

I am thankful and proud of all our large family. Sometime ago at homecoming in our Okolona Baptist home church, I remarked that if the years of service of the preacher members of our family were totaled, it would be some five hundred years of Southern Baptist ministry aside from an almost equal time of loyal service from other members of our family. When Dorothy's family is added, it would again be an equal amount of time in our Lord's work. Indeed, Brother and Mrs. R. B. Patterson Sr. were the basic inspiration in all of our lives. One can see that influence for God and good in all of the above mentioned family members. What a story of Southern Baptist missions, by the grace of God. All glory goes to His dear name!

Sarah and Mary both finished high school in Mt. Lebanon High School in Pittsburgh. Martha Ruth attended school at the Thomas Jefferson Junior High School, and Charles Jr. attended the Hoover Elementary School. He repeated the first grade at the suggestion of the child study team. At the end of that second year, we had him evaluated by Dr. Irvin Chamovitz, who gave us the sad news that he was developmentally disabled and had epilepsy. He was put on Dilantin to control the latter. The Jewish doctor told us that if Charles's brain were examined, it would be no different from anyone else's. He lacked proper development in the left frontal lobe of his brain that prevented his being able to learn academically. He was placed in a special education school, one of several such schools in the Pittsburgh area. In this setting, he progressed with those with whom he was able to compete on an equal plane. He actually had his first grand mal seizure on vacation at a Holiday Inn after a long day of activity at Disney World which was followed by a good swim. This seizure was very frightening to us. He seriously bit my finger which I had thrust into his mouth to prevent him from swallowing his tongue. He was rushed by taxi to the hospital emergency room and was able to act normally by the time he got there. He threatened to have seizures several times thereafter, but I developed the procedure of sitting beside him, holding his hand, and talking with him. He would call me, often at night, when he felt such a seizure eminent. In recent years, he has rarely ever had such seizures because of proper dilantin control. He went through special school training wherever we were living and has been earning money since he was fourteen years of age—first, at the Hunterdon Occupational School in Flemington, New Jersey, and then at Goodwill in Hawaii, at nineteen, and later in Tacoma, Washington, with Goodwill, the two best such Goodwill Industries in the nation. God blessed us immeasurably in all our children.

When Sarah and Mary finished Mt. Lebanon High School, Dorothy's father was able to be present for both occasions of special joy. In the fall of 1966, Sarah went to Bluefield Baptist College in Bluefield, Virginia, facing a beautiful Blue Ridge Mountain scene. On her first day there, she met Don Reid who took her trunk to her assigned room. He later became her husband. She worked while Don was in Southern Baptist Seminary, and then he insisted she finish her college work at Virginia Tech, one of the nation's top schools. She graduated first in education and twelfth in the whole school. What a thrilling day with special Virginia friends to witness her outdoor graduation on a beautiful day. I shall never forget my forlorn feeling when we left Sarah at Bluefield College, and drove back to the Roanoke area where we spent the night with our very dear friends, Clarence and Dot Blevins. I sat there looking at the sunset over the Blue Ridge, with Sarah on the other side, and the strong feeling that I would like to go get her. Time heals and helps in this parenting business, and we are thankful. Sarah hopes ultimately to get her doctor's degree in special education. All the girls have reacted with love and faith to their only brother's handicap.

I was invited to Bluefield College to share about our mission work in Pennsylvania and South Jersey during Religious Education Week on campus. Sarah and Don's romance had proceeded at a furious pace, and Daddy was anxious to advise, which I am sure was not too welcome. I enjoyed that special week because several of the college students there had been in some of our churches.

The day of Sarah and Don's wedding came on August 24, 1968. What a time of preparation as Mary worked furiously on wedding apparel for Sarah, herself, Martha, and Becky almost to the last minute.

The people of the Pittsburgh Baptist Church were lovingly gracious in providing space in their homes for the several members of Don's family and others. People from Newport News and Ivy Memorial Church came. Helen Morris was mistress of ceremonies for the wedding. What precious friends the Tom Morrises and their family have been across these years, along with many others of that Ivy Memorial Church. We have often been guests in their homes and more rarely, they in ours. It was stormy and rainy on the day of the wedding but cleared up just in time for the ceremony. The weather did not daunt that happy occasion. Exactly twenty-five years after he performed our wedding ceremony, Dorothy's father was present to perform Sarah's service. What a nervous day for me, walking my oldest daughter down that Pittsburgh Baptist Church aisle. The church was filled to capacity, and everyone was joyous and elated. Exactly twenty-five years later, our son-in-law, Reverend Don Reid, performed our fiftieth anniversary service in the Ivy Memorial Baptist Church in Hampton, Virginia, when those same gracious people went all out to make that occasion so very special for us. Don and Sarah got into their decorated white Karmann-Ghia, lumbered slowly away from the adoring crowd, and again I had that sort of sad parenting feeling but was glad in the Lord.

Looking toward our twenty-fifth wedding anniversary, we made our first overseas journey to visit my brother Joe and family in Frankfurt, Germany. They were due back in the states in 1968, and this was the only time we could visit them. We had German friends in our Pittsburgh Church who told us about the German Club which, if we would join for a minimal fee, would make our trip half-price. We attended and enjoyed several of their sessions before our trip. We arranged for Mrs. Austra Lucis, our church librarian, and much beloved by all, to stay with and look after our family in our absence. Her husband, Peter, was not a church member but had accepted Christ. He was deceased and I had ministered to the family at that time. They had one daughter, Ruth. Finally, all arrangements made, it was time for our departure. The Jim Robbses took us to the airport for a nighttime flight. We flew Lufthanza, a German airline. When we looked at this huge plane, we wondered how in the world this thing could fly. But it did, and how! It seemed to me that we lumbered in getting off the ground and into the air but, thank God, we made it. We flew into Rhine Mein, Frankfurt, the American gateway to Germany and Europe. Joe and family met us at the airport, and we rejoiced in the renewal of family ties. They had prepared a private little guestroom for us on the top floor of the guesthouse. It was a special place for us and we loved it. Joe and Toni used two cars for us to travel. Toni, Dorothy, the girls, and Toni's mother, Mrs. Smiley, rode in the front car. Joe, the boys, and I rode behind in the second car. We would stop along the way and enjoy family outings, lunch, and such. I remember Joe was sometimes perturbed at Toni's driving, but we made it safely to every place.

We spent a whole week at beautiful Herrin Chiemsee, the rest and recuperaton military hotel in Bavaria. We went to the Herrin Chiemsee Palace constructed by Ludwig II, called the "Mad King." He built beautiful palaces which the German people sorely complained about. Today, they are the most admired and visited tourist attractions and have more than paid for themselves. The Herrin Chiemsee Palace, on an island and reached by water, had in it the beautiful Hall of Mirrors, a replica of the famous French Hall of Mirrors at the Versailles in Paris. We thoroughly enjoyed this and visits to towns and German churches around the area.

We visited one of the ruined ancient castles above the Rhine River. It was hot walking up but a crude water fountain was available just before we started down. We drank and were refreshed. This was hard on Joe's children. As we came down, there were two elderly German women sitting on a rest bench as they came up the high hill. They were fanning and fuming. I remarked, "vasser" (water) as I pointed up there. They said, "Nein, nein, vasser, bier, bier." I realized then and all through our visit the high value of the German beer. One night, Joe, the boys, and I visited a little town across the lake. The lady asked me if I wanted "heiz Kaffee." I said, "Nein, hot coffee not ice coffee." We went on this way until Joe finally said, "Charles, heiz is hot coffee." We visited famous Salzburg in Austria and all the sights associated with the musical, "The Sound of Music." Our daughter, Mary, visited there on June 10, 1996, and so enjoyed that experience since she had been Maria in her Mt. Lebanon High School production of that play. Martha Ruth had been one of the captain's children. We went up into the ancient capital and later into the underground cemetery where persecuted Christians had stayed in catacomb-like caves.

We visited the Hitler headquarters and home area. All were in ruins from World War II. We saw the place where he wrote *Mein Kampf*. It was the General Walker Hotel, a United States military hotel in 1967. We went up, up, up the

Ober Salzburg Mountain where Hitler had built his Eagles Nest. He rarely spent time there. We saw the famous railroad that carried Hitler, his guests, and soldiers in World War II. We drove as far as we could and then rode an elevator to the top. We were able to walk up behind the famous chalet,which was located on an ice-covered promontory and saw the mountain birds still in control of the area. The Hitler chalet had been demolished. I sat with my camera at the front of the General Walker Hotel, former Nazi headquarters, cesspool of evil, aimed my camera up toward Hitler's chalet, Eagles Nest, and there was Old Glory waving between the two sights. I'm so thankful for America and the allies. Oh, what might have been, and almost was, for our world.

We visited Munich and all the famous sights associated with Germany's most beautiful city where the famous bier hall Putsh took place in 1929 and where Hitler and his brown shirts got their start. We visited Dachau where thousands of Jews were assaulted, gold teeth pulled, all belongings stashed in piles, and bodies gassed and burned in the still-standing crematoriums. We read the history, saw the actual, sad pictures, and wept as we wondered about the real horrors of that effort to elimi-nate the Jews. In all, six to twelve million died. What a tragedy for our world. We went back to Munich on a Sunday morning passing by the airfield where Britain's Prime Minister Neville Chamberlain had flown back to England with his compro-mise piece of paper disclosing, "This means peace in our time." It proved to be his downfall and Churchill's ascent. We visited the mother of our Pittsburgh Ruth Hess family. She was gracious and offered us the German alcoholic drink that we politely refused. She was perturbed. We enjoyed our visit nonetheless, and her family back in Pittsburgh was happy to hear of our visit on our return.

We went some miles on the German Autobahn at seventy miles per hour. General and President Eisenhower got his dream of our interstate highway system from the German Autobahn. We attended the National Flower Show, *Karlsrhue,* a beautiful sight with all the flowers, shrubs, and experimental plants. We enjoyed the German *Wiener schnitzel* in the open-air sidewalk area. Joe and Toni took us to beautiful, ancient Wiesbaden, a favorite tourist attraction, where after a lovely dinner, we toured the city and saw the famous opera house. Joe and I later visited the military hospital to see a patient there. It is the same hospital where all the American hostages came to from Iran at the end of President Jimmy Carter's administration. We remember that joyful occasion for all Americans.

We visited ancient Worms where Martin Luther made his stand against Roman Catholic control of religion. He nailed his ninety-five theses to the door of the Wittenburg Cathedral after being turned off by climbing the step in

Rome to kiss the Pope's ring and the tragic sale of indulgences. We saw the spot where he stood to reply in his heresy trial, "Here I stand, under God, and will not recant. God helping me I can do none other." This was the start of the Protestant Reformation.

We enjoyed cones of soft ice (German ice cream) in the hot weather. We also visited the ancient Church of the Holy Roman Empire where Charlemagne was crowned as well as others who followed him. These were special privileges for us. We also saw the ancient Roman walls. We attended church at the base chapel in the morning with Joe in charge. In the evening we attended services in the little town of Waldorf. The German/American Baptist Church was located in rented space above a German Bier Hall. There was a full house and it was a wonderful worship experience. As we left I saw an old crippled man sitting against his shack to listen to the singing. I spoke to him, expressed appreciation, and witnessed about our Lord. We visited a German Lutheran Church on Saturday afternoon. It was a nice building, well furnished, yet active only on special occasions such as religious holidays.

One other experience we had prior to leaving the Hotel at Herren Chiemsee on the second-largest lake in Germany, Lake Chiem, was to visit a shop of ancient German clocks of every description. We were in the hotel on German/American Friendship Day, July 4, 1967, and enjoyed a beautiful Tyrolian German mountain music presentation. A tent was set up outside and the German band played all day, with many consuming only tall bottles of German *bier* brought in by trucks. The next morning there was a terrible odor of the effects of that *bier*, in the restrooms especially. I realized at once why our American soldiers in World War II called the Germans "Krauts." They always said, "You can smell the Germans." Often their positions were given away by this odor of rotten cabbage. We are ever grateful that we got to see all of these unusual sights of Germany on this visit with my brother and his family.

One other impressive sight was the Black Forest. People would stop along-side the roads and go into the forest for personal rest stops. At the time we were there, the blight of the once beautiful trees was sadly in evidence. Also, most impressive was to see the German villages, homes with boxes of flowers in the windows, the red-tiled churches in the centers of the towns, surrounded by red-tiled homes. We shall never forget the unusual beauty of Germany. There will be more about Germany in our 1975 trip from New York/New Jersey with Dr. Jack Lowndes's tour of Europe.

We had planned for two more weeks to go to Paris on Bastille Day and to Basel, Switzerland. We had returned to Joe and Toni's for a break time when we received a telephone call from our sister, Mary Frances Stewart, in Memphis, Tennessee, that our father was in the Baptist Hospital in Memphis and very ill from a diabetic-related infection. All the joy of anticipation of the next two weeks was at once cancelled as we made our plans to come back to the states. His illness proved fatal.

I had been extra careful about our spending, and now I knew why. We had to get back home and didn't have enough money for a regular airline, and there was no hope of recovering a refund from the German-American Club. Joe suggested we try a military flight; maybe seats would be available. I only had my military ID as chaplain to the Civil Air Patrol from Roanoke, Virginia, days. I was a first lieutenant then. They accepted that card, and we were able to fly back to New York without mishap. We had enough money for a ticket to Pittsburgh and five dollars left over. Praise the Lord!

When we arrived at our home on Bower Hill Road, our girls, with help, had a beautiful, welcome home banner strung up and greeted us as only loving children can greet their parents. We also greeted them. Austra Lucis had done a beautiful job—bless her memory. We were prayer partners to the end of her life. When she married Harold Rikvailis, they lived in the Syracuse, New York, area. Harold, formerly from Latvia, had gotten out before the war engulfed and took over his country. He gave me thirty silver monetary pieces from Latvia which were in use prior to the war. I do not know the value of them, but treasure them highly. I shared them recently with Alex Rasmussen, our Becky's oldest child, after he earned one of my American silver dollars for memorizing Vacation Bible School Scriptures perfectly. He had started his own coin collection. We saw the Rikvailises later in Hawaii when they came on vacation bringing us a bushel of delicious, New York, Rome Beauty apples. Later, we saw them in Toronto, Canada, in 1980 at the Baptist World Alliance. We stayed in the home of Harold's Latvian friends and family—lovely, gracious people. What blessings God has given us through His people across these years.

We took our girls to see my father in the Baptist Hospital in Memphis. We stayed with my sister, Joanne, and her family. I had my slides developed from the Germany visit and was able to share some of them with my father. However, I noticed that he soon tired and fell asleep. We had hardly gotten back to Pittsburgh from Memphis when a call came, relayed to us through Deacon John Holder, that my father had died. We left the children in Pittsburgh while Dorothy and I made the trip back to Mississippi. Brother Joe had flown back to Germany, just laid his tired body down to sleep after crossing the time zones, when he got the telephone message. He then went back to Mississippi via the Memphis area military air base.

My father's body lay in state in our Mississippi home place where he and his second wife, Mrs. Effie Mae Anderson Jolly, had lived for the past seventeen years. People from all over knew my father. He had been called to preach early in life but did not acknowledge the call until early retirement from the Postal Service in 1959 because of a foot ailment that was diabetes related. He had restarted and rebuilt the old Union Baptist Church near the site where his grandfather, John Jolly, Civil War veteran, had been, among other things, the local postmaster. My father was Sunday School director when his pastor and stepson, Mack Rutledge, was preaching in a revival. God spoke to my father for the last time as he described to me later. For the last years of his life, he pastored Mississippi country churches. He was ordained and encouraged by Dorothy's father. It was in hot July and all the throng of people, including family and friends, were in and out of our home. My father had worked with RAs in his churches and some of them, in tears, told of my father taking them on fishing trips, the first time away from home for many of them, and other outings. He had just accepted a church a few months prior to his death near Water Valley, Mississippi. The people of that flock were in attendance. I recall standing and looking into his face in the casket. I noticed especially his hands so active all his life in making a living for his family of thirteen people including his younger sister, Pearl Christine Newell, at an early time. She had been with him in the hospital and told of how he was going to tell "his old Daddy" how mean she was to him by not giving him food, kidding, as he often did, to the last. I thought, looking at those hands that had worked so hard, of how often he punished us by switching, led us in plowing, hoeing, trimming fruit trees, and delivering the mail, and how Joe and I had helped at Christmas.

We had some disagreement in our immediate family as to where he would be buried. Should it be in Buena Vista, Mississippi, beside my mother who was buried beside my brother, John Merrill, or in Troy, Mississippi, where his father, Lawrence, had gone to school and where our sister, Yvonne, was buried? She was the apple of my father's eye. My sister, Marguerite, and I had heard him say he wanted to be buried beside her since she was, in body, all alone there in that country cemetery. That proved to be the place agreed upon. Today, his second wife, Effie Mae, her daughter and son-in-law are buried in the same area near Yvonne's grave. Our mother is next to brother Merrill and loved ones who rest in body, but in spirit are with our Lord until all these bodies will arise, in Glory, at the first resurrection, and so be with the Lord and all His saints forever. What precious memories, overshadowing the sad, we cherish until this day.

We came back to Pittsburgh and to our family and to our church family, older and wiser in experience. Our people were solicitous and comforting to us as we took up our ministry and mission. Both my mother first, and then my father seventeen years later, died unexpectedly. We never know when our time will come, so be ready!

There was some complaint in our church body about my too-explicit preaching to the young people. Today, the then warnings are moot considering what has come to pass. I was asked to hold a revival in the First Baptist Church of Danville, Kentucky. The interim pastor, Dr. Merrill Aldridge, had recommended me. I struggled all week with what decision to make about a possible move back to Kentucky. I finally felt led to write two letters—one to accept and one to turn down. I was to get back to Pittsburgh on a Sunday afternoon, preach that night, and leave the next morning at 4:00 A.M. from New York with a select group on our first tour of Israel and the Holy Land. Dorothy asked me what I intended to do. I told her about the two letters and that I would know in the morning which letter I would mail. She looked questioning and unbelieving.

That afternoon, there were rumored complaints about my being gone too much from the pulpit and then leaving for a trip to Israel. It was the same people who had complained about too-explicit preaching to their young people. That night the pulpit search committee from Madison, New Jersey, was in our audience. They met with me after worship and talked long and excitedly about why they felt I was needed in Madison. Ralph Shanahan, son-in-law of Mary Crowley, who in her Home Interiors gift business had often attended our church in Pittsburgh, had recommended me highly. She had exulted in the ministry of Dr. F. Crossley Morgan, who was criticized to me, and I, in turn, was criticized severely for having a non-Baptist in our pulpit.

The next morning on our way to New York, I mailed the "no" letter to the First Baptist Church Pulpit search committee, in Danville, Kentucky. Later on, after our return from Israel, I checked with the Danville committee chairman. They were already far along in their search for their new pastor and had just the right man they thought—and so they did. God's timing and leading are perfect for all His people, as we listen and utterly rely on His leading. He truly knows best, and I have never regretted my decision to go to the New York/New Jersey area, the great Madison Baptist Church, the base church for all our work in North Jersey and New York City area.

———◆◆◆◆◆———

How does one describe a first trip to Israel? We got up very early as aforementioned and all were ready without delay. We picked up our friend, Alice Kelley, close neighbor all our years in Pittsburgh and special friend across these

years since. We picked up Mrs. Iva Townsend who had had real health problems, and we felt shaky about taking her. However, she was the one who never
gave up and insisted that we go. She had a disease from potassium deficiency
that could cause utter collapse. She finally found the true value of bananas. We
made it to New York and Kennedy International Airport on time where we met
Ruth Sims from Ivy Memorial and Newport News, Virginia. We left Sue
Trotman, our capable associate in the church, in charge of our children. We met
our larger group at Kennedy Airport, a pastor, and his group from Kentucky.
They were a fun-loving, eager, expectant group, and we thoroughly enjoyed our
relationship. There was never a dull moment.

We were a little apprehensive about the anticipated long night trip, but it
was fine. We saw Dr. W. A. Criswell who was on the flight going to Egypt to
participate in an archeological dig. He was enthusiastic as always. We flew from
New York to Paris, and when we came in over the river Seine, there was a heavy
fog making it difficult to see anything. Mrs. Iva Townsend somehow misplaced
her boarding pass as we got off the plane for a little time. Dorothy had to put up
the pleas of a Philadelphia lawyer before they would let her back on—describing
her special health needs and she, Dorothy, had to assert that she did indeed have
a boarding pass and "I am her traveling companion." They let us go. We flew
up over beautiful, famous Mt. Blanc and over the red-tiled roofs of Switzerland.
We came across the island where on that day Jackie Kennedy married Aristotle
Onassis. We could only imagine the scene below as all the women and girls on
the plane oohed and aahed. We flew over the Mediterranean in the afternoon,
crossed the Israeli coastline, and excitement was raised to the highest peak.

We landed at Lod Airport in Tel Aviv and had no trouble at the airport. We
got aboard our bus, and I sat toward the front with my camera and got some very
good pictures as we traversed the Israeli territory—evidence of recent war, the
manifest tree reforestation projects, camels, drivers, little cities, people in mid-
east regalia, and finally Jerusalem. We almost held our breath as we came to the
King George Hotel in the Arabic sector of Jerusalem. Getting off the bus, we
were immediately met by a horde of Arabic children and others asking for
baksheesh coins. Everywhere we went in the Arabic sector, we had to face this
problem and were warned not to be too suckered in or we would be stripped bare.
Only in the Jewish capitol, Tel Aviv, were we not so besieged. The Jewish people,
proud, haughty, non-communicative, went about their business with obvious
pride. We were assigned our hotel rooms after our meal. The first course was
mushroom soup, Dorothy remembers. We slept the sleep of the utterly weary,

only disturbed by some loud noise and shouting down the hall that soon stopped. Next morning, I was awakened by the sound of a rooster crowing. I thought how Peter must have jumped every time he heard the rooster crow after his thrice denial of Jesus. We later visited the place where Peter had denied Jesus, home of the High Priest where they flogged Jesus and then washed his wounds with pots of salt water, only to flog Him some more with his arms outstretched upward and tied. What pain he must have borne that dread morning as Peter looked into the home to see and the suffering eyes of Jesus met his as if to ask, "Didn't I tell you?"

As we looked out our hotel room, we saw down below a fully dressed Arabic man reading his Holy Book, the Koran. There was a fig tree close by, and we could see the value of its shade. After dressing and breakfast, the ladies and most of the others wanted to shop for trinkets, some of which are beside me as I write. I decided I would like to go out by myself and so took off. As I came out of a shop, I saw an Arabic man, with his fully decorated camel, who offered me a ride. We were at the edge of the area where the terrible battle had been fought for the city of Jerusalem between the Arabs and the Jews.

I recalled the story of Robert Lindsey, our Southern Baptist missionary to Israel, married to Margaret, daughter of former Presbyterian missionaries. As the battle raged, a little Arabic boy was seriously hurt. Robert Lindsey risked his life to rescue this little boy and lost a leg in the effort. Ever thereafter, Robert Lindsey, leader of our Jerusalem Baptist Church, was called Mr. Christian, loved and admired by all, Jew and Arab. Later, some unknown people burned the church. The Jewish people erected a tent until the church could be rebuilt.

I made the Arabic man with the camel upset because I did not wish to ride his camel but took a picture of the situation. I walked on down the street not knowing it led toward the famous Damascus Gate, entrance to the old city of Jerusalem. A little Arabic boy came up and walked alongside me. He said in clear English, "You remind me of John F. Kennedy." He got the *baksheesh* coin he was really after. As I walked on, I came to the sign that said, "The Garden Tomb" (I went in later). Three Arabic men came toward me. They were selling some cards, and I bought some. In conversation they said, "We are Christians but cannot openly reveal that we are." I noticed one holding back. They said, "His name is Avocado and we are trying to help him become a Christian." I told them that that is the name of a fruit in our country, and I will pray that he will become the next fruit of your witness. I rejoiced in my heart as I walked on. Arabic people were coming into the Jewish sector of Jerusalem to work. I noticed a young Arabic woman just ahead of me, dressed in full regalia, basket on head, with something to sell and heard her softly saying, "Baksheesh, Baksheesh." I remembered my first college Bible professor, Dr. M. O. Patterson, telling us that was the Arabic term for alms please, alms please. I had the strongest impulse to give her some coins but thought it could be a serious risk for me, an American male, to be seen giving money to an Arabic woman. She walked on, and I walked toward the thronging, busy, Damascus Gate.

I saw herds of sheep, donkeys, people riding in Cadillacs, et cetera. The odors and smells, to me, suggested blood sacrifice. I crossed over the street in front where some young men were about to have lunch of wine and bread. There were trays of this everywhere, and it looked and smelled delicious. I became aware of the huge, skull-like rock in front of me, up above the busy bus station, and on the ancient Jericho road, I later learned. I engaged the young men in conversation and pointed up to the top of the skull hill. "Do you know about Jesus who died up there?" "No, we never heard that. It's an Arabic cemetery." I noticed an old, Arabic man working silently in a rose garden at the foot of the ancient north wall. I asked the young men if they knew about Ibrahim buried with wife, Sarai, over at Hebron. The old man put down his hoe, came over, and they all talked excitedly about Father Ibrahim. I said he is special to Christians and to Jews. As I talked of Christ as related to Abraham and his willingness to sacrifice his only begotten son, Isaac, they listened and shared as we talked their language about Ibrahim. To this very day, Hebron is very sacred to Arabs for these reasons.

I walked on. It was about noontime now and bright and sunny. A huge iron gate was on my left and was the entrance to the skull—Arabic cemetery. I took my life into my hands and climbed the hill Jesus might have climbed to the spot where He might have died. I sat down on the tombstone. Arabs and Jews bury so as to insure a fast decay of body back into the soil. I read my Bible and prayed. I had prayed as I sorrowfully climbed the hill, "Father, if this be the spot, show me a sign." In that moment, a dove flew down, lighted on the iron enclosure to a gravesite, and I got a picture. I looked around—Mount of Olives to the east, toward the place where Catholics say He died, half a mile away, with the City of Jerusalem all around. I got a sprig from a nearby thorn bush. I saw a large, mustard tree shrub. I saw down into the possible garden tomb nearby where He might have been buried. I walked back down the hill overcome with it all.

By this time the gardener had returned. I gave him fifty cents, and he was pleased. I walked out the heavy, iron gate and crossed the street to where a man was standing next to a church building. He smilingly greeted me, shook my hand, and in perfect English asked, "My friend, do you know the way to the New Jerusalem?" I replied, "Yes, I do. I'm a saved man and a Christian. Who are you?" He replied, "I am a Baptist preacher," and we rejoiced in the Lord. I lost my way to the King George Hotel, walked up the street, and asked some Arabic young people for directions. One young man took my arm saying, "I, Salim. I show you." He and two other young men took me to my hotel where Dorothy and others were waiting. They couldn't believe my story. *Salim* means peace, and *Ur Salim,* or Jerusalem, means City of Peace. But yet, it has been such a city of violence for almost two thousand years.

We later visited the Garden Tomb and stood trembling in the tomb which was perhaps back then Joseph of Aramathea's new tomb. We saw the evidence of an ancient winepress nearby. It had to be owned by a wealthy man if it was that close to Jerusalem. We saw locust pods that may have been the locusts, they suggested, that John the Baptist ate (somewhat like dried persimmons). We saw the slot where the huge door was which was rolled away by God's hand in the early dawn of the first Easter by an earthquake. We visited the temple area, thirty plus acres, Court of the Gentile, about fifteen acres, where Jesus overturned the money changers's tables and drove out those who had made God's house a den of thieves. We saw the Place of Healing Waters; the temple area where King Solomon judged rightly between the two women who claimed the same child; climbed to the pinnacle of the temple where Satan tempted Jesus to jump off saying, "God will protect you." Jesus replied, "It is written, thou shalt not tempt the Lord, thy God." We saw the Eastern Gate where the Prince will return, sealed until that day; visited the ancient temple wall where Jews won in the recent war and have prayed ever since, and placed their prayer strips in the walls. We wept as the then Jewish general wept as he first saw the sacred wall.

It came time to enter the Mosque of Omar/Dome of the Rock covering the ancient place where Abraham assayed to sacrifice his "only begotten son, Isaac," and the place where the Prophet Mohammed, on his horse, had ascended to heaven, according to Arabic tradition. "See," they said, "there is his horse's hoof," which I couldn't make out. When we went into this sacred Temple area, they told us we must take off our shoes. Dorothy hesitated and the armed Arabic guard assured her and us that the shoes would be okay and they were. We saw the huge, square hole where the blood of Jewish sacrifice flowed down and into the Brook Kidron, three hundred and forty-five thousand sheep in one Passover, according to Josephus, an ancient Jewish historical writer. We saw where the Masons, who reverence the Temple of Solomon, had chipped away some of the rock as relics in years gone by. All of these in more recent years have been a place of turmoil and tragedy.

We saw the Tower of Antonio where Roman soldiers were placed to keep down riots, as in the time of Paul's arrest by the soldiers, and he was also kept from being killed. We saw the Garden of Gethsemane, the rock where Jesus prayed and sweated the great drops of blood, and the ancient olive trees where the tired disciples slept and left Him alone. We saw the road leading up to the Mount of Olives where King David wept as he and his retinue went up to escape Absalom's effort to take the kingdom away from his father, David. I picked up some of the rocks where Jesus rode the donkey as he entered the city on Palm Sunday and could all but hear the children singing. We saw the Brook Kidron in the older, original ancient city of David, and the Pool of Bethesda, still clear, the ancient water duct into the city. You could stand in the pulsing cold waters and see the place where those who dug the tunnel so many centuries ago, from both ends, met. What a time of celebration it was to see all these sacred sights for ourselves.

We rode the bus to the area of the inn where the man fell among the thieves and left for dead was rescued by the Good Samaritan in Jesus' story, "Who is my neighbor?" We saw the Dead Sea and tasted its salty waters. I retrieved driftwood covered with salt residue and have kept it to this day. We visited the ancient city where the walls of Jericho fell down and the Mountain of Musa (Moses) above the valley where Moses could only look and not go in. An angel buried him on the mountain. We saw the Springs of Jericho that were poison until Elisha threw in the tree and salt to purify the waters. It is pure to this day and still the source of water for the area. We could imagine Jesus and the crowds ascending from Jericho into the city of Jerusalem. Jericho was the beautiful city of palms. It is always summertime there, when thirty miles up it could be snowing in Jerusalem. We could hear the cries of the crowds as He healed old blind Bartimaeus; and where he met Zacchaeus in the sycamore tree and went to his house for dinner, and Zacchaeus gave away his evilly accumulated fortune. All of these sights were a constant excitement as we walked where Jesus walked.

In our tour we went to the beautiful Sea of Galilee where some of our Kentucky party were baptized. We saw the ruins of the ancient city of Capernaum, Jesus' headquarters for Galilean ministry; the ruins of the ancient synagogue where Jesus read from Isaiah 61; and the Hill of Execution where they assayed to throw Him over and He walked away unhurt. We saw the city of Tiberias, city of Roman rulers, Jordan roll, the area of Mt. Lebanon where the snows melted and ran down to the Jordan and into the Sea of Galilee; and the area of the ten cities, volcanic eruptions manifest everywhere as Jesus prophesied. We saw the area of the Sermon on the Mount and the place of the feeding of the five thousand and the four thousand. All of these places were in close proximity.

We visited Nazareth where Jesus grew up and saw the place which is ostensibly His family home and Joseph's carpenter shop; the rock table in the cave area home which is always seventy degrees, where He might have met with His disciples; and the place where the angel Gabriel met Mary, possibly on the way to the city water place. I stood there and quietly worshipped and thanked God anew for His great love so manifest. We drove through Ain Karim where Elizabeth and Zacharias lived, home of John the Baptist. We visited the Valley of Megiddo and the ancient city where King Solomon had some of his stables of horses (chariot). We climbed down into and walked through the ancient water area; saw the Valley of Megiddo where tradition says that in the Second Coming of Christ two hundred million soldiers will be involved and have seven years to clean up the area of death and violence.

We visited the city of Sychar where Jesus met and ministered to the woman at the well and drank from the still, clear, cold water. We saw the area from which she came at noonday to find Jesus resting while the disciples went into Sychar to get kosher food. Up above Sychar is ancient Mt. Crag (Mt. Gerrizam) where the Samaritans worshipped in their temple and still have a church. On one mountain long years before, the people of God under Moses and Joshua stood. One half on Mt. Gerrizam under Moses, the other half on Mt. Ebal under Joshua. One group, in choral fashion, sang out the Ten Commandments; the other group, in choral response, choraled the penalty for breaking the Ten Commandments. All of this happened in the area of Sychar.

We passed by the site where an Arabic boy looking for his goat found the Dead Sea Scrolls. We visited the area of the Knesset (Jewish government building) and saw the National Museum of the printing and preserving of the ancient scrolls. The lettering looked as if it had been done only yesterday, due to the so-careful work of the ancient scribes, all for our posterity, under God's hand.

On our return trip, we landed on Nicosia, the Island of Cyprus, where Paul ministered on his first missionary journey. We went on to Athens and saw the ancient Parthenon with the city of Athens all around; and the Mars Hill area where Paul gave his sermon on the ten thousand gods, and he wanted to tell of the unknown God, and they laughed him out of school. We visited the city of ancient Corinth where Paul was defended before the Bema (judgment seat). We saw the ancient temple area where the temple prostitutes came down to the city to meet the sailors (there were always ships in port) and to lead them in orgies in the sacred Temple Cerenthus (Corinthus). We saw the ruins of the shops alongside the main street, and right next to the ancient baths's public areas were the ruins of the Christian church which ministered the gospel to all the people who had come there.

Pittsburgh Baptist Church,
Charles A. Jolly, Sr., pastor,
October 1, 1964–January 8, 1969.

We flew out of Athens on Olympic Airlines back into New York. The final touching scene for us was our dear friend, Iva Townsend, with tears coming down her cheeks. She said she felt she was "leaving home" when we left the Holy Land. You really did feel that you had been on holy ground and felt the greater reality of Bible truth. All of this was in October and on the first Sunday in November, we went to Madison, New Jersey.

We had made an earlier visit to Madison and stayed with the Jim Kitchens. We met with the pulpit committee and the hosted dinner with the Joe Hights in Chatham. Charlie and Elsie Leamer had us for lunch on Saturday and drove us out to the Masonic Hall in Bernardsville where Ben Hall's mission met for a long time.

Again, I had been in a fall revival with Brother Walter Burcham in Conowingo, Maryland. That week God blessed us. I worked with an auto dealer to trade in my car for a new blue Plymouth station wagon for my enlarged family. The dealer and his wife delivered the wagon to us just before we were to finally leave for Madison. The revival closed in Conowingo on a slightly rainy Sunday morning. Dorothy had already flown to New Jersey by prearrangement with the Madison people and was picked up by Joe and Patsy Hight. Joe was in charge of the Sunday night dinner fellowship for all the committee at the William Pitt, a famous local Chatham, New Jersey, restaurant. Brother Burcham had taken me by auto to the Baltimore, Maryland, Friendship International Airport where I took a plane to LaGuardia Airport in New York. Deacon Jim Heldebrand met me. I recall the trip with him to Madison, crossing the Verazzano-Narrows Bridge and coming into Madison at night. He remarked that Madison was known as the Rose City. The chairman of the pulpit committee was Charles Leamer who did not come to Pittsburgh with the committee because he had formerly been a member in Pittsburgh and was a very close friend of Joe Waltz, our associational director of missions. The Leamers and we have remained close friends across these years, and just recently they gave five thousand dollars for our new Mountain Highway Baptist Church building. Praise the Lord! We had a very good session with the pulpit committee and mission pastors: Ben Hall, Ike Byrd, and Ron Leisman. They were all concerned, questioning, and gave a general review of Madison Baptist Church background. It was all a very challenging and stimulating experience.

The Leamers finally took us under their wing, showed us all the local sights, and were most encouraging, as were all the others. All of us were convinced that God was assuredly leading. The Leamers took us back to the old Newark Airport for our trip home to Pittsburgh.

Thereupon, we began to close our ministry in Pittsburgh and start the transition to Madison. The Pittsburgh people were actually challenged with us about the move to the New Jersey/New York area and were loving and generous toward us in the transition. All of the church and my brother Fred and his family, who were left behind in the Pittsburgh area with a great mission work ahead for them, were a part of our final service and fellowship time.

The Pittsburgh Baptist Church later called Paul Maxie as their pastor. Paul's wife, a lovely musician, left her husband and created a problem for Paul. Paul later became associational director of missions following Joe Waltz's sudden death and served very effectively. He later came to our New York area after marrying Rosemary, a lovely Indian girl, the secretary of the Pennsylvania/South Jersey Convention in Hershey, Pennsylvania, who worked with Joe Waltz. Paul and Rosemary did a fine job as pastor and wife of one of our most difficult and needy areas in New York—Park Slope Baptist Church in Brooklyn. His first wife and family stayed on in Pittsburgh where she taught music.

It was really difficult on our family to leave the Pittsburgh/Mt. Lebanon area where so many gracious blessings of God had been on our lives and ministry. We stayed with Shirley Williams and Bonnie Bell on our last night in Pittsburgh. We had been with them in the sad loss of Bill Williams from a heart attack which was followed soon thereafter by the death of the baby daughter, Ann, who apparently died of a broken heart over her father's death. We have remained close to the Williamses across these years until Bonnie's recent death in California where Dorothy was supposed to meet her. Now they'll meet in Glory.

10

Madison, New Jersey

1969–1978

Finally, on a rather cold day with lingering snow around us and the moving van come and gone, we loaded our family into our new station wagon for the drive to our new home in Madison, New Jersey, at the pastorium at 18 Lewis Drive. It became our home for the next nine years. We stopped several times along the way and finally at Friendly's Restaurant in Madison. The Madison church family was most generous, helpful, and loving in our welcome and in helping us to get established in our new home. Mary Margaret was with us on her Christmas break from Georgetown Baptist College in Kentucky.

Aside from getting acquainted and pastoring the church family, I was immediately involved with our mission work. Brother Ralph Shanahan was mission committee chairman and enabled me to relate to the work. Ben and Mae Hall became very special to us and remained so all the remaining years of our ministry and even to this day. He and I would attend the meetings in New York City together along with Ron Leisman, pastor of the Roxbury Chapel. We went once a week into the city and were involved in special social studies. There would be a special guest lecturer, and it involved much of the religious leadership in "the City." In this way, we became acquainted with the Riverside Church, the New York seminary and excellent bookstore, and the Jewish Theological Seminary. This gave us a perspective of the city that greatly increased our ability to cope with the vastness of the work. Sharing with one another as we drove back and forth was always a special blessing. Later on, Don and Debbie Morris came to Drew University for studies and became involved in one of our mission areas. This area did not develop as we had hoped, and he later became pastor of the Montclair, New Jersey, church where Harry Emerson Fosdick was pastor before going to Riverside Church in New York. The Montclair church building was a poem in structure, but the congregation had aged and had declining prospects for the future. We had some younger people who became involved and we developed a joint ministry that proved very effective. We organized into a new church structure, on a Sunday afternoon when Bill Coakley was chairman of our deacons. The black mayor of Montclair was one of our speakers, and I became aware that several of our adjacent areas had effective black mayors.

Our Calvary Chapel combined with the newly restructured Montclair Baptist Church. Charlie Leamer related to this Calvary mission. Charlie Langston later became mission committee chairman and worked very effectively with us. Charlie Langston just recently died in Surfside Beach, South Carolina, from cancer.

Another area was in Bayonne, New Jersey. There was a nice building and a Spanish pastor, Reverend Costa. Our young people helped to renovate the building when Bob Crute was our minister of music and youth. We learned that earlier there had been another Southern Baptist pastor who led in this Bayonne area. It was indeed a thrill beyond words to get enmeshed into the total mission work throughout the area.

Associational meetings were held at the Spanish Harlem Baptist Church for a time before the purchase of our associational building from the American Board of Missions to the Jews. Buddy and Becky would often go with me to these meetings in Spanish Harlem. We drove over the George Washington Bridge and parked our car in the bus terminal in Upper Spanish Harlem. We enjoyed getting pizza at a nearby Broadway street restaurant, Frank's Place, I believe. Frank was Greek.

The acquisition of the six-story building at 236 West 72nd Street in Manhattan was a tremendous asset to our work then and now. The American Board of Missions to the Jews had experienced some serious opposition to their work in the city and moved out into New Jersey. They offered us their building for $350,000 when Ken Lyle was our second director of missions after Dr. Paul James. Mary Crowley, Ruth Shanahan's mother and president of Home Interiors and Gifts in Dallas, Texas, gave us twenty-five thousand dollars to purchase the building and a yearly pay-out plan. This building proved a tremendous boon for all our work. It had a beautiful baptistry. Several of our mission churches in the city used the facilities for worship in the lovely sanctuary. I rode the Erie Lackawanna Railroad from Madison to Hoboken, New Jersey, through the tubes (Path Train) under the Hudson River into Manhattan and then up to the West 72nd Street exit. I was moderator of the Metropolitan New York Baptist Association for two years and was therefore involved in all matters pertaining to our work.

The Manhattan Baptist Church had been the initial focus of our work in the city during the time of Dr. Paul James. From that church base, with the help of our Home Mission Board, the work developed first in three strategic areas: Madison, New Jersey, a base church for north Jersey; Farmingdale, Larry Walker, pastor, as a base on Long Island; and Greenwich, Fred Boehmer, pastor, as a base for Connecticut. From these three base churches, all of our work developed. The Manhattan Church slowly declined and finally ceased to exist as a church. Some of its members are still living and their lingering influence is always there.

When we came to Madison, I attended a first association meeting at the Manhattan Church facility. Dr. Ralph Logan Carson, now professor of theology at Southeastern Baptist Seminary in Wake Forest, North Carolina, went with me. He was a blind black doctoral student in Drew University and a member and Sunday School teacher in our Madison Church. I thought I knew where we were going, but we got lost up in Yonkers somehow. I was upset and nervous as we asked directions. Logan was on my arm and said, "Now, pastor, don't you get upset. I'll get us out of here and to the right place." I wondered how on earth this blind man could help me, but he did. We got back down on the right street, met Wally McCormick, and walked together to the meeting. What a blessed relief, and to top it all off, as we drove back to New Jersey on the Garden State Parkway, we were talking a blue streak. Suddenly, Logan said, "Now, pastor, this is about where you have to turn off!" I learned that night that the blind could lead the blind.

Logan Carson and his wife, Glenwood, were very special in our church and also their two adopted children, a boy and a girl. They had been missionaries in Liberia under another mission board. They had their son then, but wanted a girl and had let it be known in rather wide circles. One day, an old African man, with the grandmother, came bringing a bundle to the Carson doorway. As they cleaned up the child from the birth experience, they learned the baby was a girl. They had walked seventeen miles through the bush to bring this bundle of life to the Carsons. The family did not want a girl but a boy. Ordinarily, in such cases, the child would have been exposed to the sun and would have died. But she was a beautiful child, hence, the unusual effort to get her to the Carsons. Both these children have grown up and married.

The Carsons later pastored in Shelby, North Carolina. I recommended him as a teacher in Gardner-Webb Baptist College to my friend from seminary days, Dr. Gene Poston, president of Gardner-Webb in Boiling Springs, North Carolina. Logan and Glenwood and family became most beloved by all of the faculty and student body while they served in the pastorate in Shelby. Indeed, some of us in

Madison would take Logan and his faithful seeing-eye dog to his teaching position at Upper Montclair State College. It was usually Martha McCormick, but I would do it when she could not. Hence, I had learned about Logan's teaching abilities. He and his family are still beloved and most effective to all who have known them at Southeastern Baptist Theological Seminary. Glenwood almost died recently. The student body rallied in prayer and God performed a miracle of healing. I believe Logan Carson was the first black professor in one of our Baptist colleges and perhaps in one of our seminaries. We hear from them every Christmas. Another black, a former Metropolitan Association pastor, Dr. Leroy Gainey, is now a professor in our Golden Gate Baptist Theological Seminary in Mill Valley, California. Perhaps he was the first.

Pastor Ike Byrd and his family were very special to our church family. He was the pastor of Twin County Baptist Church near Princeton University. His wife was employed at the nearby headquarters of the Boy Scouts of America. They had purchased some ten acres of valuable property and built a nice, first unit building. I was excited with them, and Dorothy and I made several visits back and forth. After some little time, when things seemed to lag, Ike and his family got involved in the charismatic movement. The people would use glossalalia, and saw a miracle of the cross in the sky and eminent warnings of the Second Coming of Christ.

We had had a strong element of this in our Madison Church when we first came. There were four or five families involved who were in prominent positions in the church. There was a serious cleavage. Books pertaining to this movement were placed in the hands of the people when they went to the church library. I spent much time trying to understand, and yet sensed the division that was developing. They were really some of our sweetest, most devoted people, but nothing I could say would deter them from their mission. They were the ones who were always ready to visit but with this charismatic bent. I went to each one separately and talked endlessly. Finally, we had a meeting of all interested parties. We talked and prayed. I stated that I had studied materials about speaking in tongues. Then, I stated that it was a separate program from our normal Southern Baptist program and literature. I pointed out that we could not have two separate programs in the church without serious division. Those involved all acceded to my premise, and they all left our church to go in separate ways. I must say that I personally felt heartbroken and a great emptiness at their leaving. However, the church moved on in the Southern Baptist program to which we were committed. I later met some of those who had left. One became a Methodist minister. Another became a teacher/missionary in Africa. Our church went on to greater growth.

I became involved in the community and in the Unity Week of Prayer for Ecumenism. In this program, we exchanged pulpits and got to know each other's feelings and perspectives in a positive way. I spoke in different churches, and other pastors spoke in our pulpit. We especially enjoyed fellowship around the Seder meal before Easter in St. Vincent's Roman Catholic Church. The Catholics had real wine and obviously got tipsy. The Roman Catholic priest, Vincent Puma, would come to our table where we had regular grape juice. He remarked, "I want some of your Baptist wine. Ours is too much for me." In the Unity Week experience, several of the Catholic priests, for the first time, were saved and said so. Vincent Puma visited us twice in Hawaii, once with his father and again with the Roman Catholic bishop of Hawaii with whom Vincent Puma had gone to school and with a priest from Rochester, Minnesota. We had breakfast together, talked and shared, and I felt like I had been in a good Baptist fellowship meeting as we talked about the Lord and salvation, and shared our views.

I preached one Sunday morning in the Methodist church in Madison and told of my great-grandfather, John Fowlkes, a Methodist assistant chaplain to the Tennessee troops during the Civil War, whose handwritten diary I have. The professor of history at Drew University came to me afterwards and said he'd liked to see the diary and copy it for the school's library. I gladly consented, and today that diary is in the Drew University Library. I was very close relationally to the Drew University campus. Our Mary Margaret was a very close friend to Mary Beth Oxnam, the president's daughter. I visited Dr. Oxnam once in the hospital when he had a broken leg. I had actually enrolled to do my doctoral work over a two-year period with Ben Hall had I stayed on in Madison. The Methodist Theological Seminary is located on the Drew campus.

Madison Baptist Church, the first church to come out of the Manhattan Baptist Church in New York City.

One of our special preachers for revival in Madison was Dr. Dale Moody, professor of theology at Southern Baptist Seminary. He was from Mule Shoe, Texas. Drew University Professor of Theology, Dr. Thomas Oden, a very outstanding and a national, even international theologian, asked Dale Moody to speak to his class. I was proud of Dale Moody that morning. He had a tremendous mind.

We had a community revival with evangelist Larry Walker who was based in our church. Joe Hight, our church member, at Larry's request, handled his finances. We were privileged to use the outdoor arena of St. Elizabeth's Roman Catholic College. Our attendance was poor because of unseasonable weather. On that campus, they had a prayer center and on weekends had some seven hundred people. I went to that center once and had the feeling that I was on very holy ground. We had the outstanding black evangelist Tom Skinner on Sunday night at the St. Elizabeth Chapel. Dorothy and I went into New York City to bring him to Madison and took him back afterwards. Tom died just recently after giving his life in our Lord's cause in the city.

The former mayor of Madison, Mr. Earl Reddert, a Methodist, and an executive with the Colgate Corporation, had actually intervened to help our Madison Baptist people secure their choice acreage for our church building. We became close friends through our daughter, Mary Margaret, working at the bank and were often in his home. He always felt proud that the Southern Baptists were in Madison.

When I came to Madison, Deacon and AT&T executive Joe Hunt was chairman of the new building committee for the 1970s. We developed a campaign in which our people were asked to give five percent above the tithe for three years to raise money for the proposed new building. We developed an attractive folder depicting what Madison Baptist Church would look like in the 1970s. A number of us pledged and gave, but not enough of us. I believe we raised thirty-eight thousand dollars but never built. Our Madison people said they wanted to stay as we were and give our extra money to these sponsored mission churches as needed. Often at the end of the year we had as much as fifteen thousand dollars to give to mission-church needs. We helped several struggling situations in the city which otherwise could not have made it. Dr. Paul James always referred to "that Madison Spirit." The deacons told me if I felt someone had a need, day or night, to take care of it, and they would pay the bill—again, that "Madison Spirit." A number of times I was able to help people in distress.

We had three very able and efficient secretaries in Margaret Harris, Barbara Herriman, and Jewel Weaver, assisted by Faye Buckels and Lucille Keister. Never had we had better. I never had to worry about anything pertaining to building needs or personal comfort. Joe Markovich, J. W. Daugherty, and Jim Weaver knew all about the church building and the parsonage and kept it all in perfect condition. I must mention, too, Carlos Peña and family, formerly from Cuba, our church janitor and very special friend.

On one occasion, our church basement was flooding for some unknown reason. Joe Markovich, chairman of our building and grounds committee, called me with the news that water was pouring into our basement at eighteen hundred gallons a minute. The Fire Department could not pump it out fast enough. On further checking, we found that an outlet outside had stopped up. Once we corrected it, the water flowed furiously away from our building. We also realized that our church building sat over a vast pool of underground water—like Noah's Ark.

Another community program in which I became involved, through Detective Joe Markovich, had to do with problem youth in Morris County, the most heavily populated county in the United States. We would meet first with the problem youth alone, hear them out, and warn them that this was a one-time chance. We would then meet with the parents and share with them. We would make our decision and call in the young person and the parents together for our decision. It was said that we kept eighty percent of troubled youth out of prison. Oh, for more such programs today. We would never acknowledge we were in on such cases, even if we should afterwards see them on the street.

With Charles Jr., our handicapped son, we worked with Long Hill Chapel Boy Scout Troop to have a scout troop for handicapped youth. We developed a model program. Long Hill Chapel Eagle Scouts led us and helped us. They paid the bill for activities and set up tents on our property for campouts. Doug Totel from Arizona, now married with a family in Chicago, was my helper. Mothers, who formerly had borne their burdens alone, came to our church for fellowship with other mothers and shared coffee and cake. On one occasion, Doug and I took a group of youth from broken families, very difficult and wayward, to a Boy Scout Camp in Waterloo, New Jersey. These kids were devils that week. They cut the hoses for the camp's water system. They slashed the tents with scout knives. What a bunch! Yet the camp personnel patiently bore with us. I took them home, told their mothers, no fathers around, and tried to minister. I often wonder what happened to them—I pray some good.

At Christmas, the Down's syndrome group decorated Christmas trees with their mothers' help and took them to the homes of elderly shut-ins. These little groups would sing and pray and work hard. You can imagine the utterly surprised looks, in awe, from the shut-ins we visited.

Another part of this community effort was Meals-on-Wheels every Friday. Each week, we would go by the Red Cross office and pick up the names and addresses of people to deliver to. Then we would go to the Exxon Corporation headquarters kitchen-loading area to pick up the two-meal trays to take to ones who ordered them. All were so grateful for this service. Martha McCormick, especially, worked with us on this. Again, it was an opportunity to witness and to pray. I recall, in this program, meeting Dr. Fred Moffit, who had been a speech writer for John F. Kennedy and Dwight D. Eisenhower. He was totally crippled and had to have daily help in all personal matters. He was a constant smoker but such a highly intelligent man. We were able to have him for one of our Wednesday night family suppers. He was a great and learned man. We also had Harvey Gurley's friend, Harriet Adams, multi-author of children's books: The Nancy Drew, Bobbsey Twins, and Hardy Boy series. There is no end to the unusual blessings and opportunities because of Madison. Mary Crowley, founder of Home Interiors and mother of Ruth Shanahan, is another great story.

I write rather extensively about our work in the inner city of New York. In our Wednesday night suppers, we often had guests from New York City because Madison was the key church reaching into the inner city, and "that Madison Spirit" ministered to them. The Wednesday night meals always had a missions emphasis. I recall the occasion of Larry Walker and me taking a group of our youth to the New Year's Eve service which was televised nation-wide. I recall the associational meeting at our strong Trust in God Chinese Church in Chinatown with Dr. W. A. Criswell of First Baptist Church in Dallas, Texas, as our special speaker. Another occasion was having our friend from Virginia days, George Euting, Brotherhood director, as speaker. There were others too numerous to mention except that every fall I had a standing invitation to speak on Bible stewardship in the black Mt. Zion Baptist Church in upper Manhattan (Harlem); Brother Bullock was pastor. Their worship services were always a special blessing, and we were treated royally. The January Bible Study provided another opportunity to bring in speakers from other churches in the Metropolitan New York Baptist Association and from across our convention. This was a time of great anticipation even when it was so cold and most often with snow on the ground.

We had wonderful times of fellowship at Madison. The Sunday School leadership was in charge of the annual Sunday School picnic the last Sunday in June, the deacons sponsored a homemade ice cream social in late July or early August, and the Training Union leadership led in the annual corn roast/picnic in September usually in conjunction with the Week of Prayer for State Missions. These were all held on the church grounds on Sunday afternoon with vespers following. The corn roast idea came from our Pittsburgh years. Our people there so thoroughly enjoyed those occasions in the fall, and it was an outreach event. We brought the idea to Madison. Several churches in the inner city made use of Madison Church grounds for their church fellowships. These grounds were extensive and included a softball diamond as well as basketball court on the parking lot and other areas for volleyball, croquet games, and other activities. I organized a New Year's Eve program featuring all the flags of the nations paraded into our sanctuary by our young people. What a job to get those flags to the church and return them to Paterson, New Jersey. We hardly had room for the people, but it was unforgettable.

On Thanksgiving eve, the Madison Association of Churches sponsored an ecumenical service rotating between the various churches with the host church providing light refreshments after the service. One year, Madison Baptist Church changed the format and provided a Thanksgiving Day breakfast after a 7:00 A.M. worship service. Everyone who attended commented favorably, but no other church attempted to do it.

All the pastors in the Madison Association of Churches were involved in the discussion of whether to have sex education in the public schools. There was one session at the local high school assembly. The teachers were nervous and so were we. We had no idea of the coming explosive sex culture and the effects on our society. Oh, for the good old days. As a student of history, I was invited, at Martha Ruth's suggestion, to come and speak on personal matters of Civil War history.

Becky, Buddy, and I also developed a program with the *Grit* newspaper. We learned about this little paper because they wrote up Madison Baptist Church and our developing deaf ministry program under the leadership of Kay Erickson, a deacon's wife. She sat on a stool in front of our pulpit and signed the songs and message to those who sat toward the front of the sanctuary. Our daughter, Martha Ruth, effectively learned sign language and often stood in for Kay. She later met and married her husband, Kevin Sowards, at Dallas Baptist College because of this program and her participation. When I left Madison, we had about thirty in this marvelous group. They gave me a beautiful little gold tie clasp that is my favorite to this day. Then the so-called *Grit* newspaper ministry began with Buddy and Becky. We had fifteen-plus different communities represented in our Madison Church. The delivery of that little paper each week helped me to keep in touch with these communities. The money that Buddy and Becky collected went into a little white and pink sugar bowl. It is still a keepsake. They had their own money and never had to ask me for any. They tithed and on a couple of occasions helped in our vacation times. It was tiring for them. Becky fretted but they learned to deal with people. Some took the little paper and some did not. They learned to hear "no" as well as "yes." We would get to Mrs. Leston Fate's last on Fridays. She had ice cream and cookies, and we would visit. She dubbed it the *"Grit* Newspaper Ministry." We had almost one hundred customers. It gave me special time with my youngest children and this project taught them self-confidence. The newspaper ministry did untold good.

In our *Grit* newspaper ministry, usually on Saturday morning in the Berkeley Heights area, we came to a rather run-down old home where a black man lived with his aging, ailing wife. We sensed that they had few visitors and gladly welcomed us into their meager home. These two older people enjoyed the younger children, and I always made a pastoral visit, closing with special prayer for the ailing woman.

The elderly man would attend the morning worship service at Madison Baptist. He always wore a broad-brimmed hat and greeted me cheerfully at the church door. He was always one of the first to get away. I would never fail to ask about his wife.

In 1985 we were back in Madison from the Northwest for the twenty-fifth anniversary of the Madison Church. The Jim Weavers were our gracious hosts. As Jewel drove us around the area, she was telling us about the recent happenings at the church. It came to our attention that a very surprising gift of a considerable sum had come to the church from the will of an unknown black man. It all came rushing back in memory as I recalled those Saturday morning pastoral visits to a lonely, ailing black couple, and now here was the special meaningful gift to a great church that enabled its pastor to reach across all boundaries in blessed ministry for our Lord's own. One day in Glory, I will meet these dear people, and I can tell them what an ongoing work for our Lord came from that rundown looking home and place amidst so much surrounding wealth of Berkeley Heights, New Jersey.

We developed a program for the handicapped in Madison involving full use of the YMCA facilities. It enabled these children to learn to swim and to play together. It was a great partnership that started because of Mary Fram, secretary at the Grace Episcopal Church in Madison, out of concern for her daughter's emotional handicap. She knew of my concern about our son and got in touch with me. We gradually went from there to a total community involvement called Educational Program of Children Handicapped (EPOCH). Dorothy served on the board of trustees. Initially, it involved high school seniors interested in working one-on-one with handicapped young people and children. These Madison High School students were interested in their future college education relating to this field. It then developed with Drew University involving the head of the Education Department, a woman, and a male professor, also pertaining to students interested in this field. It finally involved Fairleigh Dickinson University and St. Elizabeth's Roman Catholic College, similarly. Our own Madison Baptist Church opened its doors one day per week for this program that proved very successful utilizing arts, crafts, music, and storytelling. Only our Lord can know the untold good these programs have done. It also involved the business community, bankers, and doctors. A number of them served on the board. It also showed the value of a general ecumenical relationship between all the churches—even the Jewish community in the Madison/Morristown area.

In regard to the Jewish community, I attended a lecture at Drew University concerning the tragic implications of the Holocaust in Germany during World War II. I got to know a rabbi who, when he prayed, made us feel he really talked to God. From this, we had a Thanksgiving worship service in our Madison Church viewed as a National American event. We invited the rabbi from Morristown to come as our speaker and to bring members of his congregation. Some thirty-five of these came and what a thrilling worship service and experience. As I introduced the rabbi, I told of visiting the oldest synagogue in Europe in Prague, Czechoslovakia, on a recent tour. It was situated below ground to avoid too-obvious a presence and was meagerly furnished. I recalled going out on the streets surrounding the area where the Jews had been confined in ghetto-fashion to this poverty area. We were in tears to contemplate such a tragedy. The rabbi stood, tears in his eyes, to say that only that day he had received an ancient scroll from that very synagogue. What a quietness of reverence and worship settled over us that night. I have attended other Jewish/Christian events before and since, in connection with my assigned purpose to relate to all religious groups, but never have I had an experience quite like that night in our Madison Church. The reception afterwards, given by our women, was an event to remember. Again, as Dr. Paul James said, "that Madison Spirit."

Another excellent program in our Madison Church, English as a Second Language, enabled our Baptist Women to relate positively to various ethnic groups.

It was the time when the boat people began to flow into our area. There were many different countries and languages involving a large number of students. For example, Barbara Christjohn, a professor's daughter from Winchester, Virginia, and a graduate of Wellesley in Boston, Massachusetts, was involved. She would put English words on the stove, refrigerator, and other items and taught by association what the English words were. Ruth Shanahan, Baptist Women's president at the time, was the leader of the program. I recall events of a social nature when I was asked to come as the pastor—such lovely occasions as only Madison Baptist women could do. Ruth took Grace Abolagba into her home and taught her how to use American appliances and gadgets. We have kept in touch with the Abolagbas over these years since they have returned to Nigeria, Africa. Paul pastors a church there. He has a son called to ministry who wanted to come back to the United States. We were not able to work this out. We were present at the time Paul Abolagba received a secular Ph.D. at Drew when New Jersey Senator Millicent Fenwick was the speaker. "Those were the days, my friend."

We were in sore need of a good music/youth leader at Madison, and God sent us Bob and Holly Crute and their first daughter, Misha (now they have Gretchen and Esther, who are all grown up). Bob was excellent in every way in his work, and Holly stood right beside him. Many outstanding youth activities developed. We had Friday night lock-ins at local facilities. Bob and I attended a state meeting in upstate New York that emphasized the value of a bus ministry. We had a pastor friend, Bob Estes from Virginia, come to Madison for a weekend session on the value of a bus ministry. He had been very successful in such an endeavor. From this developed our own Madison Baptist bus ministry with two buses. Deacon J. W. Daugherty directed one, and the other was directed by Larry Newkirk and Dr. Martha Fenner. Her doctoral physics project from Rice University, Texas, is now on the moon as of July 20, 1969. Deacon Kermit Erickson, as Sunday School director, was the overall director of the bus ministry. These responsible people would visit on Saturdays and bring in the kids on Sunday.

As pastor, I was invited in on Sunday to the Sunday School classes and once a month in the sanctuary for a joint worship experience. These were always high moments. In one children's class, a little boy asked me, "Preacher, what is God like?" I thought of my father, my mother, and others—none adequate—then, "God is like Jesus. He, Jesus, is God. He shows us who and what God is like." That satisfied the child and has helped me ever since, as illustrative. They no longer have the bus ministry, but people who were reached in that ministry, are now members of Madison Baptist Church. It is still one of the outstanding churches in our New York Baptist Convention. Larry Newkirk and Martha Fenner are married. His children by a previous marriage are grown up. They have a son and live in Saba, Texas, where they are called the "Pecan Kings of the World."

Bob and Holly Crute left us about the time of the national crises in the Richard Nixon presidency. We visited them at that time in Richmond, Virginia. They have been in the Thaila Lynn Baptist Church in Virginia Beach, Virginia, for a long time, where Junius Foster was the longtime pastor. The Madison Church finally called Bob Arnold and his wife, Annette, as education and youth minister from Southwestern Baptist Theological Seminary. Our deacons all signed a banknote to help them buy an old traditional home in Morristown. Bob and Annette spent money and time fixing it up very attractively. He paid off the loan, and subsequently the house caught fire and burned down. It was a total loss. He received insurance money to pay off his loan and some for investment allowing him to go back to New Orleans, Louisiana, for his doctorate in social ministries. After Annette left him to go back to her old ways in Lexington, Kentucky, despite all our pleadings, he married Karen, a fine, young woman in New Orleans. They have one daughter, Julie, and Bob serves as chaplain of a Veterans' Hospital in Newton, Iowa. The people at Madison felt that, under the family problems, Bob could no longer be effective in our church. It was my sad duty to inform him and to encourage him to go back to school. We keep in touch and are proud of him and his ministry in the chaplaincy.

The Madison Church went all out in the lovely wedding of our daughter Mary Margaret to Jim Ragains on June 18, 1971. Always the Madison Church was solicitous and loving toward us and our family. Sad to say, they were divorced April 21, 1995.

Now, as to my New York/New Jersey association and state work in which I was heavily involved all the time we were in Madison, the church was generous to allow me this essential involvement because of who and what Madison had been in our developing work. We went with the Charles Leamers to Syracuse, New York, on September 26, 1969, for the organization of our new New York Baptist Convention in the Central Baptist Church. We recently celebrated the twenty-fifth Anniversary in 1994 in that same church, and the Leamers were there as were the Wally McCormicks, the Delane Ryals, the David Deans, and many others from our New York/New Jersey area.

I was privileged to serve on our Executive Board and as chairman for two years and as president of the convention in 1977. In that capacity, I made regular plane trips to Syracuse for Executive Board meetings. I got to know many of our fellow pastors in a more meaningful and deeper way as we roomed together. Fred Boehmer at Greenwich Baptist Church in Connecticut and I were called the "power structure," I later learned, because of the prominence of our two churches. The Wilton Baptist Church, Dr. Wallace A. C. Williams, pastor, was also a growing, prominent church which came out of the Greenwich Church sponsorship. Ed James, son of Dr. Paul and Ava James, was the organizer and first pastor of Wilton. Wallace came later from Wilton to Madison to serve very effectively as pastor. In connection with the organization of our New York Baptist Convention, the Madison Baptist Church became the only Southern Baptist church I know of to organize three of our missions into churches in one week's time.

Ralph Shanahan, missions committee chairman, led us in organizing Twin County Baptist Church, Ike Byrd, pastor, on September 20, 1969; Somerset Hills Baptist Church, Bennett Hall, pastor, on September 21, 1969; and Hope Baptist Church, Ron Leisman, pastor, on September 23, 1969. We needed to do this to meet our requirement of fifty churches to form a convention. Praise God, by his grace, we did it! We quickly upped the number to four in four months when we constituted Montclair Baptist Church on January 17, 1970.

In 1972, Dorothy and I made our second trip to Israel and Greece with the Charles Davis group from First Baptist Church of Poughkeepsie, New York. We had originally enlisted twenty people from our area and over the country to go with us, but when Arabic persons murdered the Israeli Olympic team, many of our group dropped out. We, too, had decided to cancel, but Charles Davis made it possible for our smaller group to be coupled with his larger group. We flew from Kennedy Airport in New York to Rome, Italy, and from there to Tel Aviv, Israel, Lod Airport. From there we went by bus to Jerusalem and our hotel in the Arabic sector. When we flew into Lod Airport, we were met with very tight security because of the Israeli Munich massacre. There were soldiers with rifles and machine guns everywhere. When we got off the plane, we had to be subjected to very explicit questioning and proof of travel. On our return trip from Lod Airport, we had to strip and be searched—men by men and women by women, of course.

In Israel, we saw all the sights we had seen before but in far more careful detail. For example, we went at night to the spot near Capernaum and the Sea of Galilee where we read the Sermon on the Mount by flashlight from where Jesus gave it. We spent the night in Tiberias, the beautiful city of the Caesar's Herods' summer vacations called heaven on earth. We saw the ruins of varied archeological digs in ancient Caesarea that were very interesting to us because this is the area where Dr. John Robert Bull, professor of archeology at Drew

University, and his varied groups worked for twenty years. We saw the ancient athletic field, site of the ancient games. We saw the area of the baths where the same tiles, like our modern tiles, had lasted for two thousand years, and various statues had been unearthed. We saw the beautiful amphitheater by the sea. This was the place, now probably underwater, where the Apostle Paul was imprisoned for two years before he went to Rome and appealed to Caesar.

We went from Tiberias to Natanya by the Sea where we spent the night. We saw the ruins of the ancient Philistine cities where Samson and Delilah held forth, where he was blinded and ground at the ancient mill, where he asked to go into the temple, guided by a little boy, and brought the temple down after he regained his strength. We learned that the most prolific archeological artifacts were from the ancient city dumpsites. We saw the ancient city site of Joppa where Peter prayed on the housetop, and where he saw the sheets lowered from heaven and saw all manner of four-footed beasts and creeping things, and God's command to kill and eat. We also saw the ancient port where the logs for Solomon's Temple were floated down to Jerusalem, and the place where Peter agreed to go with the servants of the Gentile Cornelius to Caesarea and the remarkable discovery that God wanted to save Gentiles as well as Jews (Acts 10). We saw in Joppa the archeological unearthing of an ancient home site.

In the afternoon, we went to the Sea of Galilee where our party had a rental boat to go out on the Sea of Galilee where Jesus and the disciples were caught in a storm. At their cry for help, He quieted the winds and the waves, gently rebuking the disciples for their lack of faith. In the distance, we could see snow-capped Mt. Lebanon and the cemetery, place of the Gadarene demoniac out of whom Jesus cast the legion of demons. The pigs rushed down, now inhabited by the demons at the request of Jesus, the pigs not consulted, and were drowned. The people told Jesus to "go away from us, leave us alone! You have ruined our hog business" and perhaps angry that He had healed the demoniac. The demoniac was probably an ancient lucrative tourist factor. We crossed the Sea of Galilee to the village site of this instance in the life of Jesus.

We went on to Haifa, the northernmost point of our tour, where we visited an ancient monastery and saw the Cedars of Lebanon. I collected some cedar cones that they took from me and destroyed on our return trip to New York.

We visited the famous site of Mt. Carmel where the great prophet Elijah took care of and fed the student prophets, and where he called down the fire of God to destroy the prophets of Baal and the prophets of the grove. Following this mighty demonstration of God's power, Elijah prayed it would not rain for three and a half years, and God answered Elijah's prayer. This all got to wicked Ahab and Jezebel, and Ahab was on Mt. Carmel at Jezebel's behest. Elijah sent his servant to the top of the mountain to see if there was a cloud. None at first. Seven times later, a cloud the size of a man's hand came up. Elijah ran down the mountain ahead of Ahab's chariot, and at Jezebel's threat on his life, he fled to the wilderness and hid in a cave and then under the juniper tree. God fed him and encouraged him and brought him back into prophetic service, until He took him to heaven in a fiery chariot. We learned that the water source for the city of Tiberias came from Mt. Carmel, down through a concrete aquaduct that we saw. The Romans discovered the principle of concrete. It was lost for centuries and, in more recent years, rediscovered.

We went to a special factory for the cutting and display of diamonds, saw the process and saw the glitter, but there were no purchases for our group. It was on September 26 and our Becky's birthday. We called her through New York from the diamond factory. It was early enough in New York to get right through to wish her a happy birthday. She was nine years old and is still a special diamond to us.

On the way back to Lod Airport, we stopped at the Valley of Elah where young David slew the giant Goliath with one smooth stone; no other paraphernalia was needed. He amazed the army, his critical brothers, and King Saul. The people, women especially, began to sing, "Saul has slain his thousands. David has slain his tens of thousands." Saul's jealousy doomed his reign while David ever advanced in God's plan of the ages. We stopped at one other spot that our tour guide pointed out as a part of one of the ancient Roman roads. I stood there contemplating the two thousand years of history A.D. and renewed my faith in Him who is the center of all creation and time.

We left Lod Airport in Tel Aviv to fly to Athens where we saw again all the sights previously visited in 1968. We were in ancient Corinth, a seaport city between two seas, where the temple prostitutes came down into the city to entice the sailors and others to come with them to the hill Cerenthus to worship the heathen gods in sex orgies. We stopped on our way down to Piraeus to hear on the radio the soccer game in progress between Greece and Italy. When we got to Athens and were back in our hotel for the night after dinner, Dorothy and I decided to go out to explore the famous city of Athens. As we walked along, "ooing and aahing," all of a sudden we were conscious of scores of autos' horns and sirens blowing, and in a few minutes there were an estimated thirty thousand people in the city center where we happened to be. A storekeeper, sensing our fright, assured us that there was no trouble. The Athenians were celebrating their victory over Italy in the soccer game. We learned that the young people would run the seventeen miles to meet their soccer team at the port of entry.

We felt better after our peaceful sleep that night and were ready to continue on our trip. Just tonight, as I write, we have seen the New York Yankees win the baseball World Series of 1996 for the first time in seventeen years. And they won over the Atlanta Braves who started out to win the first two games by wipeout scores and left folks feeling that they would win the next two. There was a let-down, it-is-all-over feeling. The Yankees went on to win the next three games, in Atlanta, and their fourth tonight in Yankee Stadium in New York. What an over-whelming excitement in New York just as that night in Athens in 1972.

On our last Sunday in Israel, we had one of our most exciting days. We drove by bus to the area of the Dead Sea where it is thought Sodom and Gomorrah may have existed before being destroyed in the sea. We passed a beautiful spring of water area surrounded by palm trees and one of the places, among many, where the camel caravans would rest and refresh both animals and people. We drove on to the place called Masada where the final siege against Jerusalem and the Jews took place. We rode up as far as we could and then walked up to the top of the moun-tain where one can see the whole surrounding area. It was the place where King Herod had his palace, obviously a place of richness where no price was spared. It looked down on the little town of Bethlehem where the greatest choral singing of all time, of the angels, sounded to the lonely shepherds when Jesus was born. Also, it was the place where the wicked Herod ordered the slaughter of the innocents.

As we had come up the mountain, there were stops where you could look down and see the places where the Roman legions had camped. One place against the stark mountain was the spot where the captured Jews were crucified. This was to let those who had escaped the destruction of Jerusalem and of the Temple see where as many as a million Jews had died in that holocaust. Looking down, they did not know what fate awaited them. Thousands of Jews had fled and many had died. When we got to the top of Masada, we saw the ruins of Herod's Palace and the remarkable hot water system where Herod and his cohorts would shower. There was the large room where they would gather after-wards. Apparently, the walls were decorated with lewd paintings of women. We passed by the spot where the Jews burned their synagogue and treasures. We saw the area where the night before the Romans had gotten to the top.

The last Jews left had covenanted not to be taken alive. They selected ones to help arrange a mass suicide effort. The men slew their own families and then they killed one another. Finally, with only two remaining, one slew the other and the final one committed suicide after arranging all the others in an orderly fashion. When the Romans came over the top to finish off those pesky Jews, there they lay in orderly fashion, not a soul alive. We stood in silence at the realization of what had happened. Up there on Masada, I saw a place for sacred baths, washings, just like a Southern Baptist baptistry. The Jews baptized before Jesus made the custom a Christian rite. They baptized those who became Jews. Jesus turned it around, following John the Baptist's example, to always remember and to show the Christian baptism depicting the death, burial, and resurrection of Christ.

From Masada, we traveled south to Beersheba and saw the area where the angel met Abraham, showed him the spring of water under the tamarisk tree, under which Ishamel with his mother, Hagar, found water and the sustenance of God. We traveled on to the Bedouin country where the people dwelt in tents and where a city had arisen out of the desert. There was a place of refreshment and we had lunch. I remember one tiny meatball as an appetizer for our meal. We met a man there who was professor of chemistry at the University of Pittsburgh and son of our professor of chemistry, Dr. A. E. Wood, at Mississippi Baptist College. We had hoped to stop at Hebron to see the Tomb of Abraham, Sarah, Isaac, and Rebecca, famous in biblical history. Our tour guide elected not to go into Hebron because it was late in the evening and there could be danger from Arabic militants. We did stop at a grape orchard where we remembered the spies and the grapes of Eshcol. Dorothy and I made the mistake of eating some of the grapes, not washed but just wiped off, and we paid the price! We were sick all night and could not eat. The next day we were able to eat some of the delectable Peter's fish at a restaurant by the Sea of Galilee.

We flew from Lod Airport to Rome where we were delayed from the middle of the afternoon into the night because of a baggage strike problem. The airline fed us a delightful Italian dinner, and we could see downtown Rome. We finally took off for our flight to New York. I remember some turbulence as we crossed the Atlantic. We finally got back to our home with Elizabeth Painter from Roanoke, Virginia, and Dorothy's Aunt Hannah Patterson-Jones.

Only today has Dorothy's Aunt Hannah Patterson-Jones been buried next to Dorothy's father in West Heights Baptist Church cemetery in Pontotoc, Mississippi. Dorothy's Uncle David Patterson died of a heart attack at seventy years of age in Indiana. He was visiting with his son, David, and family. We have the tape of his message and you can hear him drop as he came off the rostrum following his Christian testimony. We had been very close to all of them. David has retired from the military. He is married to Ola, has two children, a daughter and a son, and has moved to the home place of his father in Wesson, Mississippi.

In November of 1986, we were visiting in Nashville from Federal Way, when Buddy called us to say someone in the family was sick. Dorothy called and got a

Greenville, Mississippi, number to call. From this, she called another woman whom we knew from a visit with Aunt Hannah and found that Aunt Hannah had had a stroke. We called David Patterson in Wesson who took it upon himself to go to Greenville to visit his Aunt Hannah in the hospital where she would be until she could travel. David took a truck, went after his aunt, and brought her to his home in Wesson. Dorothy contacted all of Aunt Hannah's nephews and all agreed to help with Aunt Hannah's living expenses. These nephews are Morgan, then seminary professor and president of Georgetown Baptist College in Kentucky; Ben, professor of journalism at the University of Florida, and Palmer, Indian history professor at the University of Waterloo, in Ontario, Canada. From that day in 1986 until today in 1996, David and his wife, Ola, have faithfully and lovingly looked after their Aunt Hannah. Dorothy visited her on her ninetieth birthday celebration in March of 1995. We both visited her in May of 1996. She had deteriorated seriously, but David and Ola and his daughter and family and David III had all cared for her. Dorothy felt she could not go back for the funeral. David understood. He made all the arrangements with the Brookhaven, Mississippi, funeral home and today took Aunt Hannah's earthly temple for burial awaiting that glad resurrection morning!

Since we could not be there, my brother Fred Jolly went from our family home in Okolona, Mississippi, to be with family members and others who knew her from Calhoun City, Mississippi. Dorothy has checked with all tonight and all went as planned. Praise the Lord! We plan to be buried there one day, if our Lord tarries.

The year 1973 was a strategic year for our New York Baptist Convention. In the latter part of the year at our regular Executive Board meeting, our beloved Dr. Paul S. James announced his intention to retire as our executive director. He was our mentor from the beginning of the New York work. He asked us to set up procedures to search for his successor. He told us he would stay with us until such a person could be found. Thus began a prolonged, prayerful search for our next executive director. I recall that it was in the time of the long gasoline lines during the Nixon administration.

At the beginning of the search, we were made aware that Dr. James and Mrs. Helen Fling, our WMU leader, had some strong leanings toward one of our associates in state administration, Jon Meek. When I was secretary of the Southern Baptist Convention Pastor's Conference, our president, Dr. Landrum Leavell, later president of the New Orleans Baptist Theological Seminary until recently, asked me about Jon Meek being one of our coming Southern Baptist Convention Pastor's Conference speakers. It seems that Dr. Leavell had been his pastor earlier. I was enthusiastic to further this suggestion and was proud of Jon as he preached at that national Pastor's Conference. However, our personnel committee felt a reluctance to consider Jon at this point. He was our missions director involved at every point in our convention life. We also had a very strong person as our education director, John Tubbs, and he was also a possible replacement. Therefore, we prayerfully felt led to look in other directions. We considered Dr. Wendell Belew from our Home Mission Board. He was a longtime special friend in all our work in newer areas of our convention. He came to Syracuse for a visit and interview. The Belews finally felt that it was not right for them. We contacted several other prominent persons with a similar result.

In the meantime, I was in Atlanta for a Home Mission Board meeting. I had been on the Home Mission Board from Pittsburgh days, thanks to the nomination by my good friend, David Haney, with the concurrence of Dr. Ray Roberts, the Ohio executive director. I recall David telling what political shenanigans went on over those to serve on Southern Baptist Convention boards and agencies. Nevertheless, I was elected and served on the personnel committee with Dr. Glendon McCullogh, our board-assigned director. Glendon later became Brotherhood director for the Southern Baptist Convention. He was tragically killed in an automobile accident in Memphis, Tennessee. It was a real privilege to serve with him and others on that personnel committee. I remember I was able to get several of our Clear Creek graduates from Pineville, Kentucky, approved for service in some of our mission churches. These men have done superbly across the years. After coming to New York, I had been asked to serve similarly on the board from New York. I was seated next to Quinn Pugh in an Atlanta meeting of the Home Mission Board and asked him about a man who seemed so familiar with Home Mission Board procedures. He told me it was Jack Lowndes who had just finished a term as president of the Home Mission Board. I had lunch afterwards with several men, including Jack Lowndes. I talked with him about our work in New York and found him interested.

I came back to our committee in New York with the report. We came to a very crucial time of decision. Dr. James and Helen Fling still felt strongly about Jon Meek. We debated that issue thoroughly and were willing to consider Jon. However, there were still some strong lingering questions about Jon. The committee suddenly said to me, "Go call Jack Lowndes." Calling from Syracuse, I got him on the telephone almost immediately. He had an opening and could come the very next morning. He came in a snowstorm, and I watched for him to deplane. I thought he reminded me of Dr. W. A. Criswell, pastor of First Baptist Church of

Dallas, Texas, one of my favorite SBC preachers. The result was that our committee came together unanimously on Dr. Jack Lowndes. At our fall meeting, we had a joint farewell for Dr. and Mrs. Paul James and simultaneously a warm welcome for Dr. Jack Lowndes and his wife, Doris, and family. The Lowndeses moved to the Syracuse area where Jack served with great effectiveness for seven years.

I was involved in the coming of Bill Dunning from Columbia, Tennessee, to serve as associate in music and student work under John Tubbs, our director of education in the New York Convention. We had Dr. Lowndes for a revival later in our Madison Church along with Bill Dunning serving as song leader. Dr. Lowndes's daughter, Mary Ann, our Becky's age, was with her father that week. Later on, after some seven years, Bill Dunning and Jack Lowndes had some difficulties over some convention financial matters. Dr. Lowndes retired from his job.

When we first went to Hawaii, Dr. Lowndes came out with a group of people involved in our churches in Hawaii. Ken Lyle had resigned as our director of missions in the New York City area to go as executive director of the Maryland Baptist Convention. Dr. Lowndes talked with me about Quinn Pugh as Ken's replacement. I strongly concurred. In fact, Brother David Jones led our first revival in Waikiki, and Quinn had come through Honolulu on his way to work in several churches in an evangelism week in Australia. Quinn came to our revival services and sang in our choir that night. The next morning, I took him to the airport to board his plane for Australia. I asked him how he would react to going to New York City as a replacement for Ken Lyle. He replied, "Well, I never thought of such a thing, but it might be interesting." Quinn had been pastor of our Bergen Baptist Church in New Jersey. He had a strong charismatic element develop in the Bergen Church, and one of his close friends was involved. Quinn felt led to resign and go back to Southern Baptist Theological Seminary to do his doctoral work. He was able to stay in the home of Dr. and Mrs. Morgan Patterson, professor of church history at Southern and Dorothy's first cousin, who were on sabbatical in Oxford, England.

Quinn later came back to Bel Air, Maryland, to serve as pastor of the Calvary Baptist Church. Unknown to him to this day, that church had contacted me in Madison about becoming their pastor. I had held a revival at Calvary Baptist Church with Brother Duke Watson, the pastor, while I was in Annapolis in 1959. Dorothy's mother had come to visit us, and we took her and our girls on the tour of Philadelphia and Valley Forge, an unforgettable experience—so much for connections. I felt that I was unable to leave Madison and knowing that Quinn was soon to come out of Southern with his doctoral degree, I recommended him. He came to Maryland and was strongly involved in Maryland Convention work, president of its Executive Board, along with other positions. From there and with Jack Lowndes's recommendation, he became the replacement to Ken Lyle and later replacement for Dr. Jack Lowndes in Syracuse.

Quinn has been wonderfully used of God to purchase and refurbish a lovely building secured in a strategic area and enlisted multiple volunteer help in the central office of our new New York Baptist Convention. He has just recently retired after twelve-plus years of faithful and inspiring leadership and service. A new era faces our New York Convention, as in all of our newer work areas. The older are passing off the scene, and only God can raise up the new generation of leaders, and He is assuredly doing just that. An addendum: the present excellent pastor of the Madison Baptist Church is the Reverend Steve Holloway. His wife, Becca, is the daughter of Nathan Porter who was one of the very able associates of Glendon McCullough when I served on our Home Mission Board in 1968. What goes around comes around. I'm deeply grateful for the privilege of knowing and working with so many wonderful gifted men and women in the New York experience of a lifetime. Madison Baptist Church was at the center of it all.

With the coming of Dr. Jack Lowndes, we were invited to go with his tour group to the Baptist World Alliance in Stockholm, Sweden, in 1975. This tour included England, Wales, Czechoslovakia, East and West Berlin, Austria, and Scotland. Some chose Copenhagen, Denmark, instead of Prague, Czechoslovakia. We enlisted Alice Kelley from Pittsburgh, Ruth Sims from Newport News, and Elizabeth Painter from Roanoke. This was truly an experience of unusual meaning in our lives. Dr. Lowndes was a perfect host along with his wife, Doris. We flew from Kennedy Airport in New York City to London, England, where we were encumbered with transferring our own baggage because of the ground crew strike. I did much of it myself, and we were just in time for our continuing flight to Stockholm. In Stockholm, we stayed in a luxury hotel and experienced daylight until 3:00 A.M. every morning. July was the month. In fact, while trying to sleep, the sun was shining brightly outside as Stockholm was far north in our hemisphere. We rode buses and the trains everywhere we went. Sweden has an excellent transit system.

The Baptist World Alliance was a new experience for us. All events were televised so that every country received the events in their own language although every service was in English. We met a number of American Baptist leaders, including Owen Cooper from Yazoo City, Mississippi, businessman and special friend and president of our Southern Baptist Convention at the time. Owen Cooper came to

New York during our time there, spoke in our Madison Church, and later we were guests for lunch in the home of Joe Hunt. We learned that day that the Coopers had an autistic grandson. C. J. Humphrey, a lawyer from Amarillo, Texas, was there. He came to New York to help us set up our Missionary Millionaire Program that has been a major source of financial help for much of our Metropolitan New York mission work. We made investments that are still earning interest to benefit our work. C. J. later came to the Northwest to help us set up a similar program that has been a similar source of help for our work here. It has helped our Mountain Highway Baptist Church in the calling of our new pastor, Brother Wesley Funkhouser. There was great help with moving expenses. It was indeed a special thrill to be a part of that Baptist World Alliance in Stockholm. We met Frank and Janet Faye Campbell who had come out of our Waverly Church in Roanoke, Virginia, for whom I was privileged to perform their wedding ceremony. He became an outstanding pastor in North Carolina, president of the North Carolina Baptist Convention, and more recently, in 1986, Dorothy and I attended his inauguration as president of Averett Baptist College in Danville, Virginia. Janet was our teenage babysitter in Roanoke. We have been close to both families.

We were impressed with the open markets of fruit and vegetables in Stockholm. This was a special touch of the native people. There was a city center, a large, open area close by our hotel where special events took place. One day we shared in the Salvation Army Band and their group in a wonderful gospel singing and preaching experience—true to God's Word. That blessed our hearts. We went out into the open country one night to share in a prayer and Bible study fellowship in a local home. The son had made a lot of money buying and selling used autos from the United States. We were much impressed with the old city of Stockholm, Gamla Stan, where the royal palace was, and where the kings were crowned. The narrow streets and shops were very fascinating.

We met our friend, Clyde Bryan, who headed up tour groups. He was the former pastor of First Baptist Church of Hattiesburg, Mississippi, through my recommendation to Dr. T. D. Brown, professor New Testament at Clear Creek Bible College in Kentucky. We had known the Bryans in Gallatin, Tennessee, close to Portland, where he was pastor of the Gallatin First Baptist Church. He later went to Hattiesburg, and from there he was to organize his worldwide tour ministries—again, connections. The last time we saw Clyde was in the Honolulu Airport. Some lady in his tour group had lost her glasses. Dorothy later found them in an airport restroom and mailed them to the lady in Jackson, Mississippi. Clyde looked exhausted that night in Hawaii and also seemed exhausted in Stockholm. We knew the feeling because we had led several tour groups. We left Stockholm to visit beautiful Prague, Czechoslovakia.

Our druggist in Chatham, New Jersey, had often talked with us about beautiful Prague. It was under communist dominance when we visited, and we were aware of the tight control everywhere. We visited the famous thousand-year-old library, saw the smallest book in the world, and the ledger Lord Nelson of English Naval fame and his paramour, Lady Hamilton, had signed. We visited the museum of the Bohemian (gypsy) culture and the history of the early rulers of Czechoslovakia. We saw children marching to schools under communist control in uniforms that some see as vital to the future of our present school system.

We walked the old streets, went to the famous city square where John Huss was burned at the stake, and saw the famous Charles Bridge and the Jewish synagogue already described. We saw a wedding there in the square that day at City Hall. It was exciting! Dorothy, Ruth Sims, Elizabeth Painter, and Alice Kelley, our Virginia group, elected to stay in downtown Prague to shop. The rest of us went back to the hotel. They became lost and sought the help of a communist policeman. Dorothy drew a diagram on her hand of where they needed to go. The policeman was able to help this frightened group find their way back to our International Hotel. Our stay in that hotel was an experience in itself. The food was just great.

There were those who were constantly trying to exchange money for profit which was highly illegal, if one were caught. One day out front, I was talking with someone who understood English. Suddenly, I became aware of several around me apparently listening intently. I quieted way down. Just recently our European Baptist Seminary has moved from Ruschlikon, Switzerland, to Prague. A number of summer college students came at their own expense to help get our new facility in condition for service.

One other unusual experience for us in Prague was our meeting for prayer and worship with a Swedish Baptist group. Dr. Jack Lowndes had known the young leaders previously. We rode the inner-city train there and back, and it was a memorable experience and blessing. We had fellowship afterwards while seeing their church. In context, I need to tell about a Saturday evening worship experience in Stockholm where the Lord's Supper was beautifully observed. I recall especially the loud crack of the breaking of the specially prepared bread symbolizing the awful sufferings in the Body of our Lord.

One other interesting sidelight had to do with our flight into Prague. There were some Bulgarians who had to step aside and wait for our tour group, and we saw the surly, angry reaction on their faces. We were glad to get ahead of that group.

We flew from Prague into East Berlin that was under strong, communist dominance. We went from there by bus to West Berlin to our very nice luxury hotel. I recall their different electrical current system when I hooked up my automatic shaver with an adapter. The bathrooms were sheer luxury. We toured West Berlin the next morning and saw the damage of World War II. One of the great churches, the Kaiser Wilhelm Church, had been bombed and left standing as a monument. We saw the area where the Berlin airlift under stubborn President Harry Truman had brought food to otherwise starving West Berliners. Harry finally won the day! We were able to get several souvenirs on the streets. We saw the Queen Charlotte Palace, Charlottenburg Palace, that is very beautiful! We saw the four-power prison where the condemned prisoners from World War II were confined. The only prisoner remaining was Rudolph Hess who died there only recently. He had refused to be released.

The main street of West Berlin is Kurfurstendamm. We traveled this street and went into one of the sidewalk pubs—beer hall—where we listened to German band music. One of our favorites was "Beer Barrel Polka." The band would graciously play our requests as we drank soft drinks and ate peanuts. Some of those band members were from the United States and gave us special attention. We thoroughly enjoyed the experience and realized some of what the famous German beer halls have meant to German culture. The famous beer hall Putsch in Munich started Hitler and his brown shirts on their fateful journey to World War II and the ultimate death of sixty million people.

Next came our tour of communist East Berlin as we came to the famous Check Point Charlie. Our tour bus was held up, and we were all required to get out and line up. There was a question about one of our passengers from Virginia, Ruth Sims. She was originally listed as Ruth Cooper Sims but on her passport listed as Ruth C. Sims. Our Ruth had to argue and finally convinced the inquisitors that Ruth Cooper Sims and Ruth C. Sims were one and the same.

Finally, we got through to East Berlin, and what a contrast it was to West Berlin. Before the war, the most famous Berlin street was Unter Den Linden, named for the famous Linden tree. This street was now in East Berlin and ran along the Berlin Wall. We were able to examine this wall where street addresses were still visible. These places were where people had been shot and killed. They were marked also. We came to the area where the trains had run in the famous depot, in and out of Berlin, now in ruins, as indeed were all the notorious Third Reich buildings which were modeled on ancient Roman buildings. We saw the place where the books that offended Nazism were burned in a bonfire. This was the same area Karl

Marx had lived and written about his communist philosophy. We saw and walked through the communist cemetery that was well marked with varied communist statuary. As we drove along, we saw a high mountain area ahead. Our tour guide pointed this out as the place to which the vast ruins of once-beautiful pre-World War II Berlin had been consigned. What a sad travesty in every direction.

It was a breath of fresh air to go from Berlin to Vienna, Austria, by the famous, formerly beautiful Blue Danube and through the fabled Vienna Woods. The Blue Danube was gray with the silt and pollution of the years, and the Vienna Woods were blighted from the same pollution. However, the city of Vienna was still beautiful indeed. We traversed the famous street where the ancient emperors traveled by stagecoach in ceremonial fashion from the lovely Schonbrunn Palace and gorgeous gardens to the other end of the city and the Winter Palace, winter home of the Hapsburgs.

Prior to World War I, Vienna was the center of the world with hundreds of years of military glory, marching armies, marching bands, and soldiers on horseback. The winter scenes were said to be out of this world. There were varied, beautiful palaces where the rich and famous lived. When we got on our tour bus, our woman tour guide said, "Ladies and Gentlemen, our history is behind us, and we have to make the most of it." We understood better as we attended a typical Vienna musical dance production. There was a thunderstorm outside. We toured the famous Schonbrunn Palace where Austrian ruler, Queen Maria Teresa, had ruled and from whence her daughter, Marie Antoinette, went to marry Louis XVI of France. Both were finally guillotined during the terrible French Revolution. The people were aroused when Marie Antoinette is said to have replied to *les miserables* (the miserable ones), "Let them eat cake." She never really said such. The poor little dauphin (the Prince who was to be the next ruler) disappeared into mystery and history.

We saw where Napoleon Bonaparte and his second wife, Princess Marie Louise, had his only son. This son grew to young manhood and wasted away and died in the Schonbrunn Palace. And poor Napoleon died in disgrace on the Isle of Elba. At the time that it seemed this military genius would conquer the world, a baby boy was born in Hardin County, Kentucky and named Abraham Lincoln. We saw on our tour, in various places, where Napoleon's armies had advanced to, in his glory journey to conquer the world, until he met the Duke of Wellington on English sod and God said, "Thus far and no further."

I had read an unusual story about Adolph Hitler and his beginnings as an Austrian housepainter. He was coming out of the great Vienna museum one day and ran into a tour group. The tour guide was telling the group the story of the spear of Christ that would rule the world. Hitler, who had been in a funky depression, went back into the museum and stood looking at that spear and had a vision that he was to rule the world. The story said that at the famous Austrian Anschluss, Hitler was three hours late, as the people waited sadly to see their country taken over by this mad man. He reportedly, was late for two reasons: 1) to foil any prearranged assassination attempt and 2) to give his hated hit man, Heinrich Himmler, time to get this spear of Christ and bring it into his possession. When the war was over, General Eisenhower ordered the recovered spear to be returned to the National Museum in Vienna. I made a special trip, alone, on a hot day, to that museum in the vicinity of the Winter Palace. I inquired about its location, finally came to the spear of Christ and stood gazing at it. According to the story, King Saul had the spear in his possession and was repeatedly foiled in his attempt to slay David. It was preserved, and was the spear finally thrust into the side of Christ to insure His death. What a story of mystery and intrigue.

Of all the many unusual sights I saw in that museum that day, one stands out. All the keys of the famous palaces during the time of the Austro-Hungarian domination of the world until World War I were there. I tried to imagine all the hands, now gone into the shroud of history, that handled those keys. "Man proposes and God disposes."

We thoroughly enjoyed going into the museums, making small purchases, and just sitting outside our hotel's sidewalk coffee shop, watching the street traffic, and imagining Vienna in its glory days.

We flew from Vienna and back to London for our remarkable tour of London and the beautiful English countryside and then to Scotland and Wales. We saw the famous Tower of London and the beautiful, gorgeous crown jewels. Never before, nor since, have we seen anything like them. We saw where the infamous Henry VIII had his several wives' heads chopped off, where they were jailed in the cold austere tower until their execution date. We also saw the ravens at the tower.

On Sunday, we attended worship at the famous Spurgeon's Tabernacle/College. Thousands were saved as the gospel was preached in Spurgeon's day. At the front, there was a plaque in the floor at the spot where over five thousand people were saved as they kneeled to pray. The tabernacle had been seriously damaged during the war when one of the German U-2 bombs fell in that vicinity. There were maybe three hundred people in church on that Sunday. What a blessing it was to attend and to remember.

We visited the Westminster Abbey where kings and queens were crowned and the famous worshipped. We saw the spaces marked where the famous of

England were entombed. David Livingston is entombed there. It was he who left his heart in Africa, literally. All England stopped when this great missionary was entombed. We saw and heard the Big Ben clock.

Several of us took a walk in downtown London at night in complete safety. We stood opposite Number Ten Downing Street, the official residence of the prime minister. One policeman was on duty. You could have thrown a rock across the street. It was so close. We saw the memorial to Lord Nelson in celebration of the victory over the Spanish Armada. We saw the houses of parliament from many perspectives though we did not go inside. We walked through St. James Park in the moonlight and by Clarence House where the Queen Mother resides. Dorothy and I walked completely around the area of Buckingham Palace, official residence of the royal family.

We left London by tour bus for the countryside. We passed the area of Windsor Castle and the homes of the famous from the past, especially in the time of Henry VIII. We saw the hovels of the very poor and the little villages where they lived. We came to Wales at night for an old-style banquet just like the ancients. We all got to taste the ale from the tankards, and the food was very good. The ale tasted like watery beer. I have merely tasted that, and only once. We passed through the area of Sandringham, the summer home of kings and royalty—Edward VIII and Wally Simpson episodes, his predecessor King Edward VII, son and successor of Queen Victoria, who was always treated like an impish child under her roof. Sandringham was Edward VII's place of refuge with many women including Winston Churchill's mother, Jennie, an American, and Lord Randolph Churchill, Winston's father, who died of syphilis. We stopped at the famous Three Feathers Restaurant, the eating place of royalty, for an excellent lunch.

We traveled through the beautiful Scottish countryside and saw the sheep enclosures. The shepherd lays down to rest across the lone entrance, protecting his sheep with his life. We saw the famous Hadrian Wall from the time of the Romans. We came to the famous city of Edinburgh and the famous university. We saw the place where the Wesleys lived and preached and wrote more than six thousand hymns. We also viewed the place where Mary, Queen of Scots, sister of Queen Elizabeth I, held forth. They were children of different mothers. Mary, Queen of Scots, was the daughter of Catherine of Aragon, Catholic and the first wife of Henry VIII who would never divorce him. Elizabeth I finally beheaded her sister, Mary, and ruled undisputed for her long and successful reign. She was the daughter of Anne Boleyn, the wife whom Henry pursued for long years before she finally succumbed to his insistent wooing. Then he tired of her and had her beheaded from the Tower of London on trumped-up charges of adultery. This evil monster of a king lived and died with syphilis brought on by his numerous "sexca-pades." He, out of his evil machinations, brought England from under Catholic domain to the Anglican faith, which is now the Church of England. We visited the Scottish Castle, high above the city of Edinburgh. We saw all the ancient glory of the Scottish kings and queens. The home of John Knox was close by. He was the great leader of the Presbyterian faith who prayed so earnestly, "Give me Scotland, or I die." Scotland was deeply moved and influenced by John Knox.

The Wesleys and the Whitefields were the progenitors of the Methodist faith. Whitefield would preach in the open fields and to great crowds when he was refused the use of official buildings. Much of the influence of these great, spiritual giants has deeply affected the history and spiritual underpinnings of our own country from its beginnings. We spent several days in Edinburgh at the International Hotel that was our official domicile. The food and attention to detail were excellent not only in our hotel but elsewhere. There was an open park area right in the city center where crowds gathered for various entertainment and family picnics.

We had previously visited ancient Canterbury, the center of the Anglican faith that is still enclosed by its ancient walls. We visited the famous cathedral, a poem in architectural design as indeed were all the ancient buildings. We saw the place in Canterbury where Thomas à Beckett was murdered by his enemies on the inner cathedral steps. Many of the great Anglican saints were buried in Canterbury.

We had also previously visited William Shakespeare country in the Cotswolds, his home, the Anne Hathaway Cottage, the theatre for the original Shakespeare productions, and the place of the Shakespeare burial ground.

We visited the places of several other famous cathedrals. Salisbury is reputed to be one of the most beautiful in the world. We saw there the world's most ancient clock. The ropes and pulleys were still working. There were people from all over the world who had come to paint the Salisbury Cathedral. We visited Winchester Cathedral, spent the night at Chester, and saw that most beautiful cathedral in Dorothy's words. We saw the area where King James I killed John Wycliff, whose last words in dying were, "O God, open the King of England's eyes." God did indeed open King James's eyes, and he assembled the seventy famous scholars who brought together the most famous and most used Bible of the world, the King James Bible. This King James started the game of golf that is so prevalent every-where today—even Billy Graham plays. One of the most famous cathedrals we visited was the York Cathedral. It costs more than two million dollars a year to keep it in repair. There we were made aware of the term *Ex Cathedra*. The ancient cathedrals contained an area for all manner of barter and trade—a veritable ancient market system. It, of course, was the burial place of many of the rich and famous. All was safe inside the cathedral area—a place of sanctuary made famous by the film, *The Hunchback of Notre Dame*. We had previously visited the ancient city of Bath where the Romans had an area for healing baths from the flowing, healing waters. The waters are still flowing. The Roman system is still in existence.

We had previously visited Stonehenge, probably the most famous ancient monument in England. These were ancient stone obelisks, somehow brought in most ancient days to an area where cattle now roam. It is a mystery as to how the ancients got those obelisks there and for what purpose. The best synthesis of opinion is that they were so placed as to reflect the sunrays in such a way as to develop a time system. They are still shrouded in mystery.

Our tour of England and trip to the Baptist World Alliance finally concluded. These tremendous experiences are once-in-a-lifetime exposures. We flew from Heathrow back to Kennedy in New York where we, rather tired and emotionally spent, scattered from one another in different directions to our homes. Alice Kelley and Elizabeth Painter came home with us where we met our children who rejoiced in our homecoming. We shared our experiences with those we had left behind including our dear Madison Church people. In fact, I think some grew tired of the sharing, and we shut up.

The Southern Baptist Convention met in Norfolk, Virginia, in 1976 and tremendous goals for Southern Baptists were developed. In the next twenty-five years, we purposed to share the gospel message of God's saving grace with every person on planet Earth. It involved the developing and funding of programs, missions, and otherwise to implement this ambitious undertaking. At that convention, the president of the United States, Gerald Ford, was a guest speaker. All of us had to be inside and quiet with no moving in or out for that session.

One day in the hallway, I met Dr. Edmund Walker, a former seminary classmate and the executive director of the Hawaii Baptist Convention. He asked, "Charlie, are you stuck in New York?" I replied, "No, not necessarily." Thereby started the next phase of our journey.

The Olivet Baptist Church in Honolulu, Hawaii, was the strong base church for all of our Hawaii Southern Baptist work. The American Baptist work and Southern Baptist work started and grew simultaneously from the start of Baptist work in the islands. Our Sue Saito (Nishikawa) from Wahiawa was involved in the early days. She had been educated in the United States at Dodd College in Shreveport, Louisiana, where Dr. M. E. Dodd, one of our

Waikiki Baptist Church, Honolul, Hawaii.

outstanding Southern Baptist preachers and one-time president of the Southern Baptist Convention was founder and president. Sue, as a college special missionary speaker for Training Union district meetings in Mississippi, had visited in Dorothy's home in Calhoun City, Mississippi, on June 10, 1936. Dorothy's father was pastor of First Baptist Church in Calhoun City. Dorothy, thirteen years old, remembers that she and Sue were together and shared on that date. Also, Dr. J. Franklin Ray, father of Dr. Hermon Ray, earlier pastor of the Waikiki Baptist Church in Honolulu, had visited in the Patterson home on March 13, 1936. More about these later except to say that Sue remembered well Pearl Harbor Day, December 7, 1941, when Japan struck our ships an all but paralyzing blow. The Foreign Mission Board secretary, Dr. Charles Madry, was in Honolulu on behalf of our Southern Baptist work on that dastardly famous day.

Our initial contact with the Hawaii experience was with the pulpit search committee of the Olivet Baptist Church. The Olivet people sent one of their leading laymen, Paul Oyer, to visit us and our church in Madison on November 20, 1976. It turned out that the Olivet committee was very slow in action and never really followed through in dealing with us. There was a word to us that they had been negative toward another person they were dealing with and that I was now at the top of their list. Yet, nothing came of it. Not until later when I visited in behalf of Waikiki Church did I get to question them about their dereliction in dealing with me. They apologized and later called our very dear friend, Dr. Curtis

Askew, as their pastor for the four and a half years while we were in Waikiki.

One hot day (July 6, 1977), I was mowing my lawn in Madison when we received a telephone call from Sue Saito Nishikawa, chairperson of the Waikiki pulpit search committee. She stated that they were interested in us via Dr. Edmund Walker. Sue invited us to come to Hawaii for a visit and in view of a call. We prayed about it and decided to go in early August of 1977. My brother Joe and family were home from Germany where he had served as pastor at a German/American Baptist church for one year. They stayed with our family in Madison and preached for me while we were gone. Somehow my initial reaction in Waikiki and Hawaii was negative because of a mix-up in the pastoral support package from our Home Mission Board. Things rocked along, and the work in Hawaii kept tugging at our hearts. In the meantime, with the Home Mission Board working through Dr. Jack Redford, the committee had Bill Jenkins, whose daughter had married Dr. Jack Redford's son, doing an excellent interim job at Waikiki. The people liked him. I wrote Dr. Walker about our continued concern, and he relayed this to Sue Nishikawa. The result was that they called us as pastor and family with a moving date for January 13, 1978. This was the day after the marriage of our daughter Martha Ruth to Kevin Sowards in Dallas, Texas. What a combination of circumstances we had to work through.

The closing of our work in Madison and in our New York Baptist Convention was all involved. Matters pertaining to our move and family needs were very crucial, especially regarding our son. There had to be adequate provision for continued schooling or a work program for him.

The truth of all these matters is that God was working before, then, and afterwards to bring it to pass according to His plan for our lives as individuals, for each of His churches involved, and for all the people and circumstances. It was a propitious time for us, for our Madison Church, for Waikiki, and all matters pertaining.

In Madison, it was a time when changes were occurring, looking toward a continuing great mission and ministry. To date, many of those formerly strategic people have gone to other places, pursuits, and retirement. Yet, God has constantly raised up new people, and the work has gone on with continuing excellence and strategic blessings under succeeding leadership. The Madison Church has been strategic in all of our New York area work and still is under the able leadership of Pastor Steve Holloway. Steve was a Baptist student in Princeton University working with Deal Hudson who worked with Baptist students. Deal was formerly at Montville where Don Morris later became pastor. Steve Holloway is also the son of Southern Baptist missionaries to Japan.

I do recall the strong feeling of Larry Newkirk that we ought to move ahead in Madison, build a home for an associate on our Madison Baptist Church property, and call a good associate. This obviously was not in God's plan for that time. All of us then present have been taken away and live in different areas. Yet, God left behind such people as the Eldred Carts, the Les Dearings, and the Bill Mussers. Those formerly so able and effective in Madison are still serving faithfully in other places and in Southern Baptist churches. In the beautiful wedding of Gina Weaver and Joe Seibert on September 9, 1995, in Garden City, South Carolina, we had a veritable old home week of former Madison Baptist members, all active in their churches in places God has led them to live and serve. "That Madison Baptist Spirit" was and is still alive and well.

One of our real problems in moving from Madison to Hawaii was our beautiful wood furniture. We learned from our friends, the Curtis Askews, that termites would eat up wood furniture in Hawaii (Curtis and I dated our future wives together at Blue Mountain Baptist College, using his car). My nephew, Harry Jolly, Brother Fred's oldest son, and his brother-in-law, Bobby Rennie, brought a Ryder truck with all essential materials from Pennsylvania to move our furniture. Harry worked with Howard Johnson in Pennsylvania at the time, and they had a franchise with Ryder. Through this they allowed Harry to bring their truck and moving paraphernalia. What a very great help this was to us. Also, the George Wassilys, our Egyptian friends in New York, brought their van and took much of our unneeded "baggage" to their home and helped to meet some of our needs. It was mid-December when this all took place. Our furniture was dispersed to the Stoney Painters in Roanoke, Virginia, to daughter, Sarah, in Blacksburg, Virginia, and Harry took some of the best to his home. He now lives in Dallas, Texas. All of this furniture, highly valuable still, is with Sarah and Harry and is properly used and cared for. We gave it to them because we cannot use it where we live now in the Northwest. What a gesture of love Harry performed in a tight situation.

One final trip over our whole great northeast area came at the invitation of our executive director, Dr. Jack Lowndes. We were in the Lake Placid, New York, area for an executive board meeting, looking toward the coming 1980 Winter Olympics in Lake Placid. A new church came out of that experience with a heavy investment of Home Mission Board and other Southern Baptist involvement. We left from Lake Placid on our trip with Jack and Doris Lowndes with me driving the car.

We knew pretty well the New Jersey/New York City area but less so the upstate area. With Dr. Lowndes, we took the trip upstate to the Lakes area, especially the beautiful Finger Lakes region that we had never seen before. We went to Albany, New York, and then south. We stopped at the Corning Glass area and left with more than we came with. We visited the area where Norman and Lena Bell gave the best part of their lives in unselfish labor—the Brushton Church and other churches in the area. We visited Ithaca and Cornell University and marveled at how God had led Southern Baptists to have all these areas on their hearts, sharing now with other denominational groups the burden for God's people and those not yet His people. We were reminded of so many of our pastors and their families who had been led of God to serve unselfishly, sacrificially, and effectively, and whom God has used in these places of His kingdom, and of our work in Syracuse and Fredonia, the Joe Olivers, the Gene Fants, the Curtis Porters, the J. T. Davises, and others, whom God has blessed in these tremendous, populated segments.

We came back tired but thrilled anew as we spent the night with Jack and Doris Lowndes and family at their home in Manlius, New York, looking back to where we had been and what we had seen and rejoicing anew in our Lord. We should mention that their daughter, Barbara Lowndes, started a Baptist bookstore ministry out of their home. We saw the track of the famous Erie Canal that opened up this whole, vast northeast area to trade, commerce, and new communities. It was one of the tremendous projects of our United States government way back when.

In November of 1977, we had our state convention meeting in Albany, New York, the state capitol. I had the privilege of serving as state president and telling the people about God's leading us to Hawaii and inviting people to come to see us.

Dorothy and I had made a recent trek across the Long Island Sound to the South Hampton area where the rich and famous live and saw beautiful Montauk Point with the old lighthouse. This had been a marriage enrichment conference for pastors and wives led by Avery and Myra Sayers, involving our Metropolitan New York Association group. Even as I write now, years afterwards, our hearts warm and thrill as I pray for these vast areas of people where God has privileged Southern Baptists to plant churches to reach His people.

We were winding down now in our last days of privileged ministry through our Madison Baptist Church. We had a final state evangelism conference in Madison in early January of 1978. All the folks came despite bad weather. We were heavily involved in Madison taking care of details. My brother Joe was present. He had just accepted a small church north of New York City where Harry and Betty Watson had so faithfully and sacrificially served. They still do to this day. Harry, a pastor now, was our longtime association clerk/secretary. He has never given up though numbers have always been few. Joe decided after a short time that he was not suited for that area and finally wound up in more familiar Texas country. I can see him now sitting in the audience in Madison and my forlorn feeling to be leaving this dear brother behind. We were always close, the first two in the Jolly family of ten. He was the oldest and always had the feeling of being the protector, and I rather depended on it.

Joe is gone now. He had leukemia that he fought valiantly but lost the battle in January of 1993. I remember the funeral at Fort Sam Houston where our own father, the first Joe Jolly, had been in World War I. Indeed, our father developed pneumonia and nearly died there before any of us got started. Joe had previously showed us the barracks area where our father had been stationed. I remember our father telling of going with a group to an old abandoned church and hearing a rattlesnake as they sat atop a pile of rocks at night. As he told it, "I must have jumped thirty feet!" I also remember him telling about "Jaw Bone pay day." He never drank or caroused and tried to save money to send home to his mother and family. The more-carousing soldiers would borrow money from our father and pay back double on payday. They were always broke, and our father had more to send home.

There was a general being buried at the same time as Joe. Joe's service had to wait until the twenty-one-cannon salute to the general's memory. Joe's casket was on hold on a catafalque and in clear hearing of the cannon salute. Later, Joe had an ordinary twenty-one-gun salute. That day Joe got it all, as he would say, "so far as it went."

One of the last gestures of "that Madison Baptist Spirit" was a gift of five thousand dollars given into our Annuity Board retirement fund. That money, with our own monthly deposits, has helped us to have a more secure retirement. It was an excellent investment for us and is repaid to us many times over. Our eternal thanks go to them. Madison has always been good to us. Many individuals have continued to relate to us in God's love in Christ—even more, later, in the Hawaii experience.

11

Honolulu, Hawaii

1978–1982

Larry Newkirk brought his rented van and took our family and nineteen bags of personal belongings to board our plane from LaGuardia Airport in New York, to Peoria, Illinois, where Mary Margaret lives. Bless Larry's loving heart, we got all that baggage checked. We arrived in Peoria in below-zero weather with a wind chill factor of minus forty degrees. We were there two nights and then, with Mary, we flew into Dallas for all the events of Martha Ruth's wedding to Kevin Sowards. For the first time in a long while, there was a snow and ice storm in Dallas, but the dear folks, family, and otherwise, came from all over for that occasion. My brother Joe assisted me in carrying out my fatherly duties first and then performing the ceremony in the local Calvary Baptist Church on January 12, 1978.

Dorothy's Aunt Helen from Smackover, Arkansas, came by bus. Dorothy's Uncle Palmer and Aunt Jess from New Orleans, visiting with their son, Ben Patterson and family, were there (Ben was a contributing editor of *Guidepost* magazine but taught journalism at Northeast Texas State in Denton). It was the last time we were to be with Dorothy's Uncle Palmer, her father's brother. I recall Martha Ruth was upset that things were not perfect at the reception. The weather, being a factor, had frozen all the English ivy. All in all, it was a beautiful occasion, and Kevin's family more than made it all very special. The Joe Hunts, who were also present, made it possible for us to have a car on this occasion. They have always been special to us.

The next day, January 13, we bade our final goodbye, tired, but happy and thankful for our new home-to-be in Hawaii. I was due in Honolulu at 7:30 P.M. for a message at the Hawaii state evangelism conference. However, we had to stop in Los Angeles, California, to repair an overseas plane light that had malfunctioned. Sue Nishikawa, who was chairperson of the Waikiki pulpit

217

search committee and state WMU director, was on the same plane and we fellowshipped with her. She had attended a national executive WMU board meeting in Birmingham, Alabama. We arrived in Honolulu at 11:30 P.M. to be met by the Roger Laubes, the Lyle Campbells, Sara Schuessler, Edith Crook, secretary, and others to "smother" us with beautiful Hawaiian leis and give us the grand aloha royal welcome despite the late hour. Dr. Edmund Walker, state secretary for Hawaii Baptists, gave my message at the evangelism conference. It was a wonderful welcome.

Every place we have been privileged to live and serve our Lord has been a life experience of very special meaning. We have kept in touch with people from every place over the years through our annual Christmas letter and otherwise. People have come to see us, and we have gone back to share with them, always careful to honor the incumbent pastor. These pastors also have welcomed us back and asked us to come for special events, always taking care of our expenses. God has let us minister among the most loving, generous, and caring people everywhere we have served, even in the many places where we were privileged to minister in revivals up and down this broad land we call America. God has blessed in the saving of souls and in changed and enriched lives wherever He has allowed us to go. "What a fellowship, what a joy divine!" One day in Glory, we shall have the eternal opportunity of precious fellowship.

Hawaii was, and is, one of those unusual experiences right out in the great Pacific, the ocean around us all the time. Waikiki Baptist Church was "right in the eye of the hurricane," a tourist mecca. All the time, day and night, the people came from everywhere.

We lived on the ninth floor of a lovely condominium right across the *ala wai* (the canal) that separated Waikiki from old Honolulu. We could stand or sit on our *lanai* (deck) and see it all. Everyday, at each meal and otherwise, we looked out across a broad expanse of open space, places for fairs, athletics, and other events, and saw Diamond Head, the major landmark of Honolulu. The airplanes came and went over this well-known marker. Diamond Head is actually an extinct volcano. Honolulu, right on the ocean, sits between Diamond Head and the other extinct volcano called the Punch Bowl. It is now the National Cemetery (Arlington) of the Pacific where the honored dead of all our wars are buried at government expense, meticulously cared for, and another great tourist attraction.

Honolulu, with tall buildings in the older tourist areas of the downtown section, was separate from Waikiki with its tall hotels, churches, government rest and recuperation hotel, and museums. What a place to live and serve. I could lie on my bed at night and see Waikiki, the *ala wai,* and the constant stream of traffic. I could see the fish jumping in the *ala wai* in the daytime. The Waikiki area had originally been called a "duck pond." It was always rather marshy and wet because of the abundant waters that came down from the nearby mountains. The digging of the *ala wai* allowed this constant flow of waters to drain away into the ocean and to dry up Waikiki and make it the phenomenal place it has become. Formerly, before the airlines came, the people would come by ships into Honolulu. The Aloha Tower area was the original meeting place of the ancient Hawaiian people to plan for the islands before the constant horde of tourists came and is still in use today, but less hectic.

The first of these tourists were the Christian missionaries who came to the islands in the early 1800s. These missionaries were allowed to build a whole conclave of living quarters as the base for their operations and spiritual ministry in Honolulu. It is still there serving as a museum. The missionaries found a people who intermarried, brothers with sisters, etc., even among the ruling classes. They introduced the Bible and its teachings and slowly things began to change. The first English word spoken by an ancient ruler was *LaBibla.*

The long era before the Christian missionaries was centered in the ancient whaling industry. The whale oil was used for lighting and heating and was more desirable than any other source. The sailors would come in on the whaling expeditions on the Island of Maui, called Lahaina, to rest and to "raise hell" among the natives. The people fit right into this routine and, altogether, the sailors and the people resisted the threat of Christian teaching and change.

It was the great King Kamehameha who wrought tremendous changes among the myriad hostile tribal groups. Great battles were fought. Blood ran like water as he and his native soldiers fought and killed by the thousands. His places of exploit are pointed out everywhere in the islands, and he is still revered as the great chieftain who brought order out of chaos and all the islands under his one rule. In one mountain promontory, called the Palisades, where the wind blows fiercely and continuously, Kamehameha shoved over seven hundred resistant warriors over the cliff to their death below. Each year in June on his birthday, he is honored with a state holiday and beautiful pageants. Beautiful Hawaiian women ride on specially arrayed horses, and there are myriads of people standing, sitting, picnicking, and rejoicing as the parade passes by.

When we first came to Waikiki and to the church, I found that we had only two deacons. They met with me regularly on Sunday before the evening service. One was aging Harlan Murphy, graduate of Mississippi Baptist College, my alma mater. He had known and loved Sybil Brame Townsend, oldest daughter of Dr. and Mrs. Webb Brame, pastor of First Baptist Church of Yazoo City, Mississippi. However, Sybil married Claude Townsend who later died from an injury received in a fruit tree pruning accident. They had a son, Timothy, who married Carol Tyler, daughter of Dr. and Mrs. W. C. Tyler, who was president of Blue Mountain Baptist College, Dorothy's alma mater. We later met them in Annapolis, Maryland, where Dr. Tyler in earlier days had been pastor of the College Avenue Baptist Church in Annapolis. When Dr. Tyler taught Bible in Blue Mountain Baptist College, Dorothy was his paper grader. She had heard him talk about College Avenue and their sad experience of burying their first child there—stillborn. We shared sacred memories and rejoiced together with Timothy and Carol at the College Avenue Baptist Church celebration. Deacon Harlan Murphy married lovely Margie. They both dearly loved music, and Harlan sang in the choir. He was an author who later sent me a copy of his book, *The Freeing of Fredeau,* about Huguenot days in France. Harlan and Margie retired and moved to the Los Angeles, California, area where their daughter and family lived. He did not hesitate to give me fatherly advice on everything, and most of the time this was highly appreciated. He was truly a great spirit.

Our other deacon, a younger Chinese man, was George Ching, an international diamond merchant who was also in the insurance business. He was the chairman of our deacons and very solicitous of our welfare. He and his wife had one daughter, Jocelyn, who was married to Kenny Kitahara of Korean-Japanese descent with a daughter, Carol Ann. George, among other pursuits, was an avid beekeeper, and we often were recipients of delicious honey. With the help and encouragement of these two deacons, our deacon body grew to ten excellent men of varied community talent and interests. All of them were good, solid, Christian men, and their wives were equally talented and highly dedicated to our Lord's work.

George Ching took it on himself to take our family on a tour of the big island of Hawaii. This required a short air flight on Aloha airlines, one of the usual ways to get from one island to another. There are eight islands. We flew into Hilo, the largest city of Hawaii, which is the name of the big island. We were in nice hotel accommodations and from there, in a rented car, we were given the grand tour, all of this at George Ching's expense. He was dealing in commercial diamond sales even on that trip. We saw the local fish market where the giant tuna and other delectable fish were sold to the highest bidder. This was a very exciting experience for all of us, especially Buddy and Becky. We enjoyed the experience of seeing a wide expanse of ocean where the waters were always turbulent. This was the great whales' playground. Becky took a picture of this area of the black sand beach. From that photo, we later had a member of our Waikiki Church, Betty White, Sunday School secretary and a great artist, paint the scene of this wild ocean shore area. Her brother was a famous American artist. That painting hangs above the bed in the guest area of our home. It inspires and recalls our first visit to the Big Island.

We made several subsequent visits to the big island of Hawaii and took various persons to enjoy it. We also visited the area of the active volcano where one can smell the sulfur that makes one aware of the volcanic figure of hell. We saw the vast field of black, volcanic blocks and the lovely black sand beaches. Since our time, Kilauea has erupted continuously and has destroyed highways and whole areas of homes. This was some experience for us and also on the several subsequent times we visited with other friends. Later we visited all of the islands except Lanai and Kahoolawe, the military proving grounds. No tourists were allowed on the latter. So much for this first amazing experience, courtesy of our Chinese deacon, George Ching.

In our first exploratory visit to the islands in August of 1977, our dear friends, Curtis and Mary Lee Askew, took us on a tour of Oahu. The city of Honolulu and area of Waikiki are where nine-tenths of the Hawaiian population lives. The approximate population is one million, two hundred thousand. They had us as their guests for dinner at a lovely restaurant beside the ocean, the Crouching Lion, and it actually looked like such. Often and again, we made this tour of Oahu with various ones who came to visit us. This original tour became the beginning of many such subsequent visits, outdoor wedding experiences, and other activities for us. Indeed on our first Sunday in Waikiki, Sue and Nobuo Nishikawa took us to a lovely outdoor restaurant north of Honolulu, Waimea Falls, for lunch. It had a beautiful waterfall and verdant mountain background for outdoor weddings and became our favorite place to take guests for lunch.

In reference to weddings, I became chaplain for the large, gorgeous, new Japanese Hotel on the lower end of Waikiki with Diamond Head in the background. The Hawaii Zoo was close by, and one could hear the roar of the beasts often. This arrangement came through the fine woman social director of this hotel. She would call me when a wedding was in prospect, and I would arrange a visit with the couple. I would not marry them without first a conference in which I emphasized the Christian/biblical view of marriage. For a long time, I received messages from some of those with whom I was privileged to work. I was paid eighty-five dollars for each of these occasions at the arrangement of the social director. This helped in the expensive costs of living in Hawaii. Usually, such weddings were in a specially designated beautiful area of the hotel. Sometimes the wedding would be in our Waikiki Church. I recall one such occasion during the Christmas season in the pouring rain with Buddy and Becky as my witnesses. There was the large United States Government Hotel, Halekoa, on Fort DeRussy, a rest and recreation hotel located next to the ocean in Waikiki. We were often there as invited guests, and I had many outdoor weddings there, usually on Saturday afternoons. Curious people would often quietly and respectfully observe these special wedding occasions under the beautiful waving palms.

Our Waikiki Church was a tourist church of first magnitude. We had people from all over the world worship with us. Many were not Southern Baptists but strong evangelical Christians who loved the evangelical fervor of our worship experiences. A large measure of credit for such worship times goes to Roger and Irene Laube. Irene was the organist, Ann Edmondson, the pianist, and Roger, the music/choir director and worship leader. Roger was a lawyer and an outstanding businessman. He was from a strong, evangelical, Lutheran background. His father and grandfather were staunch German Lutheran ministers. He and Irene and their family served similarly in Alaska before coming to Waikiki. They were there during the 1965 terrible earthquake when Irene, home alone, was trapped in their home, which was later totaled and rebuilt. They were in the music ministry at First Baptist Church of Anchorage, Alaska, with Dr. Felton Griffin, as pastor, who is now deceased. Roger was in charge of our worship in the Waikiki Church, and never has there been a better, more spiritually dedicated man to work with. He easily greeted and properly recognized the host of tourists and made them feel at home. Irene was a fabulous organist and very involved in the state WMU. She was state president in their latter years in Hawaii. They became close and enduring friends. In retirement, they have moved to Sequim, Washington, where he is music/worship leader of the First Baptist Church and she serves as the organist/pianist.

We have seen that Sequim Church grow from mission status to have outstanding property and an original, beautiful building with help from various building teams, Brotherhood related, from over our Southern Baptist Convention. Mark and Paula Weatherford are pastor and wife from the Dallas, Texas, area and he the former pastor of our daughter Marti and husband, Kevin Sowards. We met them on a visit to our daughter's home and talked to them about the Northwest and missions. At first he was completely negative, but God began to work on their hearts. He preached in our Mountain Highway Church before the Sequim pulpit committee, and the church called him unanimously. They have three lovely daughters, Melissa, Lindsey, and Emily. They are building again with multiple-group help from Southern Baptist building teams from Georgia. These Georgia people recently spent a large part of their summer getting this new building under roof before winter. They observed Pastor Mark Weatherford's need for a vacation, "burnout situation," and paid all their expenses back to a lovely Georgia vacation spot.

Dorothy, Charles Jr. (Chuck), and I spent a recent weekend with the Roger Laubes, who live on a gorgeous new community golf course. We had fellowship with the Sequim people, many of whom we had known since their mission status days. I preached for Mark, and it was like a vacation for us with the Laubes and Sequim people. Again, what goes around, comes around.

The native Hawaiians have a heathen worship style to this day. They are recovering their ancient system of ancestral gods and especially the worship of Madam Pele, the fire goddess. The missionaries made an indelible impression on one young woman who became Queen Kapiolani after her marriage to a Royal Hawaiian. She was discovered, as a young woman, brushing her hair against a rock. She had several husbands. She became a Christian and was a strong inspiring person who fearlessly led others to Christ and against the heathen culture. She and a group of her fellow believers made a deliberate trip to the Kilauea volcano. Despite warnings from some in her group to fear the wrath of Madam Pele, she threw rocks into the volcano to show her derision of the Madam Pele belief—the fire goddess showed her wrath by destructive eruptions. After this trip up to Kilauea on a Sunday morning, she and her party walked the long miles back to Hilo in time for evening worship in the then largest church in the world. Pastored by Titus Cone, it claimed to have thirteen thousand members.

The Christians, therefore, had a strong influence on subsequent Hawaiian culture that led to the modernization of the islands and ultimately to Hawaii's becoming one of our fifty states with every right of the other states, though miles and hours away from the American mainland. There was also a dynamic young man from Kona who was gloriously saved. He became a dynamic witness and preacher who greatly affected the culture of the islands until he was suddenly stricken with a fatal disease. He died quite young. However, this very fact, in legend, continued to move in great spiritual power and conversion across the islands.

One instance of the resentment of the native Hawaiians is the idea that "Christians brought us Bibles and took our land and native way of life." An illustration of that type of resentment is the well-known Dole pineapple people.

The original Dole was a grandson of one of the first missionaries. The success of that company has been a strong factor in the development of the islands. It employs thousands of people and enables them to have a decent way of life. Nevertheless, the media takes sides with the old native Hawaiian way because it is mysterious and attracts the tourists who pour in the money. The majority of these tourists are probably Christians who extol the Christian influence. To see the vast pineapple fields and hundreds of workers makes one realize the value of the Christian culture. There are also the pure Hawaiian cane sugar fields and the burning of the same preceding the planting. Becky won a state Baptist youth speech contest using the essence of these facts, and she received an all-expense-paid trip to Glorieta Baptist Conference Center in New Mexico to participate in the national youth speech contest.

Another interesting fact about the big island of Hawaii is the location of the famous Parker Ranch, the largest cattle ranch in the United States and perhaps the world. It was fascinating to see this vast area that provides most of the beef for the islands, as well as much abroad. The effect of the volcanic eruptions of many years is evident everywhere on the big island. As you drive you can see where the volcanic lava made its way to the ocean, ultimately creating more land. Also, there are areas where you can see the still active volcanic fires.

I held a revival on Maui for our pastor friend and prayer partner, the Stan Shiroma family who served the Pukalani Baptist Church. Stan had been a Buddhist before becoming a dynamic Christian. I visited in the home of one of his sisters who was still nominally a Buddhist. We had a blessed revival experience. Dorothy and I thoroughly enjoyed being in the Shiroma home. Edith Crook helped with our children. Such help she was always and still is even now. The Shiromas had four lovely children, now all grown. One, Jacob (James), is a minister. Faith, the wife and mother, was a native of Okinawa. My, what an excellent cook! On a final visit to their home after they moved to Puukahea where our Hawaiian Baptist Camp is located, we enjoyed a lovely outdoor picnic next to the ocean. I picked up an old, broken, Coca-Cola wooden crate. A new Christian Japanese man, Jimmy Suyenaga, a former Buddhist, repaired and fixed this crate. It now hangs in Martha's home in Dallas, Texas. (She loves country-style antiques.)

After our revival with the Shiromas, Stan took his large van and with his family, gave us a never-to-be-forgotten trip over Maui and up to Haleakala, the long-extinct volcano. We saw the mysterious Silver Sword plant that grows only in the lee of Haleakala—no other place on earth. We went up Haleakala early in the morning, about 3:00 A.M. At ten thousand feet up, you are almost dizzy. To see the beautiful sun rise over the magnificent array of long-dormant volcanic activity all around is a thrill. Up at a higher level were several observatories in which the stars and heavens are studied and monitored in the most rarified atmosphere on earth. There is a museum there, and what an unusual, special treat to visit. We traveled the lovely, winding, one-lane bridges built at the turn of the century. This was the famous road to Hana with beautiful blooming flowers everywhere. As Dorothy says, "That was some trip!" From Hana, we traveled to the area where Charles A. Lindbergh is buried. It is just beyond the famous Seven Sacred Pools, revered from ancient times. At Lindbergh's request, the home and burial place are not well marked. You have to walk into the ancient Kipahula Church restored by Charles Lindbergh and his fellow rancher. We walked into the simple sanctuary to be arrested by the sight of a beautiful Chinese Christ painting in the window of the church. At once, you become aware that Christ is perceived in each culture in terms of that cultural experience. An old legend of the departing wise men to their native land is fascinating. According to this legend, when the wise men were asked what they saw in the manger, each one gave a different version.

Upon leaving the Kipahula Church, the tour took us to the gravesite of the famous flyer. Mr. Lindbergh came from a famous, strong Christian, Minnesota family but in later life, he was said to be an agnostic. His tragic experience with the brutal murder of his first little son always deeply and adversely affected him. I noted on his grave marker, however, a portion of Psalm 139: "Though I take my flight to the uttermost parts of the sea, even there Thy hand shall guide me." The "lone eagle" to the last. He is buried right next to the ocean with the waves lapping nearby.

Interestingly enough, when we lived in Madison, New Jersey, our son, Buddy, worked in the Flemington, New Jersey, area where he received special educational advantages in the excellent Hunterdon Occupational Training facility. We would often pass by the little courthouse in Flemington where the Lindbergh kidnapping trial of Bruno Richard Hauptmann took place. He was condemned to death for the crime. Some of the ransom money was found in his home, but his wife always steadfastly denied he committed the crime. The whole world, at the time, centered on that little Flemington, New Jersey, courthouse, as we sat by the radio and listened, enraptured. The Lindberghs left the United States for England after that tragedy, and he seemed to argue for our non-interference in World War II and the rightness of the Hitler strategy, and tragedy, in Germany and the world. What a tragic conflict there is when one leaves the Christian faith and chooses to ignore the way of the Bible. Thank God that others saw the light and, in effect, saved the world from tragic enslavement.

One sight Dorothy recalls on our way to Hana was to look way down in the valley and see the thriving taro-plant fields cultivated somewhat as rice fields, under much water. The taro root makes the famous Hawaiian poi, literally the Hawaiian bread. It is thick and eaten with other foods with one's finger. Some tourists have likened it to Elmer's glue, and that is also my experience. It is gray-pink in color and has a sort of sour taste. Coming back to the Shiroma home in Pukalani, we passed huge areas of grazing land with men on horseback herding cattle. They are Hawaiian cowboys called *paneolas*.

Our opportunity to visit the beautiful garden island, Kaui, came from the invitation of Cliff Hoff, pastor of one of our leading churches, Waimea Baptist in the town of Waimea. He was away on vacation to mainland United States. Cliff and his wife, Margie, asked us to fly to Kaui, pick up his car at the airport, spend the weekend in their home, and preach for him on Sunday. We gladly accepted this invitation, made arrangements with our Waikiki Church and for our family. It was truly a fabulous experience for us. Everything went as arranged and we were able to see the best of Kaui, truly the most beautiful island. We saw the amazing Grand Canyon of Hawaii on a beautiful sunny day, and the marvelous colors of the canyon were most impressive. We visited one of the most beautiful, still-developing golf courses on the north shore. We saw the fern grotto and the river area where wedding parties cruised with a special singing ensemble. We thoroughly enjoyed the fellowship, the church family, and especially the more informal Sunday evening fellowship and meal. We saw one of our struggling mission churches, Eleele, where our special young Japanese pastor friend, Robert Nagamine, has preached. He was a student at our Golden Gate Seminary and served with us in Waikiki one summer as an intern. On Monday morning early, we drove through rather rugged terrain to one of the most beautiful, white sand beaches on earth. We had it to ourselves except for one other couple. We drove back to the Lihue area and to one of the fabulous new beach hotels for a lovely luncheon experience. In the afternoon, we shopped around, left Pastor Hoff's car in the prearranged place, and flew back to Honolulu and Waikiki and our children. What a life for two Mississippi rebels! Cliff Hoff became pastor of the Olivet Baptist Church in Honolulu, after the Askews, for a lengthy interval.

Our visit to Molokai came as the result of our state convention meeting on this island. Molokai Island is the site of the leper colony and Father Damien, the famous Catholic priest who gave his life, literally, in the ministry to lepers. He contracted the disease, died from it, and is buried in a hallowed place. The statue of this priest is on the front grounds of the beautiful modern Hawaii state Capitol in Honolulu. We did not ride the mules down to the leper colony area. For obvious reasons, Dorothy was not interested in such a ride. We did drive around the island and observe its unique beauty. At the state convention, in our hotel room right on the beach, we heard the musical roar of the ocean surging against the huge rock formation in sight of our room. We thoroughly enjoyed the fellowship of our fellow pastors and leaders. Our good friend Dr. Hermon Ray wanted to nominate me as state convention president, but I felt negative about his kind offer. Dub Efurd, my choice, is now executive director of the Hawaii Convention. One of our state convention evening meetings was in the Kaunakakai Baptist Church. The little town of Kaunakakai is really one main street. It is famous for the legend of the "cock-eyed mayor of Kaunakakai" drunken song. We were able to see the Pineapple Island, Lanai, from Kaunakakai, just across the ocean span. These were unusual and unforgettable experiences in our Hawaii years.

One ever-pervasive factor in Hawaii is that all the islands are heavily military, though one is not ever conscious of this. This is the key bastion for our military in the Pacific and more especially so since Pearl Harbor. Beyond Waianae, where one of our strategic churches is located, is the Makakilo military hotel with a gorgeous golf course situated against the lovely mountains. We were guests for dinner several times in this beautiful area because of a chaplain friend, Lieutenant Colonel Garnett Moss, whom we had known since Pineville, Kentucky, days. He helped us in a youth revival in Pineville. We have already referred to the beautiful Pearl Harbor area where such tragedy occurred on December 7, 1941, that started World War II for the United States. We always took tourist guests to this area. A free boat tour was provided by the Navy to the sunken battleship *Arizona.*

In connection with our Hawaii Baptist Convention, I was privileged to chair one of the three areas of work—program. Therefore, I was always involved in board meetings, decisions, et cetera. When State Executive Director Edmund Walker, now deceased, retired to return to his home in Sacramento, California, the name of an interim successor came before our board. It was a shaky time. Edmund Walker was a legend. The man under consideration was J. N. Evans, formerly in our Maryland Convention and involved from Maryland in our Pennsylvania/South Jersey Convention. There were questions about who, what, and where about this man coming from the mainland to take over such strategic responsibilities. I recommended him strongly. He and his wife came and worked with us to plan for the ongoing mission strategy for the islands—a work that has borne rich fruit in the growth of our work since. The Evanses were living in the condo owned by our good friends from Phoenix, Arizona, the Lee Jacksons.

Mrs. Evans suddenly died one morning of a major heart attack and is buried in the islands.

The Hawaii Baptist Convention subsequently called one of its own very successful pastors, Dub Efurd, to be its next, and present, executive director. He was pastor of a new church in a brand new town, Mililani Town. It was a growing church reaching new people with a strong family emphasis. Dub married a native Chinese-Hawaiian. Also, Veryl Henderson, who had worked in Waikiki in special missions and resort ministries, later became state missions director. I was Veryl's pastor and recall making a late-night tour with him of all the night places in Waikiki. Veryl had a ministry to those who worked in those places. Veryl had formerly pastored in Lahaina and came to Waikiki with his wife, Cheryl, and two lovely daughters, who are now grown up and married. Cheryl, daughter of Dr. Roy Owen who was state missions director in one of our western states, served in Waikiki with us as part time educational director. She was very effective and helpful. She later went on to the Olivet Baptist Church in a similar capacity, but also worked in Olivet's preschool and as secretary. The Hendersons serve in Colorado now where he is the state missions director. Dr. and Mrs. Roy Owens are retired there.

One other outstanding local Waikiki ministry developed by the Hendersons was a rented catamaran, a large tourist boat, with a strong emphasis on reaching youth. These boats were usually filled and a minimum price charged. There were skits, musical productions, et cetera, in the context of a tour of the Waikiki area, and all manner of refreshments were available. It was truly a great and effective ministry that was expanded later to include an Easter sunrise service. Our two children loved this experience. This took place on Friday evenings, usually.

One person we came to know in downtown Waikiki on late-night occasions was a minister's son from Knoxville, Tennessee. He played the piano beautifully and made short talks. We would purchase a large soft drink, with peanuts readily available, and thoroughly enjoy his excellent entertainment. He played for us at our final Waikiki morning worship service. He was the most popular musical artist in Waikiki.

I would visit in Waikiki, as in any other place, usually with the chairman of our deacons. I recall Ed Lewis especially, who with his wife, Dorothy, had lived in the Seattle area where he had charge of an expansion program for the Seattle Veteran's Hospital. They helped us initially to know a great deal about Seattle. They had a son, highly gifted in music, in the Phoenix, Arizona area.

In Waikiki, our church building had a down-under parking area because space was so scarce in Waikiki. We had a developing problem with homeless, hippie-type youth. Some of these hippies provided a spiritual ministry to the hippie, beachcomber type. This posed a problem when they came into our underground church parking area. I bore the adverse criticism for being sympathetic to this group. In fact, it became a negative factor in the end of our ministry. However, in more recent years, a building was purchased and personnel were forthcoming to minister to the down and out people on the beaches. Under our ministry in Waikiki, we reached many local people who became involved in our educational programs, and remain so, even to this day.

The tourists are called "snow birds" because they come to Waikiki and the islands from cold climates in Canada and Alaska to winter in Hawaii. Many of these are regular attendees of our church, morning and evening. One unusual occasion involved the murder of one of these people. Dorothy ministered to the wife of this murdered man, a Mr. David Milne, and later both of us to his family. We have stayed in touch with Gwen Milne who lives in British Columbia, Canada. She was recently a stand-in for us at the funeral service of Dorothy's sister-in-law's Canadian father. He was in his late nineties and very alert. Florence and Bob Patterson were deeply grateful to Gwen for standing in for us.

One other very upsetting event in our Waikiki Church was the death of an oriental doctor that involved our van and our youth director, Teresa Petty. We were sued for two million dollars. It took two years to resolve and twenty-thousand dollars to hire the best lawyer. Our people became afraid of the potential danger of the two tour buses we owned that provided a number of good ministries, including the regular ministry of older adults to a nursing home high above the Waikiki area. Teresa Petty was from Tyler, Texas. Her former pastor was Paul Powell, later the executive director of our very important Southern Baptist Annuity Board. Her brother, Perry Joe Petty, was the pastor of our Moiliili Mission, the first new mission work started in the Honolulu Association in the last thirteen years, as of our time in 1978. After Teresa left our church for a youth ministry position in another Baptist church, Beverly Turn came to our youth ministry. Beverly and Teresa both are now married. We reached a number of fine young people in our youth work.

Our son, Chuck, worked very effectively at a YMCA restaurant as a bus boy. The woman manager lived in our condo and took a great interest in Chuck. He learned his job well and did it well until the restaurant closed due to financial difficulties. He then rode a bus early in the morning to the airport area where he worked in the restaurant/cafeteria area in a new Goodwill building. His boss was Okinawan Japanese and somewhat harsh to Chuck in running a tight ship. He was later in a horrible auto accident, and we prayed for him daily.

His attitude changed toward Chuck. Chuck learned all about the dishwashing machine that included sixteen steps. He earned fifty cents an hour and rarely complained. Chuck still often mentions Joe Shimobokura.

Our Becky attended the Hawaii Baptist Academy and graduated from there in May of 1981. Several people helped us with tuition expenses for Becky. Edith Crook, our seventy-year-old secretary, was one. Sara Schuessler lent us her car until ours came from the mainland. She was a special friend of the Owen Coopers in Mississippi. Becky worked effectively in several downtown Waikiki area businesses. It was a sad occasion for us to send her off to Dallas, Texas, to attend Dallas Baptist College. She lived with Martha and Kevin Sowards and helped to look after baby Ryan while Martha worked.

One very vital matter had to do with our financial support in Waikiki. We thought we were assured of Home Mission Board support when we were negotiating with Waikiki Baptist Church. Every assurance was given. However, we found out at the last minute that the Home Mission Board could only support one full-time worker. It turned out that Veryl Henderson was already far along in his coming to Waikiki through Sam Choy, our state missions director. Dr. Earl Kelly, executive director of our Mississippi Baptist Convention, had been in Hawaii and heard about our dilemma. He agreed to ask our Mississippi Baptist Foundation director, Harold Kitchings, for a grant in the amount of five thousand dollars to assist in our salary package in the beginning of our ministry. This money came every month in gradually diminishing amounts. Harold was the son of Dr. A. A. Kitchings, professor of languages at Mississippi Baptist College, who was instrumental in our seminary pastorate in Salvisa, Kentucky. He was a special college friend of Dorothy's father. Connections again helped us.

Earl Kelly and his wife, Marjorie, came to Waikiki while we were there for a very effective revival meeting. Always when he came through the islands for any event, he would treat us to breakfast. He is retired now but still a powerful influence in Mississippi Baptist life. Along with his support, Joe Hunt was instrumental in enlisting help from several of our Madison Baptist businessmen to set up a trust fund that helped to support our Waikiki ministry. Without the help of these dear people, we would have been in trouble financially in Waikiki. Gradually the church was able to assume more of the pastoral support package. We developed a building fund while there. Many people from all over gave, and there was about one hundred thousand dollars in that fund when we left, I believe. It has been used for additional property development for Waikiki Baptists.

We were sad when Roger and Irene Laube went back to the mainland to Arizona, where he later became ill from breathing air in which the bird droppings contaminated the atmosphere. They were a long time finding this out, and he nearly died.

Chris Looke, chairman of our deacons, moved into Roger's place of leading music and worship. He and his lovely wife, Marian, were our dear friends. He has since died, and I am not sure about Marian.

Every New Year's Eve night we were invited to the lovely Laube home, high about Waikiki, where we watched all the fireworks below—like a war zone. The orientals believed these fireworks warded off evil spirits.

Other revival preachers during our ministry in Waikiki besides Earl Kelly were Ken Lyle and his wife, Judy, from New York; Dr. Allen Webb and Lena Mae, now both deceased; Fred Boehmer, Florida; Dr. Lee Jones and Miriam from Virginia; and Brother David Jones and Barbara who helped us set up a puppet ministry and gave us the puppets that we used in our beach ministries. All were special and effective for our Lord's work in that strategic area.

We were privileged to be in on a number of events regarding the Hawaii Baptist Academy. There were times when they hosted a spring fair and other special occasions to raise money. It had a superb group of teachers and offered the highest quality education in Hawaii.

I recall on occasion when Becky learned first-hand about the dangerous undertow of the ocean currents. She and a young military man had gone swimming on the north shore near the Bellows Air Force Base. The under currents pulled her down, submerging her head underwater. She had presence of mind to flow with the undertow to the nearby shore where she was able to get her head up. Becky was also elected manager of our local church basketball team. All the guys were connected to our church. She did an excellent job.

I learned the meaning of cremation of the dead. In most cases, it was too expensive to fly a body back to the mainland United States. Cremation was the answer. I would be given a small two-pound box of cremated ashes and these, with a local memorial service, could be sprinkled on any property that was not private. Usually such memorial services were held in the volcanic crater of Diamond Head.

I close my writings about our Hawaii years with an emphasis upon the one great overwhelming natural environment aspect—the mighty Pacific Ocean completely surrounding the islands. We would take family trips around Oahu, and I would stand and gaze out across monstrous waters, always in wonder. All our mainland weather patterns begin in the Hawaiian Islands area of the

Pacific. I remembered Dr. W. A. Criswell's view of why the ocean waters do not freeze. It's because of the salt content of the waters. By the way, as President John F. Kennedy once observed, the salt content of the ocean waters is the same as human blood. Therefore, the never-freezing ocean waters always allowed the operation of God's amazing weather systems. The warm air, drawing up the ocean waters by distillation, made up the clouds, and the ever-present trade winds would send them everywhere to come down as the rain for crops and for life. Also, the salt caves are so essential to all of life. These were put in the oceans from the time of creation.

We might have spent the remainder of our lives in Hawaii, but we felt that we needed to be back on the mainland to be closer to our family in our waning years. I wrote to our friend Dr. Jack Redford of our Home Mission Board who was responsible for Home Mission Board relations in the islands. I told him of our feelings, and he agreed to pray with us about it. The result was that he talked to us about two areas of need for a director of church extension—the matter of giving leadership to starting new work for Southern Baptists. One area was Kansas City and the other one was Seattle, Washington. As we prayed and thought about it, and having heard so much about the weather and other desirable factors in the relatively newer areas of Seattle and the great Puget Sound, Washington, God fixed this section of our country on our hearts.

12

Seattle, Washington

1982–1986

Dorothy and I flew to Seattle on February 1, 1982. It was a bitterly cold week. On this trip we went to an associational pastors and wives retreat, east of Federal Way in the Maple Valley Camp Baraca area. A wonderful man, Bill Peters, was there to meet us and spend time with us. He later took us back to the airport. He just recently died of cancer. We knew mutual friends in Ohio. He was in charge of our area of work on the Northwest Baptist Convention state level.

At Camp Baraca, we were going through the chow line at dinner when we mentioned our daughter, Marti, from Dallas Baptist College days. The young woman in front of us, Nicky (Mrs. Eddie Ernsting), a pastor's wife in our North Bend Mission, yelled out, "Marti Jolly! She was one of my suitemates in Dallas Baptist College." She had been very close to Marti and her roommate, Paula Weatherford, wife of Mark, our fine young pastor and family at Sequim, Washington. We spent several wonderful Sundays in the Eddie Ernsting home and meeting facility, the Grange Hall, in beautiful North Bend. One morning sometime shortly afterwards, Nicky was cooking breakfast and suddenly dropped to the floor from cardiac arrest. Eddie had been taking CPR and immediately gave her CPR. She recovered and was taken to the hospital and today is still a busy pastor's wife with two children and ten years now in our Green River Church.

We made a trip to Atlanta in June of 1982 for a week of interviews with the Home Mission Board including psychological testing and personal interview. Carol Darnell from First Baptist Church of Atlanta met us. She was formerly in our Waikiki Church. We saw Ken Lyle, by chance, when out walking in our hotel area. Ken had left New York and was pastor of the Tabernacle Baptist Church which Dr. Paul James had left to direct our work in the New York City area. Ken left Tabernacle to assume the position of executive director of the

Maryland Baptist Convention and now is executive director of the New England Baptist Convention following the sudden death of our friend, Jim Currin, who was the first director of the New England Baptist Convention.

We made a brief stop in Birmingham, Alabama, and my younger brother Don and his son Joe met us at the airport. Then we flew on to New Orleans for the Southern Baptist Convention. Becky flew in from Dallas to be with us for the weekend. She left us in a thunderstorm, and we worried about her. We had fellowship with the Tom Morrises from Ivy Memorial Baptist Church, and they took us to see Dorothy's Aunt Jess Patterson, wife of her father's brother, Palmer, one of our favorite uncles. Uncle Palmer is the father of Morgan Patterson, Ben Patterson, and Palmer Patterson Jr. This was our last time to see Aunt Jess who was so fragile and frail. Uncle Palmer died in 1981. Bob and Karen Arnold were there and took us out to a Cajun dinner. He was our associate in Madison and was now in the New Orleans Baptist Theological Seminary.

On our second visit to the Seattle area in June of 1982, we were privileged to be in the home of Willie and Lucy Oaks and family. Willie, you will remember, is the son of our dear friend Mildred Oaks Barringer, who served twice as our education and youth director in Virginia. I actually was his pastor in Pineville, Kentucky, when he was fifteen years old. They gave us the grand tour of the area, especially beautiful Snoqualmie Falls. I enjoyed Willie's work on his family history from a Mormon source in Salt Lake City, Utah. Willie has retired as a colonel in the Air Force. They later sold their home in Renton, Washington, and now live in Redmond, Washington. We recently visited with them there and spoke by phone with Mildred who was visiting Janice Oaks Mims in Myrtle Beach, South Carolina. Dr. and Mrs. Holden, he a director of missions, took us all for dinner atop the Space Needle, a leftover relic from the 1962 World's Fair.

When we visited Seattle in February of 1982, we were in a close-by local motel and walked up the hill to Federal Way and nearly froze. Dorothy's hip was a problem then. We met our real estate lady, Edna Fletcher, who worked diligently to get us into the right house, and she did the prefect job. However, it was not until later in June that we really found our home after seeing all that was available. We wanted something in Federal Way because this was the area of our new associational office building. We came at the time of a Boeing Aircraft depression when the sign read, "The last one to leave Seattle, turn out the lights." Our home was one of a very few in a new area of development, Hillside Heights. It had stood empty for two years. Since then, the property has developed like wildfire and all around us are lovely homes at a relatively livable price.

Our home was listed at $73,000. Today, it is worth close to $175,000.

When we took possession, only the upper floor was livable. The lower level had a concrete floor with all the pipes showing. As time went along, we obtained the expert building skills of Brother Ralph Overton, a Baptist minister without a church. For fifteen dollars an hour, half the price of a regular carpenter, plus mine and Buddy's help, we made that whole lower floor into two extra bedrooms, an office space for all my books upon my retirement, and extra storage space. Ultimately, because of the special skills of Rick Gazaway, a retiring Army officer from Ft. Lewis, a full bath with shower was built. We placed our washer and dryer in the large guestroom behind bi-fold doors. Rick and I worked all night to get all of this renovation ready when all our children and most of our grand-children came in 1991 for my seventieth birthday. All of this has added great value to the home plus the fact that we had Revere Ware steel siding put on the home for sixty-five hundred dollars (we saved three thousand dollars because we agreed to be a model home for Revere Ware steel siding).

Two things we love about our home are the space and the natural setting. We have twenty- to thirty-foot-tall trees: fir, alder, red cedar, and two holly trees just behind us. Most people are afraid of trees around them because the root systems are shallow, right on top of the ground, unlike the tree root systems in the south where root systems are deep with a taproot. People are afraid of the trees blowing down in heavy windstorms. However, when there are several trees, as in our case, the trees tend to hold each other up. Hence, we have not had any trees to topple in the fourteen years we have been here to date, nor in a recent December severe storm (1996). In the heat of summer when we often have 90-degree weather with the sun blazing in the mornings to our front, the south, we are cool until noonday. We are cool in the afternoons because the trees to the rear shade us from the sun. There is no air-conditioning except in stores and business places. And another good thing about our home is the small yard space, bounded by trees. It makes it easy for Buddy and me to care for the flowers and shrubs.

My work required the bringing together of mission pastors, summer mission-aries, Praxis teams (practical experience of starting a new church while in seminary), and student revival teams. Our home has perfectly suited this need, plus we enjoy having our local grandchildren in and out when Becky, our daughter who lives here, visits. We thank God for the place He gave us and for our Pittsburgh Baptist Church enabling us to have our own home there, at a sacrifice. That home was rented out during our Madison and Hawaii days, thus making the payments and upkeep. It finally sold on the day Becky married in 1984. The money, some sixty thousand dollars, was invested and has helped each of our children in varied ways. Many times that money helped in keeping a roof over their heads in difficult economic times. Plus, there has been money for improvements on our home here.

It was some hassle to get all our things together and to move across the ocean to the Seattle area. Our Home Mission Board paid for our moving expenses, some seventy-five hundred dollars. Thank God for its help and support. Another major problem was getting my books and library materials boxed for shipment via the post office at library rate. This saved money. The Waikiki Baptist Church had a lovely reception for us on Sunday evening, August 15th. Cheryl Henderson was in charge, and it was great. They gave us a check for fifteen hundred dollars that bought our refrigerator, washer, and dryer at Sears on our arrival in Federal Way. These utilities are still serving us well, thanks to Sears's yearly upkeep from a maintenance policy. We had to take our car to the shipment place with very little gas in it for shipment via a large crate to Seattle. Dorothy had to pick it up from Harbor Island. She was taken there by Charla Johnson and left there. The battery was dead and the storage people jumped the battery for her via their roving car detail made for such jobs. Later on in Honolulu, the moving company called Dorothy about our moving. They said the insurance on our furniture was still due them. Dorothy asked if our household furniture was covered by insurance on the way over. They said, "No." Dorothy replied, "We are not about to pay for insurance when we are not covered and all is A.O.K." They agreed and we dropped it. Finally, the moving van came. The household goods were not delivered to us until October 8.

We spent our final night in Mildred Johnson's lovely condo at her invitation. She took us to dinner earlier. I remember one time watching an eclipse of the moon from her condo. Our last night was a rainy one.

On leaving Honolulu, we went to the home of our song leader and pianist, Don and LeVon Womack, who took us to the airport for the long flight to Seattle. He was in the Navy. He is now retired and lives in Atoka, Tennessee. Arriving in Seattle on August 17th, we were met by Betty Dean, formerly a member in our Waikiki Church. She was a longtime librarian and taught library science in the public school system in Washington. She had been on loan to the Honolulu school system. She had often told us about the glories of the Seattle area, one of five marine temperate climates in the world. One other is England, and the other three I do not recall.

Our first night in Betty's home we received a telephone call from Martha and Becky. Becky had been diagnosed with cervical cancer and was to have a cryo-freezing technique procedure the next day to kill the squamous cells. We were in shock and fear when told this. This procedure was successful. In fact, she has had similar surgery here after the birth of her first child, Alex. (She had no other troubles in the births of Erik and Lauren. She had tubular ligation after the birth of Lauren.)

On the first Tuesday night here, we went to a world missions conference planning meeting at the 44th Avenue Baptist Church in Lynnwood, Washington. This world missions conference in September was to be part of my responsibility. We picked up a loaner car from Ken Hockett, a preferred risk insurance man, which we used until our car came. We later bought this same car for Becky.

Becky's first job in Seattle was with Ken Hockett's company. Kitty Wilson, a strong Southern Baptist was in charge of property, fire, and casualty insurance with the main insurance company—Bayly, Martin, and Fay. This paid one thousand dollars a month, and Becky was fortunate and delighted that it was the same salary she had made in Dallas working for Henry S. Miller, a realty management corporation, in accounts receivable. Becky dropped out of Dallas Baptist College and lived with Martha and Kevin Sowards who really stuck by her.

On our first Sunday in Federal Way, we joined the First Baptist Church. Gordon Green was pastor. He and wife, Charlotte, and two boys became our dear friends, and we shared many mutual blessings under their ministry. At the close of the first Sunday morning worship service, Dr. David Holden, our excellent associational director of missions, came by the church to ask me to go with him to a new mission opportunity. I gladly went. I was excited to get involved in my work, right off. A new Samoan group was meeting in the home of Paul and Betty Patu. We had had wonderful fellowship with a Samoan church group in Hawaii, the Happy Valley Baptist Church. Our missionaries in American Samoa who were also from American Samoa were Ray Viliamu and wife, Lena, a graduate of Blue Mountain Baptist College in Mississippi. These Happy Valley people had come to Hawaii from American Samoa to give their testimony and to sing as a choral group. Their leader was a village chief, and what a testimony they made for Christ. When we got to the Patu home, the house was filled with people for this visit with Dr. Holden and me. When I greeted them, after an introduction by Dr. Holden, and told them about the Happy Valley group in Hawaii, it was like old home week. What a blessing in sharing.

We made plans for a new church start and got Calvary Baptist Church in Renton, Washington, with Sam Harvey as pastor and dedicated mission strategist, to sponsor this group. It later proved to be unsatisfactory because the Samoan people would tend to spend what money they took in for parties and eating out. We did maintain close contact as long as I was in my job as director of church extension. Betty Patu has become an outstanding person in our Seattle school system. Later they drifted back into the Church of God group they came out of and ceased to be Southern Baptists. Ray Viliamu came from Hawaii to visit us and to encourage the group earlier on.

Later on, Ray Viliamu's son in American Samoa contracted a strange disease that completely emaciated him. He had no appetite and lost weight alarmingly. There seemed to be no answer to what was wrong. Finally, the Foreign Mission Board sent him to Hawaii to find better medical facilities to solve their son's problem. After a long, meticulous study, it turned out to be what they called Cat Scratch Fever. The boy had carried cats around next to his bare skin, Samoan style. With the development of a special serum, the boy improved, and Ray Viliamu started a Samoan work in Hawaii. We still need to reach this group of Samoan people here in our area that reached out to us.

The Puget Sound Baptist Association is the largest association in the Northwest Baptist Convention, encompassing the two-state area of Oregon and Washington. Southern Baptists' growth and development in this vast, beautiful area roughly parallels the growth and development of similar areas in other newer areas of the United States.

Dorothy and I made an auto tour of the area in June of 1951 when we attended the Southern Baptist Convention in San Francisco. Southern Baptist work in California was recognized in 1940. There are now more than fifteen hundred

Ministry Center of Puget Sound Baptist Association located in Federal Way, Washington.

churches and missions. Work for Southern Baptists began in the Portland, Oregon, area in 1947. When we visited in 1951, there were relatively few Southern Baptist churches, some one dozen. We visited several of these in Salem, Oregon, and Bakersfield, California, because of our mission interest from living in the mountains of southeast Kentucky. We were in First Baptist Church of Pineville, Kentucky, at the time and were sponsoring an ambitious missions program there.

The base of our work in the Northwest kept developing from the Portland, Oregon, area. Hence, our Southern Baptist headquarters is in that area, some two hundred miles from Seattle, Washington. Some thought has been given to a Washington State Convention. With the building of a new six-million-dollar, two-state convention center in Vancouver, Washington, just across the mighty Columbia River, that includes commodious space for our new Golden Gate Seminary campus with some one hundred plus students, the idea is in deep abeyance. Our two-state convention extends into northern California, Idaho, and to Spokane, Washington, which is across a desert area of ancient volcanic origin to the beautiful mountain ski area. This is all across Washington and south into Oregon. What a complex of people! Washington is just over one hundred years old (1889) as a state in the union. Oregon was only a territory when Abraham Lincoln was offered the job as governor of the Oregon Territory before he became the president. The Southerners would have relished his acceptance of that job! Oregon became a state in 1859.

I failed to mention the beautiful and ancient Washington/Oregon coastline which we visited and gloated over in 1951, or the vast acres of golden wheat fields, then and ever since a breadbasket wonder of the nation and the world. Nor did I mention the great Columbia River development from Franklin Roosevelt days and the Columbia River Dam with scenic wonders you cannot believe. All of this we saw in 1951 including the marvels of San Francisco and the new Southern Baptist developing work there and throughout California.

<hr />

Now back to the focus of the Puget Sound area of Washington when the Jollys had the privilege of coming on board as director of church extension. We loved to compare our area with Palestine in the time of Jesus—ninety miles long, forty miles wide, and more than one million people, with some eighty-plus churches when we came in 1982. Our job was to cover this vast area, relate to existing churches and pastors, lead in the strengthening of existing churches, and sponsor and start new mission churches. This involved innumerable association-wide planning sessions in harmony with every phase of our existing work—education, explosive ethnic work,

Brotherhood, Royal Ambassadors, Woman's Missionary Union, and you name it! It was a breathtaking, enormous challenge, and we hit the ground running without knowing how to start. Dr. David Holden was relatively new himself in the area but highly knowledgeable about the work and the area. He told us to get a good map of the area and go to it! That is precisely what we did, day and night. Dorothy sat next to me, the map in her lap, telling me exactly where to go and how to get there and how to miss the negatives. Believe you me, she was a wonder, as she always was, wherever God called us to serve.

In October of 1982, we went back to Atlanta for Home Mission board orientation and the appointment service as missionaries of that board in the Northwest. After flying from Seattle to Atlanta, Dorothy and I drove in a rented car on a rather extended trip to visit relatives and former church members in Mississippi. We drove to Birmingham, Alabama, where we sought to have breakfast at a local restaurant with my brother Don. We were unable to do so because of a scheduling conflict, but we did visit briefly by phone. We had lunch in Northport, Alabama, with Dorothy's stepmother and her daughter, Bonnie Gene, and husband, Bill Fesmire, and their five children. This was the last time we were to see Mrs. Eddith Boland Patterson, Dorothy's stepmother, for four years following her mother's death. She and her family had been so very close to Dorothy's family in Calhoun City, Mississippi, across the years.

From there we drove to our former New Hope Baptist Church in Lauderdale/Meridian, Mississippi, country. We had dinner with James and Ruby Williams from the Union Church. Both Union and New Hope were a joint church field, and each had what was called half-time pastoral preaching and ministry—two Sundays a month for each. From James and Ruby's home, we drove to the home of Mrs. Luther Walker, called "Sweet" by her friends because that was her beautiful nature and spirit. I was her family's pastor from Mississippi College days and often stayed in their home on weekends. She had two lovely daughters. At that time, Maylon, the oldest, was married and Mignon was still at home. Mignon in 1982 had married, had a family, and lived in a beautiful country home just in front of her mother's home. The father, Luther, was deceased. He was a prominent Lauderdale County commissioner when I was their young pastor. The Luther Walker home was relatively new and very beautiful in 1941 when I first knew them. Now, it had obviously aged. It was a cold night in 1982, and we had the gas space heaters on, a godsend in 1941 when I had been used to fireplace heat and going to bed in a cold room and under icy covers. Now, we were conscious of the gas space heaters taking oxygen out of the room. We thoroughly enjoyed our final visit with Sweet who died in February of 1986. I remember that Sweet gave us a special container of old-fashioned pepper (green) sauce at Dorothy's request. We used it for some length of time afterwards.

We drove from the Walker home south, four miles, to the new-to-us, all-brick Union Church house for the celebration of the seventieth anniversary of the church. James and Ruby Williams had written us about this anniversary to come, sometime previously, and said we were invited if we happened to be back in the state of Mississippi at the time. Little did we realize at that time that we would be back in the area because of our new job as Home Mission Board missionaries. It was a beautiful, sunshiny, autumn day at old Union. I went out to the nearby cemetery where so many I had known and loved and served as pastor were now at rest, as to their earthly bodies. I was one of several to preach just before the delicious noon meal in the new fellowship hall. At that meal, all from the church fields were invited, and so many former and newer members came.

It was the last time we saw Vashti (Mrs. Grady Brunson), now older but still a beautiful lady and superbly dressed. She was not the sharp lady I had known when she and Grady were just five years married and still sweethearts. They would always hold hands when they prayed at the table. Vashti and Grady married late in life, never had any children of their own, and took care of Vashti's aged mother and Grady's Aunt Kate, two very special, sainted, lively, giving ladies to their young pastor. Dorothy had always felt that Vashti and Grady Brunson never quite accepted and approved of her. I cannot fathom why except they may have thought of her as too young to be their pastor's wife. I might venture that a tinge of jealously may have entered in when I brought my beautiful, young, vivacious, capable-in-every-way, bride to be their new pastor's wife, and all things changed.

After the morning worship service at the Union Church, we were in the evening worship service of the New Hope Church. I showed slides of our mission work in the Northwest at New Hope and brought the message.

We spent the night with James and Ruby Williams. James's younger, preacher brother, Thomas Elijah Williams, came by to visit and to share old times. T. E. had lost his wife, Mary, and only child, a severely handicapped girl. He was planning to marry a local widow. We have previously shared about T. E. and Mary and their generous love in Louisville, Kentucky, during our Portland, Tennessee, years. T. E. was a superb evangelist, a wonderful Bible preacher, and we had had him in each of our churches. He was a great squirrel hunter, and we had shared several squirrel hunts in his company. It was great to share many precious memories with this dear preacher brother. In a more recent telephone conversation with his even younger, preacher brother R. M. Williams, retired longtime pastor in East Sherman, Texas, Baptist Church, we learned that T. E. is still alive and doing well. The larger Williams family had been such a strong, vital part of the Union and New Hope communities during my time as pastor. In fact, it was this R. M. Williams, our fellow student in Mississippi College, who had so warmly recommended me as pastor of these two churches.

In 1990, my brother Joe, his son Tim, and I made a long trip over the country before he was diagnosed with the leukemia that cost him his life on this earth in 1993. I shall always treasure that trip. Toward the close of that trip, we came by the old Union Church and met and talked with one of the former members, Jewel Williams Taylor (Mrs. Lamar). Jewel was the daughter of Mr. and Mrs. Richard Williams, a very special and loving family. She was able to fill us in on some of the people long since gone at New Hope. All had changed.

Dorothy and I drove back to Atlanta from Mississippi for orientation week and the Home Mission Board appointment service. During that week of intense work, we had the grand tour of Atlanta led by Nelson Tilton, our former New York pastor friend and once-president of our New York Baptist Convention and executive board member. He is now employed by our Home Mission Board. We were most impressed by that night tour of Atlanta. On another delightful occasion, we were dinner guests at a lovely restaurant with Paul and Janice Mims at that time pastor of the famous Druid Hills Baptist Church, the long-time church of beloved Louie Newton, outstanding and loving president of our Southern Baptist Convention during its dynamic years. Dr. Newton had been such a special blessing to the late Dr. George W. Truett of First Baptist Church of Dallas, Texas, and led Dr. Truett's funeral service on his death in 1944.

Dorothy's Uncle Knox Lowther, his wife, Aunt Fannie, and beloved daughter Martha Anita (Marnita) were with us on the final Sunday of our memorable week of missionary orientation for our thrilling appointment service at one of Atlanta's most outstanding black churches. We were there for morning worship when the whole worship hour was given over to the impressive appointment service. The house was full, the worship service most inspiring, and as Dorothy says, "We were most honored to be a part of that blessed hour!" After the appointment service, we were all feted to a marvelous meal served in the banquet hall of that church. Nothing was left out. I recall that Dr. and Mrs. Wendell Belew from Salvisa and Georgetown, Kentucky, days were close to us in the food line that Sunday. He asked, "How is it that you people have been so fortunate to be in so many outstanding and lovely pastorates/places?" I replied, "We are thankful that God has allowed it to be so!"

Following that great Atlanta experience, we flew to Roanoke, Virginia, where Lynn Painter met us and took us to her home for dinner. Elizabeth, her mother-in-law, was there, and we had a good time sharing our recent experience. It was national election time, Tuesday, November 2, 1982, and after Elizabeth voted, she took us to Sarah and Don's home and church in Hillsville, Virginia. We enjoyed every experience of worship in Hillsville. The people were special. The historical aspect from earlier days in this little Virginia mountain town was of special interest to me and four-year-old Timothy Reid. He knew all about it. He knew where the bullet holes were and more especially, where we could get good ice cream. The trouble was that he was pretty heavy when he got tired of walking and wanted Granddaddy to carry him.

We came back to the Roanoke airport on Thursday, and Elizabeth Painter bought lunch for all of us. She was one of the most unusual and generous people we have ever met. She was a nurse by training and experience. Some of the truly fun times of our lives were spent in the old farm home of Stoney and Elizabeth Painter. Buddy and Becky were little, and both had some great times with Stoney on the farm.

We came back to Seattle from our mountaintop, lifetime experience to get more fully involved in the work God had called us to do. A number of things came to pass. We attended our state convention meeting in Portland, Oregon.

We had been involved with Al Engleman in his Pine Chapel Mission start in Issaquah, high on the Samamish plateau. Al and his people had purchased an ideal piece of property with the sponsorship of the Calvary Baptist Church in Renton, Washington, under the leadership of Sam Harvey, the strong mission-minded pastor. At the state convention on our final morning, we had fellowship with Al, a heavy-set man and always the life of the party. Al came home from the Portland convention and was checking his telephone messages when he suddenly dropped dead of a heart attack. What a dire shock to us all. It was sad to bury such a boisterous, positive man like Al, and it was hard on his wife and family members. The mission that he had so confidently led in a burgeoning growth area was never the same. Several tried but soon the cause was lost and the property sold. We, among others, really tried but no one quite had Al's vision and hard-work formula. One of the very important contributions Al made was to lay the groundwork for the present chaplaincy program at the world famous Fred Hutchison Cancer Clinic. Al paved the way by constancy of dedication, and today we have two outstanding Southern Baptist men as chaplains, Percy Randall and Bruce Johnson.

Percy came from Morgan City, Mississippi, for treatment of leukemia. I met him and his family. His brother had bone marrow that matched, and he stayed six weeks for this procedure, as did others in his family. The cure rate is 50 percent at the clinic, and in Percy's case, it was positive. He lived, but with a crippled thigh. He became involved with Bruce Johnson up on Capitol Hill in our Capitol Hill mission, again sponsored by the Calvary Baptist Church. They were able to get a large, white, two-story house well-located in the university general area with other colleges and hospitals close by. This house served as living quarters and worship/teaching space for the Johnsons. Dorothy and I were there several times in an encouraging capacity. They were reaching a rather composite group that no one else was reaching. We were impressed and blessed. The group came on one occasion to our First Baptist Church, Federal Way, prayer breakfast and fellowship. Bruce and his wife, Ruth, daughter of a Lutheran pastor/chaplain and a superb musician, were our leaders. They had a little girl, Bethany, who they adopted and is now ten. Bruce is part Indian and had as his ultimate goal to start an Indian congregation. There are many Indians in the area who were paid vast sums for land preempted by the early settlers. Bruce was reaching people on drugs, homosexuals, and those with not much stability. Somehow interest declined, and we lost this work when Bruce left it.

However, as the chaplaincy opened up, he and Percy Randle were ready. When Percy inquired of the hospital authorities about such a position, they said, "We want you. Who better can minister to these people than someone who has come through our program successfully?" Percy walks into a room, greets the person and his/her family there for treatment, and is able to say, "Look at me. I lived through it and can understand all you are feeling first hand." Jose Carreras, one of the three great tenors, was there in recent years and has lived to sing again. So it goes. As Buddy says, "You win some. You lose some." They lost the church but gained as chaplains.

When we came, Fred DeBerry was the chairman of the Calvary Baptist Church missions committee and also our Puget Sound Association missions committee chairman. He is also the pastor of the Calvary Baptist Church's very successful deaf/hearing ministry. He worked carefully and prayerfully with us and in envisioning the association's needs. The person who replaced Fred was another Calvary Baptist outstanding layman, Cy Swartz.

We gradually developed an ambitious church starting program—starting five new works each year, using seminary students, couples who had a conviction to start new churches in the Northwest for Southern Baptists.

A part of my responsibility was to go to Southwestern Seminary in Ft. Worth, Texas, to interview and enlist these students. It was a great privilege and responsibility. It involved working with sponsoring churches in a ten-week summer program. In the process, we spent the first three weeks getting acquainted in a selected community. The first week, we left literature at the door and said we would return. The second week, we left specific literature about our plan and said we would be back the next week to solicit their interest. The third week, we knocked on the door and 50 percent responded positively. The remaining seven weeks were spent getting things started, including arranging for a meeting place and regular schedule.

I was also responsible for summer student missionaries who helped in youth activities in existing churches. In all, I worked with more than one hundred of these students who did a great job and have gone on to serve in various new churches in the West and Northwest. Every Friday I would bring them in to our commodious associational building's general large area for sharing and praying and to hear one of our local pastors tell about his specific work. It was a strong tie-in program and met with the full approval of our executive director, Dr. David Holden, and other association staff persons: Gerry Wittenmyer, church development; Vince Inzerillo, language/ethnic work; both men who were superb in their responsibilities. Vince is now state director of ethnic work and has done a monumental job in many outstanding ethnic works. One, First Baptist Church in Tacoma, is Korean with some married to Anglos and has a marvelous new building and another enlargement in process with twelve hundred each Sunday and the largest financial contributors in the association and state. Before the new building, I remember two hundred on a hot Wednesday night in the sponsoring church, Lakewood Baptist Church. First Baptist, Bothell, is right alongside them in association and state support. Dr. and Mrs. Sam Friend, the recently retired pastor, are heavily involved in Romania and foreign mission work. Dorothy was involved with me in all this work and supervised the meal we would serve every Friday—which was always outstanding.

We fell in love with the Praxis team members. We also had groups in our home for meals and special training such as the mission pastors I related to, which was about one-third of our association's pastors. It was a tremendous example of what Southern Baptists are all about. Dorothy and I would visit these places and churches, usually at least three churches a week, Sunday morning and evening and Wednesday nights. It was a rather tiresome, rugged schedule, but we really loved it. When I went to the state planning and orientation meetings, which were always at the beginning of the summer program, our Puget Sound group was always the largest; I was elated to be a part of this thrill of a lifetime.

In connection with all this work, our executive director, David Holden, suggested we develop a special financial program to assist new work and new churches. I remembered C. J. Humphrey and his wife, Ophelia, dynamic laypersons—she, especially in our women's work. He came to New York and helped us develop our outstanding financial assistance program in that vast area, which we called Missionary Millionaires. I wrote to Delane Ryals, and he sent me all the materials and related how much the program had undergirded his work in New York. The Humphreys came and helped us develop a similar program that has produced some twenty-five thousand dollars in assets. We have lent this money. It has always come back and been ploughed right back into the program. Some of it was outright gifts under direction of a special board of associational leaders. For example, at Mountain Highway Baptist Church, all of our Jolly family has given some twenty-five hundred dollars (five hundred dollars each over five years at about ten dollars a month). In turn, Mountain Highway has been given two thousand dollars on land purchase, and more recently, this money helped to move our new pastor and family, the Wesley Funkhousers, from Southwestern Seminary to the Northwest. The fund has helped to move several mission pastors to their fields of work. C. J. Humphrey has gone to Glory, but his faithful layman-led program has blessed the world in Texas, New York, and here.

In one case I know about, his Texas board lent nine thousand dollars to our Woodinville Mission area for a more beautiful small sanctuary and a brass chandelier. When the mission got down to one faithful family, aside from the pastor and his wife, it went out of business. Word has come to us that the loan is in the process of being repaid. It was done on an individual basis between the mission and the C. J. Humphrey Texas Board. This does point up a fact about starting new churches—about half succeed and about half falter. It also points up a very basic point about those that succeed. The pastor must stick with a work through thick and thin, good times and bad times, ups and downs, and God will ultimately develop a faithful, hard corps of people who become the nucleus and "seed corn" for a developing New Testament (Baptist) church. Most all churches go through up and down times. One group moves on, and another group comes in to take their place. Usually it is an improvement on the base left by the former group.

Another vital principle I have discerned in this new work area is the matter of a cooperative relationship with all other Christian groups and denominations. Southern Baptists are the largest denominational group in the United States and even in worldwide missions. Some other groups tend to feel threatened by this. Yet, I have found that all of these God-breathed and God-blessed groups will find a rapprochement with us as we express a desire to work together with all who seek to build the kingdom of God on earth. I have found this to be true in every place God has been pleased to let us make our contribution to the total cause of Christian missions. When we can love each other in the Lord and rejoice together when others excel, we make for a stronger community of faith, and all are blessed thereby. Somehow we need to understand that we are not in competition except to help build the whole kingdom of God, never failing to uphold our strong beliefs in whole Bible truth, as we understand it. Some have thought the name Southern Baptist is a detriment in other than traditional southern areas. However, I have found that in other than southern climates, we can be considered warmhearted people. We love and work together with all of God's people and find that they need us to improve the cause. I have found, therefore, that in every place we have been privileged to serve, we can bring renewal of increased faith, hope, and love among God's great people everywhere. Our mission is always bigger than we can ever envision. We need to go and flow with the moving of God's grace and His spirit— "rejoice with those who rejoice; weep with those who weep!"

We welcomed our two youngest, Buddy and Becky, to the Northwest and to their new home in mid-November of 1982. They had been in Texas where Becky had gone to Dallas Baptist College, thanks to help from Mary Crowley and Joe Hunt. Becky dropped out, to our sorrow, and went to work for Henry S. Miller Realty Management in accounts receivable, where she did well. Buddy had been working well at Goodwill Industries in Hawaii, as he has continued to do here. They had special fellowship with their Uncle Joe and family in Marshall, Texas, as well as with Martha Ruth and family in Dallas, prior to coming here. Becky was special to the Soward's oldest, Ryan, when he was a little fellow, and now he is quite grown up. For a time, Buddy and Becky went with us here in the Seattle area, especially on Sundays in our constant tour of churches and missions. Buddy and Becky came about a week before Thanksgiving and attended with us the Thanksgiving service, dinner, and fellowship at South Hill Baptist Church with John Atkins as pastor. We were warmly received.

In December, just before Christmas, we were with the Reverend Fred Jewel in Port Angeles, Washington. I became acquainted with the Jewels in my brother Fred's church back in Pennsylvania at University Baptist in Monaca, where the Jewels' daughter Freda May and her husband were members. Fred Jewel was an Army chaplain in World War II and was involved in the Battle of

Italy. In 1982, he was the pastor of the mission group in Sequim, Washington, which is now located in a beautiful new church facility. Our friends, the Mark Weatherfords from Texas, are the fine pastor and family. That is also where our worship leaders in Waikiki, Hawaii, the Roger Laubes, are involved in the same capacity in Sequim. We were several times in the Jewel home. Helen, his wife, has subsequently deceased but not before she gave Dorothy a small holly tree. That tree is now in our front yard and filled with beautiful holly berries each year just in time for Christmas. We call it our "Helen Jewel" tree. We enjoyed the grand tour of the magnificent Olympic Mountain range several times in different seasons, courtesy of the Jewels and later a lovely occasion in the Ft. Lewis Officers Club dining room. Fred has subsequently remarried, and we were privileged to be present at that wedding. He hunted in Alaska and in the nearby Olympic Mountains until his health became a negative factor.

Becky was married to Richard Rasmussen on August 10, 1984, at the First Baptist Church in Federal Way, Washington, on a miserably hot day. She worked at Cal Worthington Ford Company in Federal Way as an excellent credit manager for several years. Richard first met her there when he sold her a car. I had been concerned that the vehicle she drove did not have adequate windshield wipers as she drove back and forth to Seattle. In Seattle, she worked for Kitty Wilson in insurance. She got a job right away largely through the influence of the Ken Hocketts who lived in Lynnwood and were in our 44th Avenue Church. She later worked in Bellevue for Kitty Wilson who moved her insurance agency from Seattle to Bellevue. Later, Becky got a job in Renton where she sold insurance policies for autos, with Richard's encouragement. Cal Worthington, in Federal Way, used her insurance services.

Richard's father, Paul Rasmussen, owned the former family home in Renton where Richard and Becky first lived following their marriage. Richard had an older brother, Bruce, who was in special treatment for alcohol and drug problems. It was a sad Friday night when Becky and Richard called us to say that Bruce, out of treatment, had taken his life at the former family home place where they had lived. I had the sad experience of sharing with the family in the funeral service. The home was never the same to Becky and Richard, and it was sold later on. Richard's mother, Nancy, and his father, Paul, were divorced in 1975 when Richard was fifteen. Both parents have lovingly and steadfastly stood by Richard and Becky.

Richard has stayed home with their children while Becky worked, and he did a great job of teaching, training, and stretching the children's minds. This has put them far ahead. Becky and Richard, by common agreement, felt it best to keep the children in the home they were used to. Becky gave up her rights to their home, and Becky has provided support and maintenance until Richard could get on his feet. Richard and his mother have the main responsibility for caring for the three children: Alex, nine; Erik, six; and Lauren, five. At this point, it seems the best arrangement. Richard's mother helps him look after the children while he works in car sales.

Sometimes with Becky and Richard, the car sales business goes through terrible dry periods. Richard's father, Paul, has been most loving and helpful with his Eileen. Paul has given repeated financial help, as have we, to maintain their home. Richard has attended church, has even come forward but has not followed through. He and Nancy do permit us to take the children to church on Sundays when it does not interfere with other planned Sunday activities. The grandchildren do seem to love to go to church with us and are happy in varied children's activities. Presently, Becky lives in Issaquah and is the credit manager for a large Acura dealership in Lynnwood, Washington.

I must say here that Charles Jr., "Buddy" to the family, has lived with us across the years, thirty-seven at this writing, and has been one of the greatest inspirations in our lives. He prefers living with us rather than in a special home and is beloved by his sisters and their families.

Chuck, as his coworkers at Goodwill Industries know him, has worked at Goodwill Industries in Tacoma, Washington, ever since we came to the Northwest. He worked previously for Goodwill Industries in Hawaii. The Tacoma facility is the largest in the west and one of the best in all of the Pacific Rim. He gets up at 5:45 A.M. each workday morning, Monday through Friday, and wakes us up. He catches a bus to Tacoma at 7:00 A.M. in all kinds of weather—rain or shine, sleet or snow. He stands on his feet eight hours a day and rarely complains. He had a low-paying job initially, cleaning and scrubbing for a long period of time. Finally, he moved to the used-clothing area where he has proved very effective and has graduated to minimum wage and just recently was voted a fifteen cents an hour increase. He is beloved by all at Goodwill who view him as a loving, unselfish person who encourages others. He gets along well with his bosses and just recently was voted employee of the month and received a beautiful award emblem suitable for wall hanging. Because of him, we have enjoyed many special outings with him and the whole contingent of Goodwill employees and employers at their annual outdoor picnic.

Dorothy manages his financial affairs, which have many government requirements because of his handicapped condition, works on his taxes, and takes care of his needs.

At the same time, he is a great help to us at this stage in our lives. He does lifting, garbage management, and yard work at home. He is a very special person to have in our home and looks after us with the greatest care and concern, especially his mother. Wherever she goes, he is always by her side and is always upbeat, entertaining, and helpful. He looks after his mother when I am not around and even when I am! We feel very fortunate that we have had him with us during these aging years of our lives.

Buddy is a self-assured young man and holds his own in conversation. He has an astonishing ability to remember and to tell of events long ago. He never meets a stranger and can talk with the best on most any subject. He uses very good English. Yet, he cannot read or write. He can write his name by printing, deals with the Washington Mutual Bank, and votes with guidelines in every election. He always brings whatever the bank is giving away for children for Becky's three children. These children love Buddy and make a beeline for his room when they come to our home for a visit until he tires of them. He has varied videos, uses equipment originally given to us by Richard and Becky, and enjoys the same with his two nephews and niece. He loves *Star Trek*, *Apollo 13*, and many others. He steadily works at learning to read, and I believe he will, in time, as God wills. Buddy has never driven a car but makes sure I keep everything in order. He could possibly drive and maybe one day he will.

He knows all the neighbors and each Christmas delivers a beautifully wrapped Christmas gift to each one and to the garbage collectors. All of the neighbors love him, and he gets along well with them.

We read the Bible through every year, and each morning at our devotional, he prays for our missionaries and for our family members, by name. On Sunday mornings, we pray for all our scattered family over the nation, both sides, and for many of our former church members by name and for all, in general (see Appendix F).

We are keeping in mind his future and consult with him as to which of his sisters he wishes to live with ultimately. All of them want him to be with them. He will pay his own way, whichever, and will be a decided asset. Each of us has paid up burial insurance and plans to be laid to rest, as to earthly body, beside Dorothy's father and mother in the West Heights Baptist Church cemetery in Pontotoc, Mississippi, close to our Mississippi relatives. We do not know the future, but we know Him well, "who holds the future in His hands." We cannot imagine what we could have ever done without Chuck in our lives, having him with us and sensitive to our every need. God has blessed us in all of our children and their families—five children and ten grandchildren, nine boys and one very special little girl, Lauren, the youngest.

A further word about Dorothy's brother Bob Patterson Jr., and his family. Bob had a great ministry as pastor and worker in our Southern Baptist Sunday School Board's, Vacation Bible School department and later as associate sunday school director of the Tennessee Baptist Convention. Bob later became director of the Sunday School Department for the Tennessee Baptist Convention. His two children are unusually gifted and have done so well with their own families following in their parents' footsteps. Bob and Gloria are justifiably proud of these fine children and their families.

Daughter Robbie Ann is married to Dr. John M. Williams (Mike), D.Min. graduate of Southern Seminary. Mike, with Robbie's help, had a fine career as pastor, director of missions for the Chattahoochie Association, Gainesville, Georgia, and more recently, has been associate executive director of the Georgia Baptist Convention. In a recent visit in our home here in the Northwest, he shared his missions vision about the future of our Southern Baptist mission work. Their son, Matthew, is in Shorter College and in the Marine Reserves. He plans a Marine chaplaincy career after seminary. A younger son, Kenneth, is still at home finishing high school. Their daughter, Elaine, is a dental assistant and with her husband, an electrical engineer, lives in the Mason/Cincinnati, Ohio, area.

Son Philip Patterson lives in Nashville, Tennessee, and is married to Beth Roberts; her parents were friends of ours from Portland, Tennessee, days. Phil and Beth have two children, Amy and Andrew. Phil, a CPA, has his own business and is in association with an accounting firm in Atlanta, Georgia. Phil has done well and is the treasurer of the great Two Rivers Baptist Church in Nashville that his father helped to found and was instrumental in my brother Fred becoming its first pastor.

After four years as church extension director of the Puget Sound Association and having reached sixty-five and mandatory retirement from the Home Mission Board, we faced a great change in our lives.

For our retirement, the associational staff, consisting of Dr. David Holden, director and wife, Joy; Gerry Wittenmeyer and wife, Osa Marie; church development director, Donna Bendure, efficient, dedicated associational office secretary and husband, Ken; Charles and Daisy Joyner, new work starters; Vince and Marilyn Inzerillo, language missions director; and our daughter, Mary, and husband, Jim Ragains, gave us a tremendous and happy occasion and a lovely meal and fellowship atop the new Holiday Inn in Sea/Tac, Washington. It was a memorable time we shall always cherish. The waiters and waitresses at the restaurant provided special music and singing. We are all scattered now, only the Joyners and the Jollys are still around but the afterglow of precious memories still lingers.

Dorothy had hip replacement surgery in July of 1985 performed by Dr. Thomas Green, an exceptional orthopedic surgeon. Edith Crook, our secretary at the Waikiki Baptist Church, came at her own expense and out of special love, to look after our family during Dorothy's recuperation. Dorothy had suffered pain from this malady for some twenty-three years. (A "toothache in my hip" is Dorothy's assessment.) She has done marvelously well in recovery and care, with family help, for some eleven years. It was good to have her by my side, free of this pain, that memorable night of celebration, August of 1986.

Shortly before my retirement in early 1986, at Dr. Holden's request, I had followed through on an assignment to relate our new churches to sponsoring churches of the San Antonio, Texas, Baptist Association of churches. This proposal was done with the permission of the San Antonio director of missions, but not as an associational relationship, only on an individual church basis under the leadership of the Northeast Baptist Church which with the pastor worked out the details. I flew first into the Dallas/Ft. Worth Airport on February 28 to meet and share with my five summer Praxis teams from Southwestern Baptist

Ivy Memorial friends from Hampton, Virginia, attending Charles's retirement party in 1986. Seated in front, left to right, are: Dorothy Brockwell, Mary Jolly, Dorothy, Charles, Marti Jolly, Becky Jolly, and Buddy Jolly.

Theological Seminary. All of their work had to be on track and under my supervision before my retirement in August.

Following my mission in Ft. Worth, I flew to San Antonio on March 1, 1986. By prearrangement, I was met by our longtime, Patterson family friend, Colonel Warren Earl Ferguson, United States Air Force. He and his lovely wife, Norma, were my host family and he served as my driver during my stay in San Antonio. They were members of our Ivy Memorial Baptist Church in Virginia when he was stationed at Langley Air Force Base. My brother Joe had served as interim pastor of Northeast Baptist Church. Joe and Toni came from their home in Marshall, Texas, and took us to lunch. Colonel Ferguson and family were members of the great First Baptist Church and taught the younger adults in Sunday School. Their pastor was the young grandson of Dr. Barney Walker, outstanding longtime Mississippi Baptist evangelist. His associate in education was J. C. Hatfield, our friend and former associate state executive secretary in Virginia. We enjoyed lunch together after the morning worship service. Their former pastor, Dr. Frank Pollard, left to become president of Golden Gate Seminary and then went to First Baptist Church of Jackson, Mississippi, where he is at present. We had fellowship with the Marshall Seese Family, formerly in our Pittsburgh Church. Marshall was on the Weather Channel in San Antonio but is now in Atlanta, Georgia, doing the same work. They attended our church in Pittsburgh, and Marshall and Carole were saved and baptized. We have kept in close touch over the years. They had one son, Marshall Jr., who is now grown.

Colonel (Chaplain) Ferguson and I went over to the Northeast Baptist Church for a long sharing with Dr. Wilbur Long, pastor and my host pastor while in San Antonio. That evening we went to the Cebile Valley Baptist Church where I shared pictures about our work and made my presentation that was very well received.

On March 3, 1986, my mother's birthday, we visited the famous Alamo, and I purchased 150th anniversary commemorative stamps from the post office for my brothers, sisters, and family members. They were mailed later and received with special appreciation. Colonel Ferguson and I later visited with sixty-seventy San Antonio pastors in the dining area of Northeast Baptist Church and were served a lovely lunch. I shared with the interested pastors afterwards. I first played for them our daughter Martha's *Challenger 25* song/tape commemorating the sad explosion a short time before. Her song has been widely received by all the family members and the Houston Space Center. She has been asked to come and sing it on several occasions.

In the San Antonio/Puget Sound Partnership and with my mandatory retirement, somehow the ball was dropped in the follow-up. My notes reflect that I carefully set up the process, including personnel involved, et cetera. "Saddest of all in tongue or pen, saddest of all, it might have been." If only I could have stayed on an extra year as Jack Redford, our Home Mission Board key person and my special mentor, had suggested that I consider, but associational and state convention policy did not allow this.

One of our greatest joys over the years is that God allowed me to be involved as preacher, by actual count, for more than eighty-five revival meetings, in small mission churches, in middle-size churches, and some very large and prestigious churches. From the college and seminary years, the mountains and blue grass of Kentucky, the hills of West Virginia, the valley of Virginia, the coastal area of California, rural Mississippi, Alabama, and Louisiana, the cities and towns of our vast broad land from New York, Pennsylvania, New Jersey, and Hawaii, and here in this great Northwest, God has allowed me this privilege. In place after place, God has been pleased to bless the preaching of His word in the saving of souls, the revival of the church spirit, and completely changing churches and their mission, especially in preaching the message of stewardship tithing. I am humbly grateful for this privilege and grateful to my former churches that allowed me this special privilege. A number of these churches sought to call me as their pastor, and with deep sadness I had to decline often because God was leading elsewhere. Thus far, I have no regrets as to His leading and will forever praise Him for His unspeakable blessings and mercies until one day I do so in Glory.

On Labor Day weekend, Dorothy and I made a trip to Vancouver, British Columbia, Canada, to enjoy Expo '86 World's Fair. We spent the night at the Holiday Inn in the Bellingham, Washington, area. Our Becky made all the arrangements for this special, informative, and joyful occasion. It was truly fabulous! I had been responsible for promotion of this outstanding, international event to help tourists traveling through our area to become acquainted with our Puget Sound Association work. In this context, we became acquainted with Dr. and Mrs. Bryan from Amarillo, Texas, former missionaries to China, and their daughter, a former missionary to Kenya. These three stayed in our home and left their van at our home while they took a cruise to Alaska. They were lovely guests, and we enjoyed them thoroughly. They came back from Alaska, retrieved their van, drove to Alberta, Canada, and toured in the area of Lake Louise. They spent the night in a cabin after hiking in the nearby area. Early the next morning, Mrs. Bryan heard Dr. Bryan cough, went in to check on her husband, and he was gone. We were doubly glad we had the privilege of hosting and getting acquainted with these wonderful former Southern Baptist missionaries in the last days of Dr. Bryan's life. What a privilege for us and no trouble, the sharing of rich experiences, worth all the work, attending many meetings, and et cetera. They came because we had advertised that we would provide room and board on their travels further north. The Bryans were really the only ones to accept. What a rich blessing of our great God and Savior.

In our Expo '86 experience, Dorothy had arranged a visit from her first cousin's family, the Palmer Pattersons. The visitor, their black adopted son, Llewelyn, was to meet us under the famous Swiss clock. We found our way to this spot and had not told Mary and Jim that he was black. Llewelyn walked up and greeted Dorothy with a hug and a kiss. Jim and Mary stood gawking, and Jim wondered later about Mary's family background that he wasn't aware of. We went to a nice restaurant and had a lovely meal together before Llewelyn had to go back to his job at the World's Fair.

We had been privileged to attend the Baptist World Alliance in Toronto in 1980 when we met all of the Palmer Pattersons' unusual family mix. Palmer, professor of Indian history and author of same, and Nancy, professor of art, at the University of Waterloo, Ontario, lived in a large, colonial-type home with one bathroom for a family of nine, including seven children. On the day they moved into this home, with the moving van in the process of unloading, their little daughter, Jennifer, ran down a slight hill to the van and into the street. An oncoming car struck and instantly killed her. In their grief process, they elected to take in children in need of a home, no matter the race, creed, or color. Llewelyn was one of those children. He told us that day in Vancouver that his birth mother was German and his birth father was black. The Palmer Pattersons are the only real parents he has ever known as well as several others in this unusual family. There were two other children of their own.

Nancy and her sister came to Seattle University, and Palmer was a student in the University of Washington. They met, fell in love, married, and had this lovely family. Her sister lives in the Lynnwood area, and we visited there with Nancy on this occasion. A marvelous array of art was in that home. In Nancy and Palmer's home in Waterloo, the whole home is filled with fabulous art treasures. That day in Seattle, she had come to lecture on the world famous C. S. Lewis. It was a happy occasion for us as we had lunch at the famous Ivar's on the Seattle waterfront. Every Christmas, Nancy does a lovely art production as a Christmas card. As you can see, we are proud of this unusual family and love them dearly and keep in touch.

Dr. Palmer Patterson is doing research on the history of the Patterson family that is very fascinating. One was an engineer on board the frigate Sumter during a Civil War battle in Memphis, Tennessee. The Confederate Navy boat and the Sumter were rendered unserviceable, and this Robert Townsend Patterson escaped. He was Dorothy's great-grandfather. Another, Charles Patterson, a merchant marine, married Louise, a woman from Chile, who lived and reared a family in Monterey, Mexico. Later, they settled in San Francisco. Dorothy's father kept in touch with them, and when we were in San Francisco at the Southern Baptist Convention in 1951, we looked up the deceased Aunt Louise's family. She had died in March before our visit in June. They were of the Catholic faith and had a candle altar and a candle burning in her memory.

There was a James Patterson in the old Birmingham area of Pittsburgh, Pennsylvania. Dorothy's father found the death announcement of this James Patterson in the Carnegie Library of the University of Pittsburgh, on special tape as if it happened yesterday. We tried to find a gravesite but had no success. This Patterson family was involved in the hardware business and also in early shipbuilding, according to recent research. Dorothy's Uncle Palmer, visiting us in Madison, New Jersey, told us that the family was related to the Bond Bread people on his mother's side, Fanny Bond Rain. The Pattersons were also related to the Rain family who settled in Mobile, Alabama. Mr. Benton Cato Rain was treasurer of the Mobile City school system, and the B. C. Rain High School is named in his memory. More recently, on the occasion of my Uncle Peden's funeral service, and while staying with my father's sister, Pearl Christine Newell (and Uncle Peden's sister), I called and talked with the surviving daughter, Carrie Lee Rain. Such are important family connections for one, myself, greatly interested in history and those who have come before us.

Thus comes to a termination of our task as church extension director, Puget Sound Baptist Association, truly one of the most exciting and rewarding of our works in Christ's kingdom.

13

Interim Pastoral Service
Washington

1986–1987

Dorothy and I, like others before us, felt that we were still in relatively good health and couldn't see ourselves as ready for retirement. In prayerfully discussing these feelings, we felt that we wanted to help some of our new and smaller churches to get on their feet. It was only a short time before Claude and Erma Kinard gave us a telephone call about helping the Sunrise Baptist Church in an interim period. We had been very close to this church in a rapidly growing and developing area in South Hill. Claude was close to retirement himself as an outstanding electrical engineer and was involved in the building of hundreds of homes all around the Federal Way area. Schools and other institutions were also a part of his work. We were to be in their home and enjoy their hospitality several times in the next three months.

We had known about the Sunrise Baptist Church through the previous beloved pastor, Harry Hannah. I had known and worked with him since Mississippi Baptist College days. He married Grace from Missouri whom he met in Southwestern Baptist Seminary in Fort Worth, Texas. Harry invited me to preach at Sunrise on a couple of occasions, and we had been the recipients of their lovely hospitality and got to know the members of their family.

The church building was nice. It was a circular structure with office space, classrooms, larger recreation/kitchen area, all surrounding the worship space in the center. This structure had been built when Jim Gantenbein was the pastor. We had worked with Jim and Betty in the Port Orchard Baptist Church. Harry Hannah had been a vice-president of the Northwest Baptist Convention, highly respected by all, and the Foreign Mission Board representative for our Northwest State Convention. In this capacity, Harry and Grace had gotten in on all of our Foreign Mission Board work, become acquainted with our friends from Virginia, the Charles Joneses, who served on the Foreign Mission Board in Virginia, who always sent their greetings via the Hannahs.

As a part of my responsibility in church extension, I would receive the long list of read-outs from the Home Mission Board loan agency on the financial loans of our churches and missions that we might encourage and pray for them. I recall that Sunrise had a loan payback of two thousand dollars a month before they could pay the pastor. It was a real struggle. It was a privilege to pray for the people at Sunrise and all over our association since some one-third of the missions/churches were in my area of responsibility. We were involved in our missions and churches from one end of the association, Everett on the north, to the other, Olympia on the south. We were privileged, in effect, to be pastor and wife to our pastors/wives.

Now as the interim pastor of Sunrise, we were really to get to know this special group of people. Ward and Sarah Hathaway were from Greenville, Mississippi. He was in the Philippines during World War II as a photographer and shared his innumerable photos of that experience. Farris and LaRue Ashe were another special couple. She worked part-time at the Tacoma Pantages Theatre and kept us aware of the many fine programs of this old, historic theatre. They have since moved to the Dallas area where he found a job after a longtime lay off in the Tacoma area. Harvey and Margie Engles were a very positive couple who were heavily involved in the teacher-training program of the church and in the association. They were famous for their roast beef and lumpy gravy even on the associational level with Church Growth Development Director Gerry Wittenmyer. He is now director of missions for the Capilano Association in Vancouver, British Columbia, Canada. Our pastor at First Baptist Church in Federal Way, Gordon Green, had a sister involved in Sunrise (Gordon Green, now a director of missions is about to retire in Springfield, Oregon). We were often in the home of Bill and Sandy Starr who came into Sunrise while I was interim pastor.

We traveled back and forth from Federal Way to the church on Sunday morning and evening and for Wednesday night prayer service with training sessions in between. Also there was one special revival time. Martha Vonderwahl had given a beautiful baby grand piano in memory of her deceased husband. Dorothy loved playing the piano for worship and prayer services. Our son, Chuck, would often go with us for these occasions and loved it. They also loved him. At Christmastime in 1986, the church had a lovely Christmas party for us at the very nice community building to close our ministry with the incoming new pastor, Jay Chambers. Under Jay, the church experienced a tremendous spurt of growth and more recently, a triple growth experience under the recent pastor, David Barteau. He came as a revival preacher for our Mountain Highway Baptist Church and felt a leading toward Sunrise even before they ever met him.

Claude Kinard called about a reference to Alan Smith, one of our mission pastors, strongly involved in a new church start and later an associate at Mountain Highway Baptist Church. He and his wife, Carolena, were pastoring in Grants Pass, Oregon. We were very close to them. They were and are doing well in this pastorate. In response to Kinard's question, I told them about David Barteau who had wide experience in student work in Canada. He was a graduate of Southwestern Baptist Theological Seminary. Later the pulpit search committee came to our Mountain Highway Church to hear David preach and were impressed to call him as their new pastor. Under David's leadership, the Sunrise Church removed previously constructed inadequate buildings and has built a beautiful education center. They have a debt of thirty-five hundred dollars a month, and they are meeting that payment and still growing. Praise the Lord!

We were really sad to leave Sunrise because we had come to feel the special pastoral relationship to the people. This is impossible to explain. We have continued to feel the warm love of the people and of the new pastor and family.

We were not to wait long for our next call and experience at the Tahoma Baptist Mission in the rapidly developing Maple Valley area. They were meeting in the Maple Valley Grange Hall, a very nice facility with adjoining kitchen and good educational space. Their developing mission strategy was "by the Book" and was carefully detailed to the sponsoring Enumclaw Church. There was an inside chart enabling one to see the strategy. The Enumclaw Church had allowed us to enjoy their fellowship on several occasions. The pastors and members served as fill-in preaching assignments in connection with their mission strategy. By the time they asked us to come as interim pastor, the lay pastor felt he could not adequately lead in the work because of his job with Boeing and heavy family responsibilities. Later there was a sad breakup of his family and a second marriage. We love the family dearly. Here again we traveled considerable miles on Sunday morning and evening and Wednesday nights. On Wednesday nights we met in the Mitchell home that was some additional distance from the Grange Hall. We enjoyed the hospitality of this home and of others at times. Usually we had a houseful for Wednesday prayer time and Bible study. Here again we were dealing with the matter of a permanent pastor for this excited growing group. They finally called Paul and Emily Butterfield and family from Missouri. We were with them in their initial move, and the Butterfields were faithful until the breakup of the mission. This came from some problems in the pastor's family— a sad terminus to such a marvelous beginning work. We are just now getting back into that Maple Valley area. The Butterfields have continued faithful service at our North Auburn Baptist Church.

The North Auburn Baptist Church is a story in itself. We were involved with this fine group of people almost from the beginning of our work as church extension director of the Puget Sound Association. Pete Whitt, along with his wife Melva, was and is the strong lay leader for North Auburn Church. The church had so declined that the group had considered disbanding. A former outstanding retired pastor, Estes Mason, and his wife, Gertrude, from First Baptist Church of Crystal Springs, Mississippi, had heard about North Auburn and felt led to come in their home trailer to conduct a Vacation Bible School as a last resort to closure. God blessed in that Bible school. Dorothy and I went out to visit them and were so impressed with the children's response in the community and their obvious love for the Masons. From this Vacation Bible School arose a new impetus to survive. The people met in a nice, rented home that was fairly adequate for a teaching and worship center. We were often in their worship services. Here again a lay pastor and his lovely wife and family had a marriage breakup. This left a heartbroken people. The lay pastor, Brother Mike Smith, was an insurance man, and it was a terrible strain holding a full-time secular job and really a full-time pastoral role. The strong lay leadership survived this internal trouble and carried on.

There was a very desirable, two-acre piece of property available from two older sisters for an asking price of ninety-five thousand dollars with, hopefully, additional acreage for future growth. The payments seemed impossible but God worked a miracle! Every month for six or seven months, a check for $650 would appear on the door of the interim facility to meet the payment. Talk about angels! Until this day, it is unknown as to who this was, but the payments were made, and things moved onward and upward. They called Garry Benfield as pastor who was married to a daughter of longtime pastor and wife, Andy and Doris Seago. Garry moved mobile units on the property from former longtime pastor, Bob Berg, a timber and building expert at our Chapelwood, Black Diamond area church. Bob built these self-contained units to accommodate fifty-plus people for some twelve thousand dollars. We worked closely with the Bergs and were often invited to Chapelwood. What blessed privileges were ours in the work.

The work at North Auburn continued to grow. Building teams, via our nationwide Brotherhood people, came to assist in building a facility. Here again, those monthly payments, some four thousand dollars a month, are a real struggle, especially with a change of pastors. Garry Benfield is now director of missions with our state convention. Paul and Emily Butterfield from the Tahoma debacle and others have kept things moving. Pete Whitt, our longtime Brotherhood associational director was instrumental in bringing in the building teams. I was later asked to serve as associational Brotherhood director and served for three years and on into retirement.

These heavy loan paybacks have been a major hurdle as in many areas of our convention. We have lost churches because of this. It means that for every dollar we borrow through our Home Mission Board Loan Division, we have to pay back two for one over a thirty-year loan program. At Mountain Highway Baptist Church, we have sought to raise money, invested at interest, to avoid long-term financing. We have felt a sadness because of these financial problems, but so many of our Southern Baptist friends have helped tremendously in these situations. We would have never made it in so many areas, even today, without the generous help of traditional Southern Baptist areas. We thank God for the tremendous networking among Southern Baptists. State conventions, in relationship with our struggling new-work areas, have provided over and above the requested needs. This has made the difference in our survival in the newer areas of our Southern Baptist Convention penetration. Has it been worth it? It will turn out that Southern Baptists invented "spiritual networking" even as older conventions have kept growing and giving in our God-blessed, God-breathed networking system. Praise His dear name!

14

Mountain Highway Baptist Church Wasington

1987–1996

We had worked closely with Elmer and Rheva Mundy in the Mountain Highway area. They are a very special couple who know how to do mission work from beginning to end. When I first came to the Puget Sound Association as church extension director, we were invited for fellowship with the Mundys at our East Lake Baptist Church near the beautiful state capitol in Olympia, Washington. The church property was located near a lovely wooded area, and it was a special joy to walk among the tall evergreen trees. They are now all cut away to make room for residential homes and the East Lake Church. The Mundys came to a decision to go to another area of our Northwest Baptist Convention work on Orcas Island, a rather land-locked resort area, north toward San Juan Island. It had been hard work to create a stable, sustaining, spiritual ministry in this resort/fishing area, but the Mundys thought they could do it.

I was asked by the East Lake Church to be their interim pastor, and our director of missions granted me a one-month period. We enjoyed the experience and were instrumental in helping to obtain a young pastor and his wife from Texas, Jimmy and Nancy Petty, and their young family. They stayed with it in a bivocational capacity. He was a roofer and she, a dental assistant. They worked with the state organizational people, the legislature, and others to obtain permits to build. They were finally successful, and with outside Brotherhood teams they constructed a very nice building with a corresponding highway entrance for a very minimal financial outlay of some thirty thousand dollars. Every one of our mission works is a tremendous story of faith, brawn, and dedication.

The Mundys on Orcas Island became bogged down in apathy and came back our way seeking the will of God for their future life and ministry. The Olympic Association director, Weldon Stevens, had invited us to a pastors and

262

wives retreat, an Olympic Association event. We had supplied at the Port Orchard Baptist Church, and this retreat was a joint Puget Sound/Olympic Association effort. It is presently altogether in the Olympic Association Fellowship and still going strong—hence, our invitation and the opportunity to be with the Mundys. As we sat together for lunch, the Mundys told us of their experiences and feelings. We immediately told them of the Mountain Highway opportunity and suggested they come by our associational office and talk with the executive director, Dr. David Holden. They did and thus began their ministry at Mountain Highway Baptist Church as the first long-term pastor.

Dorothy and I had already been much involved with Mountain Highway as church extension director for our association. It was one of our areas scheduled for a Praxis Team from our Southwestern Baptist Theological Seminary. Dr. Tom Sykes from our Home Mission Board had come for a visit relative to some five Praxis teams early on and to check out the various areas we had targeted. Of course, the Home Mission Board was paying the bill for these five teams. Dorothy and I took Dr. Sykes on the tour of these areas, and Mountain Highway was the number one area. Tom was impressed, along with us, about God's leading, and we sent Van and Beth Sanders to the Mountain Highway area where they worked the entire summer of 1983 in home Bible studies and visitation. They were warmly received and laid the groundwork for the future church. In our relationship with these Praxis teams and also college-age students who were summer workers in our churches in Vacation Bible Schools, I had some negative reaction to the Sanders. It turned out that he had allergy problems. I had a further positive impression of Van. He was a man of deep prayer, and this made all the difference. Since that experience, the Sanders and children have been our foreign missionaries in Kenya.

Elmer and Rheva Mundy went to work. They knew what to do, and, above all, God blessed. We held our first service in the Smalley home on January 15, 1984, a cold, icy, sunny day. They had a roaring fire that heated the whole house. We had a full house, I preached, and we had a positive response on that Sunday. From that, things have never let up. Most of those people became active members. I was asked to hold a revival in April of 1984, and God saved people. Among them was the precious youngest Smalley boy. Something happened later in this child's life. He sniffed some glue, and it cost him his life. We met in homes for the most part.

The Mundys found a very suitable piece of land, and with help from varied outside sources, purchased some two and a half acres in the midst of a rock field. Dorothy and I were invited to come for the first service on the property, which was held under a tent on a glaring hot Sunday. God blessed that service, and our first member was Kathy Lorey; later, her husband, Jim, came. Kathy was from a broken-home situation with a Canadian background. We later met her children from a previous marriage and her mother, one of the best fruitcake makers ever.

Elmer was led of God to lock in a commitment from the landowner for the right of first refusal on an additional one and half acres on the lower end of our property if and when it was for sale. After I became pastor in 1987, I received a telephone call from the Realty Company that they had been offered thirty-eight thousand dollars for this piece of property, and they were honoring their commitment to us of first refusal. We had no money! How could we possibly take advantage of this offer? (The owner of the Sundown Realty Company was a native of North Dakota from the farm where Lawrence Welk began his meteoric career in their family barn. When I would go in to make our payments, he would show me pictures and share.)

The First Baptist Church of Euless, Texas, with Dr. Jimmy Draper as pastor (now president of our Sunday School Board—LifeWay Christian Resources—in Nashville, Tennessee), had sent its best men to help put up our present building, quite a chore and a marvelous job of skill and brawn. We were in and out during that time and got to know these workers very well. Rheva had been in Seattle early on in the courthouse and heard about a Port Authority building available for forty thousand dollars. The Mundys looked in on this two-section building, which was very heavy and in two halves. Finally they were hauled to our property on heavy trucks. There were four breakdowns because of weight. These Euless laymen had put it all together. Dorothy and I were out there with food and other provisions in the cold wintertime. We had thought to purchase and put up this building for forty thousand dollars and were in the business meeting in the Jim Lorey home when the "go" decision was voted and serious questions were raised. It had actually cost us an additional forty thousand dollars to get the building onto the property and up to code. Elmer and Rheva sold California Church Bonds to raise the money and personally bought half of them. Those bonds have begun to come due and will be finished paying out in 2003—Praise the Lord!

Now, here we were, heavily in debt, no money for the needed additional acreage and the real possibility that a convenience store would go up on this property. I prayerfully sought God's leading, and I felt impressed to write Euless and ask for their prayerful help. I felt that at the most they might give or lend us six thousand dollars. Lo and behold, they send us a check for twelve thousand dollars through the leadership of their mission chairman, Brother Fowlkes.

(Fowlkes was my great-grandfather's name on my father's side. He was a Methodist chaplain's associate in the Civil War and was captured at the Battle of Fort Donelson. Bill and I could never quite make the connection, but it is bound to be there.) Their stipulation was, "You raise the balance." We took the list that Elmer and Rheva had been using for support and wrote them of our need. Orlena Hebel, eighty-plus years of age, formerly a commercial subjects high school teacher from New Mexico and daughter of a Baptist minister, was our secretary and treasurer who became our correspondent and official accountant. We never missed a monthly payment until this property was finally paid off. These friends over the country gave and gave generously. Others in my family and acquaintances from former churches also gave. Their names will be on a plaque in our final, new building that we hope to see come to pass in the next five years. For example, fifty-five hundred dollars came in the Christmas of 1996 from friends from Roanoke, Virginia, and Madison, New Jersey days. Some of these have given repeatedly and generously. All the way, God has blessed us in this Mountain Highway work verifying that Van and Beth Sanders's deep missionary prayer life was God's way to grow and to build His churches.

Elmer Mundy held a revival at Mountain Highway in the spring of 1987. Dorothy and I were in attendance the last night of the revival, and I was asked to lead the singing. At the close of the service during the invitation, one of the men of the church, who did not like the way the pastor was doing things, suddenly came to the front and openly confronted the pastor/evangelist. All of us were shocked! This man and his wife, who had been faithful, subsequently left the church along with several others, including some who were not Southern Baptist and wanted to take over the church.

Later in the summer, the Mundys led in a very successful Vacation Bible School. On the last night of the school, July 2, Dorothy and I were present for the occasion of parents' night when 110 people were present. Every seat was taken. Parents of children were there, and a high state of exhilaration was in evidence. I was to become the new pastor on the next Sunday, July 5. You can imagine our shock on our first Sunday when only twelve of the church members were present. We had as our guest Yvonne Helton, foreign missionary in Guatemala, who had been at a boy's camp at our association's Mount Baker Conference Center. She had been with us in an earlier world mission conference in September of 1982, and we were greatly blessed by her sharing. We had planned a July 4 picnic and because of heavy rain had to have this picnic at our home around our dining table. It was truly great fun with Dorothy's bountiful eats and a thoroughly enjoyable occasion.

We knew we were in for a great adjustment in our pastorate at Mountain Highway. Mountain Highway has been through every imaginable struggle, but God has continued to bless until this very day. Here we were, committed to the ministry ahead, and Brother and Mrs. Mundy were moving away to their new ministry, first in Minnesota/Wisconsin and later to Nebraska, which is closer to their family. We have kept in touch and have sought to build on the work they did in our area.

The chairman of the pulpit search committee was John Martin, the only deacon and also Sunday School director. He was a local construction engineer and also had plumbing skills. His committee asked us to come for one Sunday; then for one month; and then called us as full-time pastor.

The associate pastor, Alan Smith, was a fine young man, newly married to a fine local girl from East Lake Baptist Church. I had worked with him in his student work at the Golden Gate Seminary Extension Center at the Portland, Oregon, state convention complex. He met with me once a week for review of his seminary work and in a new church venture that we subsequently lost because of the financial costs of borrowing from our Home Mission Board Loan Division.

Another fine Baptist group later bought this property and has a beautiful building with payments of four thousand dollars a month. They are meeting these payments. I have been involved with this pastor in a ministerial fellowship, and he is doing a great job in a community where Alan Smith saw the future potential. Alan worked with Brother and Mrs. Mundy after this disappointing mission experience. He did an exceptionally fine job in a community-wide survey and set up an excellent card file for subsequent visitation. Brother Mundy had thought of Alan as the next pastor of Mountain Highway, but the committee turned to me, and Alan was deeply disappointed. This was the start of our ministry. Alan and his young family faithfully stayed beside us until God called them to a pastorate in Oregon where their ministry has been greatly blessed. There are gains and losses always in the work, but God moves on in His great work for His churches and in our individual lives and ministries.

Following the thrilling commitment from First Baptist Church of Euless, Texas, where Brother Mundy had paved the way and cultivated excellent relationships, I was on the way with a much lighter heart for a world missions conference in the Omaha, Nebraska, area. Dr. Harold Hanrahan was, and still is, the director of missions for Southern Baptists in the Omaha area. I was at first welcomed into their home and later into the home of Brother and Mrs. Jimmy Furr, fellow Mississippians. They are now at our Home Mission Board in Atlanta,

Georgia, where he works in the Interfaith Witness Department, Central Region, United States and in the general Omaha area. From the Furr's home, I was given the use of an auto that I used to travel to various areas of the Omaha Association. I told about our Northwest mission work and showed slides in several Omaha-area churches. I was able to visit the beautiful new building of the great Calvary Baptist Church where Dr. Calvin Miller was the pastor. He is now teaching and writing about churchmanship in our Southwestern Baptist Theological Seminary in Ft. Worth, Texas (soon to go to the Beeson Divinity School at Samford University). He was not involved in the world mission conference. He had given a special scholarship to my brother Fred for his highly successful mission work in our Pennsylvania/South Jersey Baptist Convention. I was most impressed with the beautiful Calvary Baptist Church sanctuary, the encircling foyer, and the beautiful paintings done by Dr. Miller of the Omaha area Indian culture.

From Omaha, I traveled to the east and was in an older church with the pastor and family who were doing a fine job. I traveled west in the company of a fine Indian pastor who told about his difficult task among the Indians who were so often victims of alcohol. I left this pastor in the Lincoln, Nebraska, area and drove on a far distance to Grand Prairie, Nebraska, where I was an overnight guest in the pastor's home. It was on the occasion of the shocking stock market crash in the fall of 1987 when the whole country held its breath. I traveled back to the Lincoln area and was in our lovely church there for fellowship, meal, and presentation on Wednesday night. Later on that night, I went to a young church in a home fellowship for presentation of our work. I stayed the night and drove back to Omaha the next day for more presentations. On the weekend, I traveled south with Mr. Lilley, one of our other world mission conference leaders from New Orleans, and had a good sharing visit. I made a presentation in a beautiful new church which was based in the home of a lovely older couple. He was very much into antique clocks. I gave a presentation in a relatively new church and congregation on Sunday morning, had lunch with the young, enthusiastic pastor and family, and then drove in the rain to my final presentation in the evening. It was the final night of the World Series Baseball playoffs. The older church building was rather away from the downtown center. I thoroughly enjoyed this experience and meeting the fine people. I went to the home of some of the members after a late dinner and then back to my home base to spend the night. The next morning was cold with bright sun for my trip back to Omaha to the Furr home.

I left the next day for Peoria, Illinois, to visit with our daughter, Mary, and husband, Jim Ragains, for his deacon ordination service at the Woodland Baptist

Church, pastored by Jim Donahue. The ordination service on November 1, 1987, was a very special event for all of us. Dorothy was there and others of the Jim Ragains family, including his father and mother. We all were guests in Mary and Jim's lovely home for a meal and fellowship. Afterwards, Mary had everything in lovely array with beautiful gifts and furnishings from her Tupperware management job and prizes. Mary and Jim were active together in their church, mission work and Brotherhood work, and Jim was rather heavily involved in counseling. They were happy but probably got overextended and reached a burnout point and things sadly fell apart. Jim was called to preach at about nine years of age according to his testimony. They had made a decision to go to seminary and had been advised to sell their Peoria home before coming to seminary, which did not materialize. This sad disappointment surely had an adverse effect on the marriage and family. Two other deacon marriages in the church fell apart about the same time, devastating families and the church. The church pastor has stuck by Mary who has kept singing, has given up her beautiful home, is bereft of Jim's family, and has the burden of the children in their bitterness. Mary did not want a divorce. She did all she could to avoid it, but Jim insisted and resisted. This deeply hurt her and the children. It has been a long hard trek for Mary, but God has blessed and led. The boys have had love from all concerned, and Zachary is doing fine in college.

Mary has met a fine Christian man, a Methodist layman. This Methodist layman and his wife had been very impressed with Mary's singing. They had two adopted children, Nicholas and Natalie. Rick Hulva lost his dear wife about a year ago from complications after surgery. Rick and Mary have since become close and have enjoyed each other's company and the pursuit of Mary's love of music including singing, attending special community events like a country music concert, Peoria Civic Chorale events in which Mary is involved, and being a soloist in Rick's and Mary's church. Mary recently was invited as soloist for a deacons and wives Christmas banquet and to special events in Rick's Methodist Church. The future seems bright with the promises of God on which Mary has stood steadfast and true. Mary has recently made a European concert tour with her chorale group to three countries: Austria, "Sound of Music" country, Switzerland, and Germany. She is presently employed at a bank within walking distance of her home. Rick is a Caterpillar employee and greatly respected in his company.

———◆◆✕◆◆———

I had an understanding with the Mountain Highway Baptist Church at the beginning of our ministry that when I felt the need for time off for revivals, world mission conferences, vacations, or special trips, that I would have that privilege. In so doing, I would always make proper arrangements for capable persons to fill in for me, and I would be responsible to pay for pulpit supplies. It always worked beautifully. I did not feel restrained or cramped in anyway at any time, and rather felt that it was good for the church to be exposed to other good servants of God. I never received more than one thousand dollars per month while pastor, having worked up from six hundred dollars per month over a period of time. I never intended to make any money from the church. Dorothy and I felt it was our privilege in retirement to serve our Lord further in this manner.

I must say that had it not been for our son, Chuck, working at Goodwill and from his scant earnings brought home, through his mother's management, what it took to put bread on our table and to help with essential home expenses, we would never have made it. We have repeatedly told him this, and he has been proud of the privilege also, freely shared with our church people; and they have made him to feel the vital, important person he is. He has no family except us, his parents, his sisters, and their families. All have loved him and been blessed indescribably by his utterly unselfish lifestyle. He faithfully attends his own local church, First Baptist Church of Federal Way, and pays his tithe and offerings. He serves as an usher and helps with the sound system. He effectively serves as a deacon, though not ordained.

John and Rubye Martin, a husband and wife team, were very special and completely dedicated in our early years at Mountain Highway. He was our Sunday School director, and she taught older adults in Sunday School. Every Tuesday night, regardless of the weather, he came from his work to go visiting with me. The drive from our Federal Way home is seventy miles round trip, one hour each way, generally four times a week for nine years as well as other special hospital calls, funerals, weddings, et cetera. The Martins were a blessing to the whole church until they left us to move back to California and closer to their family.

There were others. For example, Doug and Sherry Willis were our very special youth leaders until they moved to Portland, Oregon. He moved to a new job situation, and she, though physically blind, went to college. God has since called them into full-time ministry, and we were present for Doug's ordination service. They have worked closely with Brother Troy Smith in a very special Home Mission Board partially supported, inner-city ministry for needy people who learn to earn their own way. We touched many youth under Doug and Sherry Willis and their son, Gary. Doug Willis took John Martin's place in visitation ministry with me.

We had two subsequent youth leaders who did very effective work until there were serious internal spiritual problems and the destruction of an effective ministry. The church family and the families involved were devastated. By my count, I baptized some 180 people of all ages in Mountain Highway. Many of these were youth whose families, often broken homes, have moved away and scattered. I pray wherever they are, they may be finding and doing God's will for their lives. I must say that the church sought in every way to be redemptive in these failures, and God continues to bless to this day.

Our Mountain Highway Church has always been in a field of great need and potential. It is a changing community—from a very rural community to a beautiful modern development in housing and property. This places our church in a most strategic position to minister in the future.

We had two revival meetings and an excellent Vacation Bible School each year. In the spring, we have had good men from our Southwestern Baptist Theological Seminary through a spring practicum experience with Dr. Dan Crawford, Southwestern Seminary professor of missions, as coordinator. Money for their basic expenses and travel was furnished through a fund created by lawyer and Christian layman C. J. Humphrey from Amarillo, Texas, referred to previously in our Puget Sound ministry of funds for new church extension. We have had excellent men, well trained and prepared, who usually stayed in our home because of local transportation needs. Also, there were usually summer student missionaries from our Baptist colleges to help us in Vacation Bible Schools. We always participated in the world mission conferences sponsored by our Puget Sound Association. And, we used many of our local pastors for revivals, all of whom were very effective and shared the rich blessings of their ministries. I was never disappointed in the ministry of any of these men, and God blessed and enriched in each case. They often brought their own people to participate and share in the ministry. Most recently, under our new pastor, Reverend Wesley Funkhouser, Brother David Young from our Trinity Church in Tacoma, Washington, was our evangelist and brought along a number of his own faithful people—especially youth.

I had the privilege of marrying a number of couples in the area. Several of these are active in the church. Others have moved away and are serving our Lord elsewhere. There have been a number of situations of broken family relationships and the problem of how to cope with Social Security restrictions. Of course, there have been others that did not last. However, the church has reached out, in love, ever careful to uphold the teaching of God's Word about marriage and the family. The Word of God in its wholeness has ever been proclaimed and faithfully taught. God has continued to send us capable, dedicated people who know our Baptist work and have served faithfully and effectively elsewhere. The roll call of our present church membership and their previous backgrounds would indicate the excellent, dedicated people God has sent us to replace others who have moved on.

I was privileged to serve in two other world mission conferences while pastor at Mountain Highway. In March of 1989, I was with Director of Missions Bill Hunke in the Sedona and Flagstaff, Arizona, area. Bill and Naomi Hunke had worked in our Home Mission Board in Atlanta before coming to Arizona to retire. They elected to keep serving and have a beautiful retirement home in the Sedona area. He has always been a special friend to those of us who have served in home mission work. I had never been in the gorgeous Sedona area down from awesome Oak Creek Canyon where one can vividly see the scraping of the ice age that made the canyon. The Hunke home is right in the center of the Sedona, huge, Red Rock Monuments that are all around. To take my morning walk amidst such natural beauty was simply breathtaking. I was privileged to stay in the Hunke home the first part of the week. Their lovely daughter Dixie was at home that week from California where she was the WMU executive director. It was a joy to share her spiritual insights. From that home, I was privileged to be in the churches of the area and to share the superb hospitality of the people as I told our Northwest missions story.

The second part of the week, I was in the Flagstaff, Arizona, area. The two weekends I was in that area, there were vivid, deep snowstorms. What a time trying to travel in deep, blowing, soft snow, but I managed to make it by getting behind huge trucks, following their tracks, and staying clear. I traveled south to the Williams, Arizona, area and was most impressed with my accommodations in a lovely home. I was by myself, since the owners were away on vacation. I recall the night scene looking out and down a beautiful snow covered wooded area where one could see the deer. It was a joy to be in the home of others for fellowship and meals and to wade through the snow to the church and meet the fine people.

I took the occasion to travel some seventy miles to Prescott, Arizona, where our dear friend and coworker from Hawaii days, Roger Laube, was in the hospital being treated for a strange malady called Bird Drop disease and a resultant shoulder problem. Bird droppings across the ages in dry Arizona affected Roger, seriously threatening his life until the doctors developed a suitable treatment. His present problem was shoulder surgery that was very painful. He and Irene had moved to the Tucson area to retire for life and were involved in two churches where Dorothy's brother, Bob, was involved as associate pastor and then pastor at Prescott Valley in a new church. You can imagine the surprised look of consternation on Roger's face when I walked into his hospital room for that most important hospital call. Roger has had other health problems, but that trouble is under control. Irene has also had health problems since coming back to the Northwest. They are closer to all their very special children and grandchildren. They recently celebrated with Irene and Roger on their fiftieth wedding anniversary on March 30, 1996. We were invited and joyfully shared with them and all the family and friends on that special occasion.

From the Williams area, I traveled back to Flagstaff where I was privileged to share a motel room with our foreign missionary, Ross Collier, from Kenya, Africa. What a privilege it was to share with this man. On a day of "break" from mission responsibility, we took an unforgettable tour of the amazing, mile-deep crater area where thirty thousand years ago a meteor crashed into the earth at forty-nine thousand miles per hour. One is supposedly in the far north of Russia, but there is no positive proof. There was complete devastation all around for two hundred miles and one can still see the effects. We went out into some of these open fields to examine more closely the effects. I purchased a sterling silver piece of Indian jewelry crafted by a Mormon gentleman and his son at a special price that I cherish as my favorite bolo tie. On a later occasion, I was in a public area when an Indian gentleman walked up to me, touched my beautiful redbird emblem bolo tie, pronounced deep satisfaction, and walked away. Ever since, I have felt an extra special pride in wearing it. I have several others now, beautifully crafted from ancient rock by some of our own rock specialists in our church family, Dave Wilson and Ken Dillard. They study our Northwest rocks that are multi-million years old.

On my last day in Arizona, where half the great natural monuments of the United States are located, I journeyed all the way up to the Grand Canyon and to Page, Arizona, for the presentation of our Northwest story. What a lovely trip. How I wished Dorothy was by my side to share the tremendous beauty. My presentation was well accepted in Page where there are tremendous monuments as far as the eye can see. I spent the night in a lovely home with the family. The wife made some delicious cookies.

The next day, I went all the way around the rim of the Grand Canyon to have an evening presentation and all the way back to Flagstaff. My last presentation was in a brand new church start in Flagstaff in a rented business section—right down my alley. What a blessing that time in Arizona was with the Hunkes, Ross Collier, pastors, and their church families. I came back home thankful for God's great and gracious people called Southern Baptists all over our nation and world. What a thrill to be part of God's great people through mission giving and sharing.

The other world mission conference experience was in the Salt Lake City, Utah, area and all across Idaho where Director of Missions Earl Jackson from Sumter, South Carolina, and recently retired back there, was our host. It was early spring, May of 1992. I flew to Salt Lake City arriving on Sunday morning and was met by pastor Chet Little, of the Roy, Utah, Baptist Church in whose home I was to be for the first part of the week. He was a former businessman who was later called to full-time ministry. He and his wife, Barbara, were very special people. She shared with me about some earlier marital problems. Their marriage and ministry were now on the right track, and they were happy in ministry at Roy Baptist Church. The evidence of their effective ministry was clearly in evidence in their church on that Sunday morning and on Wednesday night when I was a guest for their Family Night. I was very much impressed with their successful ministry in Mormon country with an Air Force base nearby. I later toured this air base and saw the varied military aircraft on exhibit, especially the no-longer-in-use Black Bird Bomber. The pastor and wife and others of their flock were very much into basketball, and every night their exuberance for their national champion Utah team, the Jazz, was rampant. I had a private room in the basement area and could be excused for quiet and private time.

From their home, I was in several of the Salt Lake City area Southern Baptist churches. I was in an ethnic church on Sunday evening with a lovely meal. Our fellowship was a very special occasion with the highly motivated pastor. On Wednesday evening, I enjoyed fellowship and a potluck dinner with an enthusiastic younger congregation in an older building where the people had come and gone. I felt at home. It was a joy to witness the renewal of this church fellowship. I was privileged to be in the leading church in the Salt Lake City area for my presentation and to be in the pastor's home for a meal and fellowship with his family.

I was in an auto service place close by and shared with the Mormon business personnel and sensed their regard for the local Baptist church and pastor. I learned somewhat as to why the Mormons are so dedicated. It inheres with regard to what they call "their recommends" up the Mormon Ethereal Ladder, literally their place in eternity. They will do everything the Mormons teach and believe to enhance "their recommends in eternity," faith by works really, and to enhance their business growth and development under a rigid, demanding system.

I thoroughly enjoyed my bus ride with others of our missionaries, especially the foreign missionaries. Several of these foreign missionaries expressed deep concern about the prevalence and spread of the AIDS virus among the people they work with. We cannot comprehend how devastating this disease is on many of our foreign mission fields. Our missionaries have to be in close contact with their people. Through the courtesy and arrangement of our host, Earl Jackson, we toured an additional Air Force museum on our way to visit the famous Great Salt Lake Basin where the first transcontinental railroad met—east and west. At this historic spot there is a museum of great interest. I learned that perhaps twenty thousand Chinese lost their lives driving this strategic railroad through the mountains and across the continent. The museum has exact replicas of the original locomotives that they brought out that bright sunny day to replicate the event of driving the golden spike to connect the lines. We all left with treasured mementos.

We came back for a tour of Salt Lake City and the Mormon Tabernacle where the famous choir briefly performed for us. We were given a highly structured tour of the tabernacle area, carefully linking the Mormon works system with our basic Christian beliefs. There was a huge statue of Christ and His crucifixion body. We were treated with every respect and given a Book of Mormon at the end, if desired. I was impressed with our tour guide, an attractive young woman from an Episcopal background in Canada, turned Mormon, and leading the tours as part of her student summer job. She was obviously dedicated to her job and aimed to leave every good impression of her new Mormon faith. A young woman in our group that day, a former Mormon, became highly volatile in her public refutation of the Mormon system. Almost immediately, we were aware of the presence of a sort of Mormon secret service expressing concern at this situation. They moved us on through without further incident.

We learned of the Christian ministry of one of Brigham Young's granddaughters and her husband who had developed materials refuting the whole Mormon system and openly distributed them right outside the Mormon Temple Square. No non-Mormon, of course, could enter the Great Temple. I was impressed with its beauty, and it reminded me of the great Riverside Church in New York City. Harry Emerson Fosdick, a deeply poetic, special man, had designed and built the beautifully situated building in Montclair, New Jersey. This church dwindled after he left. The older American Baptist congregation joined with our younger Southern Baptist group and became one of our mission churches as previously related. As I looked at that Temple in Salt Lake City that day, I was sure that Harry Emerson Fosdick got his idea for the beautiful Riverside Church from the Mormon Temple including the trumpet angels, blowing the last trumpet sound high atop each of these buildings. You can observe the deep, deliberate impression the Mormons leave on their tourists. We had pointed out to us several of the Brigham Young homes where his multiple wives and children had lived. We became acutely aware of how vital our Southern Baptist people are and the pressures they work under in this attractive Mormon country.

The story is told of the gulls that miraculously saved the early Mormons from crop disasters by hordes of grasshoppers. Those gulls are highly symbolized around the Great Temple area along with the one-man operated, simple carts that the hordes of Mormons carried across the hot, burning sands. They carried all the belongings the people had as they traveled to this then-desolate, God-forsaken country nobody else wanted at the time. It certainly gave me a deeper insight into the mundane appeal of Mormonism, heavily in evidence here in our Northwest. There were gorgeous buildings, all owned by the church which is headquartered in Salt Lake City under the domination of a board of aging white bishops. The younger ones were always pushing to succeed someday in this line of succession and control, never daring to veer from deep Mormon history and convictions. I recall once in Hawaii, visiting in the home of one of our local Baptist churches and meeting the son of one of our cherished Virginia Baptist leaders, our highly respected and beloved state treasurer. This son of his, who married a Mormon girl, turned totally Mormon and was extolling the virtues of Mormonism.

The Mormons own and control much of American industry, are greatly influential in the popular *Reader's Digest*, as the epitome of the great American system, the American dream. You had only to visit the famous Brigham Young University there in Hawaii and the popular Polynesian cultural center to be impressed with their diligence in pursuit of popular appeal and control from cradle to grave. Marriage is forever in the Mormon Church. You will have celestial children forever, and good Mormons will inherit and populate the planets out there with celestial life like the angels. I've never known any others even to hint about this use of the myriad number of barren planets. It is fascinating, and one day in Glory we can visit, unfettered, in the vast solar system created by our God.

Only yesterday, here in Federal Way, as Dorothy and I rode away from our home, two attractive young Mormon men, who always travel in pairs, usually riding bicycles, came walking behind us. They stopped at every home, including ours, talked with Buddy, offering him a Mormon Bible. Buddy refused saying he was not a Mormon. These young men and women must raise twenty thousand dollars on their own, with family help, to be eligible for these mission forays of two years duration. They live among the people. It appears the women are rather subverted to this Mormon system of a male-dominated society. Dorothy reports, however, that young women do some "on mission," and she had talked recently with a young woman in our bank who was now on a two-year mission in London, England.

The last half of our conference was in Idaho. Dorothy, Buddy, and I had been to Idaho in July of 1990 to beautiful Priest River, Idaho, and the lake country, not far from the Canadian border. We visited with my sister Marguerite and her husband, Hubert Hammett, and their daughter Karen (Mahli). Marguerite and Hubert were spending the summer working in the local Baptist church in Vacation Bible School and other ministry. In general, they filled in for the pastor who was away trying to raise money. They were living in the pastor's home that he had built himself, and we stayed with them. We had traveled across Washington through the beautiful rolling wheat country, a desert, and across ancient volcanic fields, to beautiful Spokane, Washington, a city of beautiful buildings, and then north to Priest River. It was a most pleasant visit with my sister and her family. It was our first and only time yet to visit that area. What a terribly hot trip back across that desertlike country we had because the air-conditioning went out on our car.

Our mission conference was crossing into the southern part of Idaho for the last half of the week. We took a tour bus up to Pocatello, Idaho, home of the state university, with various stops in between. A potluck lunch was prepared for us in the First Baptist Church, and it was good. I was met by my host pastor, Brother Ray Runner, for the ride to American Falls, a lovely little city, to the home of my hosts, Mr. and Mrs. Lyle Eliasen, he a lawyer from a Mormon background. His wife, Barbara, is a nurse. I thoroughly enjoyed being in their company and home. He was my host driver to various churches in that area.

Every church visited and shared with was a special blessing, and the people were enthusiastic. I was impressed with our lovely new church in Idaho Falls, the oldest Southern Baptist church in eastern Idaho with three hundred members. There are ten thousand Spanish people in the area. They had a lovely meal for our group. We came back to American Falls and were in their church for an early morning breakfast. Their building is small, but well used, and sits beside the ancient wagon tracks of the Oregon Trail. Our last church on Sunday morning was an Indian church. Two lovely ladies from American Falls were my host drivers. The Indians were slow in coming, but I had been warned. They were a wonderful group and had prepared a delicious meal amidst a warm loving fellowship. Our last Sunday evening service was across the state to the east in famous Soda Springs, a small house church with a beautiful, though small building nearly finished and a few people present. The pastor was from Hot Springs, Arkansas, and knew our former Mississippi and Southern Seminary friend, James Fairchild, who had encountered the gambling interests in Hot Springs. The Soda Springs pastor knew about these gambling people from personal experience. I was impressed with the beauty of the land, the farms, and the Mormon love of the land. Then, we went back to American Falls for our return bus trip to Salt Lake City to catch planes back to our various destinations.

I arrived back home about 4:30 P.M., and as always when returning from afar, I received a warm welcome from my dear wife and family. What a privilege to have seen this part of our great country—to see the area where the famous Idaho potatoes grow prolifically, the makings of most of our french fries, and to hear Lyle Eliasen tell about his early Mormon background among the poor, who resisted the Mormon priests coming to insistently collect their tithes, usually early on Sunday morning. Southern Baptists are ministering to such people and making great inroads. Praise the Lord!

15

The Present and Future

1996————

I have continued as pastor emeritus at Mountain Highway Baptist Church and have supplied in various churches for pastors.

We are restoring our family home place in Okolona where we own five acres of our original land where I was saved.

Dorothy leads in her high school reunions with two thus far and hopefully plans on one in the year 2000 in Okolona, also, in Calhoun City, Mississippi, whence they came to Okolona.

We actually keep in touch with those we have known and loved and worked with across the years. The people call us and we call them and share in sickness, death, and other events. Dorothy keeps a running correspondence with many, and our annual Christmas letter touches many bases.

I will be with my Brother Fred and his family and other family members in the Memphis, Tennessee, area October 4–7, 1997, for the 125th anniversary of Mt. Olive Baptist Church that Fred serves as pastor in his retirement, and where our father was a member at sixteen years of age. This is also where my father's mother was an early member. This church helped me financially in college when it was so needed, especially to send Dorothy a daily three-cent letter, and that was sometimes hard to come by.

I have been asked to hold a revival in Atlantic, Virginia, for former Ivy Memorial member Robert Reese, on October 12–16, 1997. We are very close to his family there, and to his sister, Alice, now full-time in seaman's ministry, and her husband, Doug Thomas. These younger children were left behind when their mother died of cancer and the father had a sudden heart attack.

We will continue to do such ministry as time allows. We still have the full-time responsibility of our son, Chuck, who just turned thirty-eight. We are

Charles and Dorothy Jolly celebrate their fiftieth wedding anniversary at the Ivy Memorial Baptist Church in Hampton, Virginia, June 26, 1996. Pictured with them are their four married daughters and their children. One son-in-law and four of their ten "grands" were not able to be present.

looking at future relationships for him with his sisters. We enjoy many happy occasions with him—eating out and special treats that he enjoys with money he earns at Goodwill Industries. We enjoy the yearly Goodwill picnic in beautiful Spanaway Park, which has a beautiful lake, swimming, and large native trees all around which are hundreds of years old. Perhaps three hundred-plus people are present and they all know and love Chuck. I have the devotional service every first Wednesday.

Truthfully, Dorothy and I just enjoy our home—our love, which still flowers—and the blessed quietness after so many years of listening, preaching, praying, and ministering. I walk four miles a day and do wayside witnessing along the way.

My pacemaker does its remarkable work well, and my heart is okay. My feet give me some trouble but like old Dr. John R. Sampey, longtime president of Southern Baptist Theological Seminary, remarked, "My feet are a little numb but I'm glad it's not my head." This was spoken to me one day as I was working in Dr. Sampey's garden on a seminary-assigned work project. Praise the Lord!

Afterword

A TRIBUTE TO OUR ANCESTORS

Throughout our story we have referred to various ones of our ancestors on both sides. We are a part of all we have met, known, and loved! These have all been a constant encouragement and inspiration. We glorify our Heavenly Father for giving us the loving heritage of all of these from time to time. Dorothy has remarkably kept up with remembrances, birthday occasions, and other important happenings.

To all of those we never knew, we know you left a legacy on the lives of those who have blessed us. One day, in the sweet by and by, we shall meet on that Golden Shore and rejoice in the gracious blessings and mercies of our Heavenly Father through Christ our Lord! And, we shall see all of God's people who have so blessed our lives.

We would challenge our own and those of each of our varied families to uphold the ideals of God's grace and mercy and to be sure to meet us in that glad day of rejoicing in the matchless grace of God!

Appendix A

THE CONSTITUTION IN A CHANGING CIVILIZATION
Charles A. Jolly

In our present world where strife and uncertainty preside, and where every individual seems to be intent on defrauding the other fellow, it has become necessary that the citizens of our great and powerful nation do something to check the mad rush, which is hurling us onward, at break-neck speed, toward the destruction of the nation which our forefathers started.

George Washington was indeed right when he said before the signing of our Constitution: "We stand now an independent people—experience, which is purchased at the price of difficulties and distress, will alone convince us that the honor, power, and the true interest of this country must be measured by a continental scale and that every departure therefrom weakens the Union and may ultimately break the band which holds us together."

Since the signing and the ratification of our Constitution, which provides for justice, domestic tranquility, the common defense, the general welfare of and the blessings of liberty for the American people, many changes have occurred in our national life. The cross-hatching of the entire nation with railroad lines, the universality of the telephone, the telegraph, and the radio, the unparalleled structure of automobiles and the paved roads they require, and the introduction of aviation have all added to the complexity of American life, keyed it to the idea of haste, whether in the rush of business or in the pursuit of happiness, and tended toward the elimination of localism and the prejudices of its ignorance and toward the primacy of nationalism.

Public supervision of and control over private affairs, as well as sharp consideration of the rights of the individuals and the welfare of the many or of the whole, consideration of the claims of property and of humanity, of material and human conservation and reclamation, consideration of the right and requirement of education, of representation and more direct control by the American people themselves, consideration of the right to a healthful life and sufficient leisure, of the justifiable place of amusement, both indoors and out—these are also phases of our present national life. The youthful pioneer spirit died down with the disappearance of the frontier and the end of free land. Our nation approached maturity, took on dignity and international responsibility as it became a world power and brought to the forefront of the American people the teeming problems of greatness—of which the framers of our Constitution had no perception. They did not dream of the complexity of the problem of keeping peace with all nations, nor of the numerous later problems when the Supreme Court of the United States was forced to use its own perception of the Constitution in legislating on the main issues of the day.

But even though the framers of our Constitution could not see the many changes which were later to occur in their nation, they exercised judgment and sagacity in writing the Constitution for the United States of America. That Constitution, with its Bill of Rights and its provision for amendments, has been able to meet every situation dealing with the social, economical, and political problems of our nation since 1789. This famous document has served as the very foundation for the government of the greatest democracy on earth, and at present it offers the 130,000,000 American citizens the glorious privilege of living in the ONLY land of the free and the home of the brave.

Today our nation is, as in 1914, faced with the problem of how to keep out of the affairs of foreign nations. Our position as a world power and as one of the world's three greatest democracies, demands of us certain duties and responsibilities which cannot be disregarded. The recent Pan-American Conference, in which the United States was the leading figure, has done much to cement the bond of friendship between our nation and our Latin-American neighbors.

Conditions in Europe are greatly affecting the lives of the American people, even though we little realize it. In Germany and Italy, every effort is being concentrated into the building of vast and powerful war machines with the idea of imperial expansion in view. These totalitarian powers are already dominating Central Europe with their barbaric uncivilized scheme of government. It is necessary, in order to promote the general welfare of the American people, for the United States, as the leading figure in the Western Hemisphere, to do her part in preventing those nations who love land and war better than peace and happiness from gaining a foothold in the new world. In order to maintain the peace and the happiness of our citizens, our government must provide an ample army and navy to protect the rights and the liberties of the American people. Europe is on the verge of a major catastrophe; anything can happen; and only a few more of Herr Hitler's land grabs will thrust the entire world into a war which will destroy the civilization of all nations.

In addition to our problem of foreign relations, our nation is faced with the grim reality of having the worst criminal record of any other nation in the entire world. When the United States was still very young, our vast undeveloped resources attracted many classes of people to our shores. As a result of these numerous immigrations, our population increased so rapidly that not enough employment was to be had for our citizens. Hence, the illiterate, uneducated classes of our population turned to crime for a livelihood.

But since our federal Constitution provides justice for all, our government has done much to remedy these deplorable conditions. When Franklin Delano Roosevelt and the Democratic Party came into power in 1933, a vast public works progress was started; as a result, unemployment has been greatly reduced, and we are gradually emerging from the depression which struck our nation in 1929.

But even with the unemployment question temporarily taken care of, there are still fraud and corruption in our government which must be reckoned with. Our government is both necessary and dangerous. It is necessary to control and to punish those anti-social individuals who refuse to live according to the rules of the society of which they are a part; and it is dangerous when those who are made officials and are entrusted with power abuse that power to the injury of other members of society whom they are supposed to protect. One of these dangers we call lawlessness, the other tyranny—the best government will protect us from both.

Our federal Constitution, which became the model for all later constitutions, was drawn up at a time of great reaction against the tyranny of officials which caused the American Revolution. Our ancestors wrote strong safeguards such as due process of law, habeas corpus, and prohibition of excessive bails and unreasonable searches and seizures into our constitutions, both national and state. But as our society has become more complex, the anti-social individuals have come more and more to use these constitutional safeguards to escape punishment from their crimes.

The protection of people against impure, unclean, adulterated foods, against dishonest weights and measures, and against unsanitary standards of living have made great progress. We have come to realize the untold value of our natural resources, and the grave danger threatening the unbalancing of nature is being checked with the transplanting of our forests and the conservation of our wildlife.

All in all, our nation is making more progress toward the betterment of civilization than any other nation in the entire world. The rights of our citizens are fully taken care of by the Bill of Rights which compose the first ten amendments to our federal Constitution. We are not in constant dread of being carted off to an accursed concentration camp, there to be beaten and starved until death relieves us from our unendurable agony; we are not forbidden the right of free speech nor is our press dictated to or controlled by our government; we are not told when and how to worship our God; we are not denied the right to assemble nor the right to petition our Congress for a redress of grievances; our homes and our property are not in danger of confiscation by our government; we are not facing an economic crisis because our government is spending every penny that she can beg, borrow, or steal from the common people to build murderous implements of war.

Ours is a democratic form of government guided by our federal Constitution and operating for the common good of the American people, granting to them the rights and the liberties for which their forefathers fought and died. It is our moral duty as citizens of this great and powerful nation to prevent the safety of that form of government from impairment by the radical elements of our population, and may God continue to guide the steps of the leaders of our nation in order that that form of government may be maintained forever.

Speech presented at the National High School American Legion Oratorical Contest in Springfield, Illinois, on April 14, 1939. Charles Jolly tied for second place out of a field of 24,000. The booklet *Youth Speaks* prepared by Charles A. Jolly includes this speech with the other top four speeches presented by their authors along with their photographs, biographies, and a history of the American Legion. This booklet was published in 1939.

Appendix B

MEMORIES OF MY LITTLE BOY, MERRILL

I am alone and I feel the urge to put on paper the thoughts that crowd my memory on this lovely autumn day. Poignant memories of days that are gone, never to return. Autumn drawing on apace, the sun brightly shining in a sky of heavenly blue, goldenrod swaying gently in the breeze, leaves of scarlet turning the summer's green to gold.

Oh! My darling little boy. You must know that the memory of you prompts me to write these words. It seems that I would only have to reach out my hand to touch you. You seem so close. How you loved to ride the cotton wagons to gin. All the darkies loved you. You were so kind and gay, though you suffered much. It seemed you had not a care in the world. Now is the time, too, for the annual fair, and I am reminded of how you looked forward to this occasion with joyful anticipation. I especially remember the last one you ever attended. You had so much sympathy for the man who was slowly turning to stone. I still have the little knife you purchased from him in order that he might continue his medical treatment. It almost broke my heart when I looked at you, as you gazed upon him with such infinite pity. And, I thought that you, too, might never overcome your affliction. So, now my darling, you can understand why I had to write these thoughts as they came to me. But, I am not unhappy. I have long since found the lovely peace that follows tears, an echo sounding down through the years.

The words you spoke often lift my heart when deep unrest would tear my every hope apart. I thank God for the privilege of having you with me for awhile.

I thought that when I told you my last goodbye it would break my heart, but I know that God still reigns supreme, and that He does all for the best. And so I dream of another spring when my soul's lonely quest for rapture shall end in white transcendent flight to that heavenly choir in the realms of the blest of which I know you are a part. And, dying, I know that I shall live again, and too shall say, "I have not lived in vain."

Your Mother
Fall of 1941

Appendix C

Following are some meditations I wrote in verse at the time of the home-going of my mother-in-law, Mrs. R. B. Patterson Sr., on January 13, 1964.

A tribute written on the train on the way home from the funeral.

DEAR MAMA PAT

Many memories flood my mind as we travel today,
Your only son-in-law and your dear Dorothy Faith;
To attend what we have long known had to come,
The service of welcome to your Heavenly Home.

    I remember you first as my pastor's wife,
    Standing always beside him and giving your life;
    In homes, in hospitals, with people along the way,
    Pointing them to the land of never-ending day.

To my own family you ministered so well,
The cheerful word, the bright friendly smile,
Helped lift our load of sickness and trial;
When first a dear brother, then mother, then sister,
Went Home to live with our Lord, now Risen;
You made me to feel that my burdens were your own,
As you blended your tears with mine.

    I remember when I, a timid farm boy,
    Loving your daughter with a secret joy;
    Found your sympathy and words of approval,
    That made even me to feel that I could win her love and find
        God's Will.

As my mother-in-law, you were truly the best,
There were times when your rebukes gave me no rest,
But as the years went by I loved you the more,
Because I knew deep inside you all you were;
You loved me and inspired me—
I never doubted where you stood,
To God's Word and His Mission you were ever true.

I remember you as Mamaw to my children dear,
Who today far away shed the silent tear.
You were good and sweet and kind, yet firm,
Your influence in their lives will ever be warm.
Even Rebecca Ernestine will be told of the one whose name she bears.
And, Buddy though too young to remember you well,
Will be a finer man indeed because of what you were.

    I remember many vivid details—
    Red hats, pretty dresses, and champagne music of Lawrence Welk;
    Midnight vigils on Saturday nights,
    When would-be Miss Americas were beauties in white;
    And you shared with my girls this part of yourself,
    That will help them remember Mamaw in a human depth.

I remember good cooking, bright decorations—a cheerful home,
Where I always loved especially to come;
Always clean, always welcoming, always warm.

    I remember your singing, with others, and alone.
    Your voice was sweet and clear as bell tones.
    You lifted and blessed many a heart,
    And helped young and old to make a new start.

I remember your pride in us all,
Husband, son, daughter, grandchildren;
Those things, and many more, I can never forget
And pray that I may be more yet;
Because it was my privilege, in a special way,
To call you Mama Pat.

    Three things stand out as I reflect,
    You taught your children that to eat right one should not neglect—
    The difference in good health, and that of blight.
    You always told us at each letter's end,
    Love each other real good for me as mine I do send,
    And, last but not least, just good horse sense: "Help us, Dear
        Lord, to get over the fence."

Dorothy and I had to ride the train because of extreme winter weather—snow and ice were everywhere. We stopped in a little village and everyone wondered why.

THE LONESOME TRAIN

The iron monster paused briefly in its southward flight
belching steam and smoke from every vent.
A blanket of new snow in the sun glimmered white
as life gently idled in the village street.
Mine eyes wondered, what place is this,
as a mid-winter trip paused a brief time.
Then was seen the town's most popular Miss,
bearing the mail sack in her arms entwined.

    The train moves on to its journey's end,
    those riding its rails each lost in his thoughts;
    For many on this earth will meet their kin,
    still others will meet theirs in Heaven's vault.
    Ride on, lonesome train till your labor is done.
    You were made by men's hands to serve a day.
    But, up there 'tis Glory with God's dear Son,
    where those living with Him, for us here, do pray.

On the return trip we rode back through the mountains of East Tennessee. This little verse was written as we were coming through the mountains in the vicinity of Chattanooga, Tennessee, about 3:00 A.M.

THE NIGHT TRAIN

The huge locomotive with its wheels on fire,
was snaking the long train through the wild mountains high;
Midst soft moonglow and the twinkling stars,
hurling its hoarse call into the distances afar.
The lights across the mountains were like sentinels fair,
helping those on board to know that life was there.
And then the great city burst in full view,
and all breathed easily that we were safely through.

On the return train trip, Dorothy remarked about the overwhelming finality of death.

DEATH

Death is a huge door on hinges closed,
And beyond it is mystery in eternity's abode;
For all who enter never return,
And those left behind grieve and yearn.
But through Christ our Lord the mystery pales,
Because every step of the journey is a blazed trail.
And at the end of the road, He will welcome us Home,
Where we will never be parted from those we have known.

The following was written on our return trip as we came through several places where our loved ones had lived, and where we had visited them. This was the same train that Mrs. Patterson had caught to come see us in Annapolis where she spent five weeks in a most happy visit. We went to Philadelphia and Valley Forge. It was on this trip that she started to have trouble with her heart, a sort of asthmatic attack for which a doctor in Iuka, Mississippi, gave her some medicine.

I REMEMBER

I remember Okolona where many things began,
I fell in love with Dorothy Faith,
And you told me of her name,
Gift of God through faith.*
Where I learned some special manners, as your table I did share,
And I felt the Call of Jesus to preach the Gospel clear.
    I remember Memphis where I married your daughter dear,
    Where her father stood before us and brushed back the tear.
    And, as we left the home with hearts eager and glad,
    He said, "Always remember she's the best gift I had."
I remember Bruce, and the hills so red,
Where we went one year for Christmas after we were wed.
Our hearts rejoiced together as a secret we shared.
A new one was on the way, and we were kinda scared.

I remember Pontotoc, and two homes there,
And when we came to see you many joys we did share.
Sarah Pat was with us and Mary on the way,
My dear mother left us and with you we had to stay.

    I remember Corinth, and two little girls so dear,
    The church we loved to go to had a steeple tall and clear.**
    The pastor there baptized me, and was glad to know us anew,
    For when he left Okolona for you to come we thought we were through.

I remember Iuka, and the gushing springs around,
And the lake where fishing and good times did abound.***
And Martha Ruth was with us to comfort our hearts
Because from dear Aunt Martha, we had to depart.****

    I remember Amory, and the beautiful home you loved,
    Where a peaceful feeling seemed to lift us above;
    Where Buddy, our only little boy,
    Came to live with us and to fill our lives with joy.
    And we came one Christmas, with hearts all aglow,
    Then, we had to leave you suddenly back to Annapolis to go;
    Because a dear young deacon, who was so sick when we left,
    Went to be with Jesus and from his dear ones was bereft.

I remember Grenada and the last sweet years.
There were joys aplenty, but there were also many tears.
Yvonne went suddenly to heaven, to her mother who was there.
You put your arm around me, and wept with me in care.
And, we came to see you, in the hospital small,
From where you left us also, to ascend to the final home of us all;
But not before you got acquainted with little Rebecca Ernestine,
Who is such a comfort to our hearts, because for you she was named.

    I remember Pontotoc again, where we laid you to rest,
    Midst rural scenes and among the people you always loved the best;
    And the people from the church, your husband helped to start,
    Had prepared a lovely meal for us before we had to part.
    We enjoyed delicious food, and fellowship so sweet,
    As outside beautiful flowers adorning your grave our eyes did meet.
    And as we left the house you lived in, in the churchyard behind,
    We knew that you were at last in Heaven, with our Saviour, so kind;
    And all of those you have helped to be there, and loved awhile on earth,
    You have joined in sweetest fellowship eternal, and the only one of worth.

Notes:

*Her mother almost died in childbirth—born of caesarian section.

**As I wrote this we were actually passing through Corinth and we could see the beautiful steeple of the First Baptist Church outlined in white against the night sky.

***Iuka is an Indian name given to a place of healing, boiling springs where the Indians used to come and later on a sort of resort center that people from great distances would come to. Iuka is now a sleepy little village.

****Aunt Martha was Dorothy's mother's only full sister to whom she was very close. She had no children of her own but helped to rear Dorothy who was very close to her and her husband when a little girl. Her husband found her dead in her chair after taking an afternoon bath and reading a book awaiting his return home—a sudden heart attack on November 8, 1955. Martha Ruth was named for her and for a dear friend in Portland, Tennessee, Mrs. Annie Ruth Massey. This dear friend met our train at Bowling Green, Kentucky, on our way home from Mrs. Patterson's funeral. She drove thirty-five miles in snow and ice to get to be with us about twenty minutes.

That next night after the funeral service, we had some special fellowship with Brother Patterson who was going through a file of old writings, et cetera. As he sat there, I realized that he had so many friends and people so interested in him and concerned about him that I wrote the following lines.

THE MEEK SHALL INHERIT THE EARTH

The Prophet of God who truly gives,
His utmost to Christ on this earth;
Is one, whose investment always lives,
And never ceases to bring "new birth";
To countless souls across the ages,
To the glory of God's Grace.
    The Prophet of God may lack material things,
    Since his service is sown in love;
    He may have little of gold to ring,
    Yet He has all in the Home above.
    And, there are friends—there are homes by countless score,
    Across the length and breadth of this land,
    Where he is always welcome at every door,

Because of the rich blessings of his spiritual stand;
Surely this Prophet is one of those,
Whom Jesus meant by His precious words;
When he spoke on the Mount in Heavenly Prose,
"The meek are those who shall inherit this earth."

THE SILENT OLD PIANO

An old piano sits posing in the living room,
Where it has been many years in home after home;
The good pastor's wife made it ring with many fine tunes,
As she played the keys softly in the twilight gloom;
Or, as she waited patiently for him to come,
Who had been busily working for Jesus away from home.
>   An only precious daughter made the same keys trill,
>   With the best of music that makes the heart thrill;
>   Grandchildren have likewise played it well,
>   As the heart of grandmother with pride did swell;
>   And, now it sits silently waiting its time,
>   To blend its earthly music with the heavenly chime;
>   As we join our dear loved one in our final Home,
>   Where there'll be no separations around the great white throne.

Mrs. Patterson collected little pitchers from many happy places.

THE LITTLE PITCHERS

Many little pitchers rest on the shelf,
Brought from many travels by happy hands, and well;
Placed in neat patterns with a loving touch,
To many they have no meaning, but to others much.
The one who collected them has now gone Home,
And rejoices with God's Angels around His throne.
Each of those pitchers still speaks to us here,
As we gaze on them fondly through the glistening tear.

I watched a porch swing from the living room as it swayed in the icy wind.

THE OLD PORCH SWING

I gaze at the swing as it sways on the porch
And memories flood the mind as if put to the torch;
I see a young couple pledging their love so pure,
As the Hand of God's Mercy guides their lives so sure.
I see the same couple in the twilight gloam,
As the years go by in the place they call home.
I see their children playing at their feet,
As the same truths of their fathers they often repeat.

I see another couple in the springtime of life,
Pledging their love in the beauty of soft light.
Then the children are gone to do the Lord's will,
And the couple sits quietly in the same swing still.

The grandchildren come to visit those they love,
And the old swing moves faster, back and forth;
While grandmother and her daughter share their joys,
The little ones play happily with their toys.

And now grandmother has gone to that Heavenly Home,
Where she awaits the coming of those she has long known;
Perhaps there in that place so beautiful and bright,
She sits in a swing of eternal light;
But the old porch swing sways softly in the wind,
With precious stories to tell like an old-time friend.

Appendix D

THE BIRTHING OF THE FAMILY
Dorothy Patterson Jolly, January 21, 1997

The story of the times of our life together would not be complete without my adding something about each of our five children.

When Charles and I married in 1943, I had recovered from major surgery the summer before. Dr. Robert Sanders performed the operation to correct longstanding problems I had experienced since my early teen years. Dr. Sanders told my parents he always tried to do constructive surgery on young women instead of destructive work. He advised my waiting a year to be married and also told my parents he found that I was possibly sterile because of endometriosis. Charles was told all of this but I was not—not until after we had been married several years and I had finished college at the University of Louisville, Kentucky, in 1946. Dr. Carl Sanders, brother to Dr. Robert, was the diagnostician to whom our family went for physical checkups at the Sanders Clinic, located in the Baptist Hospital in Memphis. Dr. Carl "lowered the boom" on me when we were at home during the summer of 1946. He encouraged me, however, to try taking wheat germ oil capsules to perhaps overcome the inability to conceive. He also laughingly added that wheat germ oil was a substance fed to cows to make them fertile. That was the ray of hope for us at the time.

By early December of 1947, we were eagerly looking forward to moving from our apartment to the brand new home the church in Portland, Tennessee, had built for the pastor. In and through all of the disruption of the move, I thought I was managing quite well. However, the stench of the newly painted interior of our house was making me deathly ill. I couldn't shake it, day or night. I imagined that I had a walking case of the flu.

While we were at home in Okolona, close to the Christmas holidays, I decided to get a physical checkup at Sanders Clinic in Memphis. Charles's mother had to go in then, too, for a follow-up check on surgery she had had earlier. To our great surprise, and joy, Dr. Carl examined me and announced that I was pregnant. Oh, joy! We established that the delivery would be due on or about July 31, Charles's birthday, and that was the day our first child, Sarah Patterson Jolly, was born at Vanderbilt Hospital in Nashville. Several wonderful friends were named Sarah, and we used my surname as Sarah's middle name, thinking that would please both my mom and dad.

I knew absolutely nil, nada, nothing about babies. I was greener than June apples in May—truly! And, on top of that, I was scared of being a mother. There was nothing in all of my twenty-five years of living that had prepared me for this experience. I even set the alarm clock at night for a 2:00 A.M. feeding, never understanding that when a baby is sleeping, one does not wake her for that early morning bottle. I was so afraid my baby would be contaminated by all the visitors we had come by to see our new addition that I placed the crib in the far corner of our room and let the visitors look at her from the door entering the room. She was beyond three months old and had all her required shots when I ventured out to church with her. Even then, I would sit way at the back, under the balcony, in order to be able to exit quickly should she become a disturbance.

There's no experience common to women like the inauguration of becoming a mother. I soon loosened up and came to enjoy this precious little girl the Lord gave us. She did all the usual things that babies do—cry, wet, poop, scream, coo and goo, and cut teeth. By the time she was a year old, she began walking—took her first steps on her first birthday. Over time, I began to relax and understand this new little being who had changed our lives so radically.

By Christmas of 1949, I knew that I was going to have a second child. This time, it would be a boy. Famous last thoughts! I had majored on blue for every detail when I was expecting Sarah, but now that we were living in Pineville, Kentucky, and I had so many more duties to see to, the color of anything mattered the least. I had baby clothes left over from Sarah's arrival, but the women in our church gave us a lovely shower of new things for our coming baby, due on August 31.

Charles's mother died in early March 1950, and that summer his fifteen-year-old sister, Joanne, came to live with us. What a boon this was to have this dear sister-in-law. She was such a help in every way, and Sarah Pat loved her tremendously.

We purchased some new furniture to prepare a room for Joanne and Sarah to share. I was working into the night to have it all ready and finally decided I had better give it up and go to bed. I recall standing at the front window of our bedroom and seeing Dr. George Asher, my doctor, come in from a long day. He lived at his sister's house across the street. Poor guy, I thought, having to be out so late. I lay down to go to sleep, then but I was up again immediately. Guess what! We had to make a quick trip to the community hospital where our second daughter, Mary Margaret, was born on August 30, 1950. I was overjoyed that Sarah now had a playmate (I have remarked many times that I learned on having our first child, practiced on our second, enjoyed the third, threw away the rules and did the best I could with the fourth and fifth). That is a quip that perhaps has more truth than poetry in it!

Mary was a much calmer baby than Sarah, but I feel that I was the one who was more into the matter of motherhood. I had lost many of my hang-ups by then and was a lot more relaxed. Of course, I had a tremendous amount of assistance from Joanne and various ones in our church who so willingly gave help.

I would be remiss if I didn't state that my mother came when I had both girls. She was a brittle diabetic and was hampered in so many ways by this ailment, but she worked like a Trojan to help keep up the house, prepare the meals, do laundry, and act as hostess whenever church members would come by to see us. Her greatest joy was when she could sit and rock her granddaughters (the rocking chair we purchased when we first moved to Portland has been the one used to rock each of our five).

We moved to Roanoke in March 1953, just prior to Mary's third birthday in August. She and Sarah had a room together upstairs adjacent to our room. The room directly across the hall from them was their playroom. Before they would go to bed at night, I would insist that they pick up any scattered toys and put them in the playpen that was the size of a regular crib. There were some days when the room was so cluttered I didn't see how on earth they made any sense at their play. Their big thing was to call each other by fictitious names—Mrs. Jonkers and Mrs. Possydoots. Where in heaven's name those handles came from was one up on me.

During a youth revival in late summer of 1954, I began to feel queasy again. Uh oh, our "boy" was surely to be this one. Famous last thoughts! On May 20, 1955, little Miss Martha Ruth made her entrance into the world at Lewis Gale Hospital. She was due on June 3, our wedding anniversary. I had no choice at this time but to go on to the hospital at my doctor's instructions. He was Dr. Rufus P. Ellett. We entered at noon and by 5:00 P.M. when nothing happened, Charles said to me that I might as well get up and go on back home. Not to be daunted, I remarked that if I could have this baby, he could surely sit and wait. I can't recall if he had reading material with him this time, but when I was in labor with Sarah, my obstetrician, Dr. Joseph D. Anderson, got a real charge out of the fact that Charles was in the family waiting room and reading a Civil War book by Douglas Southall Freeman (to each his own, *c'est non?*).

Martha Ruth was soon to develop allergies that plagued her for long years. I really liked our pediatrician, Dr. Ruth Barnhart, a Canadian, who had never married. She was the doctor I looked to over the years and used her advice when doctoring subsequent children. I recall her being so baffled by Marti's failure to respond to an antibiotic prescribed for a horrible old cold. She advised me to resort to "our grandmother's remedy," as she called it—castor oil. Ugh! But, let me tell you, that turned the trick!

I must tell about the time I had to go to the hospital to deliver Marti. Sarah had recovered from a horrible case of the red measles, on top of which she broke out with a bonafide case of poison ivy. What a sight she was—bless her heart! She had sat down in a patch somewhere while at play. Mary was due to come down with the measles, and already she was running a high fever as I prepared to go deliver Marti. One of our church members, dear Mary Trent, had volunteered to help at the house while I was in the hospital and after I came home. She truly got more than she bargained for but what a love she was in every good way. Mary's measles were the "red-est."

Sarah Pat was seven and Mary five when Marti was born. They loved their little sister and were ever so helpful to look after her.

We moved to Annapolis, Maryland, in July 1956, right about the time Marti was beginning to try her wings at walking. I had hoped she would not do so until after we settled, but that was not to be. Our across-the-street neighbor, Shirley Knowles, kept her while the movers loaded the van. When Shirley returned Marti to us, she was elated that Marti had begun walking on her watch. From then on, there was no holding back on this little independent miss.

The older girls were into all the children's activities in our church at Annapolis. Sarah had begun school while we lived in Roanoke, Virginia, and dearly loved her first and second grade teacher, Miss Corrine Williams. For all of Sarah's life, this fine young woman has been a model for Sarah, and she is now a teacher. Our fine choir director at church, Jackie Owens, was the girls' first piano teacher. She was able to get them started, and then a professional teacher, Katherine Grimes, took over. It was evident, early on, that the girls had musical abilities, and we tried to encourage their love for studying piano and participation in choral activities at school.

I realized in the fall of 1958 that we were due to have our fourth child the next summer. It was not easy to help execute a move to Newport News, Virginia, in June 1959, but move we did. Five weeks later, Son #1 was born. Charles had always promised me he would have an orchid pinned to my pillow if we had a son. Enroute to the hospital that Sunday night (early morning July 27, really), he asked me if I still wanted that orchid. The reason he asked was that the ladies of the church prepared a lovely orchid corsage for me, given at the time of our welcoming reception on Sunday afternoon, July 26, at our new church, Ivy Memorial. Charles had always given me one dozen red roses when the girls were born, but by now, who cared? I think I recall his giving me more roses. Oh, well, we had our boy at last! This was four years after our third child. I just knew he was our last, and I relaxed in that thought for sure.

I had some physical difficulties in the spring of 1962 and tried to get in to see my obstetrician, Dr. Benjamin Harrison Inloes, who delivered Charles Jr., or Buddy as we called our son. I was unable to get a needed immediate appointment and chose to go to another very reputable doctor, a Dr. Baggs. He performed a D and C and told me he also saw some other needed areas of concern but to be careful or I would end up on the other end of the floor by next year—obstetrics. By March of 1963, I called Dr. Baggs to see if he was taking O.B. cases. When he told me "no," I retorted I didn't know whether to shoot him or kill my husband. To be sure, I was rather perturbed. I went back to Dr. Inloes and felt perfectly at ease doing so. Because of my having serious allergies and asthma for long years, he advised my having my tubes tied after our fifth child's birth. The Virginia law then was that one must have both parents' consent and four live births to have this procedure done. Our baby was due in mid-October but because of the necessity to set up a date for the surgery, Dr. Inloes set my delivery for October 1. This was to ensure the child's ability to begin school by its sixth birthday. October 1 was the cut-off date for beginning school in first grade. On Wednesday, September 25, I went to a luncheon with friends from our church but had to leave early to keep my doctor's appointment for my weekly checkup. Dr. Inloes was appalled at my condition. He announced I was "sitting on a keg of dynamite and the fuse was lit." He told me to go home, sit in a chair, take any moves slowly, and meet him at the hospital at 8:00 A.M. the next day. He had to reschedule the surgery for September 27, for I was to deliver on September 26. All went well and by 3:00 P.M. the next day, we had our fourth little girl. She was the largest of any of my babies even though I only had a total weight gain of five pounds (it sounds unbelievable but it's the truth).

Charles called my parents immediately, and my mother was overjoyed that we had four "Little Women" (secretly, I had always wanted that fourth girl). Mother was somewhat chagrined that I had never named one of our girls for her, especially since Marti was named Martha after my mother's only sister who had no children of her own. I had thought Anna Elizabeth would be such a pretty name, but my mother suggested Rebecca Ernestine. Rebecca was my mother's grandmother's name, and my mother was Suzie Ernestine. So! Rebecca Ernestine she is, and what a comfort it was to have that little namesake, for my mother died on January 13, 1964.

Time and circumstances do not permit or allow me to tell more about each one of our children. Each one is so very special, but by the same token, so very different. Their differences have made our lives richer and more complete as we have seen them grow into their maturity. We try not to dwell on or question what we could have done differently in their developing years. I feel, as my mother used to say to me, that the next generation should be an improvement over the last. I take comfort in the wise admonition of my father when he would quote the Scripture verse, "Train up a child in the way he should go and when he is old, he will not depart from it."

Appendix E

ABOUT OUR CHILDREN AND GRANDCHILDREN

Sarah is married to Dr. Donald Preston Reid Sr. They presently live in Fredericksburg, Virginia. Don has been pastor of churches in Virginia for his entire ministry and presently pastor of Blue Ridge Shores in Louisa County. Don graduated from Bluefield College and then got his B.A. degree from Carson-Newman College. Don has his D.Min. degree from Southern Baptist Theological Seminary in Louisville, Kentucky. Sarah is a Bluefield College graduate and received her B.A. degree in education at Virginia Tech. Sarah received her master's degree in special education at Radford University in Radford, Virginia. She presently teaches at the middle school level at Chancellorville Middle School in Fredericksburg, Virginia. Don now is pastor of Blue Ridge Shores Baptist Church in Louisa County, Virginia.

Mary was married to James Michael Ragains from June 18, 1971, until April 21, 1995. She attended Georgetown Baptist College for two years and then went into banking in Madison, New Jersey. She has worked in banking also in Lexington, Kentucky, and in Peoria, Illinois. She was in Tupperware sales for a number of years and subsequently worked in a manager's position quite a long while. She has taught in her church's preschool program, worked for Ruppman Technologies, and presently is back in banking in Peoria while going to night school to obtain a college degree in business management. Mary retained her maiden surname Jolly at the time of her divorce. She is engaged to Richard G. Hulva of East Peoria, Illinois. They plan to be married on April 17, 1998.

Marti married Kevin Philip Sowards on January 12, 1978, the night before we flew to Honolulu, Hawaii, to become pastor at Waikiki Baptist Church. They were married at Calvary Baptist Church in Dallas, Texas, in the midst of an ice storm. She and Kevin met at Dallas Baptist College in the fall of 1976. After they married, Marti worked as an activities director for quite some time in various nursing facilities prior to developing her own business as a choral music teacher for children in private preschools and private schools, kindergarten through grade six. Severe health problems led to her developing, along with her physician, a fitness program for his obese patients. She presently works in marketing for an imaging firm while still counseling people who seek her services relative to weight loss. Kevin is employed by the United States Postal Service and is a residential carrier in Mesquite, Texas. The family lives in Cedar Hill, Texas.

Charles Jr., or Buddy as he's known to family members, lives at home with us. His co-workers at Goodwill Industries in Tacoma, Washington, where he has been trained and employed since February of 1983, call him Chuck. He was diagnosed early on in his childhood as having a developmental disability with epilepsy. The latter is controlled with a monitored dosage of proper medication. He was placed in special education classes by the child study team of the Madison, New Jersey, Public School System when we moved there in 1969. When we moved to Hawaii, he was then eligible to be placed under the services of the Hawaii Department of Vocational Rehabilitation.

Through its services, he was placed in vocational training using Goodwill Industries of Hawaii, where he was a trainee until we moved to Washington in August of 1982. He began as a trainee at Goodwill in Tacoma, Washington, reputed to be the best facility in all of the Pacific Rim. Since July of 1984, he has been an employee at the Tacoma facility and has repeatedly received pay raises, though not much, on an average every six months, based on his productivity progress. In essence, and in actuality, he helps to put bread on our table.

Becky married Richard Rasmussen on August 10, 1984, and was divorced May 24, 1995. She graduated from Hawaii Baptist Academy in May of 1981 and came to the mainland to live with her sister Marti prior to entering Dallas Baptist College in the fall. College was not for Becky, and she went to work in the accounts receivable division for a large realty management company in Dallas, Texas. Following some major medical difficulties, she chose to come to Washington to live with us and went to work for a large insurance firm in Seattle. She later began work in Federal Way as a credit manager for Worthington Ford in the fall of 1984. Since then, she has been credit manager in a number of dealerships but is presently working in Lynwood, Washington, north of Seattle. Her home is in Issaquah. She was married on November 2, 1997, to Matthew Zuckerberg.

OUR GRANDCHILDREN

See photos on following page.

Children of
Sarah and Don Reid

Donald Preston Reid Jr.
    June 15, 1971
    Louisville, Kentucky
Timothy Joseph Reid
    June 21, 1978
    Radford, Virginia
Charles William Reid
    May 10, 1986
    Galax, Virginia

Children of
Mary and James Ragains

Zachary Ryan Ragains
    August 2, 1976
    Peoria, Illinois
James Robert Benton Ragains
    June 8, 1989
    Peoria, Illinois

Children of
Marti and Kevin Sowards

Ryan Christopher Sowards
    March 12, 1981
    Dallas, Texas
Spencer Christian Sowards
    June 24, 1988
    Dallas, Texas

Children of
Becky and Richard Rasmussen

Alexander Paul Rasmussen
    July 11, 1987
    Federal Way, Washington
Erik Lawrence Rasmussen
    January 30, 1990
    Federal Way, Washington
Lauren Deann Rasmussen
    January 10, 1992
    Federal Way, Washington

Donald Preston Reid Jr.

Timothy Joseph Reid

Charles William Reid

Zachary Ryan Ragains

James Robert Benton Ragains

Ryan Christopher Sowards

Spencer Christian Sowards

Left to right: Erik Lawrence, Alexander Paul, and Lauren Deann Rasmussen

Appendix F

OUR SUNDAY MORNING PRAYER TIME

Around our breakfast table

We read the Bible through about every year for Chuck's sake who cannot read. We read the missionary prayer list each day, and Chuck prays for them and for all our family members, both sides, by name.

Sunday morning is a special time of prayer. We remember our missionaries for that day and again all our family members, brother, sisters, cousins, etc., by name, and each of their families as well and any unusual circumstances prevailing.

We remember our former churches in Mississippi (as pastor):

> Franklin School House and especially the Talmadge Purvises who still survive.
> New Hope Baptist Church, Lauderdale County, the pastor and people we still know.
> Union Baptist Church, Clarke County, the pastor and people we still know, especially the Williamses.

We remember in prayer:

> The Mississippi Baptist Convention, Dr. Bill Causey, executive director, who served as pastor of the Kirkwood Baptist Church near Salvisa, Kentucky.
> Mississippi Baptist College, Dr. Howell Todd, president; Gene Fant's son, professor of English; Dr. John Jolly, Fred Jolly's son and Charles's nephew, professor of psychology at the college.
> All the Mississippi Baptists who have been so good and generous toward us, especially to help us financially in our Hawaii days and our friends in Hawaii.
> First Baptist Church, Wesson, Mississippi, especially the pastor with family problems.
> All our colleges, seminaries, faculty and student bodies.

We remember also:

> The conventions where we have served and the churches by name; those we have known and worked with who are still there and new ones who have come in.
> We pray especially for our New York Baptist Convention and changes in leadership. Our Madison Baptist Church, all we have known and loved because of this church, those who have gone out and are living and serving elsewhere, most by name.
> We pray the same for the Pennsylvania/South Jersey Baptist Convention; our strong Pittsburgh Baptist Church and pastor, Danny Crow, and people we know and love.

We pray for:

> Our Northwest Baptist Convention officers, leaders, retired and active, by name.
> Our Northwest Baptist Convention associational mission directors and families, active and retired, by name.
> Our Puget Sound Association Director of Missions Don Beall.
> Our Puget Sound Association office secretaries, Ruth Ann and Dee.

301

We remember family:

Brother Fred and wife, Maxine, and family: Jimmy, a teacher in Philadelphia, Pennsylvania, and wife and two children; Harry, a steel company executive in Dallas, Texas, and family Lillian Ann and family; Ladye and her two boys, Nolan and Titus.

Brother Don's family in Dallas, Texas, and former wife, Zi, in Birmingham and his personal situation.

My oldest sister, Laverne Webber, and husband, Bob, and family: Robbie, a telephone executive in Atlanta, Georgia; Susan, an art teacher in Lake Charles, Louisiana, and family; Jimmy, a lawyer in Jackson, Mississippi, and Marty, an M.D., and their Methodist Church.

My sister, Mary Frances, and husband, Joe Kelley, in Olive Branch, Mississippi, and family and his auto body shop business in Memphis, Tennessee.

My sister, Joanne, and husband, Darold, in Walls, Mississippi, and each of his and her families, their children.

My sister, Marguerite Jolly Hammett, in California and family; Rose and Jim in Portland, Oregon; Ed and Karen in California.

My deceased sister, Yvonne's husband, Harry Lloyd Rye, and two daughters; Ann McCaa and husband, Bobby, and family; Melissa Davis and husband, Charles, and three boys.

Mildred and Brownie Brown in Bridgewater, Virginia, Dorothy's first cousin; Mildred's Brother, Murphy, and wife, Marie, in West Point/Cedar Bluff, Mississippi; her mother; and their new church situation. Mildred's sister, Martha Anita (Marnita) Lowther and Mildred and Brownie's son, Bobby, on his move to Bridgewater, Virginia; daughter, Martha Lynn, and family.

Dorothy's cousins and families in Arkansas and Alaska; Nancy Burley, a teacher in Barrow, Alaska, and her daughters, Amber and Brianna; Nancy's mother, Kathryn Box; sister, Janie, and family in Odessa, Texas; Becky and family in Smackover, daughter of Kathryn, and family; Glynn and Gordie Givens.

Our relatives in Mobile, Alabama, formerly from Mississippi; Christine Jolly Newell, my father's only sister; Dovie Lee Floyd whose child, Dorothy Jean, died recently and left behind ten lovely children and their families.

My father's niece, Geraldine Pugh McNeeley, daughter of my father's oldest sister, Ellen, who is deceased, and all of Geraldine's family.

Isadora Powe Jolly, wife of my deceased Uncle Peden, and all her family especially Pam and John and families and others in Mississippi.

We remember more family:

Our daughter Martha, husband, Kevin and sons, Ryan and Spencer; those they work with; Kevin's brothers and families, et cetera, Kevin's parents, Phil and Barbara Sowards.

Dawn and Donna McMillian, cousins on my mother's side in Houston, Mississippi; her Roman Catholic Church, her brothers, John Merrill and family in Houston, Texas and Tony in Arizona.

Cousins Beth and Frank in South Dakota; for their deceased brother, Leon's family in the Houston, Mississippi area.

My deceased Uncle Bill Freeman's family in the New Albany, Mississippi area.

Claiborne Freeman's family (deceased) in Van Vleet, Mississippi, and for his daughters, Fauna Ruth and Kay, in the Memphis, Tennessee, area.

My mother's sister, Thelma Alexander's (she is deceased) son, Ted and Gail in Olive Branch, Mississippi.

Donna's sister, Sandy Porter, and husband, Robert, in Tupelo, Mississippi.

Dorothy's brother, Bob, and wife, Florence, for his children and their mother in Nashville, Tennessee, and their churches. Bob's daughter, Robbie Ann, and husband, Mike Williams and family in Atlanta, Georgia, where Mike is associate executive director of the Georgia Baptist Convention, strongly tied to our New York Baptist Convention. Philip, Bob's son, and his wife, Beth, and their two children.

We pray for others in Mississippi:

The churches in Mississippi pastored by my father where I was privileged to help him in revivals.

All the people Dorothy has worked with twice in Okolona, as her high school class leader for two very meaningful class reunions.

All the Okolona people—black and white.

All the churches—not just Baptist.

The Boland family in Calhoun City, Mississippi, their step-sister, Bonnie Gene Fesmire (now deceased), and her family in Northport, Alabama.

The John Stones who have been close neighbors and friends since childhood. Their family, brother Richard and sister Idanelle, back on the farm from Dallas.

We pray for:

Mrs. Dellanna O'Brien and the national Woman's Missionary Union in Birmingham, Alabama.

The Elmin Howells who came to the Northwest to work with and wrote about the advantages of small churches.

Dr. and Mrs. David Holden, our former executive director, who moved to Dallas after retirement to pastor a church, most of their family there.

Dr. Bill Pinson who came to New York for special work while we were there. Since has becqme president of Golden Gate Baptist Theological Seminary and now is executive of the Texas Baptist Convention.

The Weavers, Deena Langston and Lucille Keister, Brother Denley Caughman, Van Segars and his mother, Norma Vincent, formerly in Hawaii, and all others we came to know in the lovely Weaver-Seibert wedding in Garden City, South Carolina.

The Ocean View Baptist Church in Myrtle Beach, South Carolina, and pastor, PaulMims, and wife, Janice. Her mother, Mildred Oaks Barringer; Paul's mother, "Bubba" and for Mildred's daughter, Carolyn, who recently lost her husband, Raymond Winstead, to cancer in Morristown, Tennessee, and their churches and pastors.

The Jack Stewarts, retired from banking in Morristown, Tennessee, whom we knew in our Pineville, Kentucky, days and his family in the timber/coal business.

Carson-Newman Baptist College, Jefferson City, Tennessee, where so many of our early youth went to college and where my beloved brother in Christ and friend across the years, Dr. Clarence Watson and wife, Frances, and family formerly from Yazoo City, Mississippi, taught religious education, now retired in Jefferson City, Tennessee.

Dr. Frank Campbell, president of Averett Baptist College, Danville, Virginia, and Dr. Fred Bentley, Baylor alumnus, retired as president of Mars Hill Baptist College, North Carolina, and where his wife, Doris, went to college. I married both of these lovely families and several older families deceased from Waverly Place Baptist Church in my Roanoke, Virginia, days. All our dear friends in the Roanoke, Virginia, area.

Our Salvisa and Pineville, Kentucky, days and friends there.

Our Annapolis, Maryland, Newport News and Hampton, Virginia, friends.

We remember various others by name from time to time as we know of special needs. Dorothy says we cover this ground in some twenty minutes. Can you believe it? How does our Father in Heaven, with ours and all other petitions, cope? But He does! Praise His name! And how!!

Appendix G

PARTIAL SUMMARY OF OUR TOTAL WORK
From Pastoral Record Book

Total Baptisms   986

Members Received   853
(other than baptisms)

Weddings   411

Funerals   484
(Does not include a number not in Pastoral Record Book.
Does not include missions, Hawaii days, or since Puget
Sound.)

Messages   14,250
(Averaged five messages per week for fifty-seven years
minus vacation days. Does not include revivals, radio, TV,
et cetera. Does not include innumerable conferences, counseling sessions, business involvements, endless meetings
regarding total work.)

Appendix H

Certificate of Ordination

We, the undersigned, hereby certify that upon the recommendation and request of the Okolona Baptist Church at Okolona, Miss. which had full and sufficient opportunity for judging of his gifts, and after satisfactory examination by us in regard to his Christian experience, call to the ministry, and views of Bible Doctrine.

Charles Jolly

was solemnly and publicly set apart and ordained to the work of The Gospel Ministry by authority and order of the Okolona Baptist Church at Okolona, Miss., on the 1st day of September, 1940.

Ordaining Council   W. C. Stewart, Moderator
                     F. U. M. Fatridge, Clerk

Index

309

310